Keywords in the Social Studies

Studies in Criticality

Shirley R. Steinberg
General Editor

Vol. 527

The Counterpoints series is part of the Peter Lang Education list.
Every volume is peer reviewed and meets
the highest quality standards for content and production.

PETER LANG
New York • Bern • Berlin
Brussels • Vienna • Oxford • Warsaw

Keywords in the Social Studies

Concepts & Conversations

EDITED BY
Daniel G. Krutka
Annie McMahon Whitlock
Mark Helmsing

PETER LANG
New York • Bern • Berlin
Brussels • Vienna • Oxford • Warsaw

Library of Congress Cataloging-in-Publication Data
Names: Krutka, Daniel G., editor. | Whitlock, Annie McMahon, editor.
Helmsing, Mark, editor.
Title: Keywords in the social studies: concepts and conversations /
edited by Daniel G. Krutka, Annie McMahon Whitlock, Mark Helmsing.
Description: 1st Edition. | New York: Peter Lang, 2018.
Series: Counterpoints; 527 | ISSN 1058-1634
Includes bibliographical references.
Identifiers: LCCN 2018012617 | ISBN 978-1-4331-5643-4 (hardback: alk. paper)
ISBN 978-1-4331-5642-7 (pbk.: alk. paper) | ISBN 978-1-4331-5639-7 (ebook pdf)
ISBN 978-1-4331-5640-3 (epub) | ISBN 978-1-4331-5641-0 (mobi)
Subjects: LCSH: Social sciences—Study and teaching.
Classification: LCC H62 .K438 2018 | DDC 300.71—dc23
LC record available at https://lccn.loc.gov/2018012617
DOI 10.3726/b13499

Bibliographic information published by **Die Deutsche Nationalbibliothek**.
Die Deutsche Nationalbibliothek lists this publication in the "Deutsche
Nationalbibliografie"; detailed bibliographic data are available
on the Internet at http://dnb.d-nb.de/.

The paper in this book meets the guidelines for permanence and durability
of the Committee on Production Guidelines for Book Longevity
of the Council of Library Resources.

© 2018 Peter Lang Publishing, Inc., New York
29 Broadway, 18th floor, New York, NY 10006
www.peterlang.com

All rights reserved.
Reprint or reproduction, even partially, in all forms such as microfilm,
xerography, microfiche, microcard, and offset strictly prohibited.

Printed in the United States of America

To our students and colleagues. Thanks for learning about the world with us.

Table of Contents

List of Tables... xi

Acknowledgments xiii

Foreword: Innovations in Knowledge Construction............................xv
    Anne-Lise Halvorsen

Introduction: Unsettling the Social Studies..................................... xxi
    Mark Helmsing, Daniel G. Krutka, and Annie McMahon Whitlock

Section I: Culture

Chapter One: Indigenous 3
    Sarah B. Shear and Christine R. Stanton

Chapter Two: Ethnic 17
    Tommy Ender

Chapter Three: Spilling the *Lemonade* in Social Studies:
    A Response to the Culture Section.. 29
    Amanda E. Vickery and Delandrea Hall

Section II: Time, Continuity, and Change

Chapter Four: Time 37
    Mark Helmsing and Annie McMahon Whitlock

Chapter Five: Not So Fast!: A Response to the Time,
    Continuity, and Change Section 47
    Gabriel A. Reich

Section III: People, Places, and Environments

Chapter Six: Borders 53
    Sajani Jinny Menon and Muna Saleh

Chapter Seven: Environment 65
    Jodi Latremouille

Chapter Eight: Home 79
    Gabriel P. Swarts

Chapter Nine: Place 91
    Whitney G. Blankenship

Chapter Ten: Space 101
    Stacey L. Kerr

Chapter Eleven: Between There and Here: A Response to the
    People, Places, and Environments Section 113
    Jason Harshman

Section IV: Individual Development and Identity

Chapter Twelve: Gender 119
    Megan List

Chapter Thirteen: Race 131
    Kristen E. Duncan

Chapter Fourteen: Sexuality 141
    Daniel T. Bordwell, Ryan D. Oto, and J.B. Mayo, Jr.

Chapter Fifteen: On and On: A Response to the Individual
    Development and Identity Section 153
    Ashley N. Woodson

Section V: Individuals, Groups, and Institutions

Chapter Sixteen: Community 159
    Erik Jon Byker, Amy J. Good, and Nakeshia N. Williams
Chapter Seventeen: Family.. 169
    Erin C. Adams
Chapter Eighteen: Religion.. 181
    Colleen Fitzpatrick and Stephanie Van Hover
Chapter Nineteen: Embracing Complexity in the Social Studies:
    A Response to the Individuals, Groups, and Institutions Section 191
    Sara A. Levy

Section VI: Power, Authority, and Governance

Chapter Twenty: Democracy.. 197
    Jane C. Lo and Amanda Geiger
Chapter Twenty-One: Freedom 207
    Eli Kean and Jeffrey Craig
Chapter Twenty-Two: Terrorism 217
    Wayne Journell
Chapter Twenty-Three: Passwords to Citizenship?: A Response to
    the Power, Authority, and Governance Section........................... 231
    Cathryn van Kessel

Section VII: Production, Distribution, and Consumption

Chapter Twenty-Four: Consumption 237
    Kim Pennington
Chapter Twenty-Five: Class.. 249
    E. Wayne Ross
Chapter Twenty-Six: Entrepreneurship 261
    Matthew T. Missias and Kristy Brugar
Chapter Twenty-Seven: How Should We Teach the Children?: A Response
    to the Production, Distribution, and Consumption Section................ 273
    Mary Beth Henning

Section VIII: Science, Technology, and Society

Chapter Twenty-Eight: Technology 279
    Daniel G. Krutka

Chapter Twenty-Nine: Media 293
    Lance E. Mason

Chapter-Thirty: Cyber Salvation and the Necessity of Questioning:
    A Response to the Science, Technology, and Society Section 305
    Scott Alan Metzger

Section IX: Global Connections

Chapter Thirty-One: Global 311
    Kenneth T. Carano and Robert W. Bailey

Chapter Thirty-Two: Immigration 325
    Dilys Schoorman and Rina Bousalis

Chapter Thirty-Three: Crossing/Erasing Borders: A Response
    to the Global Connections Section 335
    Cinthia Salinas and Melissa Rojas Williams

Section X: Civic Ideals and Practices

Chapter Thirty-Four: Discourse 341
    Rory P. Tannebaum

Chapter Thirty-Five: Citizenship 351
    Sarah E. Stanlick

Chapter Thirty-Six: Teaching Civics Amid New Discourses of Citizenship:
    A Response to the Civic Ideals and Practices Section 365
    Beth C. Rubin

Afterword: Keywords, Windows, and Content Selection 369
    Walter C. Parker

Contributors 373

Tables

Table 1.1. Resources for Indigenous Education 13
Table 12.1. What Does It Mean to Be a Masculine/Feminine/Meta Person in Ancient Spartan Culture? 125
Table 12.2. What Does It Mean to Be a Masculine/Feminine/Meta Person for Indigenous American Peoples? 127
Table 31.1. Teachers' Definitions of Global 319
Table 35.1. Knowledge, Skills and Attitudes for Global Citizenship Competency 360

Acknowledgments

We would like to thank all the contributors to this book. To Anne-Lise Halvorsen and Walter C. Parker for beginning and ending this book with wisdom and spirit. To our respondents for their thoughtful contributions and quick turnaround times. To our chapter authors for their care in unsettling their keywords and challenging us with compelling, provocative, and fascinating ideas. Thanks to Shirley Steinberg, Sarah Bode, and others at Peter Lang for helping shape this book into a final form. Finally, we would like to thank our friends, families, and local coffee houses. Without each of you, this could not have been possible.

Foreword

Innovations in Knowledge Construction

ANNE-LISE HALVORSEN, MICHIGAN STATE UNIVERSITY

In its vision statement, the National Council for the Social Studies (NCSS) declares, "Meaningful social studies builds curriculum networks *of knowledge, skills, beliefs,* and *attitudes* that are structured around enduring understandings, essential questions, important ideas, and goals" (NCSS, 2016, emphasis added). In recent years, many educators have developed and promoted innovative methods for teaching skills, such as conducting inquiry (e.g., Grant, Swan, & Lee, 2017; NCSS, 2013) and discussing (e.g., Hess, 2009; Hess & McAvoy, 2015).

However, less attention has been paid explicitly to the first dimension: knowledge. Although educators have emphasized the critical role of disciplinary knowledge (e.g., Dimension 2 of the C3 Framework is Applying Disciplinary Concepts and Tools [NCSS, 2013]), and knowledge construction can be embedded in pedagogy focused on skills (e.g., Parker et al., 2011, 2013), direct focus on students' development of knowledge has not been foregrounded in recent pedagogical innovations. Perhaps the explanation is that, traditionally, knowledge is viewed as "fixed," rather than as dynamic and fluid. Or, perhaps educators are pushing back against traditional teaching approaches that are fact-based and involve memorization.

The notion that knowledge building tends to be lower-level than other forms of social studies learning is dispelled by *Keywords in the Social Studies: Concepts and Conversations*. This book demonstrates that knowledge is complex, contested, and "unsettled." Chapter by chapter, social studies scholars review the meanings of 26 keywords used in historical and current social studies teaching and scholarship.

They examine the competing perspectives and debates on these keywords. The result is an imaginative, impressive, and thoughtful examination of some of the principal concepts and conversations found in the thinking on social studies. Rather than separating knowledge from beliefs and attitudes, the authors show how our collective understandings and knowledge of these keywords are driven by diverse beliefs and attitudes.

The inspiration for this book, as coeditors Daniel Krutka, Annie McMahon Whitlock, and Mark Helmsing explain, was Mark's ambition that the ideas and methods found in cultural studies can motivate social studies educators. Specific reference is made to Raymond Williams' *Keywords: A Vocabulary of Culture and Society* (1976/1983) and to Walter Parker's (2015) interest in the dynamic and contested nature of knowledge. In my reading of the book, I found connections to curricular reformer Hilda Taba's work on concept development (Fraenkel, 1994; Taba, 1966). Taba argued that teachers should understand three levels of knowledge: facts, basic ideas, and principles and concepts. The 26 keywords of this book reflect complex, sophisticated, and multifaced concepts as used in conversations about the social world.

To me, the task of creating and refining a list of 26 keywords seemed simultaneously exciting and painful. What should drive the criteria for inclusion? Whose voices should determine what gets included and what gets excluded? Whose knowledge (Apple, 2014) should be featured? There are myriad ways to approach the process of assembling keywords. State and national content standards list the fundamental ideas that social studies should present. Indexes in social studies textbooks list commonly used social studies words and terms. In my social studies methods classes, I ask teacher candidates to find the keywords (i.e., concepts) in newspaper articles needed to make sense of the articles. I also ask teacher candidates what passions, worries, and curiosities their students have about the social world, and we generate concepts that are important to young people.

The decisions for the keyword selection in this book were driven by the editors' beliefs that "the social studies is unsettled and unsettles us." Dan, Annie, and Mark, whose collective areas of expertise and experience span a wide swath of keywords, explain that in their call for proposals, they suggested a list of keywords from which the authors could choose. Many of the suggested keywords were taken up and others, such as "equality" and "utopia," were not. Authors even suggested their own keywords, such as "home" and "borders." Although some of the book's keywords are expected choices for social studies, such as "democracy," "global," and "race," others are more unexpected. "Consumption," "discourse," and "media" are novel choices for keyword listings. Thus, the final selection of keywords, as constructed jointly by the editors and authors, is current and relevant.

The keywords come from the fields of anthropology, communications, cultural studies, economics, geography, history, political science, religion, and sociology.

The editors organize the chapters around the NCSS' ten themes (NCSS, 2010). Although they admit this structure may be "too settled and settling" for this very diverse range of keywords, this organizational scheme offers two benefits. First, readers learn a few of the keywords associated with each of the ten themes. For example, "borders," "environment," "home," "place," and "space" are keywords associated with the theme of "People, Places, and Environment." This is a welcome alternative to the keyword lists typically highlighted in traditional geography lessons (e.g., "region," "maps," and "location"). Second, this structure can support teachers who are bound by curricular mandates and accountability reporting. For example, teachers can focus on the keywords "democracy," "freedom," and "terrorism" in the "Power, Authority, and Governance" theme.

All the chapters are well-researched, engaging, and provocative. A powerful quotation related to the chapter keyword introduces each chapter. Some authors provide some historical context for the keywords; others draw on autobiographical narratives and historical genealogies; some chapters explore the figurative use of the keywords. The chapters offer examples of the keywords, discuss their misuse and abuse, describe past and present conversations on their interpretation and use, and conclude with a list of discussion questions. For example, the chapter on "home" discusses how bell hooks uses "home" as a space for healing and a community of resistance for Black women in a White society. The chapter on "freedom" describes the many constraints on people's freedom and the ways they have resisted such constraints. Some chapters, such as the chapter on "place," situate the keywords in pedagogical strategies such as place-based education. The chapter on "entrepreneur" invites the reader to take a noneconomics perspective of the keyword, for example, by viewing Harriet Tubman as an entrepreneur.

A significant contribution of this book is the chapters' inclusion of related keywords. For example, the chapter on "Indigenous" explores the keywords of American Indian and Native American, which the authors explain are problematic because they reinforce settler colonialism. The chapters also encourage readers to consider additional keywords. The chapter on "environment" suggests "sustainability"; the chapter on "race" suggests "power"; and the chapter on "entrepreneurship" suggests "innovation."

A "response" follows each thematic section. Readers are asked to continue the conversation about the keywords and the interaction among the keywords. These responses offer yet another perspective on how educators and society understand and apply these keywords. This provokes the editors to comment that certain interpretations may "unsettle" readers as they think about the 26 keywords. Any reader who looks for a definitive agreement on the meanings of the keywords will be disappointed. Moreover, Hilda Taba's concept formation activity in which students agree on the critical attributes of a key concept would be challenging to use with these chapters. Yet, consensus on these keywords is not the editors' objective.

Instead, the chapters' complex conceptions of the selected keywords reflect the dynamism and fluidity of knowledge. Innovative and interactive instruction cannot represent knowledge as "fixed." Moreover, the keywords tend to be "transformative academic knowledge" (Banks, 1993)—knowledge that challenges mainstream paradigms.

An easy critique of the book is that the keyword list is too limiting, much as critics have criticized E.D. Hirsch's ideas on cultural literacy (Hirsch, Kett, & Trefil, 1988), for example. Yet the book is not intended as an exhaustive listing of important keywords for social studies research and instruction. Instead, the book is a fascinating collection of keywords that reflect both classic and contemporary social studies interests. Fifty, twenty, and even ten years ago, the list would have been different. And ten and twenty years from now, the list will also be different. We can expect new examples of keywords and new conversations on the meanings of old examples. The focus of social studies will naturally evolve as society changes.

Keywords in the Social Studies: Concepts and Conversations is a critical resource for social studies scholars who seek to understand contemporary research and theory on the 26 keywords, for other scholars who are interested in the 21st-century mission and vision of social studies education, and for social studies educators who seek to show preservice teachers and K–12 students how to understand and use these keywords. Even the book's structure of 26 chapters could serve as inspiration for students to think about what 26 keywords drive current thinking in their social studies lessons and courses. In both structure and content, this book is engaging and unsettling—just as the editors hoped it would be. I anticipate that this book will become a "primary source" in social studies for the values we argue about and cherish at this particular moment in time.

REFERENCES

Apple, M. W. (2014). *Official knowledge: Democratic education in a conservative age* (3rd ed.). New York, NY: Routledge.

Banks, J. A. (1993). The canon debate, knowledge construction, and multicultural education. *Educational Researcher, 22*, 4–14.

Fraenkel, J. R. (1994). The evolution of the Taba curriculum development project. *The Social Studies, 85*(4), 149–159. doi:10.1080/00377996.1994.9956294

Grant, S. G., Swan, K., & Lee, J. (2017). *Inquiry-based practice in social studies education: Understanding the inquiry design model*. New York, NY: Routledge.

Hess, D. E. (2009). Controversy in the classroom: The democratic power of discussion. New York, NY: Routledge.

Hess, D. E., & McAvoy, P. (2015). *The political classroom: Evidence and ethics in democratic education*. New York, NY: Routledge.

Hirsch, E. D., Kett, J. F., & Trefil, J. S. (1988). *Cultural literacy: What every American needs to know.* New York, NY: Vintage Books.

National Council for the Social Studies. (2010). *National curriculum standards for social studies: A framework for teaching, learning, and assessment.* Washington, DC: Author.

National Council for the Social Studies. (2013). *The college, career, and civic life (C3) framework for social studies state standards: Guidance for enhancing the rigor of K–12 civics, economics, geography and history.* Silver Spring, MD: Author.

National Council for the Social Studies. (2016). A vision of powerful teaching and learning in the social studies. *Social Education, 80*, 180–182.

Parker, W. (2015). *Social studies today: Research and practice* (2nd ed.). New York, NY: Routledge.

Parker, W., Lo, J., Yeo, A. J., Valencia, S. W., Nguyen, D., Abbott, R. D., … Vye, N. J. (2013). Beyond breadth-speed test: Toward deeper knowing and engagement in an Advanced Placement course. *American Educational Research Journal, 50*(6), 1424–1459.

Parker, W., Mosborg, S., Bransford, J., Vye, N., Wilkerson, J., & Abbott, R. (2011). Rethinking advanced high school coursework: Tackling the depth/breadth tension in the AP US government and politics course. *Journal of Curriculum Studies, 43*, 533–559.

Taba, H., & San Francisco State Coll., C. A. (1966). *Teaching strategies and cognitive functioning in elementary school children.* Distributed by ERIC Clearinghouse.

Williams, R. (1976/2014). *Keywords: A vocabulary of culture and society.* Oxford: Oxford University Press.

Introduction

Unsettling the Social Studies

MARK HELMSING, GEORGE MASON UNIVERSITY
DANIEL G. KRUTKA, UNIVERSITY OF NORTH TEXAS
ANNIE MCMAHON WHITLOCK, UNIVERSITY OF MICHIGAN-FLINT

> [This] is not a dictionary or glossary of a particular academic subject ... [i]t is, rather, the record of an inquiry into a vocabulary: a shared body of words and meanings ... I called these words Keywords in two connected senses: they are significant, binding words in certain activities and their interpretation; they are significant, indicative words in certain forms of thought ... Certain other uses seemed to me to open up issues and problems, in the same general area, of which we all needed to be very much more conscious.
> —RAYMOND WILLIAMS, *KEYWORDS: A VOCABULARY OF CULTURE AND SOCIETY* (1976/1983)

> You keep using that word. I do not think it means what you think it means.
> —INIGO MONTOYA, *THE PRINCESS BRIDE* (1987)

(UN)SETTLING THE SOCIAL STUDIES

Teaching and learning the social studies is unsettling work. Far from being a simple, "easy" subject taught as part of a school's curriculum, social studies education requires wading through multiple overlapping fields of study from the social sciences, the humanities, the arts, media studies, and, increasingly, STEM fields such as ecology, environmental science, and science studies. Social studies educators must then take their understanding of the ideas, methods, and debates from those fields of study and translate them into knowledge and skills for learners to put into practice in various roles: as students, as citizens, as future historians or geographers. In reading the C3 Framework for Social Studies Standards (2013)—the most recent attempt at providing organization to the field—you do not have to read for long before reaching a section titled, "What Is Not Covered." Knowing the field well, the authors anticipated the persistence of a century of wrangling about what our field is.

To understand what it is that social studies education does, we must map out how the work of social studies education took its shape and how it has been defined. If you were to go to a local bookstore, you would find sections of the store that mirror the names of subjects found in most school curricula. A bookstore's section titled "science" would shelve books about animals, gemstones, weather, space exploration, and perhaps books on infamous epidemics of diseases around the world. A bookstore's section titled "art" would shelve books on painting, drawing, sculpture, and architecture. A bookstore's section titled "literature" would shelve books of fiction and essays, many of which appear on reading lists in schools. But few, if any, bookstores will have a section titled "social studies." You may find sections titled "history," "geography," "current affairs," or "society and politics," but social studies is one of the few fields of curriculum that appears to be something created especially for use in schools. This curious characteristic of social studies education exists partly because social studies has a different genealogy and a different disciplinary anatomy from most other fields of knowledge. Because of its amalgamated nature, it has always been an unsettled field of study (Evans, 2004; Halvorsen, 2013; Thornton, 2005).

Not only is the social studies unsettled, it also unsettles us. The social studies unsettles us because engaging with both the explicit and hidden curricula of social studies can be confusing, frustrating, and upsetting. When we traverse down the social studies rabbit hole, we might be disoriented by the world we find. To learn that a familiar map carries a Eurocentric bias (Schmidt, 2011; Segall, 2003; Subedi, 2010); to grapple with how to interpret sources from times and places vaguely familiar to our own (King, 2014; Wineburg, 2001); and to uncover the myths and fantasies of historical actors (Loewen, 2007; Santiago, 2013; Woodson, 2015) are all ways to unsettle our knowledge and our relation to the world. Content in our field often resides in contexts that are disagreed upon, contested, or sometimes traumatic—violence, genocide, and oppression in the past, present, and our foreseeable futures result in difficult histories, spaces, and narratives (Epstein & Peck, 2018; Garrett, 2017; Helmsing, 2014). When we wrestle with difficult topics we must consider what it may mean for us to take on the role of perpetrator, bystander, victim, and/or upstander. We hope the chapters in this book continue the unsettling of the field and unsettle us into new possibilities for the social studies and ourselves.

We do not presume that settling and unsettling are inherently good or bad conditions; rather, we support a stance for our readers and authors that questions, disrupts, plays, affirms, troubles, and honors the concepts and conversations threaded in the project of social studies education. Because the social studies is a field of study that integrates and transcends different disciplines and approaches, the field continually defines itself through a cycle of settling, unsettling, and resettling along specific lines of disciplinary content and topics for inquiry and study. As an act of settling, unsettling, and resettling, the reflective process of debating and deliberating what the social studies *is* and *can be* is a healthy process, one that enacts and honors our commitment to democratic association as members of a learning community. We hope this book contributes to this ongoing process of settling and unsettling the social studies by offering conversations we hope cultivate forms of citizenship that are inclusive, participatory, and more just and democratic ways of living.

One widely settled version of the social studies is found in the *National Curriculum Standards for Social Studies: A Framework for Teaching, Learning, and Assessment* (NCSS, 2010). This framework anchors approaches to social studies education by organizing the social studies curriculum across ten themes. We use its ten themes to organize the keywords for this book as an example of a settled form of the social studies curriculum. Within each thematic section are keywords we believe most closely match and correspond with each section. While we do not unsettle these ten themes that help structure and settle the social studies curriculum, we do unsettle the language and assumptions that are commonly taught and associated within these curricular themes. To take one example, Section III of our book surveys the NCSS theme "People, Places, and Environments." Within this section, keywords on borders, environment, home, place, and space are themselves unsettled. The authors of these chapters contemplate how concepts associated with these keywords appear in the social studies curriculum and offer compelling conversations for how to think in multiple, diverse ways about these concepts, unsettling the ideas and topics within the settled frameworks within which we teach social studies education.

THE ORIGINS OF THIS BOOK

This spirit of this book materialized in a casual conversation at the 2015 National Council for the Social Studies (NCSS) annual conference in New Orleans. One of the coeditors of this book, Mark Helmsing, had wanted to collaborate on a book that would draw voices and perspectives from what he saw as different corners of the social studies education field. While he identified with voices and perspectives associated with critical theories of education, curriculum theory, and history education, Mark sought out Annie Whitlock to represent the corners of the social studies field identified with elementary and entrepreneurship education. Mark also contacted Dan Krutka because of his scholarship on media and technology in social studies education. Mark, Annie, and Dan discussed ideas for this project and decided to set about drawing up plans for the book that would solicit contributions for these varied (although by no means exhaustive) areas of the social studies education field. What should the book be that we were to edit? We were authors in search of stories to write.

We believed that cultural studies offered ideas and methods to help unsettle how we approach social studies education. As a field of study, cultural studies is often seen as an outgrowth of ideas from the Welsh public intellectual Raymond Williams. In his *Keywords: A Vocabulary of Culture and Society*, Williams (1976/1983) employed the idea of "keywords" to illustrate how concepts and ideas in cultures change over time, demonstrating how words we use as a society grow and change over time as a result of various political and social forces. Williams took concepts (e.g., "writing") and made attempts to explain them through a historical and analytical lens, exploring how the words are used both popularly and academically. An attention to the language we use is critical for social awareness, Williams argued, because "our vocabulary, the language we use to inquire into and to negotiate our actions, is no secondary factor, but a practical and radical element itself" (p. 323). We adapt Williams' approach to examine how the field of social studies education puts to use "our vocabulary, the language we use" across and through the different contexts of our field.

Walter Parker (2015) draws upon Williams' concept of keywords in helping educators consider the changing dynamics of concepts in social studies education that "are central to our thinking but fundamentally ambiguous" (p. 2). For Parker, in the spirit of Williams, the concepts that animate the questions with which we grapple in social studies education are "always in flux" and "subject to argument." We wanted to model an approach with this book in keeping with Parker's application of Williams' keywords idea in social studies education. The chapters in this volume unpack and unsettle the evolving, contested workings behind keywords that give shape to much of the curriculum and pedagogy within social studies education. Our authors' keywords invite readers into conversations about collections of impressions, imaginations, and implications grounded in the keywords we use to talk social studies in classrooms, books, lecture halls, films, museums, web sites, literature, television, the arts, digital media, memorials, parks, playgrounds, zoos, supermarkets, shopping malls, family reunions, military zones, courtrooms, border checkpoints, and more.

To provide the shape of our book, we undertook an extended process to select a list of keywords to suggest as possible chapters. Many keywords we identified as important to developing a broad outline for social studies education did not make our list sent out as a call for proposed chapters. Keywords such as *equality*, *heritage*, *nature*, and *utopia* each resonated with us in different ways, but were not taken up by authors when we solicited chapters and ended up not appearing in this book. There are also keywords we did not initially consider and their absence from our call for chapters generated critiques and conversations about what is foundational to the social studies. One senior scholar rightly asked how a word such as *culture*, the cornerstone of Williams' own keywords project, could be missing from a book as culture lies at the heart of the social studies. This critique forced us as coeditors to consider what we missed and could not see existing right in front of us. Which other keywords did we fail to recognize?

The initial call for chapters insisted, however, that our proposed list of keywords was not exhaustive and we welcomed submissions for keywords we did not mention in our list. Fortunately for us, our book includes chapters that address important keywords we suggested to prospective authors, keywords such as *home*, *religion*, *gender*, and *borders*. We believe these negotiations with authors have resulted in contributions that even unsettled our ideas of what this book might be. And so this book should be seen as an invitation, not a declaration. Rather than declare that these are the most central and important keywords to be found in social studies education we ask readers to instead see them as invitations to think in new and different ways about the social studies, and to reexamine and reconsider what social studies education looks like now and how it may look differently in futures we have yet to imagine.

With this goal in mind, we edited these chapters to experiment with what could happen in our classrooms if we unsettle words seen as central to social studies education that are either taken for granted (e.g., *environment*) or are words that need to be forcefully confronted in our teaching (e.g., *terrorism*). Each chapter attends to a specific keyword selected for both its contemporary applicability to social studies education and to its nearly universal presence in the curriculum structured by social studies education. The authors of each keyword chapter discuss the complex and contested components of the keyword by way of offering diverse accounts for the keyword's abilities to move throughout the social studies curriculum. These accounts range from autobiographical narratives of the authors' lived experiences to creative, historical genealogies of the concept. Narratives also range from suggesting implications of the concepts in specific curriculum contexts to offering vignettes of classroom teaching in which authors account for the keyword in an example of instruction. In all of the chapters in this book, however, the authors deconstruct and reconstruct the keyword in order to galvanize new positions, new stances, new approaches, and new orientations to both the keyword and the concepts the keyword makes possible to think and teach within social studies education. We offer these chapters to help social studies educators play with the ideas, impulses, and ideologies that stitch together democratic ways of living and being in the world as citizens.

Our chapters urge readers to reread, reconsider, and readopt pedagogical practices attending to the keywords in social studies education so that we can, as Parker (2015) urges us, "construct social studies education, again and again, by enacting it, describing it, and debating its means and ends" (p. 3). These keywords and concepts upon which social studies teachers and teacher educators rely in their daily enactments of the work guide the framing of curriculum, the questions posed to students, and the assumptions underlying these conversations. For example, when teachers make reference to "Indians," time as the past, borders as lines between nations, the environment as something "out there," gender as male or female, technology as the newest gadgets and gizmos, and media as something transmitted to us, we have taken a side in social studies debates, sometimes without realizing it. With their unsettling of keywords, our authors pose a challenge to the social studies as Inigo Montoya posed to Vizzini in *The Princess Bride* (1987) in saying, "You keep using that word. I do not think it means what you think it means." We hope these keywords challenge social studies educators to see the field anew.

PRESENTING THE KEYWORDS

Anne-Lise Halvorsen began this book by arguing that social studies knowledge can be overlooked and viewed as "fixed," but that the concepts and conversations in this book encourage us to see knowledge as fluid and conversations as ongoing.

Section I: Culture

In unsettling around themes of culture, Sarah Shear and Christine Stanton take up the word *Indigenous* and ask, Indian? Native American? Indigenous Peoples? In doing so, they challenge settler colonial narratives and suggest ways social studies educators might engage Indigenous cultures and histories in social studies curriculum and pedagogy. Tommy Ender examines the role of the keyword *ethnic* through autoethnography by drawing ethnicity out of invisibility and into more visible and centered positions in discussions of social studies education. Amanda Vickery and Delandrea Hall brilliantly respond and extend the conversation on culture by pointing out how Beyoncé's *Lemonade* offers the social studies an illustrative example of how to affirm and center complex histories and experiences of Black women.

Section II: Time, Continuity, and Change

Mark Helmsing and Annie Whitlock unsettle the commonly understood meanings of *time*, continuity, and change by questioning what counts as "historical" and worthy of consideration in the social studies curriculum, offering two areas of inquiry: how teaching Millennials (and teaching about Millennials) requires us to confront what we determine to be historical events and how the teaching of different time periods as periodization opens space to consider the subjective ways we classify and organize time as "the past." As Helmsing and Whitlock unsettle how we think about organizing time, Gabriel Reich astutely responds by arguing that the settling of time periods—even if oversimplified—"allow students with limited historical knowledge to begin wrestling with continuity and change over time" (p. 48).

Section III: People, Places, and Environments

Jinny Menon and Muna Saleh foreground their experiences as women of diverse heritages to unpack the pluralistic nature of thinking about, with, and within *borders*, border making, and border crossing. Jodi Latremouille challenges binary conceptions of the *environment* as empty lands and bottomless reservoirs that exist "out there," contests corporate greenwashing pedagogies that "download eco-guilt onto consumers" and dominate environmental work in schools, and shares "love stories" of teachers doing environmental work. Gabriel Swarts complexifies our conceptions of what counts as a *home* by pointing out how common sense understandings of home limit our views to physical spaces, safe and comforting, familial and familiar, and places the keyword into larger contexts. Whitney Blankenship illustrates the ubiquitous centering of *place* by pointing out how we often ask people we meet, "where are you from?" She argues that place is more than physical or cultural characteristics because the places from where we live and the experiences we have in different places frame how we think about ourselves. Stacey Kerr challenges the idea that *space* is a static container for human activity, and instead shows how space can be understood through movement. Jason Harshman deftly responds to these chapters by engaging the subjectivity of borders, environment, home, place, and space as processes of ongoing meaning-making. He asks us to think of our recent travels not in terms of *what* we have done, but the geographic *where*.

Section IV: Individual Development and Identity

This section examines three keywords that are front and center in discussions about our identities, sometimes disparaged and dismissed as "identity politics." Megan List argues that *gender* is often simplified into a male/female binary and the social studies can benefit from challenging heteronormative and cisnormative assumptions in the past and present. Kristen Duncan contends *race* and racism are often reduced to examples of people mistreating or discriminating against others because of the color of their skin, but such representations ignore structural and systemic racism and a need for racial literacy. Dan Bordwell, Ryan Oto, and J.B. Mayo examine their collective experiences to interrogate how sexuality often appears in the social studies through the pervasive web of heteronormativity. In her section response, Ashley Woodson powerfully asks, returns to, and expands upon the question: what will it take to recognize a broader spectrum of raced, sexed, and gendered bodies in social studies education?

Section V: Individual, Groups, and Institutions

Erik Byker, Amy Good, and Noreen Williams examine *community* through the lens of intersectionality, probing exclusions in the "expanding environments" curriculum, and presenting a case study of community mapping podcasts produced by social studies teacher candidates. Erin Adams explores how social studies educators can explore *family* through various mediums such as television shows as well as in places that are outside the home, such as in grocery stores and markets. Colleen Fitzpatrick and Stephanie van Hover argue that social studies educators must remediate religious illiteracy in the United States so students and teachers may understand what religion is and what religious beliefs mean for society. In response, Sara Levy argues that the concepts of community, family, and religion can allow students to "study, critique, participate in, and define their own communities" beyond personal considerations, but in the shared spaces of school and in terms of the common good.

Section VI: Power, Authority, and Governance

Jane Lo and Amanda Geiger help readers appreciate the complexities and challenges of *democracy* in both historic and modern conceptions, asking what it may mean to teach students about democracy in social studies courses. Eli Kean and Jeffrey Craig reason that *freedom* is a fundamental and historically troubling concept for U.S. democracy as they explore the triadic relationship of freedom to, from, and for in relation to the First Amendment. Often contrasted to freedom, Wayne Journell argues that Western definitions of *terrorism* as exclusive and evil acts of Muslim extremists limit both a historical and contemporary understanding of the term. Cathryn van Kessel converses with these chapters by pointing out that the meaning behind these keywords must be understood in terms of who has the influence and power to shape their meanings and implications.

Section VII: Production, Distribution, and Consumption

To question consumption, Kim Pennington explores how (over)*consumption* is normalized and reinforced within social studies curriculum and presents sustainability as an alternative concept that might interrupt these narratives. E. Wayne Ross agitates *class* as a construct almost entirely absent from the social studies curriculum and clarifies the complexity and educational significance of class as a concept for curriculum and research. Matthew Missias and Kristy Brugar explore *entrepreneurship* in the context of the American Ideal and notions of innovation, critically examine characteristics of entrepreneurship, and offer a more varied pantheon of entrepreneurial examples. Mary Beth Henning expands upon the chapters in this section by connecting the concepts in each chapter to lessons, research, and ideas for teaching more "critical and compassionate approaches" to economic education and financial literacy (p. 273).

Section VIII: Science, Technology, and Society

Dan Krutka contends we should examine why and how *technology* in the social studies is often represented as historical tools and contemporary innovations that are part of the same story—a story of technological progress. Lance Mason points out how *media* is generally defined as a conduit for newspapers, radio, and television messages that students should analyze, but students and teachers should understand how mediums also create social environments. Scott Metzger responds to these provocations with keen ideas and examples to extend conversations in this section by calling on the social studies to ask critical questions that weigh the benefits and limitations of media, gaming, and technologies that supposedly offer cyber-salvation.

Section IX: Global Connections

Kenneth Carano and Robert Bailey demonstrate how the term *global* has become widely used, arguing that the social studies field has struggled to construct a meaningful definition for the word. To address *immigration*, Dilys Schoorman and Rina Bousalis contend that because the underlying tensions surrounding immigration are deep-rooted and persistent, discussions of the concept require historical, cultural, economic, and social contextualization that reveal ideological underpinnings. Cinthia Salinas and Melissa Rojas Williams carefully reflect on these chapters, advocate for reconceptualization of these discourses around citizenship education, moving us toward a politics of belonging.

Section X: Civic Ideals and Practices

Rory Tannebaum reexamines civic ideals and practices when he unpacks *discourse*, arguing students should learn discourse, more so than debate or dissent, as critical to a progressive collective sphere in which parties work together to construct knowledge and grow as citizens. Sarah Stanlick questions a weighted and ambiguous keyword that is most often associated with the purpose of social studies: *citizenship*. She argues that citizenship should be conceived of as an iterative process—rather than a singularly bestowed right—in an inquiry-driven field that critically examines our world and ourselves. Beth Rubin expands on the constructs offered by the authors in this section by arguing that "we construct our worlds through talk" within contested contexts that can connect students to longer histories and different visions of citizenship.

In the afterword, Walter Parker, a scholar who influenced our thinking for this volume, adds his voice to our conversations by unsettling *social studies* as a keyword. He closes this book, but leaves open the conversation, by making clear that keywords and concepts are practical matters for teaching and learning that necessitate care, criticism, and curiosity. We hope this book unsettles the social studies for you as it has for us.

REFERENCES

Epstein, T., & Peck, C. (Eds.). (2018). *Teaching and learning difficult histories in international contexts: A critical sociocultural approach*. New York, NY: Routledge.

Evans, R. W. (2004). *The social studies wars: What should we teach the children?* New York, NY: Teachers College Press.

Garrett, J. (2017). *Learning to be in the world: Difficult knowledge and social studies education*. New York, NY: Peter Lang.

Halvorsen, A. L. (2013). *A history of elementary social studies: Romance and reality*. New York, NY: Peter Lang.

Helmsing, M. (2014). Virtuous subjects: A critical analysis of the affective substance of social studies education. *Theory and Research in Social Education, 42*(1), 127–140.

King, L. J. (2014). Learning other people's history: Pre-service teachers' developing African American historical knowledge. *Teaching Education, 25*(4), 427–456.

Loewen, J. W. (2007). *Lies my teacher told me: Everything your American history textbook got Wrong* (10th anniversary ed.). New York, NY: The New Press.

National Council for the Social Studies. (2010). *National curriculum standards for social studies: A framework for teaching, learning, and assessment*. Silver Spring, MD: Author.

National Council for the Social Studies. (2013). *The college, career, and civic life (C3) framework for social studies state standards: Guidance for enhancing the rigor of K-12 civics, economics, geography, and history*. Silver Spring, MD: Author.

Parker, W. (2015). *Social studies today: Research and practice* (2nd ed.). New York, NY: Routledge.

Santiago, M. (2013). Teaching a new chapter of History. *Phi Delta Kappan, 94*(6), 35–38.
Scheinman, A. & Reiner, R. (Producer), & Reiner, R. (Director). (1987). *The princess bride* [Motion Picture]. United States: MGM Home Entertainment.
Schmidt, S. (2011). Who lives on the other side of that boundary: A model of geographic thinking. *Social Education, 75*(5), 250–255.
Segall, A. (2003). Maps as stories about the world. *Social Studies and the Young Learner, 16*(1), 21–25.
Subedi, B. (Ed.). (2010). *Critical global perspectives: Rethinking knowledge about global societies*. Charlotte, NC: Information Age Publishing.
Thornton, S. J. (2005). *Teaching social studies that matters: curriculum for active learning*. New York, NY: Teachers College Press.
Williams, R. (1976/1983). *Keywords: A vocabulary of culture and society*. Oxford: Oxford University Press.
Wineburg, S. (2001). *Historical thinking and other unnatural acts: Charting the future of teaching the past*. Philadelphia, PA: Temple University Press.
Woodson, A. N. (2015). "What you supposed to know": Urban Black students' perspectives on history textbooks. *Journal of Urban Learning, Teaching, and Research, 11*, 57–65.

Section I: Culture

CHAPTER ONE

Indigenous

SARAH B. SHEAR, PENN STATE UNIVERSITY-ALTOONA
CHRISTINE R. STANTON, MONTANA STATE UNIVERSITY

> The terms indigenous[1] and First Nations Peoples still generalize the identity of the more than 500 indigenous groups in the lower 48 and Alaska. However, I believe they are empowering 'generalized' descriptors because they accurately describe the political, cultural, and geographical identities, and struggles of all aboriginal peoples in the United States. I no longer use Indian, American Indian, or Native American because I consider them oppressive, counterfeit identities.
>
> —Michael Yellow Bird (Sahnish, Arikara) quoted in Pewewardy (2000)

We are often asked, "which term should I use when teaching about Native Americans?" This question is complex, and the answer depends on whom you ask and your purpose(s) for teaching about Indigenous Peoples. The topics described in this chapter, including those presented in Mr. Yellow Bird's quote, cannot possibly encompass the beliefs of *all* Indigenous Peoples. Furthermore, while we, the coauthors, have extensive experience researching and teaching about these topics and advocating for/with Indigenous Peoples, we are non-Indigenous educators and scholars, so our perspectives are limited. That said, we hope this chapter will provide a foundation for teachers (and others) to initiate conversations with Indigenous community members about the terms used to reference this land's First Peoples. First, we will unpack why names used to identify Indigenous Peoples should be central in our efforts to unsettle social studies terminology, given the widespread and lasting effects of colonization and settlement by non-Indigenous peoples. Second, we focus on specific terms, their histories, and their continued influences today. Third, we suggest strategies and resources for social studies educators seeking additional information.

The histories and experiences of Indigenous Peoples are some of the most often misrepresented, inaccurately portrayed, and silenced in social studies education (Journell, 2009; Rains, 2006; Sanchez, 2001; Trafzer & Lorimer, 2014; Vasquez-Heilig, Brown, & Brown, 2012). Textbooks often describe Indigenous Peoples from a single Euroamerican viewpoint, instead of honoring the experiences and perspectives unique to diverse Indigenous groups and individuals. Even when Indigenous perspectives are included, they are often presented in a way that suggests inferiority or obstruction to the assimilationist goals of the United States. For example, in her study of U.S. history textbooks, Stanton (2014) found that "inclusion of Native primary accounts does not necessarily result in the validation of Native perspectives" (p. 660). Similar findings were found in Shear, Knowles, Soden, and Castro's (2015) national study of K–12 U.S. history state standards. States by and large presented Indigenous Peoples as barriers to U.S. expansion (i.e., Manifest Destiny) and all but erased Indigenous Peoples and Nations from U.S. history after the year 1900.

Fortunately, several states are developing resources to confront and challenge the problematic ways Indigenous Peoples are represented in curriculum. For example, Montana's "Indian Education for All" constitutional amendment and Washington's "Since Time Immemorial" standards encourage a more accurate, culturally sustaining/revitalizing (McCarty & Lee, 2014) presentation of Indigenous Peoples, through multiple perspectives and counternarratives. Even in places where teachers may not have much control over their curriculum, there are ways to support anticolonial work. Being purposeful in our use of terms, and of the terms used by our students, is an important first step to support social justice, anticolonial education. In the following section, we describe several foundational terms (i.e., imperialism, colonialism, settler colonialism) and concepts (i.e., naming, self-determination) that underscore the need for purposeful terminology within social studies education.

FOUNDATIONAL IDEAS

Settler Colonialism

To begin talking and thinking about terms surrounding Indigenous Peoples, we need to talk and think about how the United States *became* the United States. While we cannot delve into every decision that took part in this creation, we can acknowledge that this land was invaded by Europeans and, over time, was settled by Europeans-turned-U.S. Americans. Within this acknowledgement is the essential understanding of imperialism and colonialism. Sometimes used interchangeably, imperialism and colonialism are in fact distinct, albeit connected, issues. Summing up their differences and similarities, Maori scholar Linda Tuhiwai Smith (1999) wrote, "Imperialism was the system of control which secured the markets and capital investments [of European nations]. Colonialism facilitated this expansion by ensuring that there was European control, which necessarily meant securing and subjugating the indigenous populations" (p. 21). In the American context, Hixon (2013) explained, "What primarily distinguishes settler colonialism from colonialism proper is that the settlers came not to exploit the indigenous populations for economic gain, but rather to remove them from colonial space" (p. 4). In other words, Americans fulfilled not only the imperial goals of economic expansion but also the colonial goal of land theft.

Hixon (2013) noted that settler colonialism in the United States is like the actions taken by settlers in Australia, including ethnic cleansing and cultural genocide via education reforms (i.e., boarding schools). Unlike Australia, however, settler colonialism in the United States turned to legal maneuverings—in particular, carefully worded treaties—to forcibly remove Indigenous Peoples from their lands. Furthermore, American settler colonialism used these legal provisions to justify war on Indigenous Nations. Notably, at the dawn of the United States, "The Americans streaming into the borderlands joined by land speculators and the 'founding fathers' back east were determined to take the land and to kill or remove those who stood in their way" (Hixon, 2013, p. 62). Unfortunately, we do not often see social studies education confronting this violent and complicated history, particularly in a way that values and centers the voices and experiences of Indigenous Peoples. It is important, as we move forward, to challenge ourselves to reread our histories, curricula, and pedagogies as intimately tied to a carefully crafted story of who we are as Americans. Purposeful consideration of how we name ourselves— and each other—allows us to more fully confront our country's complex history, including the efforts to erase Indigenous Peoples.

Naming

For many Indigenous groups, names are intrinsically linked to identity. Kiowa author Momaday (1996) explains that names are powerful: They have multiple meanings, they shape interpretations, and they contain historical and cultural knowledge. Indigenous individuals may introduce themselves by sharing their name in their own language, identifying their tribal affiliations, and/or explaining their relationships with other individuals. Young people may receive a name in their Indigenous language as part of a ceremony, and adults may be given a new name following a transformative experience.

Given the culturally significant role that languages, names, and identities hold, it is not surprising that naming served as a tactic of colonizers and settlers. Indigenous Peoples who met certain federally determined requirements (e.g., blood quantum, connection to a land base) were named and enrolled in specific tribes to justify policies such as relocation to reservations. The naming of Indigenous Peoples by governmental agencies, popular media, and teachers has been, and continues to be, complex and often politically or economically motivated.

Since Indigenous words frequently have multiple meanings that cannot be accurately expressed in English, it is problematic to assume that single English words adequately represent the diverse identities within and between Indigenous groups. However, social studies standards, textbooks, and other curricular resources often use single, generalizing terms such as *Native American* and *Indian* without providing explanations. Therefore, educators may need to look beyond their most accessible resources when considering terminology. One way teachers can easily and efficiently encourage students to think about the importance of naming is to explain their own rationale for using one name over another.

Self-determination

Historically, Euroamerican officials, settlers, and educators ignored or misunderstood the names Indigenous groups chose for themselves. For example, the Apsáalooke (a word that does not translate directly to English, but loosely means "children of the large beaked bird") were inaccurately renamed the Crow. Indigenous groups also had names for each other that conflicted with those names groups chose for themselves. The Anishinaabe referred to the Lakota using a word that means "enemy" or "snakes," and through permutations of Anishinaabe and French words, this name became "Sioux" (Makes Good Ta Kola Cou Ota, 2009).

It was not until 1975 that, through the Indian Self-Determination and Education Assistance Act, the U.S. government expanded authority for tribes to revitalize Indigenous languages and identities, particularly within educational contexts. However, today Indigenous Peoples note that there is still much work to be done in terms of *self-determination*. To truly end the "hegemonic voice-over of indigenous experiences" (Tuck & Fine, 2007, p. 149), Indigenous Peoples need to be able to determine their own individual and collective identities.

When asked about the traditional meaning of the names tribes call themselves, many translate to "the People" or "the Children." Today, more tribes are actively replacing settler-colonial names with their traditional names (e.g., "Apsáalooke" instead of "Crow"). Educators can promote interest in and respect for self-determination of Indigenous identities through inclusion of Indigenous languages, knowledges, and ways of knowing in their curriculum and instruction. For example, teachers can refer to resources created by members of the Indigenous communities under study or—better yet—actively collaborate with Indigenous communities and individuals to identify the terms and descriptions preferred by the Indigenous Peoples themselves.

"INDIAN": ORIGINS AND COMPLICATIONS OF COLUMBUS' INVASION

Ojibwe[2] scholar Anton Treuer (2012) aptly wrote, "The word *Indian* comes from a mistake: on his first voyage to the Americas, Columbus thought the Caribbean was the Indian Ocean and the people there were Indians" (emphasis in original, p. 7). We begin this section with a discussion of the term *Indian* because it is a term embedded within a broader history of genocide and confusion. Gerald Vizenor (Anishinaabe) (1994) wrote that "Indian," as a word used to encapsulate hundreds of unique cultural groups, was inherent in the language of dominance. Likewise, for Roxanne Dunbar-Ortiz and Dina Gilio-Whitaker (Colville Confederated Tribes) (2016), the term "is Eurocentric because the word was a term of convenience for the interlopers who couldn't distinguish between differing cultures and languages and because it suited centuries of European newcomers rather than respecting the nations' words for themselves" (p. 146). Two issues center our problem with the term "Indian": (1) It is associated with Columbus, who brought death and destruction to the Americas, and (2) it denies Indigenous Peoples agency to name themselves.

Use of the term *Indian* is made more complex in that some Indigenous Peoples have advocated for "taking back" of the term (sometimes also seen as NDN). For example, Spokane/Coeur d'Alene writer Sherman Alexie said, "The white man tried to take our land, our sovereignty, and our languages. And he gave us the word 'Indian.' Now he wants to take the word 'Indian' away from us, too" (quoted in Treuer, 2012, p. 8). The last few decades saw a rise in the use of "American Indian," which is also problematic according to Dunbar-Ortiz and Gilio-Whitaker (2016) because "qualifying the term 'Indian' with 'American' adds another layer of imposition by inferring the centrality of U.S. ('American') legal domination, a concept many Native people today still find highly offensive" (p. 146). In sum, whether to use *Indian* is a personal decision, one that should be thoughtful and deliberate with full knowledge of the history it carries with it.

"NATIVE AMERICAN" AND "AMERICAN INDIAN": RESPONDING TO THE CIVIL RIGHTS MOVEMENT

Our preservice teachers often ask about the use of *Native American* as a substitute for *Indian*, and they understandably scratch their heads when told that that name, too, is problematic. Dunbar-Ortiz and Gilio-Whitaker (2016) wrote:

> "Native American" is a term that arose after the civil rights movement in response to a need for unbiased terminology regarding historically maligned ethnic groups. While perhaps a step in the right direction, it still highlights a relationship of historic domination. The Eurocentrism inherent in all of the terms defines the racism at the root of them all, especially given that the terms are imposed by outsiders in Native peoples' own homelands. (p. 146)

Often tagged with being *politically correct* because of the social and political climates of the time, the use of *Native American* became increasingly popular among both Indigenous and non-Indigenous Peoples, especially in the 1980s and 1990s, to move away from the blatantly racist language of the past. Unfortunately, such terms as *Native American* and *American Indian* (as briefly mentioned in the previous section) still situate Indigenous Peoples and Nations as dependent upon the United States, which reinforces settler colonial mentalities in two critical ways: (1) these names deny Indigenous sovereignty and self-determination, and (2) these names erase an essential history of acknowledgement for the peoples who lived on these lands long before the names American and United States ever existed.

The debates about whether to use one name or another reflect the complex history of Indigenous–U.S. relations. Comanche-Kiowa scholar Cornel Pewewardy (2000) noted:

> During my undergraduate years in the seventies, many people in this country felt that a major new paradigm shift had been made when "native" in Native American became popular, with the predictable addition that "n" in native would be capitalized.... We wrestled with the ascribed terms—Indian, American Indian, Amerindian, Native American—as if we had no power to define other choices. (pp. 12–13)

Taking this into consideration, the use of *Native American* or *American Indian* brings us again to the importance of centering Indigenous Peoples in social studies and being deliberate in our teaching of why names matter.

"WARRIORS," "BRAVES," AND "R**SKINS": THE PROBLEMS OF CULTURAL (MIS)APPROPRIATION

When it comes to representations of Indigenous Peoples, confusion frequently surrounds the distinction between cultural appreciation and cultural appropriation. Because Indigenous Peoples have long been excluded from curricula and media, some people argue that any representation is better than none. This sort of claim is evident when sports fans dressed up in warbonnets argue, "I'm honoring you!" While we rarely see problematic terms such as "R**skin"[3] within contemporary social studies curriculum, they continue to plague educational discourse more broadly. These terms are rooted in genocide, colonization, and violence, and they have a continued effect of Indigenous youth and communities today. As William Mendoza (Oglala-Sicangu

Lakota), director of the White House Initiative on American Indian and Alaska Native Education (Obama Administration), explains, "Harmful stereotypes affect students' lives, day in, day out" (quoted in Anderson, 2016).

A nationwide database reveals that over 2,000 sports teams—most of them at high schools—have mascots referencing Indigenous Peoples (Munguia, 2014). These include generic terms (e.g., Braves, Warriors, Indians), as well as specific Nation names (e.g., Apaches, Mohawks, Sioux, Utes). Most notably, the database lists continued use of "Squaw" (a highly offensive term that encourages sexual violence against Indigenous women) and R**skins (a term which refers to the sanctioned slaughter of Indigenous Peoples for scalps). A common thread across terms—including more "positive" terms such as "warriors"—is that they urge predominantly non-Indigenous fans to "dress up like Indians" and use stereotypical behaviors, such as "tomahawk chops" or "war chants." Tolerance for these behaviors often neglects critical historical, cultural, and political context. For example, fans may not know that warbonnets are part of the ceremonial regalia worn only by leaders of some (not all!) Nations for important events.

Sometimes, schools serving predominantly Indigenous populations choose mascots that align with the community's traditional views or specific Nations names (e.g., Wyoming Indian Chiefs, Piikani Blue Thunder). In these cases, the Indigenous community plays an important role in the selection of the mascot, the choice reflects the student body's identity, and the imagery is historically accurate and respectful. It is vital to work with Indigenous communities to determine if Indigenous imagery is culturally appropriate, or if it is cultural appropriation. However, it is also important to remember that many Indigenous communities hold knowledge collectively, so support must come from the community, not only from a few individuals.

NOT ALL THE SAME: CHALLENGING COLONIALISM BY HONORING INDIGENOUS NATIONS BY NAME

Referring to specific nations (e.g., Lakota, Choctaw) is often preferable to using generic terms (e.g., Plains Indian, Native American). For instance, musician and activist Radmilla Cody prefers to be referred to as Navajo or Diné, instead of "Native American," which, as she argues, suggests assimilation and sameness (Blackhorse, 2015). Use of specific nation names also promotes more accurate understandings of history. For example, textbook authors frequently imply that *all* "Native Americans" fought against Custer's forces at the Battle of Little Bighorn. Such generalization neglects the complex reality that distinct tribes and bands (e.g., Oglala Lakota, Cheyenne, Arapaho) formed a powerful alliance, while other Indigenous individuals (e.g., members of the Apsáalooke and Arikara nations) served as scouts for the U.S. Cavalry.

To further challenge misconceptions, advance self-determination, and reinvigorate Indigenous languages, many scholars and activists urge revitalization of *traditional* nation names (e.g., Diné, Apsáalooke) instead of relying on names created and used by settlers (e.g., Navajo, Crow). For example, during early contact with European settlers and traders, the A'aninin (which translates loosely to "White Clay People") made a sign depicting a waterfall (likely the Great Falls of the Missouri). The sign was misunderstood to mean "Big Belly," which inspired the French name for the nation ("Gros Ventre"). Teachers can share this information to confront historical misconceptions, encourage revitalization of Indigenous knowledges, and support social studies content and skills. As illustrated by this example, traditional names often offer insights to geographic places and oral histories.

To use a nation name appropriately, we must first know with which group a person identifies. This task can prove difficult, because we may not be able to ask the individual directly, he/she may identify with more than one tribe, or he/she may not identify with any particular tribe. Several tribes have divided (e.g., Northern Arapaho and Southern Arapaho), with key distinctions between groups, so it may be insufficient and inappropriate to refer to an individual by the broader name (e.g., Arapaho). Because, historically, most Indigenous languages were not written, people may use various spellings (e.g., Piikani, Pikuni, Pikani) to refer to the same group. Therefore, it is important for educators to determine the terms, spellings, and pronunciations preferred by members of Indigenous communities.

"INDIGENOUS": BREAKING COLONIAL LANGUAGE BY ACKNOWLEDGING FIRST PEOPLES

To show solidarity within and between diverse groups, many scholars advocate for the terms *Indigenous*, *Indigenous Nations*, and *Indigenous Peoples*. The use of capitalization emphasizes community and sovereignty, as it does for other cultural or ethnic groups (e.g., Latinx, Hmong) and nations (e.g., New Zealand, Peru). Furthermore, capitalization also distinguishes peoples from plants and animals that are *indigenous* to a specific place. It is important to also note the use of the plural forms to acknowledge diversity between and within groups.

These terms are especially powerful when thinking beyond the political, sociocultural, and geographic boundaries of the United States, as they can also refer to First Nations (Canada), Aboriginal (Australia), and other Indigenous Peoples around the world. At the 2011 meeting of the American Educational Research Association, leading Indigenous scholars from around the world called for use of the term "Indigenous" to generate strength and solidarity within educational research and practice (Smith, Wong, Brayboy, Grande, & Cowan, 2011). Linda Smith (1999) noted that *Indigenous Peoples* stems from the 1960s

Civil Rights Movement, which marked a turn in the discourse toward expanded self-determination and decolonization efforts around the world. We advocate for the use of *Indigenous Nations* to draw attention to the collective, political power of Indigenous Peoples, instead of *tribes* or *tribal nations*, which may evoke stereotypical images of primitive peoples.

Aside from supporting solidarity and sovereignty, these terms directly resist settler-colonial discourses, because they provide "a more accurate description for peoples with existences that long predate modern states and histories of colonial intrusions into already occupied territories" (Dunbar-Ortiz & Gilio-Whitaker, 2016, p. 147). Unlike *American Indian* and *Native American*, *Indigenous* does not imply dependency upon the *American* or settler-colonial political context. Instead, the term recognizes an inherent connection to place of origin, given that "Indigenous peoples have sustained themselves on their homelands since time immemorial" (Brayboy, Fann, Castagno, & Solyom, 2012, p. 23).

Like the many terms discussed in this chapter, *Indigenous*, *Indigenous Peoples*, and *Indigenous Nations* should not be used without purposeful consideration, even though they are widely respected. Sometimes, there are locally dependent reasons for preferring certain terms over others. Therefore, we urge educators to learn about the complex and specific experiences of distinct groups or individuals and, if appropriate, to use the most specific terms possible when referencing those experiences.

CONCLUDING THOUGHTS

Settler colonialism in the United States sought to erase the complexity and uniqueness of millions of Indigenous Peoples, and the development of language by which *to know* and *to name* a person or group of people was central to that endeavor. As Philip Deloria (Dakota) (1998) wrote, "Race has, of course, been a characteristic American obsession—and the racial imagination has been at work on many different groups of people, Indians included" (p. 5). Identifying people by racialized names was and continues to play an integral role in U.S. education, government, and society, with the names associated with groups of people rooted in insidious histories.

While there is no easy way to challenge the complicated history of settler colonialism in the United States, social studies teachers have a unique responsibility to share historical, political, economic, and sociological contextual information with their students. Teachers can provide background about names assigned to Indigenous Peoples and those preferred by the Indigenous Peoples themselves. They can engage their students in community-based research to learn about the histories of Indigenous Peoples and their names within the local setting. Together, students, teachers, and community members can compare and contrast the different terms used to identify specific groups of people. These approaches are possible even in classrooms where teachers have limited flexibility in terms of curriculum.

Teachers can further support Indigenous self-determination in many ways. For example, they can confront inappropriate terminology and imagery in curriculum and school environments. In many schools, teachers and youth have led efforts to ban the use of inappropriate Indigenous imagery or to replace inaccurate content. Such initiatives offer opportunities for educators to lead discussions regarding civic engagement. The nationwide mascot debate provides powerful, engaging opportunities for educators to connect to current events and media. These conversations also support integration of multiple social studies disciplines, such as history, economics, government, sociology, and geography.

Even when faced with time constraints and curricular pressure, teachers have many options to teach about terminology used to identify Indigenous Peoples. Specifically, we can:

- Work with Indigenous Peoples to determine preferred names and appropriate usage of names and identifying terms;
- Avoid activities that trivialize names and identities (e.g., *What would your Indian name be?*);
- Engage students in thinking critically about identity, naming, and self-determination (see example activities from Montana and Washington curricula websites in Table 1.1);
- Question and unsettle terms, and their related stereotypical images and behaviors, in and beyond schools (e.g., advocate for elimination of Columbus Day and recognition of Indigenous Peoples Day);
- Teach about ongoing efforts of Indigenous Nations to advance sovereignty and self-determination (e.g., nonviolent direct action by water protectors in Standing Rock, relocation of Indigenous Peoples from Newtok, Alaska and Isle de Jean Charles, Louisiana due to climate change);
- Be purposeful in our own choices; and
- Explain our choices to others (e.g., model criticality in terms of reading, viewing).

The purpose of this chapter was to open critical dialogue about the terms we use, see, and hear within social studies education and advocate for the use of "Indigenous" when addressing the collective of peoples who have lived on these lands since time immemorial. In addition, because of the complexity of settler colonialism and Indigeneity, this dialogue must extend beyond these pages, so we encourage educators to engage with each other, their communities, and resources (see Table 1.1) to continue learning. As educators, we can best support decolonization efforts led by Indigenous Peoples by pushing ourselves as learners, openly challenging the colonizing language of our nation, and becoming purposeful in our use of naming terms related to Indigenous Peoples.

Table 1.1. Resources for Indigenous Education

Resource type	Title	Author/ producer	Why we recommend it
Website	*Native Knowledge 360*	The National Museum of the American Indian	http://www.nmai.si.edu/nk360/ Provides an "Essential Understandings" Framework, lessons, resources, and information about professional development opportunities for teachers
Website	*Indian Education for All*	The State of Montana	http://opi.mt.gov/Programs/IndianEd/Curric.html Provides teacher resources, including lesson plans, across content areas and grade levels. Resources have been developed in partnership with members of Indigenous Nations and align with seven "essential understandings" related to Indigenous experiences. Montana's IEFA mandate requires all teachers, including those outside of social studies, to teach about the essential understandings to Indigenous and non-Indigenous students alike
Website	*Since Time Immemorial*	The State of Washington	http://www.indian-ed.org/ Provides curriculum materials for K–12 teachers to teach about Indigenous sovereignty, self-determination, histories, and current events. These curricular materials were developed as a partnership between the State of Washington and several of the 29 federally recognized Indigenous Nations of Washington
Website	*Oyate*	The Oyate Organization	oyate.org Provides resources about and reviews for books written by and about Indigenous Peoples, as reviewed and evaluated by Indigenous educators and community members. Includes criteria for evaluating books and a list of books to avoid. Also see the book *A Broken Flute* (published by Oyate). Especially useful for pre-K–6 teachers
Book	*Rethinking Columbus*	Rethinking Schools	Offers in-depth resources, including lesson plans, to teach about the European invasion of the Americas

Continued on next page

Table 1.1—*Continued*

Resource type	Title	Author/producer	Why we recommend it
Book	*Playing Indian*	Philip J. Deloria	Provides a thorough examination of U.S. history in relation to the impact of colonization, assimilation, and appropriation of Indigenous Peoples. Recommended for development of content knowledge
Book	*An Indigenous People's History of the United States*	Roxanne Dunbar-Ortiz	Provides a rich counternarrative to the creation of the United States. Recommended for development of content knowledge
Book	*All the Real Indians Are Dead and 20 Other Myths about Native Americans*	Roxanne Dunbar-Ortiz and Dina Gilio-Whitaker	Offers evidence and commentary about Indigenous stereotypes. Recommended for content knowledge and useful in secondary social studies classrooms
Book	*Everything You Wanted to Know about Indians but Were Afraid to Ask*	Anton Treuer	Provides evidence and commentary on commonly asked questions about Indigenous Peoples. Recommended for content knowledge. Also useful in secondary social studies classrooms
Book	*The Earth Shall Weep: A History of Native America*	James Wilson	Provides an examination of the impact of settler-colonialism on Indigenous Peoples in the Americas, and is critically acclaimed for including Indigenous worldviews alongside archeological and historical research
Film	*Reel Injun*	Neil Diamond (Cree)	Documentary film traces the history of Indigenous Peoples in movies and provides evidence and commentary on the impact of (mis)representations of Indigeneity. Recommended for content and film literacy development; useful in secondary social studies classrooms
Film	*In Whose Honor?: American Indian Mascots in Sports*	Jay Rosenstein	Documentary film tracing controversy surrounding the U of Illinois mascot. Provides commentary from multiple sides of the issue. Recommended for content and film literacy development; useful in secondary classrooms

DISCUSSION QUESTIONS

1. Given the information in this chapter, what are specific ways teachers can engage their students in thinking critically about the use of the terms *Indigenous Peoples, Native Americans, American Indians*, etc.?
2. How can teachers, parents, museum personnel, and other community members confront settler-colonial terminology and representations in their community's learning environments? What are some ways to expand awareness on a community-wide level?
3. Given the complexities presented in this chapter and the continued problem of misrepresentation of Indigenous Peoples in curriculum and teaching, how can social studies education research work in solidarity with decolonization efforts in education?

NOTES

1. It is important to note that preferences of naming terms, including how they are spelled and capitalized, varies depending on who is speaking/writing. In direct quotes from reference material, we use the original author's terminology. The use of lowercase "i" versus uppercase "I" will be discussed in subsequent sections of this chapter.
2. We use the Indigenous Nation names identified by the scholars we cite within the chapter. Anton Treuer self-identifies in his work as Ojibwe. The traditional name of this nation, as will be discussed in subsequent sections, is Anishinaabe.
3. In solidarity with leading Indigenous scholars, policymakers, and educators, we have elected to use this spelling. Given this term's historical call to violence, we refuse to provide direct, full attention to it. However, by using this spelling, as opposed to omitting the term altogether, we also strive to recognize its history and its continued influence in the United States today, particularly as connected to sports teams.

REFERENCES

Anderson, J. (2016, April 18). Report released on Native American mascots' use in schools. CBS Denver. Retrieved from http://denver.cbslocal.com/2016/04/18/report-native-american-mascots-schools/

Blackhorse, A. (2015, May 21). Blackhorse: Do you prefer "Native American" or "American Indian"? 6 prominent voices respond. *Indian Country Today*. Retrieved from http://indiancountrytodaymedianetwork.com/2015/05/21/blackhorse-do-you-prefer-native-american-or-american-indian-6-prominent-voices-respond

Brayboy, B., Fann, A., Castagno, A., & Solyom, J. (2012). *Postsecondary education for American Indian and Alaska Natives: Higher education for nation building and self-determination*. San Francisco, CA: Jossey-Bass.

Deloria, P. J. (1998). *Playing Indian.* New Haven, CT: Yale University Press.
Dunbar-Ortiz, R., & Gilio-Whitaker, D. (2016). *All the real Indians died off and 20 other myths about Native Americans.* Boston, MA: Beacon Press.
Hixon, W. (2013). *American settler colonialism: A history.* New York, NY: Palgrave Macmillan.
Journell, W. (2009). An incomplete history: Representations of American Indians in state social studies standards. *Journal of American Indian Education, 48*(2), 18–32.
Makes Good Ta Kola Cou Ota, S. (2009, March 12). Sioux is not even a word. *Lakota Country Times.* Retrieved from http://www.lakotacountrytimes.com/news/2009-03-12/guest/021.html
McCarty, T., & Lee, T. (2014). Critical culturally sustaining/revitalizing pedagogy and Indigenous education sovereignty. *Harvard Educational Review, 84*(1), 101–124.
Momaday, N. S. (1996). *The names: A memoir.* Tucson, AZ: University of Arizona Press.
Munguia, H. (2014, September 4). The 2,128 Native American mascots people aren't talking about. *Five Thirty Eight.* Retrieved from http://fivethirtyeight.com/features/the-2128-native-american-mascots-people-arent-talking-about/
Pewewardy, C. (2000). Renaming ourselves on our own terms: Race, tribal nations, and representation in education. *Indigenous Nations Studies Journal, 1*(1), 11–28.
Rains, F. V. (2006). The color of social studies: A post-social studies reality check. In E. W. Ross (Ed.), *The social studies curriculum: Purposes, problems, and possibilities* (pp. 137–156). Albany, NY: State University of New York Press.
Sanchez, T. R. (2001). Dangerous Indians: Evaluating the depiction of Native Americans in selected trade books. *Urban Education, 36,* 400–425. doi:10.1177/0042085901363005.
Shear, S. B., Knowles, R. T., Soden, G., & Castro, A. J. (2015). Manifesting destiny: Re/presentations of Indigenous people in K-12 U.S. history curriculum. *Theory & Research in Social Education, 43*(1), 68–101. doi:10.1080/00933104.2014.999849.
Smith, G., Wong, L., Brayboy, B., Grande, S., & Cowan, G. (2011, April 9). Presidential session: Standing our ground/Standing on our ground: Indigenous research as an act of defiance and enlightenment. Panel presentation for the Annual Meeting of the American Educational Research Association. New Orleans, LA.
Smith, L. T. (1999). *Decolonizing methodologies: Research and Indigenous Peoples.* London: Zed Books.
Stanton, C. R. (2014). The curricular Indian agent: Discursive colonization & Indigenous (dys)agency in U.S. history textbooks. *Curriculum Inquiry, 44*(5), 649–676, doi:10.1111/curi.12064.
Trafzer, C. E., & Lorimer, M. (2014). Silencing California Indian genocide in social studies texts. *American Behavioral Scientist, 58*(1), 64–82. doi: 10.1177/0002764213495032.
Treuer, A. (2012). *Everything you wanted to know about Indians but were afraid to ask.* St. Paul, MN: Borealis Books.
Tuck, E., & Fine, M. (2007). Inner angles: A range of ethical responses to Indigenous and decolonizing theories. In N. K. Denzin & M. D. Giardina (Eds.), *Ethical futures in qualitative research* (pp. 145–168). Walnut Creek, CA: Left Coast Press.
Vasquez-Heilig, J. V., Brown, K. D., & Brown, A. L. (2012). The illusion of inclusion: A critical race theory textual analysis of race and standards. *Harvard Educational Review, 82,* 403–424.
Vizenor, G. (1994). *Manifest manners: Post-Indian warriors of survivance.* Hanover, NH: University Press of New England.

CHAPTER TWO

Ethnic

TOMMY ENDER, LOYOLA UNIVERSITY MARYLAND

> To continue to move toward greater cultural and linguistic responsiveness in schools, teachers must see themselves as part of a community of educators working to make schools more equitable for all students. Teaching is an ethical activity, and teachers have an ethical obligation to help all students learn. To meet this obligation, teachers need to serve as advocates for their students, especially those who have been traditionally marginalized in school.
>
> —Villegas and Lucas (2007)

I attended an urban high school just outside of New York City. If you walked on Bergenline Avenue, the business thoroughfare in our neighborhood, you would hear business owners, customers, police officers, firefighters, and others all speaking Spanish. While we all shared a common language, we also had differences. I could go into one clothing store owned by an Argentinian and hear Argentinian Spanish or enter a different clothing store owned by a Colombian and hear Colombian Spanish. I could eat mofongo at a Puerto Rican restaurant or eat mangú in a Dominican restaurant. Both dishes were the same—fried plantains with olive oil and garlic. I could attend worship services at a Cuban synagogue or a Mexican Pentecostal church. However, attending high school brought a different experience.

It started with my first day of 9th-grade U.S. history. As I entered the classroom and sat down, the teacher, a white woman who taught for more than two decades, took roll by reading last names in alphabetical order. When she said "Ender," I responded with "present." She then said, "I thought you were somebody else." Surprised by the comment, I asked her, "What do you mean?" "Well, you have an American name, but you look Hispanic." It was the first time an educator had addressed me in that manner. I felt conflicted, angry, shame, and sadness. I loved history, and up until that day, I devoured historical knowledge without questioning it. That initial interaction foretold the rest of the school year.

The yearlong course focused on U.S. history from Columbian exploration to the U.S. Civil War. While the majority of the students identified as either Hispanic or Latino, the class revolved around white male perspectives. I learned about Columbus, John Locke, Thomas Jefferson, Andrew Jackson, and Abraham Lincoln. Her stories about these men deemed them infallible. We often challenged her by asking about Jefferson's alleged children born in slavery, Columbus's treatment of the Taíno people, and Lincoln's political reasons behind the Emancipation Proclamation. The teacher consistently refuted the arguments, calling them "speculation." By the end of the year, I just gave up and skipped the final. I felt marginalized because the teacher falsely assumed I lacked the knowledge to contribute to the class (Cammarota, 2016). I also felt conflicted about the history I learned in the K–8 setting. That 9th-grade history class helped me realize that learning history came from only white perspectives and other perspectives were permanently silenced (Halagao, 2004).

In this chapter, I connect my personal and traumatic experiences to the keyword *ethnic* through autoethnography. Autoethnography encourages the individual to study the self and present different perspectives (Hughes & Pennington, 2017), but the approach differs from autobiographical writing. Autoethnography allows the writer to "retrospectively and selectively write about epiphanies that stem from, or are made possible by, being part of a culture and/or possessing a particular cultural identity" (Ellis, Adams, & Bochner, 2010, p. 4). My 9th-grade history class experience served as the foundation for the examination of the keyword *ethnic* in social studies. I specifically drew out that experience to illustrate the concreteness of cultural conflict (Muncey, 2010).

I will explore *ethnic* in three ways: (1) tracing *ethnic* as identity, (2) disrupting *ethnic* as a concept, and (3) supporting *ethnic* in the social studies. My experiences as a Latino social studies K–12 teacher and scholar helps explain the phenomenon of interpreting *ethnic* in social studies (Wall, 2005). The isolation I felt in 9th grade, the community we developed as resistance toward the teacher, and the constant self-reflection years afterward are all part of the struggle in engaging *ethnic* within social studies (Winkler-Morey, 2010).

TRACING *ETHNIC* AS IDENTITY

Being a Latino, Latina, Latin@, or Latinx reflects the multinational and varied social group of a people reconciling and/or decolonizing with dominant cultural practices (Valdes, 2000). I experienced attempts to singularize the term as a K–12 social studies student and teacher. At one high school and one middle school, I was the only Latino on the entire school staff. At another middle school, I was one of two Latinos. During Hispanic Heritage Month at one school, a school administrator asked me to illuminate the highlights of being Hispanic for a one-hour school assembly. When I informed him that one hour would not be sufficient for identifying as a Hispanic or Latino due to different cultural cues and practices and that more representation was needed beyond one month, he thanked me for my thoughts and asked a teacher in the Spanish department to organize the event. The tokenism the school administrator wanted to project to the school audience contributed to a prevailing mindset at that school—that ethnic groups were monolithic (Halagao, 2004). The social studies department at the high school where I taught reflected a similar approach when it came to discussions of *ethnic*.

The social studies department required the use of a textbook for instruction. At the same time, they placed a significant value on democratic citizenship in teaching social studies (Busey & Waters, 2016). Democratic citizenship connected to, as Shiveley (2014) argued, the purpose of the discipline—developing students to actively and efficiently participate in a democracy. I firmly agreed with that approach; however, in department meetings, I pushed for an additional focus on ethnic identity. Discussing ethnic identity in social studies supported the department's concentration on democratic citizenship. The department chair instead suggested I rely on the textbook for assistance. Rather than make critical adjustments to our democratic society by addressing keywords such as *ethnic*, the textbook instead utilized a "rhetoric of certainty" (Loewen, 2007). While the textbook discussed ways students could become active citizens in the United States, the book also promoted "Americanization" (Hernandez Sheets, 2002). "Americanization" refers to the concept of assimilating immigrants into a single culture, thus altering their ethnic identities (Hernandez Sheets, 2002). The text was perceived to be correct since the department used no other textbooks. Any attempts to engage with *ethnic* needed to take place during class discussion.

I chose to engage with the students as knowledge holders. As Villegas and Lucas (2007) argue, the need to bring in students, especially those who have been marginalized by other teachers, is vitally important for conversations on *ethnic* to occur. Because I did not view myself as an educator who acted as all-knowing about *ethnic* (Freire, 1970/2000), I resisted teaching *at* the students (Maloy & LaRoche, 2015). Instead, I encouraged students to lead these conversations.

The students, as a result, made connections between the keyword *ethnic* and historical events. Typically, on the first day of class, I asked the students the following question, "What do you want to learn about yourself and your community?" Students often responded with the following phrase, "I want to learn about history I can relate to." The conversations then transitioned to the students' ancestral backgrounds. Stories of great-grandparents and other family members from

Ireland, Greece, Germany, Mexico, and China experiencing prejudice from nativists due to their ethnicity, such as being shut out of employment opportunities, residential areas, and houses of worship. These conversations uncovered the incidents of oppressed individuals, not elevating myths of immigrants achieving the American dream (Loewen, 2007; Winkler-Morey, 2010).

Extending into the academy, my ethnic identity informs my understanding of social studies research. I view the literature through critical lenses. I perceive limited scholarship on the application of critical theories or ideas in social studies. The research I conduct provides opportunities for change in the literature (Cammarota, 2016). I incorporate concepts from Critical Race Theory (CRT) and Latino Critical Theory (LatCrit). I challenge race and other forms of prejudice. The work firmly places *ethnic* as part of that critical theoretical framework. While comments from leading scholars exemplify the subtle resistance toward the work (e.g., "You are the person for that"), finding critically minded scholars is central in bringing awareness to different topics.

DISRUPTING *ETHNIC* AS A CONCEPT

Exploring historical uses of *ethnic* might provide clues into its usage in social studies. I recognize the prevailing view of *ethnic* as an individual connected to a particular group of people different from the dominant culture. Even though my father grew up in the Canal Zone of Panama, his European last name and physical appearance (white skin, light brown hair) afforded him access to the dominant culture. He also referred to himself as an "American," not "Panamanian" since he also spoke English. Some of his cultural cues differed from American culture. He wore guayabera shirts with slacks daily. A guayabera is a fashionable shirt in Central America and the Caribbean with two vertical rows on both sides and worn untucked. He only listened to típico, Panamanian traditional music. Interpreting these as cultural conflicts, I perceived *ethnic* as complex.

However, the accepted definitions of *ethnic* reveal simplified interpretations. According to the Merriam-Webster online dictionary, the first definition of *ethnic* is a person "relating to large groups of people classed according to common racial, national, tribal, religious, linguistic, or cultural origin or background." The second definition connects a person "to the Gentiles or to nations not converted to Christianity." The first synonym listed for *ethnic* is *heathen*.

Heathen, historically, has been portrayed in negative terms. In teaching social studies, I often came across curriculum narratives of individuals using Christianity to convert the *heathens*. The narratives viewed these *heathens* as unsophisticated or uncivilized. My mother immigrated from Colombia. She has always credited the Church for helping her learn "proper Spanish." She also attended services daily and spoke out against those who did not attempt to learn English in the United States. She also resisted when I asked her about her Indigenous background—she was proudly Colombian. She situated her perceptions of *ethnic* within the negative views of it.

Extending beyond *heathen*, additional words support the cynical viewpoint of ethnic—*barbaric, savage, uncivilized*, and *uncultured. Ethnic* descends from the Greek meaning *national*. Montagu (1942) describes *ethnic* as a "number of people living together, a company, a body of people" (p. 186). How did *ethnic* go from the Greek meaning of *national* to the definition of *heathen*?

According to the Merriam-Webster online dictionary, the "first known use" of the word *ethnic* in American English came in the early 1940s. Woofter, Jr. (1933) illustrated the social trends of ethnic groups in the United States. His report, part of his work with the President Hoover's Research Committee on Social Trends, provides details on the "ethnic character of the United States" since 1900 (Woofter Jr., 1933, p. 1). He examined a variety of topics, such as immigration, urban occupations, education, and assimilation. However, Woofter scrutinizes the role of education. He characterizes schools as institutions most appropriate of "assimilating the various groups to American culture" (Woofter, Jr., 1933, p. 163). He also emphasizes the political power of ethnic groups in some areas of the country concerning education:

> The Negroes, disenfranchised in the South, are subject to marked discrimination, but in North, where they constitute a powerful minority bloc, they receive much greater consideration. The Mexicans, who seldom vote, are neglected in Texas and given good facilities in California. The Orientals, however, suffer little discrimination on account of their ineligibility of citizenship, though unsuccessful efforts have been made to place them in separate schools. (p. 163)

Montagu (1942) dismisses the social acceptance of race in identifying human diversity. He begins by saying that "the idea of 'race' represents one of the most dangerous myths of our time and one of the most tragic" (p. 1). He argues that researchers, politicians, and other individuals need to use the term *ethnic* in place of *race* and that human beings share a wide variety of genetic and physical traits (Montagu, 1942). The constant reliance on race is, thus, scientifically invalid. By using *ethnic*, "it eliminates all question-begging emphases on physical factors or differences and leaves that question completely open, while the emphasis is now shifted to the fact—though it is not restricted to it—that man is predominately a cultural creature" (p. 186). *Ethnic* allows an individual to study societal inequities without relying on race as a biologically justified term (Montagu, 1942).

Warner and Srole (1945) contend that the dominant culture in the United States, rooted in English culture, places labels on ethnic groups. Through a case study with eight different ethnic groups in a town in New England during the

1940s, the type of ethnic an individual was placed the resident within a top-down social hierarchy. The whiter your ethnic group is, the closer you are to the top. More significant differences between white and non-white ethnic groups encourage a longer time of assimilation and greater disharmony (Warner & Srole, 1945). While Irish, Italians, and Germans experienced prejudice in the 18th and 19th centuries, they are viewed as "white" in contemporary times. Other groups, such as Mexican-Americans and African-Americans, continue to experience prejudice and dehumanizing rhetoric.

Zelinsky (2001), more recently, views *ethnic* as a social construct. The government's interpretation of *ethnic* is poorly defined since the U.S. government was slow to implement census measures based on ethnicity (Zelinsky, 2001). Only after significant waves of immigrants from multiethnic areas such as Russia and Austria-Hungary, and the annexation and occupation of Mexican lands following the end of the Mexican-American War of 1848 did the federal government start to examine it. (Zelinsky, 2001). I found Zelinsky's arguments especially disruptive since he appears to dispute other scholars' attempts at placing *ethnic* within the conventional view. Zelinsky (2001) believes that from a historical point of view, *ethnic* implies a more political reality than cultural:

> The fact that certain ancient civilizations and political states have enjoyed great longevity without fatal interruption scarcely validates the primordiality of their ethnic character. The prolonged existence of the Japanese, Chinese, Ethiopian, French, British, Iranian, Thai, Vietnamese, and other such durable polities may merit congratulation, but they are political, not ethnic, continuities. (p. 28)

As a result, *ethnic* will not necessarily lead students to a peaceful, conflict-free space within the social studies. Zelinsky (2001) points out that events of the past two hundred years warn us of attempting to establish a setting for *ethnic* learning in education that is free of conflict and disagreement.

SUPPORTING *ETHNIC* IN THE SOCIAL STUDIES

Since the 1960s, *ethnic* has been applied in schools and universities as programs resisting the "Americanization" of social studies (Hernandez Sheets, 2002). *Brown v. Board of Education* called for schools to desegregate, yet many school districts continued to discriminate against non-white students, an issue that persists today (Macdonald, 2004). The protest movements of the 1960s encouraged high school and college students in California, New York, and Texas to identify the lack of cultural, linguistic, and ethnic narratives in their classrooms (de los Ríos, López, & Morrell, 2015; Macdonald, 2004). Public school districts and higher education settings, as a result, developed courses, programs, and departments based on *ethnic*, known as ethnic studies.

Ethnic studies programs provide students with an opportunity to engage in more culturally relevant learning than their previous educational settings. Traditional curricula contain a minimal emphasis on the voices and experiences of marginalized individuals (Cabrera, Milem, Jaquette, & Marx, 2014). Ethnic studies evaluate the roles of race and ethnicity in society. The learning taking place "deconstructs the forces that contribute to the normalizing of racialized inequity" (de los Ríos et al., 2015). Ethnic studies also provide students with numerous opportunities to examine political systems, the media, and entertainment through personal narratives (Cammarota, 2016; de los Ríos et al., 2015). As Sleeter (2011) argued, it is not anti-American or acrimonious toward others. Instead, ethnic studies prepare students to be academically successful while situating and embracing their ethnic identities within a politicized space like a school (Sleeter, 2011). A recent example of this was the Mexican-American Studies (MAS) program in Tucson, Arizona.

In the 1990s, the Tucson United School District developed the MAS program to help increase student achievement, especially Latino students, in the district. The program urged students to see themselves as active learners, using that knowledge to critique the injustices occurring around them (Cabrera et al., 2014). According to Cammarota (2016), the MAS program also encouraged students to examine Arizona's "educational function of sorting students into racial hierarchies" (p. 234). Teachers used critical works such as Pedagogy of the Oppressed (Freire, 1970/2000) and Rethinking Columbus (Bigelow & Peterson, 1998) as central texts positioning students as knowledge holders. Students, especially Latino students, began to find spaces within the school setting. More students attended school on a regular basis, thus reversing decreasing graduation rates (Cabrera et al., 2014).

However, conservative politicians in Arizona denounced the program and sought to ban it. The legislative body in Arizona authorized Tom Horne, state superintendent of public instruction, to withhold state education funding if he discovered courses that "advocated ethnic solidarity rather than treating pupils as individuals" and "are designed primarily toward a race or class of people" (Cabrera et al., 2014, p. 1085). Horne's subsequent rhetoric portrayed the MAS program of being anti-American (Galvan, 2017). While hundreds of supporters attempted to save the program in the Tucson through protests and sit-ins, Horne successfully disbanded the program. Since the elimination of the program, students involved in the MAS program filed lawsuits against Horne and other officials. At the time of writing, a federal judge ruled that Horne's actions were racist and suppressive, thus violating the students' Fourteenth Amendment and First Amendment rights (Galvan, 2017).

As the fight over MAS program illustrates, *ethnic* remains a concept in heated debate. Hu-DeHart (1993) argues that the field of ethnic studies, at that time, was being institutionalized. With that institutionalization comes attempts to settle what counts as ethnic and what ethnicities should be and look like. Sanchez (1997) cites the reissues of history textbooks as examples in simplifying the role of a keyword like *ethnic*. The textbooks addressed multiculturalism through nationalistic narratives, even when addressing the plurality of the U.S. population (Sanchez, 1997). Winkler-Morey (2010) argues that more aggressive pushback to *ethnic* stems from nativists' fear of a growing diverse U.S. population.

While ethnic groups retain critical cultural practices as part of their identity, we must recognize ethnic as "an important part of our total population," a keyword that "vitally influences every aspect of American life" (Warner & Srole, 1945, p. 283). Students in the social studies need to access both ethnic studies programs *and* more culturally relevant social studies programs. I offer three suggestions.

First, social studies teachers can empower their students by encouraging them to speak. Halagao (2004) recommends teachers develop activities that encourage class discussions, presentations, and small group work about themselves. Teachers should ask, Who are the students in your classes? Where do they come from? How would you describe their communities? What languages/dialects do they speak? Whether a class reflects a diverse or homogeneous group, each student has a story to tell. That student's story results from the accumulation of funds of knowledge, "culturally developed bodies of knowledge and skills essential for household or individual functioning well-being" (Moll, Amanti, Neff, & Gonzalez, 1992). Au (2009) advises hybridity, a combination of the students' home cultures with learning elements. In planning lessons and units, teachers could incorporate the student narratives into the overall goals and objectives of the grade and curriculum.

The second suggestion is for the preservice teacher in elementary and secondary social studies methods courses to engage in self-reflection regarding their ethnicity. Branch (2004) encourages preservice teachers to look inward: what are the connections between social studies and ethnic identity? Hammond (2015) advises a systematic approach when engaging with the term. Start with some surface questions like "How did your family identify ethnically?" and "What are some of your family traditions—holidays, foods, or rituals?" and work to deeper questions like "What physical, social, or cultural attributes were praised in your community?" and "Which attributes were you taught to avoid?" (Hammond, 2015, p. 57). As Au (2009) argued, there is no simple formula. However, the engagement of self-reflection allows the preservice teacher to disrupt the fears associated with *ethnic*. Highlighting the positive and successful contributions of ethnic groups historically and contemporarily fosters further discussions on *ethnic* (Branch, 2004). Relying on self-reflections can encourage a development of a culturally responsive teaching framework.

The third suggestion is for the academy to incorporate *ethnic* research into the mainstream. Similar to race, *ethnic* is a struggle for many social studies scholars (King & Chandler, 2016). In their comprehensive *Handbook on Research in Social Studies Education*, Levstik and Tyson (2008) include a chapter on diversity and citizenship education, but no central chapters on *ethnic*. Nevertheless, a small group of scholars generates research based on *ethnic*. One example is the growing number of presentations at the College and University Faculty Assembly (CUFA) annual conference. For the 2017 conference, four scholars situated *ethnic* as a central focus of their presentations (CUFA, 2017), whereas the previous year there were none (CUFA, 2016). While the number of scholars situating *ethnic* grows within social studies research, mainstream support needs to be given to scholars choosing to engage with *ethnic* in other spaces. Ethnic studies is a dynamic field, reconnecting higher education with K–12 settings. By uncovering the past and current narratives of marginalized students, teachers, and scholars, *ethnic* looks to eliminate encounters like my own 9th-grade history experience.

DISCUSSION QUESTIONS

1. How do you approach *ethnic* in social studies?
2. How do you challenge your own assumptions about *ethnic*?
3. How do you ignore *ethnic* in social studies?
4. How would you incorporate different ethnic perspectives into your work?
5. How can you further situate *ethnic* in social studies?

REFERENCES

Au, K. (2009). Isn't culturally responsive instruction just good teaching? *Social Education, 73*(4), 179–183.

Bigelow, B., & Peterson, B. (Eds.). (1998). *Rethinking Columbus: The next 500 years*. Milwaukee, WI: Rethinking Schools.

Branch, A. J. (2004). Modeling respect by teaching about race and ethnic identity in the social studies. *Theory & Research in Social Education, 32*(4), 523–545.

Busey, C., & Waters, S. (2016). Who are we? The demographic and professional identity of social studies teacher educators. *The Journal of Social Studies Research, 40*, 71–83.

Cabrera, N., Milem, J. F., Jaquette, O., & Marx, R. W. (2014). Missing the (student achievement) forest for all political trees: Empiricism and the Mexican-American studies controversy in Tucson. *American Educational Research Journal, 51*(6), 1084–1118.

Cammarota, J. (2016). The praxis of ethnic studies: Transforming second sight into critical consciousness. *Race Ethnicity and Education, 19*(2), 233–251. doi:10.1080/13613324.2015.1041486.

College and University Faculty Assembly. (2016). *Full program.* Retrieved from http://cufa2016.socialstudies.org/modules/request.php?module=oc_program&action=program.php&p=program

College and University Faculty Assembly. (2017). *Full program.* Retrieved from http://cufa2017.socialstudies.org/modules/request.php?module=oc_program&action=program.php&p=program

de los Ríos, C. V., López, J., & Morrell, E. (2015). Toward a critical pedagogy of race: Ethnic studies and literacies of power in high school classrooms. *Race and Social Problems, 7*(1), 84–96. doi:10.1007/s12552-014-9142-1.

Ellis, C., Adams, T. E., & Bochner, A. P. (2010). Autoethnography: An overview. *Forum Qualitative Sozialforschung / Forum: Qualitative Social Research, 12*(1), Art.10. Retrieved from http://nbn-resolving.de/urn:nbn:de:0114-fqs1101108

Freire, P. (1970/2000). *Pedagogy of the oppressed: 30th anniversary edition.* New York, NY: Continuum.

Galvan, A. (2017). Federal judge says Arizona ban on Mexican-American studies program was motivated by racism. *Update on TUSD Mexican American Studies Program.* Retrieved from https://mas.arizona.edu/news/update-tusd-mexican-american-studies-program

Halagao, P. E. (2004). Holding up the mirror: The complexity of seeing your ethnic self in history. *Theory & Research in Social Education, 32*(4), 459–483. doi:10.1080/00933104.2004.10473265.

Hammond, Z. (2015). *Culturally responsive teaching & the brain.* Thousand Oaks, CA: Corwin.

Hernandez Sheets, R. (2002). Ethnic identity development through social studies instruction. *Multicultural Education, 9*(3), 45–47.

Hughes, S., & Pennington, J. L. (2017). *Autoethnography: Process, product, and possibility for critical social research.* Thousand Oaks, CA: SAGE.

Hu-DeHart, E. (1993). The history, development, and future of ethnic studies. *The Phi Delta Kappan, 75*(1), 50–54.

King, L. J., & Chandler, P. T. (2016). From non-racism to anti-racism in social studies teacher education: Social studies and racial pedagogical content knowledge. In A. R. Crowe & A. Cuenca (Eds.), *Rethinking social studies teacher education in the twenty-first century* (pp. 3–22). Berlin: Springer.

Levstik, L. S., & Tyson, C. Y. (Eds.). (2008). *Handbook of research in social studies education.* New York, NY: Routledge.

Loewen, J. (2007). *Lies my teacher told me.* New York, NY: Touchstone.

Macdonald, V.-M. (Ed.). (2004). *Latino education in the united states: A narrated history from 1513–2000.* New York, NY: Palgrave Macmillan.

Maloy, R. W., & LaRoche, I. S. (2015). *We, the students and teachers: Teaching democratically in the history and social studies classroom.* Albany, NY: State University of New York Press.

Moll, L. C., Amanti, C., Neff, D., & Gonzalez, N. (1992). Funds of knowledge for teaching: Using a qualitative approach to connect homes and classrooms. *Theory into Practice, 31*(2), 132–141.

Montagu, A. (1942/1997). *Man's most dangerous myth: The fallacy of race* (6th ed.). Walnut Creek, CA: AltaMira Press.

Muncey, T. (2010). *Creating autoethnographies.* London: SAGE.

Sanchez, T. R. (1997). The social studies teacher's lament: How powerful is the textbook in dealing with knowledge of ethnic diversity and attitude change? *Urban Education, 32*(1), 63–80.

Shiveley, J. (2014). Teaching for democratic citizenship: Arriving at a guiding question for pedagogical practice. *Social Studies Research and Practice, 9*(3), 81–87.

Sleeter, C. E. (2011). *The academic and social value of ethnic studies: A research review*. Washington, DC: National Education Association.

Valdes, F. (2000). Race, ethnicity, and hispanismo in a triangular perspective: The "essential Latina/o" and LatCrit theory. *UCLA Law Review, 40*, 305–352.

Villegas, A. M., & Lucas, T. (2007). The culturally responsive teacher. *Educational Leadership, 64*(6), 28–33.

Wall, S. (2005). An autoethnography on learning about autoethnography. *International Journal of Qualitative Methods, 5*(2), Article 9. Retrieved from http://www.ualberta.ca/~iiqm/backissues/5_2/html/wall.htm

Warner, W., & Srole, L. (1945). *The social systems of American ethnic groups*. New Haven, CT: Yale University Press.

Winkler-Morey, A. (2010). The war on history: Defending ethnic studies. *The Black Scholar, 40*(4), 51–56.

Woofter, Jr., T. J. (1933). *Races and ethnic groups in American life*. New York, NY: McGraw-Hill.

Zelinsky, W. (2001). *The enigma of ethnicity*. Iowa City, IA: University of Iowa Press.

CHAPTER THREE

Spilling the *Lemonade* in Social Studies

A Response to the Culture Section

AMANDA E. VICKERY, ARIZONA STATE UNIVERSITY
DELANDREA HALL, THE UNIVERSITY OF TEXAS AT AUSTIN

In April of 2016, artist/activist Beyoncé surprised the world with the release of her second visual album titled *Lemonade*. *Lemonade* was pioneering not only because it was a full-length movie, but more so because it was a love letter written specifically to and for Black women. In this visual album, Beyoncé transports the audience into a world where the American South, as a sociocultural and political space, is the main character. It is a reminder that it is a place that continues to play a vital role in the narrative, history, and experiences of Black women. Beyoncé reminds us of this connection through images of ominous chains hanging from sheds, cabins inhabited by enslaved persons, and large plantation porches. We see representations of the Yoruba culture, a reminder of the inexplicable link between Africa and American slavery (Reid, 2016). While these powerful visuals remind us that slavery is very much still part of American culture and collective memory, it is juxtaposed with images showing the strength, power, beauty, and resilience of modern-day Black women.

Lemonade masterfully connects the past with the present using imagery that unapologetically celebrates and affirms the cultural, experiential, and historical knowledge of Black women. It is important to note that while this album does center the cultural experiences of Black women it is not representative of *all* Black women but instead wrestles with:

> ...A history that resonates with power legacies of both oppression and resistance. Think of Bree Newsome scaling that flagpole in South Carolina to bring down the Confederate Flag on a cloudless blue sky day last summer. It was genuinely beautiful to see that flag in her hands. Then think of the nine people whose massacre precipitated that beauty. The South is both of these realities. (Harris-Perry, 2016, para. 23)

Beyoncé is unafraid to address such a complex history of the American South and the end result is a narrative of Black women that is both healing and liberating. It is unfortunate that the history that most African-Americans learn within K–12 schools fails to address both oppression and resistance within cultural communities (Brown & Brown, 2010). Montecinos (1995) argued that master narratives privileged within the social studies essentialize the complexities and richness of the cultural history of Communities of Color,[1] resulting in stereotyping and a distortion of histories that has become unrecognizable. The social studies curriculum privileges white cultural knowledge and histories that is deemed *normative* while positioning everyone else *abnormal* (Solórzano & Yosso, 2002).

Shear and Stanton and Ender call attention to the ways in which cultural hegemony (Gramsci, 1975; Hall, 1986) is oftentimes left unquestioned and perpetuated within the social studies classroom. In their chapter on the use of the term "Indigenous," Shear and Stanton demonstrate the need for teachers and students to become cognizant of terms associated with Indigenous Peoples as a way toward a humanizing and anticolonial education. Ender engages in the reflexive work of critically examining his own experiences wrestling with the term "ethnic" as a student, classroom teacher, and teacher educator. Taken together, these two chapters help social studies educators critically consider how and why teaching about culture and cultural identity unsettles us as a field. Moreover, they make a striking case for the importance of unpacking how the social studies curriculum and pedagogical practices often perpetuate cultural hegemony.

This is significant because "in a sense, everything in education relates to culture...Culture is in us and all around us, just as the air we breathe" (Erickson, 1997, p. 31). Yet, Ender questions why teaching about culture remains controversial within the social studies. Darder (2015) argued this is in part because one cannot discuss culture unless you also consider the relationship between culture and power and whose knowledge is considered truth. Within schools, teachers play a key role in teaching societal knowledge that represents the values and perspectives of those in power (white men)—stated plainly, that which is considered legitimate knowledge. This knowledge is transmitted to students via the hidden curriculum and taught as standard canonical knowledge (Apple, 1992, 2000, 2004). Those in power craft a curriculum that functions to "marginalize and invalidate cultural values, heritage, language, knowledge, and lived experiences which fall outside the purview of capitalist domination and exploitation" (Darder, 2015, p. 29). Within the social studies such historical and cultural knowledge is packaged into a curriculum premised on "uniting" students as American citizens.

Shear and Stanton and Ender's chapters speak to this troubling reality: students in social studies classrooms are forced to internalize a narrative of the past that reinforces systems of white supremacy and settler colonialism. The social studies curriculum, as a whole, dehumanizes non-white bodies and erases the cultural knowledge of Communities of Color while upholding white cultural knowledge as infallible and truth (Urrieta, 2004), resulting in the social studies becoming a site of *educative-psychic violence* (Leonardo & Porter, 2010). King and Woodson (2017) argue that it refers to a type of "psychological violence, one that keeps students of all racial and ethnic backgrounds from developing a full sense of their racial, historical, and political identities" (p. 3). This occurs when the curriculum presents white European cultures as the norm and standard, people of color are presented in simplistic and stereotypical ways, and the abuse of Black/Brown/Indigenous bodies is unquestioned and normalized (Brown & Brown, 2010; King & Woodson, 2017). In order to combat *educative-psychic violence* and the dehumanization of Communities of Color within the curriculum, social studies educators must rethink constructions of knowledge and notions of truth privileged within the curriculum. Teachers must unlearn and reject ideologies of white supremacy and settler colonialism.

Furthermore, the field must pay attention to the cultural knowledge of teachers of color and how it impacts and enhances their curricular and pedagogical decisions (Vickery, 2016, 2017). Teachers enter the field with cultural knowledge and oftentimes teacher preparation programs attempt to suppress such knowledge and replace it with the western canon. There is an extensive body of work by Indigenous and scholars of color within the field examining teachers' cultural knowledge (Salinas, Rodríguez, & Lewis, 2015; Vickery, 2016) and the importance of infusing cultural knowledge and histories into the curriculum (An, 2016; Dilworth, 2004; King, 2014; Lomawaima & McCarty, 2002; Rodríguez & Ip, 2018; Vickery, 2017). The field, as a whole, should be compelled to reevaluate whose cultural knowledge and voices are privileged and presented as "truth."

When reflecting on the significance of *Lemonade*, Harris-Perry (2016) wrote, "What would happen if we took the hopes, dreams, pain, joy, loss, bodies, voices, stories, expressions, styles, families, histories, futures of Black girls and women and put them in the center and started from there? Lemonade happens" (para. 1). By centering the lives and experiences of Black women, Beyoncé sought to redefine how society viewed the intersections of Blackness, womanism (Walker, 1983), history, and Black southern culture. Collins (2009) argued that the validation of cultural knowledge and allowing communities to redefine their own realities and truths is key to empowerment. That is our task in order to create a safe and empowering space within social studies for cultural communities. We draw inspiration from Harris-Perry's summation of Lemonade to consider what must be done in actualizing such a humanizing (Bartolomé, 1994) and culturally sustaining (Paris & Alim, 2014) framework for teaching social studies: What would happen if we took the voices and stories as well as the historical, cultural, and experiential knowledge of Communities of Color and put that at the center of the social studies curriculum? What would happen if cultural and ethnic groups defined their own realities and determined their own truths and we started from there?

DISCUSSION QUESTIONS

1. How can teacher education programs and schools attend to critiques of whiteness and settler colonialism?
2. What are some ways the field of social studies can privilege and center the cultural knowledge of teachers and communities?
3. How can spaces/structures be created within schools and teacher preparation programs to facilitate the development of critically conscious students and teachers?

NOTE

1. We intentionally capitalize the term "Communities of Color" throughout this chapter to use capitalization as a grammatical strategy to (re)claim power typically removed to describe historically marginalized communities.

REFERENCES

An, S. (2016). Asian Americans in American history: An AsianCrit perspective on Asian American inclusion in state U.S. history curriculum. *Theory & Research in Social Education, 44*(2), 244–276.

Apple, M. (1992). The text and cultural politics. *Educational Researcher, 21*(7), 4–11.

Apple, M. (2000). *Official knowledge: Democratic education in a conservative age.* New York, NY: Routledge.

Apple, M. (2004). *Ideology and curriculum.* New York, NY: Routledge.

Bartolomé, L. (1994). Beyond the methods fetish: Toward a humanizing pedagogy. *Harvard Educational Review, 64*(2), 173–195.

Brown, A. L., & Brown, K. D. (2010). Strange fruit indeed: Interrogating contemporary textbook representations of racial violence towards African Americans. *Teachers College Record, 112*(1), 31–67.

Collins, P. H. (2009). *Black feminist thought: Knowledge, consciousness and the politics of empowerment.* New York, NY: Routledge.

Darder, A. (2015). *Culture and power in the classroom: Educational foundations for the schooling of bicultural students.* New York, NY: Routledge.

Dilworth, P. P. (2004). Multicultural citizenship education: Case studies from social studies classrooms. *Theory & Research in Social Education, 32*(2), 153–186.

Erickson, F. (1997). Culture in society and in educational practices. In J. A. Banks & C. A. McGee Banks (Eds.), *Multicultural education: Issues and perspectives* (3rd ed., pp. 30–60). Boston, MA: Allyn & Bacon.

Gramsci, A. (1975). *Prison notebooks Volume II*. New York, NY: Columbia University Press.

Hall, S. (1986). Gramsci's relevance for the study of race and ethnicity. *Journal of Communication Inquiry, 10*(2), 5–27.

Harris-Perry, M. (2016). *A call and response with Melissa Harris-Perry: The pain and the power of 'Lemonade'*. Retrieved from http://www.elle.com/culture/music/a35903/lemonade-call-and-response/

King, L. J. (2014). When lions write history. *Multicultural Education, 22*(1), 2–11.

King, L. J., & Woodson, A. N. (2017). Baskets of cotton and birthday cakes: Teaching slavery in social studies classrooms. *Social Studies Education Review, 6*(1), 1–18.

Leonardo, Z., & Porter, R. K. (2010). Pedagogy of fear: Toward a Fanonian theory of "safety" in race dialogue. *Race Ethnicity and Education, 13*(2), 139–157.

Lomawaima, K. T., & McCarty, T. (2002). When tribal sovereignty challenges democracy: American Indian education and the democratic ideal. *American Educational Research Journal, 39*, 279–305.

Montecinos, C. (1995). Culture as an ongoing dialog: Implications for multicultural teacher education. In C. Sleeter & P. McLaren (Eds.), *Multicultural education, critical pedagogy, and the politics of difference* (pp. 291–308). New York, NY: State University of New York Press.

Paris, D., & Alim, H. S. (2014). What are we seeking to sustain through culturally sustaining pedagogy? A loving critique forward. *Harvard Educational Review, 84*(1), 85–100.

Reid, J. (2016) *A call and response with Melissa Harris-Perry: The pain and the power of 'Lemonade'*. Retrieved from http://www.elle.com/culture/music/a35903/lemonade-call-and-response/

Rodríguez, N., & Ip, R. (2018). Hidden in history: (Re)constructing Asian American history in elementary social studies classrooms. In S. B. Shear, C. M. Tschida, E. Bellows, L. B. Buchanan, & E. E. Saylor (Eds.), *Making controversial issues relevant for elementary social studies: A critical reader*. Charlotte, NC: Information Age Publishing, 319–340.

Salinas, C., Rodríguez, N. N., & Lewis, B. A. (2015). The Tejano history curriculum project: Creating a space for authoring Tejanas/os into the social studies curriculum. *Bilingual Research Journal, 38*(2), 172–189.

Solórzano, D. G., & Yosso, T. J. (2002). Critical race methodology: Counter-storytelling as an analytical framework for education research. *Qualitative Inquiry, 8*, 23–44.

Urrieta, L. (2004). Dis-connections in "American" citizenship and the post/neo-colonial: People of Mexican descent and Whitestream pedagogy and curriculum. *Theory & Research in Social Education, 2*(4), 433–458.

Vickery, A. E. (2016). "I know what you are about to enter": Lived experiences of African American women as the curricular foundation for teaching citizenship. *Gender and Education, 28*(6), 725–741.

Vickery, A. E. (2017). "You excluded us for so long and now you want us to be patriotic?" African American women teachers contemplating the quandary of citizenship. *Theory & Research in Social Education, 45*(3), 318–348.

Walker, A. (1983). *In search of our mother's gardens: Womanist prose*. San Diego, CA: Harcourt Brace Jovanovich.

Section II:
Time, Continuity, and Change

CHAPTER FOUR

Time

MARK HELMSING, GEORGE MASON UNIVERSITY
ANNIE MCMAHON WHITLOCK, UNIVERSITY OF MICHIGAN-FLINT

> We live in time—it holds us and molds us—but I never felt I understood it very well, (but) I know this much: that there is objective time, but also subjective time, the kind you wear on the inside of your wrist, next to where the pulse lies. And this personal time, which is the true time, is measured in your relationship to memory.
>
> —Julian Barnes, *The Sense of an Ending*, 2011

What could Barnes mean by suggesting there are two types of time: objective and subjective? If time is subjective then it must seem to be subjective to each of us through how we experience time and recollect time through memory. Objective time, on the other hand, must seem measurable, precise, accurate—all terms associated with those devices we wear on the outside of our wrists or in our pockets that display standard hours and minutes. Unlike the precision of a digital clock face, subjective time is tracked and accounted for more intimately and figuratively "where the pulse lies," where our heart is, and where our life is. To someone having a stressful week, seven days can seem to crawl past slowly. To someone getting married, a wedding day can seem to fly by even though it is only one cycle of 24 hours (also a title of a wildly popular television series that used the passing of time in a rather novel and dramatic fashion). To someone watching a loved one suffer health issues, two months can feel like a lifetime. We attach meaning to time—and its various measures of dates, anniversaries, centuries, famous "firsts" and "lasts"—in ways that may not have universal significance. Which, for example, is a more significant experience of time to celebrate: when a person reaches the age of 12, 16, 18, 21, 30, 40, 100? What about the significance of time's passing in cultural events?

At the time of this writing in 2017 the United States of America approaches the 100th anniversary of its entry into World War I. A few years ago in 2012, however, the United States had little in the way of public commemoration of the 200th anniversary of the War of 1812, especially compared to the large array of public commemorations in Canada for the war. Indeed, remembering, commemorating, and memorializing time is relative and subjective. One instance of the relative and fickle ways in which we engage in commemorating time is in the memeification of "Throwback Thursday," an Internet practice of tagging photographs and written memories in posts that are meant to elicit fondness for a past event or to cringe at the awkwardness of youthful indiscretion, indignity, or embarrassment. Similarly, we engage in the act of personalizing time and its passages through our proclivity to bond over our shared experiences that are always already unique and universal at the same time. "Where were you when…" is a familiar phrase as people socially recall with others their memories of the assassination of President John F. Kennedy, the chase on the California freeway for O.J. in a white Ford Bronco, and terrorist attacks that occurred on the morning of September 11, 2001. These feel like "common events" that are remembered in unique ways because of our experiences and, paradoxically, because of who experienced them and who did not, who has access to stored memories of these moments in time, and who does not because of their age or "where they were when" that renders them unable to engage in the shared act of collective memory.

Thus, if time is all around us and within us, it is no surprise to find "time" as a thematic concept that appears in the National Council for the Social Studies' Curriculum Standards for Social Studies with its own theme: "Time, Continuity, and Change" (NCSS, 2010). Although this theme appears to refer to the discipline of history, "time" is a construct that crosses all social studies disciplines, not only in the academic study of history. Time as a social construct can be discussed in geography curriculum in how humans divided the world into time zones or in economics curriculum in how "time is money" by analyzing time as a valuable commodity and how humans make choices with our "use" of time. Time can be explored as social concepts in sociology, psychology, and anthropology through querying how time makes an impact upon human behaviors: How do we perceive time consciously? What does it mean to be "efficient" with one's time or to be late as opposed to punctual in American life? How does time play a role in the "slow life" and "slow food" movements? How do institutions such as schools and prisons use time for various means, from punishment to promotion? How is time expressed and understood across cultures and within subcultures? What do the biological processes of time effect upon human bodies and their functions?

When we explore time in relationship to the study of history, however, it is most often through "past time" as something homogeneous, infinite (history happens every second), and unproblematic. If, as the colloquial saying goes, the past is history, the future is a mystery, and the present is a gift, it is the notion of past time that structures historical thinking and understanding. Conceptions of past time have been expanded and significantly altered within social studies education recently, as seen in how widely many schools are adopting the Big History Project as an integrated science/social studies course, with its curricular explorations of time beginning with the cosmic "big bang" through different eras of time previously studied geologically in science class and now as periodizations in most world history classes. The Big History Project presents a robust problem for social studies educators to consider: what counts as appropriate "time" to study historically? Does the past time of our planet possess the same significance as the past time of humanity? Thus, questions that appear to treat time objectively are subjective in nature. As opposed to only considering time as objective, predetermined, and settled in the past, this chapter considers how to teach and learn about time as subjective. How might we engage with determining and debating what counts as "historical" and worthy of consideration in the social studies curriculum? In considering this question we offer two areas of inquiry: how teaching Millennials (and teaching about Millennials) requires us to confront how we determine to be historical events and how the teaching of different time periods as periodization opens space to consider the subjective ways we classify and organize time as "the past."

TEACHING MILLENNIALS: WHAT EVENTS ARE HISTORY?

The passing of time is often marked by defining generations. Generations are not just defined as one's parents, children, grandchildren, etc., but are defined culturally through changes in beliefs, attitudes, social characteristics, media, and technology. The "Greatest Generation" are those born in the early 20th century and had their formative years defined by their participation in World War II at home and abroad. But why are they the "greatest?" Greatest compared to whom? Inevitably the generation that precedes us or the generation we "belong" to is "the best one"—"the good old days." The "younger generation" is different and ultimately a scourge on society. Nowhere is this more evident than the current generation of "Millennials."

What defines a "Millennial" has been mostly determined by the media and our culture, as the U.S. Census Bureau doesn't label generations other than "Baby Boomers," since they are associated with a population increase (Bump, 2015). The Pew Research Center (2016) defines Millennials as born between 1981 and 1997 so they can track statistical analyses, but other sources have listed Millennials as born anywhere from 1977 to 2000 (Garvey, 2015). Millennials are often negatively characterized as entitled, selfish, lazy, and addicted to screens and technology. The authors of this chapter were born in 1981 and 1982. By some definitions, we are

Millennials, but we often find more differences than similarities with those born in the early or late 1990s. For example, we have worked with computers most of our lives, but were in our mid-twenties when smartphones and tablets became ubiquitous. We may be savvy users of social media, but yet, managed to live our undergraduate college days mostly free of social media. (Thank goodness!) The subjectivity of time is evident in the ways that generations are defined and named. Who gives generations their names? Who gets to define them?

Cultural changes happen so quickly in the 21st century, with the immense access to information and global connectivity. There may be different ways we mark the passing of a generation in light of our faster society. Perhaps Millennials should be split into "old" and "young" Millennials? Or "Junior" and "Senior" Millennials (Orazio, 2015)? But what should mark this shift? How you answer this question depends on your subjective time and your childhood memories. Maybe Millennials born in the 1980s are "Oregon Trail" Millennials, named for one of the few computer games we had access to in elementary school (Garvey, 2015). Maybe the ages in which you purchased your first cell phone or created your first social media account define you as a generation.

One of the most significant ways to mark a generation is to define one in relationship to major events of the time period, which one can best achieve by looking back once time has passed. The "Greatest Generation" were not referring to themselves by this name at the time, but are revered as we remember their contributions in a great war. "Baby Boomers" are named reflecting back on the large postwar population increase. Perhaps this is the time to divide Millennials as we look back on arguably the most significant historical event of the 21st century—the terrorist attacks of September 11, 2001.

How you remember "9/11" marks a significant cultural shift. If you were old enough to remember what life was like on September 10, 2001 and able to process the immense shift in our culture that began almost immediately on September 12, 2001, then you may be a different kind of Millennial that was too young to remember the event at all. Younger Millennials have never known a world where there was not an intense fear of terrorism at home, where a trip to the airport wasn't a violation of personal space and property, and where Muslims were not stereotyped as the enemy.

Our suggestion of September 11, 2001 as a generation-defining event causes us to think about this idea of what makes an event "historical." To current high school students and undergraduates (young Millennials), September 11, 2001 is a historical event—something that happened either before they were born or when they were very young children. For many of their high school teachers (older Millennials or Gen Xers), that event was a lived experience, one that may not resonate as historical in the same way as World War II might. In this way, how one remembers events from the 1980s, 1990s, and 2000s has a major impact on teaching social studies in the classroom. One can recall or maybe identify with the high school history teacher that spends an inordinate amount of time teaching World War II and never gets farther than touching on the Civil Rights Movement or perhaps the Vietnam War. Is this because teachers that are Generation X or "old" Millennials don't view the "turn of the century" (21st, not 20th!) "old" enough to be history?

Since time is so subjective in this way, this way of unintentionally ignoring recent history may deprive students of learning about important historical and cultural touchstones. Units on the Reagan administration might help students better understand the 2008 financial crisis and the Occupy Wall Street movements. Learning about the 1992 Los Angeles riots and the 1994 O.J. Simpson trial can give students context for the current Black Lives Matter protests and uproar over police brutality. Studying the bombing of the 1995 federal building in Oklahoma City along with September 11, 2001 can help students better understand terrorists at home and abroad. The time and memories that are "inside our wrist" are farther away for our students and future students. It's perhaps time to make the shift. Instead of ignoring these events in the classroom because they are lived experiences to older Millennials and Gen Xers, we should embrace these lived experiences because we have access to a tremendous amount of primary source material for our students. The 1990s are now far enough in the past that pop culture treats this era as historical; *Straight Outta Compton*, *The People vs. O.J. Simpson*, *Fresh Off the Boat* (among many others) may be good places to start the conversation.

The question of what events are historical enough to include in history classrooms might be posed back to students. Perhaps we should ask students how Millennials should be remembered and what events are inside their wrists. This discussion can show our students that this construct of time is plastic and not carved in stone.

TEACHING THE MIDDLE AGES: MARKING PERIODS OF TIME

Another way in which time is an all-encompassing element of knowledge in social studies is illustrated by how we subjectively use time to mark passages of events, moments, and duration. Although the primary focus of the "Time, Continuity, and Change" thematic standard is to "include experiences that provide for the study of the past and its legacy," the theme invites learners to contemplate the contours and features of time as a force or agent of history (NCSS, 2010, p. 15). For example, including historical analysis as a feature of social studies instruction "enables" learners to "identify continuities over time" and contextualize "institutions, values, and beliefs" of different time periods throughout human history (p. 15). But before learners can engage in historical analysis within identified time periods, should we not ask how or why these time periods emerge as they do? During the years between 1914 and 1917 when the Great War waged in Europe, people did not refer to it as the First World War or World War I. To do so would presume that a second war was inevitably occurring. Yet, social studies educators often think and teach about the World War I as indistinguishable from World War II. For issues of causality, it is useful to teach the First and Second World Wars as interrelated, but only because of the hindsight of historiography, not because the events are inseparably related time. To see this point more clearly, let us consider one example—the historical period defined as "the Middle Ages"—to see how tricky it is to periodize our history and why it is important to call attention to the debates, challenges, and issues of periodization within social studies education.

During the so-called "Middle Ages" in European history, people of the time did not refer to their lived experience of their time as "the Middle Ages." I (Mark) have encountered students who think that persons living during the Middle Ages would have identified their moment as such. This is, of course, not possible since the concept of the "Middle Ages" is a periodization applied only to a set number of years long after they occurred. The concept of time inherent in the phrase "the Middle Ages" implies that something came before this collection of years and that there is a significant period of time that comes after it. But with *what* are these particular years stuck in the middle? To understand this concept I have students consider how the Middle Ages were conceptualized first during the Renaissance (itself a periodization of time). Leonardo Bruni used the Latin word for middle *medieval* to classify a period after the fall of the Roman Empire in the 5th century through the 12th century in his 1442 book *History of the Florentine People*. Similarly, Flavio Biondo distinguished the same time period as a "middle age" beginning with the plunder of Rome in 410 by the Visigoths through the 13th century until his contemporary Italy saw a rebirth of learning and culture in the 15th century. Both authors viewed history as being ancient, medieval, or modern. Even though their conception of the modern age begins in the 1400s, historians continued to follow this periodization six centuries later. Will humans forever live in a never-ending third story? Will there be a fourth period to chop up these three-part trilogy of history, and, if so, what shall it be called?

Historians and archaeologists who specialize in researching, excavating, and studying the Middle Ages (called "medievalists") are, somewhat surprisingly, the most vocal in their dissatisfaction with this three-part division, which they find conceptually unhelpful and problematic. Medievalists Tison Pugh and Jane Weisl contend that what we classify as the Middle Ages "emerges as an invention of those who came after it; its entire construction is, essentially, a fantasy," a time period that all too easily allows us to assume "cultural difference and continuity can be cordoned off from prior and subsequent eras" (2013, p. 1). Complicating the use of "the Middle Ages" as a periodizing concept in social studies education is its frequent conflation with the concept of the "medieval" and medieval cultural representations. "Medieval" connotes representations of culture that involve knights and squires, castles with monarchical families and lands they rule over, colorful banners tied to intricate heraldry, and an elaborate system of social and political behaviors that blend virtue and nobility with extreme elements of violence and survival. Medieval historian John Arnold condenses this classification by suggesting the medieval conjures images of "tyrants a pope, intrigue, torture, and magical practices" of fair maidens and damsels in distress that are found equally at home, in school history textbooks, as well as high fantasy novels (Arnold, 2008, p. 4). Indeed, many popular cultural texts our students currently consume, from *Game of Thrones* to *Assassin's Creed*, from *Braveheart* to *Galavant*, employ aspects of medievalism. As I have had to stress to some high school social studies teachers, *Game of Thrones* and the Norman Conquest of 1066 are both medieval, but one is based on fantasy literature and one is rooted in the history we associate with the Middle Ages. The fact that King Arthur and Robin Hood continue to exert wide appeal and presence in our everyday lives from movies and television to jousting-themed restaurant attractions and theme park attractions suggests that medieval culture fuels an interest in conceptualizing what historians identify as the Middle Ages while at the same time blurring its temporal reality as established in definable time.

This exploration of how time periods are constructed is true for how history education periodizes most classifications of time that we turn into teachable curriculum. As educators, we create units on the Age of Reason and the Enlightenment in Europe or Reconstruction in the United States, periods that are more a collection of ideas than a measurable event that began and ended on a certain day, at the same time creating units divided by events that have empirical beginnings and endings, such as the Civil War and World War I. We know that World War I began on July 28, 1914 and ended on November 11, 1918. Or did it? Did World War I really begin with the assassination of Austrian Archduke Franz Ferdinand on June 28, 1914? Is the assassination an origin story, a prelude, a prequel, or something else? Is there a cultural trait we can assign our students to examine with World War I in the same way we assign the mapping of cultural traits with time periods such as "the Roaring Twenties" or "the Swinging Sixties?" For that matter, why is it the case that time in U.S. history curricula during the 20th century is often neatly periodized by decades (and the ubiquitous U.S. history class assignment of dressing up in period attire for "decade days" activities), yet the periodization of decades does not appear as crystallized in the 18th and 19th centuries? The "Roaring Twenties" are associated with the 1920s, but with the exception of the "Gay Nineties" of the 1800s, what other decades are periodized by a defining trait and what would we call them if we did have names? What would it mean to call the 1850s the Feisty Fifties, which saw a booming market economy in the United States? Or could we call the 1870s the Sad Seventies, which saw a crippled United States attempt to heal the wounds from its civil war? Only time will tell.

IMPLICATIONS

In the *National Standards for World History* (NCHS, 1994), the authors pay particular attention to "arranging the study of the past into distinct periods of time" (p. 40). The many different possibilities for arranging time into distinct periods should be understood by students as "a creative construction reflecting the historian's particular aims, preferences, and cultural or social values" (p. 4). Yet it remains the case, two decades since these standards were disseminated, that the construction of time into different histories for different purposes is often rarely foregrounded or event taught explicitly in the social studies curriculum. The predominant aspects of time within practices of historical thinking render issues of chronology into objective time: "establish temporal order," "measure and calculate calendar time," "interpret data presented in time lines," and so forth (NCHS, 1994, p. 18). The narrative of civilized progress, historically presented as a driving quest toward modern life through social evolution and human advancement, allows only objective time to be marked and measured. Our chapter has attempted to show that subjective time also has an important place in social studies education as it calls attention to how we choose to think about time and the intervals and periods of time that are messy, contested, or difficult to measure and classify. The duration of a generation or the discrepant temporal ordering of historical time periods, as shown in the examples above, can reorient the kinds of historical thinking and understanding that allow us to engage with time that is all at once shared, lost, borrowed, hurried, wasted, remembered, forgotten, and much more. Rethinking time as a structuring concept in social studies education requires thinking of objective time as not the only conceivable way of experiencing time in history and the social sciences. Elizabeth Ermarth, a philosopher of history, argues that "*within* time you can differ; but you can't differ *with* time" (emphasis hers) (2011, p. 29). We might disagree with her. Reconsidering time as a tool of thought within social studies education means we have all the time in the world (and of the world), past, present, and future. A time has now come for us as social studies educators to be more creative and more critical in what we do with that time.

DISCUSSION QUESTIONS

1. How would we have students periodize today's time period? How do they conceptualize what comes after the final chapter in a history textbook?
2. Children of Millennials are now known as "Generation Z." How will we approach teaching history to them?
3. How do we modify or adapt our history curriculum to include units on the 1980s, 1990s, 2000s, and 2010s?

4. How can social studies teachers leverage recent history to better equip students in analyzing and understanding current issues?
5. How can educational researchers investigate the ways in which social studies educators approach contemporary history in their curriculum? What might be some affordances and constraints in history education increasing its attention to recent history of the late 20th and early 21st centuries?
6. What are some possible strategies for social studies educators to explore with students recent history? Is that phrase itself even possible to teach or to conceptualize?
7. How can we help learners explore the construction of time through examining the debates around classifying generations and historical time periods?

REFERENCES

Arnold. J. H. (2008). *What is medieval history?* Malden, MA: Polity Press.
Bump, P. (2015). Here's how the Census Bureau fooled you on 'Millennials.' *Washington Post.* Retrieved from https://www.washingtonpost.com/news/the-fix/wp/2015/06/25/the-censusbureau-scores-a-public-relations-coup-on-millennials/?utm_term=.f9e11360b357
Ermarth, E. D. (2011). *History in the discursive condition.* New York, NY: Routledge.
Garvey, A. (2015). The biggest (and best) difference between Millennials and My Generation. Retrieved from www.huffingtonpost.com
National Center for History in the Schools. (1994). *National standards for world history: Exploring paths to the present.* Los Angeles, CA: Author.
National Council for the Social Studies. (2010). *National curriculum standards for social studies: A framework for teaching, learning, and assessment.* Washington, DC: Author.
Orazio, A. (2015). Addressing the generation gap—junior Millennials vs. senior Millennials. Retrieved from http://theamericangenius.com
Pew Research Center. (2016). Millennials overtake Baby Boomers as America's largest generation. Retrieved from www.pewresearch.org
Pugh, T., & Weisl, J. (2013). *Medievalisms: Making the past in the present.* New York, NY: Routledge.

CHAPTER FIVE

Not So Fast!

A Response to the Time, Continuity, and Change Section

GABRIEL A. REICH, VIRGINIA COMMONWEALTH UNIVERSITY

In their chapter, Helmsing and Whitlock do an excellent job describing time as simultaneously objective, subjective, and intimately connected to memory. It is the implications of that latter aspect for social studies curricula that I suspect troubles them the most and that I would like to unpack a little further. They asked, "before learners can engage in historical analysis within identified time periods, should we not ask how or why these time periods emerge as they do?" (p. 41). They pointed out that adopting standard historical epochs leaves students with misunderstandings, turning time periods into hollow stereotypes. Their question is important for teachers to consider, but I am less sure of the answer.

Research on how students learn history does not provide much in the way of guidance when considering that question. Perhaps the most rigorous study was conducted by Lee and Ashby (2000) who presented children, aged 7–14, with two accounts of the fall of the Roman Empire. One ends in 476 with the death of the last Western Roman Emperor, and the other in 1453 with the Ottoman sack of Constantinople. They asked students how it is possible that two accounts of the end of the Roman Empire present such different information? They traced a developmental path that began with the idea that one date is right and the other is wrong, and proceeded to an understanding that historians construct criteria for making judgments about the beginning and ending of historical periods. The latter understanding is the one that Helmsing and Whitlock value more, but by the end of that study, only 40% of 8th graders had achieved it, and over 30% continued to believe one date was a factual error. Thus, if we are to follow their advice, we will need curricula that explore how historians reconstruct time beginning in early grades and continuing through high school.

Before we decide to advocate for that change, however, we should consider the value of historical time as it is commonly understood. Many cultures organize the past into *time maps* (Zerubavel, 2003) that connect people to key historical moments that define identity, and promote continuity. As in most countries, U.S. holidays are connected to the nation's origins, conflicts, and dominant religion (e.g., Christianity). The cumulative effect of celebrating those holidays throughout the year is designed to provide citizens with a sense of the nation's origins, values, and historic trajectory (Zerubavel, 2003). There is a lot to criticize about the ideology and assumptions baked into the American Exceptionalism that our national time-map reinforces. To change the shape of that collective memory, and the time map that reinforces it, is a difficult undertaking. Its effects, however, are not uniformly negative. Our national time map can help connect present-day citizens to values and ideals that, although never realized, present continuity between contemporary struggles for social justice with those in the past (Booth, 2008). For example, Dr. Martin Luther King Jr.'s (1963) "I Have a Dream" speech begins with an allusion to Lincoln's (1863) "Gettysburg Address" and continues with an allusion to the "Declaration of Independence" in order to ground the progressive change he was advocating in the collective memory of the nation's past. Like Lincoln's (1863) "Gettysburg Address," King's use of the American time map helps to communicate a set of moral values through a narrative that is readily understandable by many people that transcends time.

Despite those affordances, the unreflective use of historical epochs can hinder a deeper understanding of world and U.S. history. They are used in K–12 classrooms to simplify complex historical phenomena into easily remembered historical stereotypes that obscure the nuanced differences of time and place. Thus, *American chattel enslavement* exists in the collective memory as deep-South cotton enslavement in the decade or two preceding the Civil War. Likewise, *Medieval* becomes the in-between time of knights, warfare, plague, and chivalry. Those stereotypes, however, allow students with limited historical knowledge to begin wrestling with continuity and change over time. For example, an economy that relies on enslavement can be compared to an economy that relies on free labor, and the rigid social hierarchies of premodern Europe can be compared to the changes wrought by the growing presence of bourgeois and working-class urban dwellers. These examples lack nuance, but they offer a starting point.

All teachers face difficult trade-offs when they make choices about what they will teach. Teachers can decide to build on familiar time maps, and perhaps reframe their meaning, or they can decide to break them down so students can learn how historians construct accounts of the past. That latter choice is the more difficult one for both teachers and students, many of whom will struggle with the ambiguity that introduces. That choice should be guided by teachers' understanding of their students' needs, and their own curricular priorities.

REFERENCES

Booth, W. J. (2008). The work of memory: Time, identity, and justice. *Social Research*, 75(1), 237–262.

King Jr., M. L. (1963). I have a dream. Retrieved from https://kinginstitute.stanford.edu/

Lee, P. J., & Ashby, R. (2000). Progression in historical understanding among students ages 7–14. In P. Stearns, P. Seixas, & S. Wineburg (Eds.), *Knowing, teaching and learning history* (pp. 199–222). New York, NY: NYU Press.

Lincoln, A. (1863). The Gettysburg address. Retrieved from http://memory.loc.gov/ammem/index.html

Zerubavel, E. (2003). *Time maps: Collective memory and the social shape of the past*. Chicago, IL: University of Chicago Press.

Section III:
People, Places, and Environments

CHAPTER SIX

Borders

SAJANI JINNY MENON, UNIVERSITY OF ALBERTA
MUNA SALEH, CONCORDIA UNIVERSITY OF EDMONTON

> Living on borders and in margins, keeping intact one's shifting and multiple identity and integrity, is like trying to swim in a new element, an "alien" element. The "alien" element has become familiar—never comfortable, but home.
>
> —ANZALDÚA, 1987/1999, P. III

Sitting together and discussing possibilities for this chapter, we realized that depending on how we position ourselves and, in turn, find ourselves situated in dynamic relation to others, temporally grounded, and within the diverse worlds we inhabit (Lugones, 1987)—we could critically and thoughtfully take up the notion of borders as being the intersection and multiplicity of experience. Similar to Anzaldúa (1987/1999), whose quote we used to introduce this piece, we believe any discussion about borders is ultimately a discussion of self/selves. Framing our understandings of borders in this manner, we recognized, permits us to disrupt and reconstruct and recontextualize more traditional conceptualizations of borders; those of which may (un)consciously be used by students and teachers in different social educational contexts. In particular, understandings and constructs limited to the demarcation of geographical regions and peoples. We wondered why this might be, as globalization forces (Smith, 2003) such as the development of sophisticated technologies and their subsequent uses, combined with enhanced access to social media, would suggest the exchange of ideas and experiences is much easier than in the past. Yet, as educators we readily acknowledged numerous teacher and student resources (e.g., student textbooks, classroom maps, and even certain online sources) that constitute sociocultural artifacts representative of a simple cartography of borders that are typically interpreted, translated, and packaged from within specific perspectives.

Because social studies curricula is in part, we believe, concerned with the understanding of past and current events and how they in turn influence the present and shape the future, we deem it important to highlight the importance such evolving events can play in contextualizing a discussion on and about borders. Within the greater context of the world, we were able to pinpoint events we felt were germane to how border-making, border-crossing, and dwelling within borders are being perceived, experienced, spoken about, discussed, and storied. For instance, we wonder(ed) at the xenophobic border-making inherent in Britain's Brexit referendum (Rochon, 2016). Closer to home, the slow response to act on the issue of missing and murdered Canadian Indigenous women highlights challenges in cultural border-crossings (Smith, 2016). Suggestive of dwelling within diverse borders, Canada's actions regarding the refugee crisis evokes a maelstrom of emotions (Kanji, 2016). During the "Three Amigo Summit," a meeting among Canadian Prime Minister Trudeau, former U.S. President Obama, and Mexican President Pena Neito, a united front was presented in terms of their condemnation of the "rise of protectionism and anti-immigrant sentiment at home and abroad" (CBC News, 2016, para. 1) which hint(ed) at a dismantling of psychological borders.

Eschewing simple encapsulations, we understood that, for social studies teachers and students, this requires entertaining different views of the world around us. In essence, trying myriad lenses on to gain a more complicated and, we suggest, more humane appreciation of the term borders—whereby personal, familial, intergenerational, social, institutional, and cultural (Clandinin, 2013) stories intertwine—and where there can be an overlapping of lives (Bateson, 2000). This we recognize is no easy task and so we are mindful of hooks' (1995) still relevant words:

> Sadly, at a time when so much sophisticated cultural criticism by hip intellectuals from diverse locations extols a vision of cultural hybridity, border crossing, subjectivity constructed out of plurality, the vast majority of folks in this society still believe in a notion of identity that is rooted in a sense of essential traits and characteristics that are fixed and static. (p. 10)

Thus, in shifting attention away from a monolithic or fixed construct of borders, we *purposely* choose to unsettle the concept of borders as it is often presented in various literature and media taken up in social studies classrooms. Instead of defaulting to a singular view whereby borders act to separate geographical spaces, people, and ideas, we would like to draw attention to how by their very nature, borders can concurrently act to position geographical spaces, people, and ideas within close proximity of one another. This is a profound consideration as it serves to expand static definitions of borders to include those embedded in, and contoured by, human experience and not necessarily conceived as rigid, fixed, naturally occurring phenomena. In this light, borders can be molded, shifted, and shaped by experiences—internal and external, personal and social—over time and in relation with one another. In an ongoing state of flux, they can be messy, continually defined and redefined. Additionally, from this perspective, this amorphous quality enables borders, in both the figurative and literal sense, to be permeable and semi-permeable constructs, existing with spaces within and around them, alongside more traditional constructs or impermeable border conceptualizations. We believe that such understandings can only serve to benefit social studies teachers and encourage students to inquire more deeply into their assumptions and moreover, to foster deep and rich dialogue as they jointly work toward complicating different conceptualizations of borders.

EXPERIENCE AS STORIED BORDERS AND BORDERLANDS TO LIVE BY AND WITHIN

Our work is rooted in Dewey's (1938/1997) view of education as life and life as experience. Experience, for Dewey, is built over a lifetime of relational living, shapes future experiences, and alters understandings of past experiences. This concept undergirds the work of curriculum theorists Connelly and Clandinin (1999), who developed the term "stories to live by" as a narrative way to understand identities in their work alongside teachers who often questioned who they were within and outside the border(land)s of school. Later, Clandinin and Huber (2002) wrote, "Stories to live by are shaped in places and lived in places. They live in actions, in relationships with others, in language, including silences, in gaps and vacancies, in continuities and discontinuities" (p. 161–162). In this vein, we reposition borders and border-making as significantly experiential endeavors that are storied, fluid, multiple, temporal, relational, contextual, and perpetually evolving, and further suggest that social studies educators alongside students can rework new understandings for this keyword of borders.

Border-Crossing Does Not Always Necessitate a Passport

We are also drawn to Lugones' (1987) concepts of "worlds" and "world"-traveling. In discussing the plurality of "worlds" we may inhabit as we compose our lives, Lugones elucidated, "A 'world' need not be a construction of a whole society. It may be a construction of a tiny portion of a particular society. It may be inhabited by just a few people. Some 'worlds' are bigger than others" (p. 10). Lugones further described how the movement, or travel, between and among "worlds" may be undertaken with loving or arrogant perception. For Lugones, "Love is seen not as fusion and erasure of difference but as incompatible with them. Love reveals plurality" (p. 3). In contrast, arrogant perception is the "failure to identify with persons that one views arrogantly or has come to see as the products of arrogant perception" (p. 4).

Likewise, we see border(lands)s as emerging from a continuum of arrogance and love. In thinking about borders in this manner, we recognize that there are "worlds" where we are storied in particular ways and where we feel compelled to "animate"—or live out—certain stories of who we are (Lugones, 1987) which serve to build, maintain, and/or deconstruct borders. Simultaneously, specific narratives can invite border-crossing or enhance isolation. As such, we imagine that allowing for the sharing of diverse and personal life experiences within social studies classrooms can create invitational spaces for border-crossing. In the following sections, we employ Lugones' understanding of "worlds" to guide our autobiographical musings.

SHARING AUTOBIOGRAPHICAL STORIES AS WAYS TO INTERRUPT, DISRUPT, AND EXTEND UNDERSTANDINGS OF BORDERS AS A KEYWORD IN SOCIAL STUDIES

Through working to trouble static conceptualizations of borders in this fashion, we offer one way (of many) by which the sharing of personal narratives can facilitate important insights for teachers and students alike.

Muna: Bordering on the (in)Humane

"Look at their little tribe, they're just loading 'er up, 'eh?"

I heard his booming voice and looked at the man standing next to me, hoping that the words didn't mean what I suspected they meant. But no, his snickers and pointed gesturing confirmed my fears. The man next to me was indeed talking about, and laughing at, my family members as they retrieved my sister's plentiful luggage from the baggage carousel.

I had hoped this latest trip to the airport to greet my sister would be different than the one from the previous week when we were there to greet my Dad. They had both traveled to Lebanon over the summer and we, as always, held our breaths, praying that the horrific violence in neighboring Syria, close to where our family lives in Lebanon, would not cross over the shared border. Thankfully, it had not and we were elated to welcome our loved ones home. The week before, as we were gathering my Dad's luggage, a man waiting near the arrivals gate asked his female companion aloud, "They're coming from a *domestic* flight??"

My Dad had traveled back home via a connecting flight from Toronto and the man could not seem to comprehend why we, obviously not the sort of Canadians he envisioned, were in the same area as he. In response, I mocked his comment, turning to my brother to say, in a really exaggerated and obnoxious way, "Ha-ha, this guy can't believe we're here from a *domestic* flight!" The man looked appropriately uncomfortable and my family and I continued on our way. Later recounting the story to my siblings, we ruefully agreed to file it under our ever-expanding imaginary folder titled, "You Can't Make This Shit Up."

Today, however, I was not in the frame of mind to laugh. The despondency in spirit I was experiencing was the reason I had decided to stand a little to the side, away from the crowd of travelers and greeters. The day before, I checked my phone to see that my sister had sent the now-infamous image of three-year-old Kurdish Syrian toddler, Alan, who alongside his five-year-old brother Galib, died following a disastrous attempt at seeking refuge by sea. These beautiful boys were found lying, as if asleep, on a beach in Turkey. One of the captions above the horrific image of little Alan read "Humanity Washed Ashore."

Heart shattered and body shaking, I checked with several online news outlets to see if I could find more information about what happened to little Alan and his family. As I was reading some of the links, I looked over at Maya, who was Alan's age, and thought back to a recent family trip to Kelowna, B.C. I thought about how excited Maya and her older siblings, Malak and Ahmad, had been to board a boat on the Okanagan and I wondered about how Alan and Galib felt boarding that raft on the shores of Turkey. How and why were our experiences so different? I wondered about the boys' mother and father and if they had other children. Were they still alive? Were they now dealing not only with the angst of displacement, but also with unbearable anguish after the horrific losses of Alan and Galib?

As I was reading, I thought about the devaluation of lives in all parts of the world, incomprehensibly because of differences in skin color, income, sexual and gender identities, abilities, dress, languages, among so many other stated and not stated reasons. I wondered if my grandparents had not sought refuge from Palestine, and if my parents had not emigrated from Lebanon, could we have been among those seeking refuge today? Would our lives, our stories matter? I thought about the daily dehumanization taking place not just within sensationalist media headlines about "swarms" of refugees and "big, beautiful walls" but in everyday discourses, everyday interactions, everyday living. A sideways glance, thoughtless comment, or awkward silence in the stead of looking *at* someone, being present *with* another person, attending to each other as equals in creation, words that could have been spoken (or not) to create spaces where internal and external, real and perceived, borders could be deconstructed and/or reimagined.

Unable to sleep that night with the image of Alan in my heart, I stayed up late and followed the unfolding story. I was confused by the hateful comments on some of the online discussion sites accompanying the images and articles—sites I do not often visit because of the ugliness that often accompanies discussion threads. Many comments brought to mind African-American poet Nayyarah Waheed's (2013) short but powerful poem: "you broke the ocean in half to be here, only to meet nothing that wants you.—immigrant." Within one of the discussion threads, someone had the audacity to write that Alan died because of his parents' greed in wanting to travel to a prosperous country. For me, these unfeeling words evoked a line from a poem by Somali-British writer Warsan Shire (2011): "You have to understand that no one puts their children in a boat unless the water is safer than the land."

I then found out that Alan and Galib's mother Rehan had died in the same merciless way, seeking security in a world that couldn't, wouldn't, hold them. With my heart in my throat, I thought about those who, like the Kurdi family, feel forced to make life and death decisions in the hopes of crossing borders and finding spaces where they can maybe compose their lives in the absence of oppression. Where they may be free to *live*.

These thoughts and questions were living inside me as I heard the man in the airport continue to scoff at my family, "Look, see how they treat their women?" I looked over to see that my Mom was attempting to move one of the carts piled with luggage to the side while my Dad and my husband, Wissam, went to pay for parking. Even then I held my tongue, fearful that my weariness and sorrow, rage and guilt, would be unleashed on the man next to me. Fearful that I would allow myself to become less than who I want to be. Just then, Maya toddled over to me with an unfamiliar penguin neck pillow in her hands. I picked her up and asked in Arabic, "Maya, min wayn jibteeha?" ("Maya, where did you get that from?"), only to hear the man repeat my words in a gibberish, mocking tone. Unable to hold back any longer, I turned to him and said, with anger and exasperation, "You're funny." The man looked at me, unembarrassed, amused even, and said, "Thank you." I couldn't stop myself. His arrogance broke my resolve. I responded with, "You're welcome. Jackass."

I think he was stunned into silence that a woman wearing hijab would be so bold. I, however, was not finished. Glaring at him as the men in my family returned to push the carts of baggage toward the parkade, I made sure that every one of my family members proceeded me before I followed. They did not realize that I was engaged in a heated, if now silent, confrontation. The man would not look at me even as I would not look away from him. Finally, before walking away, I said, "It's easy to talk when you think no one will respond, hey?" He didn't say anything and I made my way to the exit with Maya in my arms, feeling the uncomfortable stares from others who had witnessed our exchange, but who had remained silent.

What type of life is of most worth? Whose? Why? What can be done? These are the questions and thoughts alive within me as I mourn two beautiful babies and their mother, and too many others who, like Alan and Galib, are born and raised in a world unable, and sometimes unwilling, to cradle them and their beautiful light.

Jinny: Bordering on Academic?

Teaching, I often found myself exchanging stories with the students under my care. Sometimes the stories that traversed between us featured the people most treasured in our lives, those we named as family and friends. Often these stories expressed hopes we shared. Of the stories that fell from my lips, one included that old chestnut of a "good" education opening doors. I believed what I espoused—having a formal education could dismantle certain borders, enabling passage to new worlds and opportunities. What I hadn't truly appreciated, until fairly recently, was that certain experiences lend themselves to easier border-crossings than others. Just as there are entry ways that open into inviting vistas, there exist others that aren't as welcoming.

Last year a friend and I had been invited to attend an academic social gathering. Moving away from the coat room and into the foyer where guests were raising their glasses in celebration, we passed a group of people. Conscious of their eyes upon us, I heard one gentleman remark, "There *must* be another event." I didn't know if my friend caught the man's words but they certainly made an impression on me. As we proceeded to join the festivities, his words echoed in my mind in subtle and not-so-subtle ways, reminding me that women of color find themselves repeatedly caught in dark borderland spaces. His comment drew me back to another disquieting moment.

"Did someone say dirty? Dirty immigrants?" she asked sitting down with a smile. In point of fact, no one had said any such thing. She had aligned the two words, "dirty" and "immigrants" all on her own. I wondered how my fellow student had come to pair those specific words, as the discussion she had walked in on was about our delight in the obvious warmth and care that existed between the school staff and the students. The blood rushed to my ears. Did she realize how offensive her remarks were? Several of us had opted to volunteer our time in a classroom as part of a graduate course related to the experiences of newcomers to Canada. This was one of my favorite courses as the instructor went out of her way to make the class interesting and welcoming. Yet, I encountered challenges that I had not anticipated in working alongside others within and outside the boundaries of the university setting.

Sitting in the school staffroom that morning, as I watched my classmate's mouth move, I barely heard what she said after that first utterance—*those words* had been a direct assault to my person, shards wounding me in untold ways. This was not the first time that I had trouble digesting her or another of my class member's remarks. I had listened to them speak and understood that they held some strong views about immigrants and people belonging to visible ethnic groups. I have faced my share of discrimination, erroneous assumptions of identity often played to the discordant tune of: "Go back where you came from!" or "You (expletive) Paki!" alongside the much-favored refrain, "You're *Canadian*?! No *really*, where are you from?" I had found through much soul-searching and heartbreak that irrespective of what you say and do, some individuals cling to their assumptions. Sadly, as time passed, I could see this student and another becoming even more belligerent and set in their views. It was as if they had placed an impervious barricade around themselves, something which effectively prevented them from meaningfully interacting with *some* of their classmates. So, while there existed opportunities to adopt new perspectives, I painfully relearned "world"-traveling (Lugones, 1987) could not occur unless there existed a willingness to attempt to cross lines whether they be self-imposed boundaries or otherwise constructed limits. Skirting the edges of these jagged-edged bordered lands, I had hoped that continued exposure to divergent views and dialogue foregrounding topics of citizenship, immigration, settlement, language, and culture among others, would permit for more open communication. Yet with each outrageous comment I heard outside of the classroom ("Sixteen years ago, we didn't have *this many* foreigners!" "Teachers have problems dealing with *these kinds* of kids!" "What are we supposed to do? Take *all of them* into our homes?") I felt tension coiling throughout me. I had wanted to afford others space and time, qualities which I had frequently been denied, to encourage a sharing of voices but I now found myself at odds with this notion of freedom to speak.

Dirty immigrants. The two words reverberated ominously in my brain throughout the day. I couldn't stop thinking. Innocuous words on their own? Except, *dirty* was a word which conjured up synonyms such as: filth, polluted, fouled, contaminated, and I could go on. *Immigrant*, at the time, didn't seem nearly as pejorative. It evoked images of a stranger in a new land. However, combining the two words resulted in a meaning which disturbed me on a visceral level. Considering the converse left me distinctly uneasy. Simple word association led me to descriptors such as: clean, pure, uncontaminated, unpolluted, and interestingly, citizen. Such a dichotomy, such a black and white manner of viewing people seemed inherently wrong. Born of immigrants, did that make me debris one generation removed or was I ascribed that same special status as an early comer? What about other family members? Friends? How would they be classified according to this typology of *The Dirty Immigrant?* What about the countless others who had bravely made their way to "O Canada! Our home" in the hopes of living their dreams? Would skin color, sex, occupation, gender, socioeconomic status, sexual orientation, language, or any other trait examined on its own or in confluence with others, determine how much of a *Dirty Immigrant* a person could be categorized as? And being labeled in such a manner was one given a life sentence with no reprieve, living in constant fear, not knowing when the sword of Damocles would fall? In essence, severing opportunities to trespass (with impunity) into bordered spaces not traversed before, crushing aspirations to travel beyond the borderlands.

In revisiting these two incidents, employing the imperfect compass of memory, I tentatively map out boundaries that I have bumped up against (and those that have bumped up against me) in my ongoing attempts to humanely navigate worlds. The incident of the get-together occurred on a university campus, arguably a bastion of higher learning, a place habitually touted as inclusive. Nonetheless, the man who pragmatically stated that there *must* be another function taking place, appeared to be upholding an attitude that diversity, heedless of the party line, is simply, disappointingly, rhetoric. Likewise, the storied moment I retold of a university classmate defaulting to a label of *Dirty Immigrants* in another educational setting, intimates a disconnect between an institutional narrative of inclusion and a deficit discourse on the same matter. Looking beyond definitive perimeters and moving toward a horizon of possibilities, I think of Okri (1997/2014) who ventured:

> The only hope is in the creation of alternative values, alternative realities. The only hope is in daring to redream one's place in the world …Which is to say that in some way or another we breach and *confound the accepted frontiers of things* [emphasis added]. (Chapter 5, Section 23, para. 2)

Is it only in the recognition and acceptance of the (in)scrutable geographies which inscribe each of us, that we may learn to border-cross? If schools, universities, and other forums are to be lauded as sites of inclusion, ought not the stories of diverse individuals (whether they be newcomers, refugees, immigrants, tourists, strangers, citizens, and innumerable others) need to be narrated and heard? In desiring to embrace the complicated multiplicities that engrave *all* experiences, I dare to reimagine borders recalibrated by hope.

DWELLING WITHIN THE BORDERLANDS: FORWARD LOOKING THOUGHTS AND IMAGININGS ACROSS SOCIOCULTURAL AND OTHER EDUCATIONAL CONTEXTS

> Borders are set up to define the places that are safe and unsafe, to distinguish us from them. A border is a dividing line, a narrow strip along a steep edge. A borderland is a vague and undetermined place created by the emotional residue of an unnatural boundary. It is in a constant state of transition.
>
> —Anzaldúa, 1987/1999, p. 3

While our respective autobiographical narratives were written and represented individually for clarity, we sought to dwell in borderland spaces alongside one another and readers as we traveled to one another's "worlds" as educators, academics, and more importantly, as humans. Along with experiencing multiple resonances, we were also struck with how concrete or imagined borders seemed to be erected or reinforced within ourselves, and between us and others, with words and actions (and/or their absence) that are often laced with arrogant perception. These are rigid borders that do not allow for, or may perhaps necessitate one-sided and perilous attempts at, world-traveling (Lugones, 1987). These experiences, alongside recent calls by a presumptive American president for a "ban" on certain people and walls to be constructed (Holpuch, 2016) and other sociopolitical events, confound us. We are particularly troubled by constructed borders that story certain lives as less valuable and/or worthy of care. In thinking about these autobiographical stories and broader historical and evolving events, we see the potential in how sharing such experiences can personally and collectively (re)shape singular understandings of borders as an important keyword within social studies curricula and beyond.

We share Connelly and Clandinin's (1988) belief that "all teaching and learning questions—all curriculum matters—be looked at from the point of view of the involved persons" (p. 4). Personal knowledge (Connelly & Clandinin, 1988), forged through the crucibles of life experiences and personal stories, shared in safe classroom spaces, can foster dialogue and enable social studies students and teachers to inquire together into their understandings of borders. In this chapter, we penned our autobiographical musings but we suggest that the sharing of personal stories can also be taken in up in myriad mediums that allow for the storied pluralities we each live. In this manner, we believe the keyword of borders can be unsettled, reimagined, and embedded within social education curricula.

As we actively and relationally imagine possibilities for the co-composing and living of social education curriculum (Menon, Redlich-Amirav, Saleh, & Kubota, 2015; Saleh, 2017), we hold close Anzaldúa's (1987/1999) understanding of borderlands—simultaneously a liminal space of pain and a place of redemption, a site of promise. It is in dwelling within the borderlands that we can experience ambiguity, dissonance, reflection, dialogue, community, and further, understand these feelings as the harbingers of a true heteroglossia (Greene, 1993) whereby diversity is honored. In (re)telling personal stories and sharing experiences of borders, border-making, border-dwelling, and border-crossing across heterogeneous social education contexts, diverse peoples can disrupt, interrupt, and rewrite dominant border narratives ... connecting with others who, too, are composing lives in the midst of multiplicities and complexities.

> To survive the Borderlands
> you must live sin fronteras
> be a crossroads
>
> —ANZALDÚA (1987/1999, P. 195)

DISCUSSION QUESTIONS

1. Having read the authors' autobiographical pieces, have your understandings of borders as a social studies keyword been interrupted? What resonates for you? What does not?
2. As social studies educators and students, how do cultural, social, personal, institutional, and linguistic narratives, among so many others, shape how we compose ourselves in our moment-to-moment living in relation to the myriad borders we embody and experience?
3. In the midst of frequently conflicting narratives, how can communal borderland spaces be created and/or sustained within social studies classrooms and beyond?
4. Acknowledging borders within ourselves, how do we engage in conversation in ways that honor instead of appropriate? Thinking about your social education context(s), how would you best convey (past and evolving) personal/sociocultural stories of border-making, border-crossing, and/or border-dwelling?

REFERENCES

Anzaldúa, G. (1987/1999). *Borderlands/La frontera: The new mestiza*. San Francisco, CA: Aunt Lute Books.

Bateson, M. C. (2000). *Full circles, overlapping lives: Culture and generation in transition*. New York, NY: Ballantine Books.

Clandinin, D. J. (2013). *Engaging in narrative inquiry*. Walnut Creek, CA: Left Coast Press.

Clandinin, D. J., & Huber, J. (2002). Narrative inquiry: Toward understanding life's artistry. *Curriculum Inquiry, 32*(2), 161–169. doi:10.1111/1467-873X.00220.

Connelly, F. M., & Clandinin, D. J. (1988). *Teachers as curriculum planners: Narratives of Experience*. New York, NY: Teachers College Press.

Connelly, F. M., & Clandinin, D. J. (1999). *Shaping a professional identity: Stories of educational practice*. New York, NY: Teachers College Press.

Dewey, J. (1938/1997). *Experience and education*. New York, NY: Simon & Schuster.

Greene, M. (1993). Diversity and inclusion: Toward a curriculum for human beings. *Teachers College Record, 95*(2), 211–221. Retrieved from https://maxinegreene.org/uploads/library/diversity_inclusion.pdf

Holpuch, A. (2016, January 4). Trump re-ups controversial Muslim ban and Mexico wall in first campaign ad. *The Guardian*. Retrieved from www.theguardian.com

hooks, b. (1995). *Art on my mind: Visual politics*. New York, NY: The New Press.

Kanji, A. (2016, March 10). The disturbing movement against Syrian refugees in Canada. *The Star*. Retrieved from www.thestar.com

Lugones, M. (1987). Playfulness, "world"-traveling, and loving perception. *Hypatia, 2*(2), 3–19. doi:10.1111/j.1527-2001.1987.tb01062.x.

Menon, J., Redlich-Amirav, D., Saleh, M., & Kubota, H. (2015). Embracing lived multiplicities as beginning narrative inquirers. *Creative Approaches to Research, 8*(3), 80–101. Retrieved from http://creativeapproachestoresearch.net/wp-content/uploads/CAR8_3_fullissue.pdf

Okri, B. (1997/2014). *A way of being free*. Head of Zeus. [Kindle Edition]. Retrieved from Amazon.com

Rochon, L. (2016, June 28). Brexit: Xenophobia, nationalism, and questions about income distribution. *CBC News*. Retrieved from www.cbc.ca

Saleh, M. (2017). *Stories we live by, with, and in: A narrative inquiry into the experiences of Canadian Muslim girls and their mothers* (Doctoral dissertation). University of Alberta.

Shire, W. (2011). *Teaching my mother how to give birth*. London: Flipped Eye Publishing.

Smith, D. G. (2003). Curriculum and teaching face globalization. In W. Pinar (Ed.), *International handbook of curriculum research* (pp. 35–51). Mahwah, NJ: Lawrence Erlbaum.

Smith, J. (2016, June 29). Provinces studying terms of reference for inquiry on missing murdered Indigenous women. *CBC News*. Retrieved from www.cbc.ca

The Canadian Press. (2016, June 29). Three Amigos say relations 'strong' amid rising protectionism, anti-immigrant sentiment. *CBC News*. Retrieved from www.cbc.ca

Waheed, N. (2013). *Salt*. San Bernardino, CA: Createspace.

CHAPTER SEVEN

Environment

JODI LATREMOUILLE, UNIVERSITY OF CALGARY, ALBERTA

> Environmentalism, in its deepest sense, is not about environment. It is not about things but relationships, not about beings but Being, not about world but the inseparability of self and circumstance.
>
> —Neil Evernden, *The Natural Alien: Humankind and Environment*, 1999

The word *environment* refers to a wide-ranging aspect of human participation in life on earth. It has long been associated with equally broad concepts (such as nature, habitat, ecology) of that which surround us. Most North Americans continue to see ourselves as self-enclosed human entities at the center of the "surrounding" two-dimensional environment (Serres, 1995, p. 33). In this perception of an encircled environment, vast tracts of wilderness or urban grasslands are easily designated as *empty* lands waiting for our development, and deep oceans seen as *bottomless* reservoirs for our effluent.

With the dominant modernist worldview in North American society, the relationship for many of us with the natural environment is most commonly characterized by a denial of relationship, which allows the Enlightenment dichotomy of romance and control to dominate. Our approach to environmentalism oscillates between the romantic naturalist and conservation philosophies and the rational management ethos of problem-solving and natural resource development (Blenkinsop, 2012, p. 354). The National Geographic Magazine (2016) *Environment* webpage, for example, on one hand encourages us to fall in love with full-color images of adorable baby orangutans so that we will be more inspired to protect them, while on the other hand, educates us on the connections between climate change, development, and the plight of refugees in hopes that we will find ways to resolve and *fix* these problems (Nixon, 2011, p. 152). Across the social studies curricula and resources in North America, the environment is consistently represented as a singular, abstract, external entity, framed in Enlightenment terms either as the object of a child's romantic and emotive care and concern, or as a problem that needs to be rationally managed and balanced against the advancement of human interests.

Based on the premise that "all education is environmental education," Orr (1991) asserts that we teach students about their place within our environment not only by what and how we teach, but also through our collective denial, that is, by what we do not teach (p. 54). I propose that our relationships with our *environment* may be much more dynamic than the dual Enlightenment mythologies of romance and control if we embrace a deep cultural shift toward an *honest participation* in Being (Little Bear, 2000, p. 80). Interpreted through Elder Bob Cardinal's Cree principles of security, love, and discipline, this honest participation is interactive and intersecting relationships with/in and through human beings, the more-than-human, and the earth.

LOVE STORY I: PROJECT ENGAGE

Stephanie Bartlett from Calgary, Alberta, works with six-year-olds to inspire entire schools and communities to action. She and her kindergarten class created *Project Engage: Living our Lives for a Sustainable Future*.[1] It is described as a school-wide project whose vision is to increase environmental stewardship within the community through authentic task design and partnerships outside the school. It includes a metal collection station, a Christmas light collection and recycling campaign, a sweater day to raise awareness around energy use, and a partnership with a local community center re-design (Chinook Park, 2016, p. 1–2). This year, the class worked on a sound sculpture from recycled metals, highlighting resource use and the relationship between art and the environment.

Stephanie has felt called to interpret curriculum, teaching, and the world through the lenses of environmental sustainability, economic justice, and community. When a teacher such as Stephanie sees herself as integral to the life of a community, she may find ways to "live and breathe moments of deep engagement and connection within the institutional contours" (S. Bartlett, personal communication, April 2016). She is asking critical questions with her kindergarten students: "what is needed here, now, in this time and place, under these particular circumstances?" Along with other teachers who take up environmental work in a deeper way at all levels in the field of social studies, Stephanie is "broadening the spectrum of what counts as environmentalism" (Nixon, 2011, p. 5), invoking place-based environmental education, inquiry, and community involvement.

"Greenwashing Pedagogies" of Romance and Control

In reviewing definitions for *environment* in Merriam-Webster's dictionary, I found the following definitions the most relevant for the social studies: 1. "the circumstances, objects, or conditions by which one is surrounded." 2a. "the complex of physical, chemical, and biotic factors (such as climate, soil, and living things) that act upon an organism or an ecological community and ultimately determine its form and survival." 2b. "the aggregate of social and cultural conditions that influence the life of an individual or community." The root metaphors of romance and control originated in Descartes' Enlightenment dichotomy, which denied relationships and created a chasm "between the mind and the whole of the material world" (Abram, 2010, p. 108). Western dualistic mythologies of mind/body, culture/nature, and so on, assert that humans are discrete beings who remain "cleanly divided from the surrounding world of persons and places" (Keller, 1988, p. 1), completely separate from the life cycles of the earth.

When we interpret the environment as merely a "surrounding," external to ourselves and our narrow human interests, North Americans may become vulnerable to the romance/control inspired "greenwashing"[2] of large corporations and industries: airlines sell carbon offset credits, grocery stores stock "all natural," yet still factory-farmed meats, and fuel stations tout hip-sounding "biofuels" such as government-subsidized, GMO corn-based ethanol. Large companies also make highly public donations to popular earth charities in order to promote an "I am greener than thou" image, while refusing to disclose or change their own large-scale environmentally destructive practices for fear that this may cut into their profit margins (Steinberg, 2013, p. 254). They skirt responsibility and download eco-guilt onto consumers, playing off the *Lorax's* dire warning that "unless someone like you cares a whole awful lot, nothing is going to get better. It's not." (Dr. Seuss, 1971). By admonishing individuals "to do our small part," to "reduce, reuse, and recycle," to "save the environment," to "go green," and to compete to see who can make the most "empowered, healthy, and guilt-free" consumer choices (Knufken, 2010, p. 1), these companies are encouraging us to ignore the more central ethical inconsistencies propping up the "bottom line" of consumer culture and environmental extortion. And meanwhile… a mere one hundred global corporations go on "torching the planet," emitting 71% of total carbon emissions since 1988 (Lukacs, 2017).

These greenwashing practices are widely encouraged in schools across North America, with recycling programs, *save the polar bears* campaigns, and quick-and-easy litter clean-up initiatives. Teachers can select from a wide range of charities, preplanned events, educational resources, and corporate-model programs, in the quest to "empower and enable youth to be agents of change," and asks the familiar question, "if we don't take action, who will" (WE Movement, 2017)? Teacher professional development workshops and curriculum support materials often uphold this model, providing practical lesson plans and printable worksheets for teachers to replicate and deliver "controlled activism" in their classrooms (see, for example, Calgary Board of Education, 2015; Calgary Catholic School District, 2015). These programs allay students' eco-guilt and offer a certain sense of satisfaction, without asking them to question the root metaphors and social narratives at the heart of environmental issues, the deeper impact of their actions in their own communities, or the complexities of the environmental challenges that we face today.

Historical Roots of Romance and Control in the Conservation Movement

Eurocentric conservation efforts in America in the second half of the 19th century were generally concerned with generating appropriate techniques and programs to maintain and utilize the natural environments in practical and beneficial way. As the 20th century approached, several prominent political figures committed to preserving the country's wilderness against overexploitation. Theodore Roosevelt, governor of New York (1898–1901), and U.S. president (1901–1909), used his political influence to protect the state's and the country's natural resources and watersheds, stating that "there can be no greater issue than that of conservation in this country" (Roosevelt, 1912, p. 29). The Theodore Roosevelt Conservation Society (2017) focuses on safeguarding public land for habitat preservation, maintaining access for sportsmen, and the outdoor recreation economy. Gifford Pinchot, the primary founder of the Society of American Foresters in 1900, argued that a practical conservation should yield "the greatest good, for the greatest number, for the longest run" (Grant, 2017, par. 6). He fought for regulation of timber companies and electric utilities, and in his 1905–1910 term as chief of the U.S. National Forest Service he was responsible for the increase from 60 forest reserve units (56 million acres) to 150 protected national forests (172 million acres). John Muir, founder of the Sierra Club in 1892, argued that Pinchot was "too pragmatic" in his willingness to sacrifice wilderness for the sake of development, most notably California's Hetch Hetchy Valley watershed in Yosemite National Park in order to provide water to San Francisco for sustainable development (Grant, 2017). Muir, a stauncher protector of wilderness, helped establish Sequoia and Yosemite National Parks.

After World War I, Aldo Leopold espoused an ecological *land ethic*, arguing that nature was the vast system with which all human activity—culture, philosophy, the arts, values—interacted, for better or worse. Any abuses of the environment could be attributed to improper social and cultural beliefs rather than inappropriate management techniques. In his influential book, *A Sand County Almanac*, he wrote, "We abuse land because we regard it as a commodity belonging to us. When we see land as a community to which we belong, we may begin to use it with love and respect" (Leopold, 1949, p. viii).

In the 20th century, however, wilderness preservation embraced a more romanticized view of nature and animals, focusing on preserving scenic parklands and "charismatic megavertebrates," while ignoring earthworms, fungi, and less spectacular but more diverse landscapes such as grasslands and river valleys (Jensen, 2002, p. 85). The romantic conservationist ethic was perpetuated by David Brower, first executive director of the Sierra Club, who "wanted to save as much as the planet as possible from humans," overseeing the exponential growth of the Sierra Club which began with 7,000 members when he joined in 1952 and expanded to over 77,000 members when he left in 1969 (Steinberg, 2013, p. 246). His group significantly expanded the national park network, and successfully protected all national parks from dams, logging, and other forms of resource extraction, most notably protecting the Dinosaur National Monument by stopping the damming of the Colorado in Echo Park. The Dinosaur National Monument, however, came under the stress of heavy tourism inspired by Brower's highly successful Sierra Club film and print publicity campaign, undermining the very wilderness he was trying to save (Steinberg, 2013, p. 246).

In Canadian elementary provincial educational curricula, this 20th century romantic ethic of "care, concern and protection" often dominates, in the hopes that if young children spend more time in nature, they will somehow naturally learn to love it and take better care of it (Alberta Ministry of Education, 2006a; Ontario Ministry of Education, 2011), while failing to address the complexities of natural relationships or the consequences of heavy eco-tourism. In the United States, many supplementary curriculum resources promote environmental education that brings awareness to over-consumption without challenging the popular belief that "the world is our oyster" (see Pennington's *Consumption* chapter for more). The Think Earth Online Curriculum Project (2016) is an American nonprofit, public–private partnership providing free curriculum resources from grades 1 to 9 which help teachers educate students to conserve natural resources, reduce waste, and minimize pollution. This site focuses on content delivery and individual lifestyle choices, encouraging students to use less paper, water, and electricity, to carpool, and to recycle and put litter in the trash. Not surprisingly, Think Earth is sponsored by companies such as Toyota Motor Sales, U.S.A., and Edison International, a public utilities holdings company.

Rachel Carson's pivotal book, *Silent Spring* (1962), helped hasten the shift from a *humans vs. nature* conservationist ideology to the more ecological *socio-environmental* outlook that served as a powerful model for environmental justice movements in the later years of the 20th century (Nixon, 2011, p. xi; also see Gadotti, 2003). The growing environmental movement served to expose the consequences of consumer capitalism, with 75% of Americans considering themselves "environmentalists" in 1990 (Steinberg, 2013, p. 241). Today, however, despite widespread awareness of environmental issues, both the conservationist and socio-environmental outlooks have given way to increasingly competitive resource exploitation. The natural environment—while still romanticized for its exotic beauty—is simultaneously gravely exploited for its seeming endless wealth in order to promote human economic activities such as resource extraction, tourism, and technological replacements for natural processes, based on the unquestioned myths of progress, growth, and development. Ever-advancing technology promises not only management but also mastery of nature, which from this perspective becomes "a standing reserve" for human consumption and wealth-creation (Jensen, 2002, p. 208). With this "environment vs. economy" mindset, the inherent conservatism of ecology is seen as a barrier to food production and resource extraction even while economic disparity increases at an alarming rate (Shepard, 1998, p. 2).

In junior high and high school, the social studies curricula shift to a more rationalistic stance that views the environment as a passive object to be studied and manipulated by humans. It is a "contemporary issue" listed alongside—and often in competition with—trade, war, poverty, debt, disease, and human rights. High school students are expected to learn about human-environment relationships order to control them more effectively (Alberta Education, 2006b; British Columbia Ministry of Education, 2016).

Aborigines in Australia have dubbed European colonizers the "future eaters," those who consume without thought to replacing the resources used (Nixon, 2011, p. 96). Now, in the early 21st century, as participants in a closed earth ecosystem, human beings in many locales around the world are being forced to face the hard limits of our environment (Gadotti, 2003; Serres, 1995, p. 32). These limits are not borne equally by all. Paul Shepard (2002), a key American conservation activist, teacher, and author, argues that we have long been in the midst of a slow disintegration of natural systems—evidenced by such wide-ranging symptoms as recessions, poverty, mental-health epidemics, suicide, disastrous weather, political conflicts, famine, social upheaval—that is nothing short of a creeping "planetary ecological disaster" (as cited in Jensen, 2002, p. 256). Some endure a gradual, attritional destruction, a "slow violence" of environmental and social degradation that too often remains invisible, buried under more sensational tales of natural disaster, war, and discrete events (Nixon, 2011, p. 2).

Although North Americans occupying privileged positions may be most responsible for these consequences, we often feel relatively disconnected from these larger issues (Blenkinsop, 2012). Teachers often agree that "we pay lip service to the environment in our curriculum" (M. Matthew, personal communication, June 8, 2016). We feel challenged and overwhelmed by deeply troubling and complex environmental problems of our times, yet distracted and paralyzed by the eco-guilt built up through greenwashing techniques and corporate environmentalist slogans. Wendell Berry (2013) responds to this trouble by reminding us that in proposing responses to large and overwhelming socio-environmental problems, we do not ultimately have the right to ask if we will be successful or not. We are each challenged to respond in the best way that we know how, for the time and place that we find ourselves in, in all its local particularities and dynamic relations. The responses are necessarily multifarious.

The David Suzuki Foundation's Blue Dot movement (2016), based on the simple principle that "this blue dot is our only home" argues that it is a human right to live in a healthy environment, and that each community is charged with upholding this right by addressing the particular needs of their locale (para. 1). Sandra Steingraber's investigation of cancer and the environment (2010) connects chemical contamination by industry to cancer incidence in rural underprivileged populations, long denied in public health campaigns. Standing Rock protests against the Dakota Access Pipeline are being described as "a new civil rights movement where environmental and human rights meet" (Solnit, 2016, n.p.). These examples evoke deep ethical questions regarding what constitutes a proper relationship for humans with/in our environment, in our localized responses to the multiple and diverse challenges that we face in our time.

What Is Not Taught? Reviving Relationships with Security, Discipline, and Love

In Indigenous philosophies and holistic ways of knowing, the divides between the mind and the body, culture and nature, humans and the earth, are false and disruptive to the *happenings* that characterize our multiple earthly relationships. Leroy Little Bear (2000), an educator and scholar from the Blood Indian Tribe of the Blackfoot Confederacy, describes the relationship between humans and the environment as cyclical. It is in constant motion, yet characterized by regular, recurring patterns. The migration of the animals, the seasons of the year, the arising and disintegration of bones, bodies and landforms, require continual nourishment by humans, through "renewal ceremonies, songs and stories" (p. 78). As we gain more nuanced and lively understandings of our environment, this seemingly two-dimensional, self-enclosed earthly sphere becomes a textured, living, breathing "circle of kinship" (p. 78) in which humans participate fully and equitably. No longer do we operate from a discrete, singular, and isolated center, but rather from diverse points within a dynamic and lively "spider web of relations" (p. 78). Elder Bob Cardinal of the Enoch Cree Nation in Alberta shares his philosophy of *security, discipline, and love* in relationships (B. Cardinal, personal communication, July

11, 2016).[3] This philosophy unsettles the root metaphors of romance and control, which deny and violate humanity's deep relationship with our environment.

Moreover, Matthew Fox (2002, as cited in Jensen) argues that the persistent separation between humans and nature, and thus the need to control nature, is rooted in a false perception of the universe as unfriendly. The underlying assumption that "there *is* something profoundly unfriendly and threatening in nature" (Orr, as cited in Jensen, 2002, p. 25) motivates the human obsession with technology that monitors and controls our lives with ever-increasing accuracy. The underlying fear of nature brings about a need to control all aspects of one's environment, and perpetuates the cycle of unnecessary destruction (Jensen, 2002, p. 71). However, Elder Cardinal's notion of security may "restory" our environment as an essentially benign and abundant place (Jensen, 2002, p. 25), opening spaces for humans to move beyond our denial of relationships with the environment to deeper appreciation of our role in the grander cycles and seasons of life itself. These understandings of the dynamic world require our honest participation, that is, to "speak the truth" in the "the spider web of relations" (Little Bear, 2000, p. 80). We cannot, for example, "save the rainforest" without listening to the people who live there. Speaking the truth requires a more grounded and disciplined recognition of our true selves, "co-extensive with other beings and the life of our planet" (Macy, 2007, p. 148).

As security grows, we may shift from a romance or control-based ethic to a deeper, more careful, more complex and loving relationship with the earth. David Jardine, following Wendell Berry (2013), says, "the secret goal of education is to fall in love with the world. You can't fall in love with something if you don't know it. And you can't know it if you don't stay put" (D. Jardine, personal communication, 2015). When educators make loving intergenerational commitments to the earthly places that sustain us, living consciously with forests, overturned soil, towns, resource industries and swampy marshes as they flourish and fade, celebrate and decay once again, we make careful judgments that require us to "say no as often as to say yes" (Orr, as cited in Jensen, 2002, p. 25). Our decisions leave marks on the land: beautiful, scarred, telling its stories through those that stay behind—in gravesites, on reserves, in stands of aspen trees, and in the plots of forgotten land that continue to yield to each new generation of living and dying. Vandana Shiva reminds us that we belong to an earth democracy, whereby the land is a sacred trust for human sustenance (van Gelder, 2017). The committed love of staying put requires intimacy and affection, but unlike romanticism, recognizes limits and defines parameters for dynamic, mutually suffering, and sustaining relationships with/in and through the environment (Orr, as cited in Jensen, 2002, p. 25). These three principles lay embedded in a deeper environmental premise that humans must participate in this world truthfully and with discipline, so that we may responsibly love the environment with "open heart-minds" (Macy, 2016) in reciprocal, responsible relationships of security, discipline, and love.

LOVE STORY II: WHAT IS A BIOSOLID, ANYWAY?

In my work as a high school teacher in British Columbia, Canada, I asked students to consider their community as they undertook socio-environmental justice projects involving localized research and real community connections. One group learned that local First Nations groups were leading protests against the applications of biosolids on farms in the valley surrounding our small, rural community. These treated human wastes, or sewage sludge, are deemed *safe* by the companies that ship them in from larger cities in the province, but these claims and the research that they are based on are considered suspect by local activist groups and independent scientists alike.

In a work period early in the project, my students were discussing a plan of action for their small group project. They had spoken with members in the community, conducted in-depth research, and were contemplating how to bring the active phase of their project to fruition. As they were debating big plans, such as organizing a community rally, writing letters to government officials, and conducting various interviews, another student, eavesdropping on our conversation, asked, "So, what *is* a biosolid, anyway?" This query evoked Wendell Berry's (2013) critical ecological question, "what is needed here, now, in this time and place, under these particular circumstances?" (n.p.). Despite their extensive research and grand plans for change, the group needed to recognize and respect the relations at play in their environment. They realized that many members of the community were not even aware of this problem contaminating our very own backyard, and they wisely shifted their focus to building awareness in our community. They decided that an informational presentation was the most reasonable starting point for their project.

Later in the year, our class attended a public forum featuring local community groups, specialized scientists, government officials, and biosolid management companies. The students found the content of the talks highly technical, and very challenging to follow. When I asked them afterward how they felt about the day, one student replied, "It was very boring, with so much information! When we went to our Me to We Day,[4] they entertained us with famous guest speakers, cool music, and fun games for the crowd. They gave us lots of swag, and they really pumped us up!" Another student snapped back, "Well, this is not about entertainment, this is about our community!" This young woman had recognized the increasingly popular "greenwashing" activism that discourages young people from deeply contemplating their relations with other human beings, natural communities, and the land. As educators, we are often encouraged to engage in these well-meaning, yet generalized, oversimplified, and entertainment-based forms of socio-environmental "activism."

Shifts in Pedagogy: "The World Is *Not* Our Oyster"

Socio-environmental justice in schools and beyond, interpreted as a dynamic and active interrelationship, asks for the *honest participation* of all those involved. The social life of social studies:

> ...is meant to provide an articulation is actually lived out in locales of great intimacy, particularity and grace. Families, practices, languages, roles both inherited and resisted, times, places, heartbreaks and joys, geographies known through the body and breath and the labor of hands, and, too, great arcs of reminiscence, ancestry, old ways barely recollected or inscribed in practices learned hand over hand, face to face, full of forgotten-ness. (Jardine, 2015, p. 1)

The principles of security, discipline, and love demand an intimate, lively, participation in the field of social studies. Elder Cardinal shows me how to expand deeply outward from learning *about* other ways of being, to learning *with and through* each others' traditions, cultures, and ways of Being (Donald, 2003). Human beings learning *with and through* our environment may perceive it not as an external, flattened sphere that we interact with and influence, but rather a dynamic, living, circle that demands our honest and perceptive participation. This participation may shift the "bottom line" from a self-referential notion of human happiness toward "peaceful interspecies and multispecies coexistence" (Jensen, 2002, p. 62).

As social studies educators entering into these open, dynamic, and intimate relationships between and among species, landforms, and ecosystems, recognizing the environment not as something to be romanticized, controlled, ignored, or even saved, but as a dynamic, participatory arc that is never complete, closed, or settled, we may be better able to see what is needed in our particular times and places. Michael Derby (2015) suggests that we are living in a time that calls teachers to restory our environment, to set "a new tone for sustainable and holistic ways of understanding in a world confronted by an escalating ecological crisis" (p. 1). If "the world is *not* our oyster" what stories will we tell as social studies teachers (Jensen, 2002, p. 212)? How will these stories be told, who will hear them, and how will we invite others to participate in them truthfully and lovingly? These questions must be deeply rooted in our own communities, as we endeavor to untangle the deeply intertwined threads of social, economic, and ecological justice.

DISCUSSION QUESTIONS

1. What examples of *greenwashing* can be seen in everyday life? How are environmental responsibilities portrayed by corporations and the media?
2. How do the principles of security, discipline, and love shift and deepen conversations with respect to the environment, in terms of conservation, resource use, technology, and human economic activity?
3. In a social studies classroom, how might one shift environmental education from learning *about* other ways of being, to learning *with and through* each others' ways of Being?

NOTES

1. I am grateful to Stephanie Bartlett for her permission to share the story of Project Engage. Details of the ongoing project can be found at https://twitter.com/cbeengage and https://www.facebook.com/Project-EngageLiving-our-Lives-for-a-Sustainable-Future-924246637631395/
2. Greenwash. (noun). A superficial or insincere display of concern for the environment that is shown by an organization, often to deflect attention from an organization's environmentally unfriendly or less savory activities (Collins English Dictionary, 2012).
3. I would like to gratefully acknowledge Elder Bob Cardinal of the Enoch Cree Nation, Alberta, whose oral teachings were shared in a 2014 graduate course entitled, "Holistic Understandings of Learning," which he cotaught with Dr. Dwayne Donald through the University of Alberta. The participants in this curriculum and pedagogy course on Indigenous philosophical approaches to holistic learning were encouraged to inquire into and share our understandings of how "wisdom teachings regarding holistic understandings of life and living [may] provide meaningful curricular and pedagogical guidance in schools today" (Donald, 2014, p. 2). I would like to thank Bob for permission to print excerpts from his oral teachings, and his ongoing and generous support of all of the work stemming from the course.
4. ME to WE is an "innovative social enterprise that provides products that make an impact, empowering people to change the world with their everyday consumer choices" (We Movement, 2017).

REFERENCES

Abram, D. (2010). *Becoming animal: An earthly cosmology*. New York, NY: Vintage Books.
Alberta Education. (2006a). Social studies kindergarten to Grade 6 programs of study. Alberta: Alberta Education. Retrieved from https://education.alberta.ca/social-studies-k6/programs-of-study/
Alberta Education. (2006b). Social studies Grade 10 to 12 programs of study. Alberta: Alberta Education. Retrieved from https://education.alberta.ca/social-studies-1012/programs-of-study/
Berry, W. (2013). *Wendell Berry: Poet and prophet*. Online interview with Bill Moyers. Retrieved from http://billmoyers.com/segment/wendell-berry-on-his-hopes-for-humanity/

Blenkinsop, S. (2012). Four slogans for cultural change: An evolving place-based, imaginative and ecological learning experience. *Journal of Moral Education, 41*(2), 353–368.

British Columbia Ministry of Education. (2016). Curriculum 10–12 drafts. British Columbia Ministry of Education. Retrieved from https://curriculum.gov.bc.ca/curriculum/10-12#ss

Carson, R. (1962). *Silent spring*. Boston, MA: Houghton Mifflin.

Calgary Board of Education. (2015). Collaborative online resource environment. [Password protected resource bank]. Retrieved from https://www.albertacore.ca/access/home

Calgary Catholic School District. (2015). Instructional media centre. [Password-protected resource bank]. Retrieved from http://www.cssd.ab.ca/staff/

Carson, R. (1962). *Silent spring*. Boston, MA: Houghton Mifflin.

Chinook Park. (2016). *Project engage: Living our lives for a sustainable future*. Calgary: Calgary Board of Education.

Collins English Dictionary. (2012). Greenwash. William Collins Sons & Co. Retrieved from http://www.collinsdictionary.com/dictionary/english/greenwash

David Suzuki Foundation. (2016). Blue dot. Retrieved from http://bluedot.ca/

Derby, M. (2015). *Place, being, resonance: A critical ecohermeneutic approach to education*. New York, NY: Peter Lang Publishing.

Donald, D. (2003). *Elder, student, teacher: A Kanai curriculum métissage* (Unpublished master's thesis). University of Lethbridge, Lethbridge, AB.

Donald, D. (2014). Holistic approaches to learning: A curricular and pedagogical inquiry. Course Outline, Fall 2014. Edmonton: University of Alberta.

Evernden, N. (1999). *The natural alien: Humankind and environment* (2nd ed.). Toronto: University of Toronto Press.

Gadotti, M. (2003). Pedagogy of the earth and culture of sustainability. Paper presented at the International Conference for Lifelong Citizenship Learning, Participatory Democracy and Social Change: Local and Global Perspectives, Oct 17–19, 2003. Toronto: Ontario Institute for the Study of Education.

Grant, S. (2017). Gifford Pinchot: Bridging two eras of national conservation. *Connecticut History Organization*. Retrieved from https://connecticuthistory.org/gifford-pinchotbridging-two-eras-of-national-conservation/

Jardine, D. (2015). "You need accuracy": An appreciation of a modern hunting tradition. *One World in Dialogue: A Peer Reviewed Journal and Focus Newsletter, 4*(1), 1-2.

Jensen, D. (2002). *Listening to the land: Conversations about nature, culture, eros*. White River Junction, VT: Chelsea Green.

Keller, C. (1988). *From a broken web: Separation, sexism and self*. Boston, MA: Beacon Press.

Knufken, D. (2010). The top 25 greenwashed products in America. *Business Pundit*. Retrieved from http://www.businesspundit.com/the-top-25-greenwashed-products-in-america/

Leopold, A. (1949). *A sand county almanac*. Retrieved from https://faculty.ithaca.edu/mismith/docs/environmental/leopold.pdf

Little Bear, L. (2000). Jagged worldviews colliding. In M. Battiste (Ed.), *Reclaiming Indigenous voice and vision* (pp. 77–85). Vancouver, BC: UBC Press.

Lukacs, M. (2017). Neoliberalism has conned us into fighting climate change as individuals. *The Guardian*. Retrieved from https://www.theguardian.com/environment/true-north/2017/jul/17/neoliberalism-has-conned-us-into-fighting-climate-change-as-individuals?

Macy, J. (2007). *World as lover, world as self: Courage for global justice and ecological renewal*. Berkeley, CA: Parallax Press.

Macy, J. (2016). It looks bleak. Big deal, it looks bleak. *Ecological Buddhism: A Buddhist response to global warming*. Retrieved from http://www.ecobuddhism.org/wisdom/interviews/jmacy

National Geographic. (2016). Environment. National Geographic Society. Retrieved from http://www.nationalgeographic.com/environment/

Nixon, R. (2011). *Slow violence and the environmentalism of the poor*. Cambridge, MA: Harvard University Press.

Ontario Ministry of Education. (2011). *The Ontario Curriculum grades 1–8 and kindergarten programs. Environmental education: Scope and sequence of programs*. Ottawa: Queen's Printer for Ontario.

Orr, D. (1991). What is education for? Six myths about the foundations of modern education, and six new principles to replace them. *The Learning Revolution, 27*(4), 52–55. Retrieved from http://www.context.org/iclib/ic27/orr/

Roosevelt, T. (1912). *A confession of faith*. Speech given at Progressive Party Convention. August 6, 1912. Chicago, IL. Retrieved from http://www.theodoreroosevelt.com/images/research/speeches/trarmageddon.pdf

Serres, M. (1995). *The natural contract*. Translated by E. MacArthur and W. Paulson. (Original work published in 1990).

Seuss, Dr. (1971). *The lorax*. New York, NY: Random House Books for Young Readers.

Shepard, P. (1998). *Nature and madness*. Athens, GA: University of Georgia Press.

Solnit, R. (2016). Standing rock protests: This is only the beginning. *The Guardian*. Retrieved from https://www.theguardian.com/us-news/2016/sep/12/north-dakota-standing-rockprotests-civil-rights

Steinberg, T. (2013). *Down to earth: Nature's role in American history*. New York, NY: Oxford University Press.

Steingraber, S. (2010). *Living downstream: An ecologist's personal investigation of cancer and the environment*. Boston, MA: Da Capo Press.

Theodore Roosevelt Conservation Partnership. (2017). Our issues. Retrieved from http://www.trcp.org/what/sportsmens-access/

Think Earth Environmental Education Foundation. (2016). It's time to Think Earth! *Think Earth Foundation*. Retrieved from https://thinkearth.org/curriculum/document/1125-summaryof-unit-objectives

van Gelder, S. (2017). Earth democracy—an interview with Vandana Shiva. *YES! Magazine*. http://www.yesmagazine.org/issues/what-would-democracy-look-like/earth-democracyan-interview-with-vandana-shiva

We Movement. (2017). Our beliefs. Retrieved from https://www.we.org/we-movement/ourbeliefs/

CHAPTER EIGHT

Home

GABRIEL P. SWARTS, UNIVERSITY OF WYOMING

> If I were asked to name the chief benefit of the house, I should say: the house shelters day-dreaming, the house protects the dreamer, the house allows one to dream in peace.
>
> —BACHELARD, 1994, P. 6

> I'm more comfortable in my home so I'm more myself. I feel free to be me... I can give in and relax into a warm hug knowing nothing can happen because this place or *these arms will hold me together when all I may want to do is fall apart*. [italics added for emphasis]
>
> —UNIVERSITY STUDENT, PERSONAL COMMUNICATION, JUNE 12, 2016

My own childhood home is one that is hard to pin down; moving seven times before I was nine years old, "home" was something that traveled. My wife, on the other hand, never knew another street, another bedroom, another kitchen table; for her, home wasn't complicated by changes and disruptions, it was simply *home*.

As adults, we are reconstructing our home life in years, months, and weeks at a time as our relationship and experiences inform our lives and way of living. The homeplace, and the process of home-*making* is undoubtedly influenced by our present world as well as deep cultural, historical conceptions of what home is and could be; from painted caves in Lascaux and Mongol yurts, Mohawk longhouses, Indonesian stilt houses, and Levittowns of suburban America these physical structures belie many deeper connections and transactive, wide-ranging experiences of the physical, social, spiritual, and ecological. As Bachelard (1994) states in the opening epigraph, home is a place for dreaming and is something deeply personal and profound, yet radiating out into the community and beyond into larger human society in an ecological partnership with Earth itself.

In this chapter, I argue home-making is an integral, transactional process that should be enhanced in scope within our classrooms from traditional domestic structures and language. Ultimately reframed within the confluence of space, time, the individual, local/global communities, and planet Earth, home is not simply a structure but is rife with layers of time, space, feeling, and living. I believe social studies teaching and learning is the academic space, the home, within which we can take up this challenge to expand our conceptions of home and place. As educators and teacher-leaders in our field we are best equipped to open the transaction among student-school-home and to allow for all involved to enable holistic visions of home-making.

WITHIN THE "HOMEPLACE"

Starting from traditional American colloquialisms such as "home is where the heart is," or "a house is not a home," one can venture into basic understandings of home in American culture, a sound starting point for this chapter. Popularly in America, and as the university student illustrates in this chapter's second epigraph, home is a place, a "castle," a personal space, a ritual, a protective shield, safety, comfort provided by humans in a familiar space. The space of home is meant for reflection, familial ties, personal choices, and privacy. Within the walls of our American classroom and physically in a school building, as teachers and students, home is *somewhere else*; a place for extra school work in the evening, for family being, for rest, far away from the work of the day. As teachers and students conduct their work in schools, home can be a resource, an escape from study, or perhaps a challenge, a barrier to a student learning. Even more codified in this country, students in the United States most often attend a school within districts of which a student's home is physically located. Home and school are explicitly tied together forming a local unit of government tasked with organizing and funding (not necessarily well) a democratic, liberal-arts education with administrative decisions made collectively by district residents. Fundamentally, the educational spaces in the United States revolve around the existence of home.

It is this popular simplicity and assuredness of home, this perceived separation from the larger world and involvement with the local one, that is rapidly changing in our world today. As social studies educators we can challenge and reframe these traditional perceptions in our schools, unsettling the structured roles involved, in order to expand our students' conceptions of their homeplace as something more complex, contested, and in-process. This home-making approach can open a variety of spaces for discussion, debate, and deliberation as students bring their own homeplace expertise into the classroom, couched in the places they know best.

To first complicate the homeplace as a bastion of safety and comfort, as embracing as the university students' "arms," I purposely selected literature that elevated the homeplace to something more; something greater than, in process, and nurturing. Four specific works by Whitlock (2005, 2007), hooks (1990), and Bachelard (1994) do just this. I selected these authors for their varied and unique perspectives as well as their specific scholarship directed at the formation of the homeplace. Their views unsettle traditional American values of home and disorient the foundation of the meaning of home.

Whitlock (2005, p. 9) describes the Southern American homeplace as a curriculum of place, one that "should consider the socially constructed sense of place that arises from homeplace experiences." This "home(be)coming" is something that is not yet, a yearning that can be familiar and of sameness, or one that can be a border to be transgressed or transcended (Whitlock, 2005, p. 19). The magical power of place, it's politics and negotiations in becoming a homeplace, is *not* all-powerful and good, but magnetic nonetheless (Whitlock, 2007).

hooks' (1990) work describes this yearning for home as a black woman in a white society. Home becomes a space for healing, for sharing history and common struggles, oppression.

> It was there on the inside; in that "homeplace," most often created and kept by black women, that we had an opportunity to grow and nurture our spirits. This task of making a homeplace, of making home a community of resistance, has been shared by black women globally.... (hooks, 1990, p. 384)

This provision of a space of resistance, of shared history and experience as an oppressed minority, this transaction of societal angst and communal catharsis through a home, paints a powerful narrative of the healing powers of the homeplace. Home as the genesis of a broader black, female consciousness jumps off the page and allows the home to take its place within a larger societal narrative of oppression, spirit, and resistance.

Neither Whitlock nor hooks claim that the homeplace is apart from, separate, immune, or isolated from society. The homeplace is very much *within* and *of* worlds as constructed either in black households under incredible oppression, Southern cultural complexities, or further, within the homeplace of Earth and local environment. This is a marked departure from our common sayings; homeplace is an isolated oasis, one that shuts out the larger world. In our society, in our literature, and in our social studies curriculum home is separate, apart from, familiar, not strange; in here not out there.

Our starting points, our American colloquialisms in this chapter, reflect the larger American acceptance that a home is a separate entity. In these texts, the home is a protected and portable feeling of love, but the environment, the social surroundings of the home are negligible, again somewhere else. Bachelard (1994) expands on his opening quote in this chapter in the work *Poetics of Space* by including the thought that "home is the human being's first world" (p. 7). Although home may be our first world, it is not an isolated one. Lines of cultural, social, local/global, civic practices flow through our homes and subsequently, our hearts. Flowing practices and beliefs enter our home through our experiences and transactions with others as well as other homes. These experiences influence and maneuver our own way of living in our homeplace. Thus, home is never static or in stasis, but e/merging and in process within and with our surroundings.

BEYOND THE "HOMEPLACE"

What does home mean for social studies teachers today? For students? For human beings today? In many ways home has been interrupted by Heidegger's (1927/1962) "unhomeliness" ... a place full of strangers, which infiltrate our spaces of safety and comfort. Modern technologies, television, and mass media have fundamentally altered our access to representations in film, music, images, art, and literature. Exposure, interaction, connection, and communication among human beings is happening instantaneously and at light speed, with further reaches into our lives at a faster rate, than at any other time in human history. Humans can view into others' worlds, governments can enact surveillance over bodies and movement, mass and social media allows for more peer-to-peer interaction with more humans than our ancient cave-dwelling ancestors in Lascaux could have ever imagined. We can see further from our homes (and strangers further into them) than ever before.

We can couple this technologically-enhanced evolution with three modern human-made catastrophes: (1) a total biospheric collapse due to climate change; (2) the sharp uptick in violent conflict in Syria and Afghanistan; and (3) economic catastrophe reverberating powerfully through this decade. Combined, these trends have forcibly displaced 65.3 million humans in 2016, a staggering record (United Nations Refugee Agency Report, 2015). This radical junction of presence, technology, violence, and ecological disaster threatens the very existence of our home, whether private, local, or Earthly. It is imperative that the way we think of our homeplace, our home-making, be expanded beyond our own personal visions, and that our students begin this thinking in our classrooms. This is done best, I believe, within social studies teaching and learning.

To thrust the homeplace out into open conversation, away from isolation and traditional meanings, the complexities of home can provide ample space for social studies work. As students (regardless of age) enter our classrooms, what better do they know than their own homes? The layered experiences and transactions our students have, whether six or sixteen, hinge on the through-lines of our local community and neighbors, our cultural productions and media, and the ever increasing importance and presence of their digital lives and social media avatars. Our students are experts, steeped in the ways of their own homes! But in order to harness this expertise and to work to expand visions of the homeplace somewhere beyond the traditional sayings, it is important to operate from a new framework. Three sets of ideas by Noddings (2011, 2013), Spivak (2003), and Dimock (2007) can provide a path forward. I selected these works as a way to envision our classrooms and teaching practices moving toward the unsettling of our comfortable homeplace.

Noddings' *Education and Democracy in the 21st Century* (2013) directly argues for home/school education. Regarding home, this work focuses on bringing the home into our teaching and learning curriculum, with critical questions regarding space, psychology, and comfort, as well as how our places shape us, and us them (p. 69). As we straddle nationalist curricula and the changing, dynamic world and its problems within social studies work, Noddings conception of homeplace and our nation has incredible value. Arguing for a re-focus of the homeplace with a "humble and critical attitude," Noddings argues that our views of home, the nation, our love place, must include recognition of where our homes exist, on planet Earth. Ecological cosmopolitanism is Noddings' final scholarly destination, a love of place connected with deep values of understanding of human connection (2013, p. 83). Noddings outlines her ideas in a previous work:

> If we love a particular place, we know that its welfare is intimately connected to the health of the Earth on which it exists… Because I love this place, I want a healthy Earth to sustain it… If the well-being of my loved place depends on the well-being of earth, I have a good reason for supporting the well-being of your loved place. (Noddings, 2011, p. 66)

The homeplace is much more than safety or our private space—for Noddings it is an e/merging place, both of and with all species of life on Earth. This interaction of human consciousness and place, and time, can be enhanced through reflection and appreciation of the local, with a wider, open mind to the larger world (Noddings, 2013, p. 85). If home is to be loved and cherished, so too we must love and cherish the Earth and its entire inhabitant species.

Enhancing, or possibly challenging, Noddings' concept of ecological cosmopolitanism, Gayatri Spivak's *Planetarity* clears a critical path toward a great "outside." To inform this troubling of home, Spivak's work on collectivities, namely the emergent inclusivity "to come," a togetherness she calls planetarity (Spivak, 2003). Thinking of our species as "of this planet" not simply "on" it can inform our visions of home; home is no longer an escape to safety (perhaps a removal from the elements on a cold, Wyoming, snow day) but within nature, of nature, inherently symbiotic. The homeplace then must include reframed thinking about our place, and being in that place. Home is not human-centered, solely for us, but exists within a biosphere in a delicate balance; and our responsibility is toward a collective "next" that includes this consciousness as an advance towards planetarity.

Finally, Wai-Chee Dimock's work on American literature has place within our discussion here as her focus on relativity as well as historical connections allows us to escape the present of a homeplace, to understand deeper Earthly, human linkages throughout the ages of time, and beyond. Dimock specifically engages a "hazard" of Spivak's planetarity, employing an attempt to "rethink the shape of literature against the history and habitat of the human species, against the 'deep time' of planet Earth" (Dimock, 2007, p. 6). Within this hazarding of planetarity, Dimock explores the lineage of home and deep time, intertwined and inescapable:

> These old records and their modern transpositions give us a "deep time" in human terms. They alert us to our long sojourn on this planet, a sojourn marked by layers of relations, weaving our history into our dwelling place, and making us what we are, a species with a sedimented imprint. Honoring that imprint, and honoring also the imprints of other creatures evolving as we do, we take our place as one species among others, inhabiting a shared ecology, a shared continuum. (2007, p. 6)

Dimock's version of the holistic approach toward our home planet lies within the framework of a global civil society, "a place not territorial but associative, and extending as far as those associations extend..." This "side-effect" of the nation-state is not linked solely to the state, but exists outside and can be a space for emergent conceptions of home/home-making... beyond nationalism (Dimock, 2007, p. 7). Further:

> ...the concept of a global civil society, by its very nature, invites us to think of the planet as a plausible whole, a whole that, I suggest, needs to be mapped along the temporal axis as well as the spatial, its membership open not only to contemporaries but also to those centuries apart. (Dimock, 2007, p. 5–6)

In Dimock's piece, Thoreau, Gandhi, and others are "seen" through their readings and interpretations of *Bagavad Gita* and the classic's lessons in a global civil society framework. Literature affected these public figures "deeply" through space and time, through culture and continents, yet within their local places and interpretations. This approach can provide ample space for our social studies work. Using the artifacts or documents of home, of democratic associated living in the most Deweyan (1916) sense, the "deep time" of home can trace our student perceptions, visions, and complications through historical work and in the space within which they live and learn. Social studies is at its very best suited to this task, to opening young minds not only to modern challenges and contexts, but through a historical lineage beyond human existence and shaped by the planet, the "plausible whole" of our homeplace.

Within this brief, specifically selected body of literature, the homeplace is a protective shield, a space for dreams, a contested/battled social construct, our own loaned, multilayered ecological corner of the world, within the long arches of time and space. This mapping of the homeplace allows us to leap forward and to ask how we can think of these ideas daily, with our students and in our lesson planning, in how we approach our curriculum, and in how we look out into our students' worlds. How do we work on our craft of the homeplace, this process, cultivation of home?

HOMING AND DEMOCRATIC LIVING

As social studies educators, our work is to teach within the context of our world today and our future existence, to teach the churning processes of our home and surroundings as students are home-making, or *homing*. Inspired by Heidegger's (1927/1962) *worlding*, homing is the making of, the construction, the sculpting of our being in home life within/of society, morality, and space/time. Far beyond traditional conceptions of Western conceptions of home-making, traditionally thought of as a gendered, female task, homing is the rooted growth through space and time within/of our most sacred home spaces, both generative and reflective, and in/of larger societal influences and changes. Within the context of our classrooms and on the larger world of Earth, traditional views of home should be challenged and replaced with more a fluid, unmoored, collective, and floating, we can think of *homing* as the making of a homeplace. And in the modern world, in a time of such human displacement and diasporic upheaval, nearing a traumatic ecological event, homing is a distinct challenge for many human beings. Constructing a subjective, "being-in-the world" or "being-in-home" can occur however, and our troubled version of home is the starting point (Heidegger, 1927/1962; Pinar, 2009).

As a social studies teacher in the United States, homing will occur within a democratic society, and I think it is important to utilize our social studies curriculum and democratic teaching approaches in how we conceptualize homing. Much as radiofrequency homing devices, or homing pigeons, work to send/receive beacons to establish a homeplace a destination, we must ask what our destination should be? Our students are doing this work on multiple levels and their homing occurs within a democratic society. How do we tie homing into general democratic ways of living and being, with regards to human beings, plant and animal species, and Earth?

Through our previously reviewed literature, selected as a method of unsettling conceptions of home, that we can advance into the "best," not how it *is* now, but how it *could* be—the best of associated democratic living; somewhere within a society where democratic aims are moral, in-process, and all-inclusive of a broad visions of Earth, it's inhabitants, and the societies they are making. As members of such a society, our own *homing* is simply imperative to the success and structure, the balance of the best of democratic work. The home is our "first world," and can be the foundation of our "best" world (Bachelard, 1994).

John Dewey's work aims to explore democracy at its best; a creative society of the public, not a government or state, of moral aims, not individual desires and physical means, as a community of communities, not isolated, bordered, and territorial (Dewey, 1916/1944, 1927, 1940). Most of all, however, Dewey started his work within the home, as individuals in situated spaces, actions and beliefs rippling out into a larger and larger democratic society.

The process of this rippling, the activation of the waves, is a transactional experience between the individual and home, and society/democracy, I interpret this as *homing*. Dewey's vision of democracy, his educational theories, his focus on experience/transaction helps to open our discussion in social studies to focus on democratic homing, both as a homeplace, and within the context of an active democratic society. Dewey's educational theories, aesthetic examinations, and pragmatism influenced his views on individual space and consciousness, society, community, and democracy, which he collectively, explicitly, and inviolably linked (Jenlink & Jenlink, 2008). Dewey called this confluence *associated living*. At once active and organic, Dewey's vision of democracy is rooted in associated living and is a way of life to be embodied in every day practice (Bernstein, 2000, p. 217). Requiring consciousness and community, sustained by deliberative action, the "conjoint communicative experience" of associated living birthed Dewey's societal ideal and open spaces for unsettling moorings and challenging assumptions. Associated living cannot be passive. It was active and communal. The individual must engage in reflective inquiry with democratic intent and must do so with neighbors, friends, and community members in a creative fashion. This has always been a challenge both in our world today, and when Dewey (1940) wrote *The Public and its Problems*, as fascism consumed Europe. Dewey's thoughts were on the home, the gathering of neighbors and friends:

> When I think of the conditions under which men and women are living in many foreign countries today, fear of espionage, with danger hanging over the meeting of friends for friendly conversation in private gatherings, I am inclined to believe that the heart and final guarantee of democracy is in free gatherings of neighbors on the street corner to discuss back and forth what is read in uncensored news of the day, and in gatherings of friends in the living rooms of houses and apartments to converse freely with one another. (Dewey, 1940, p. 222)

Writing about what he called "creative democracy," Dewey (1940) saw schools, curriculum, and societal action as contingent on the *creative local*, the neighborhood, the community; individual transactions involving creative people required to innovate and obligated to contribute to the society that they exist within (see also Ryan, 2011). Small-scale individual talents and *transactive* experiences would enable a transnational *community of communities*, filled with important creative differences and experiences of which an obligation to the public would ensure deliberation, judgment, and reflexivity.

More specifically, in his *The Public and Its Problems*, Dewey sets out to further clarify his concept of associated living; it was physical, organic, natural (he likened it to atoms), a condition necessary to create community, while the act of community itself, is moral (Dewey, 1927, p. 330). This moral condition can enable "disorderly experiences into harmonies ones that allow every participant involved the opportunity to grow" (Wang, 2007, p. 114). Each associated individual within a community can then both contribute to, and benefit from, their personal reflective inquiries; the motivation for social benefit in a democracy and the cooperative nature of human beings can again, only be encouraged and nurtured in schools; curriculum can reflect these fundamental necessities of/by/for community in order to sustain democratic living (Dimitriadis & Kamberelis, 2006, p. 8).

CONCLUSION: OUR SOCIAL STUDIES HOME-WORK

I believe social studies is the best place to address the homeplace/homing. Disrupting "home" with *homing* requires conversations in houses; conversations regarding empathy, morality, plurality, democratic living, resistance, social constructions, and transactive experiences throughout history or Dimock's deep time. The "home" can be thought of as an active process, a verb, an act of thoughtful reflection and study, and as social studies teachers we can initiate this process along with our students. The ripple effect of John Dewey's associated living, the community of communities, greater society and democracy truly beings in our homeplace as we create it. As teachers our job is to generate essential questions, to utilize our required textbooks, standards, and lesson plans, to engage our physical spaces and ecological places, in order to facilitate our students homing into something larger and inclusive, to enact "the fusion of the learners' horizons" (Waks, 2007, p. 34). Our job as social studies teachers is to tip the balance and enable our students to meet the challenges in the world as they influence larger society. We can do this from the homeplace and by using their homing experiences as openings for dialogue, conversation, and deliberation; and as social studies teachers we need to educate our students in this way, to claim the majority. As Davies (2006) proclaims:

> For conflict, only one or two people are needed to fan the fires of hostility, but for actions for peace and security, very broad and strong bandings of people are needed who are comfortable with notions of multiple identity, and who have enough in coming to work together. They also need to recognize difference to value and cope with diversity. (p. 8)

Davies' aims begin in the homeplace, our most common human space. Bringing the homeplace into the classroom and incorporating the process of *homing* into our work and study is the work of social studies.

DISCUSSION QUESTIONS

1. If you had to draw the home of one of your students, what would it look like? What items would be in the rooms, what type of neighborhood would the home be situated? What unique characteristics would emerge in your drawing details?
2. In what sense does our *homing* contribute to our sense of belonging to society, humanity at large? How does this process form our relationship to planet Earth?
3. In light of this chapter, how would you resettle the words like "home," "homeless," "refugee," "transient," "migrant," etc.?
4. How can you bring your students' home life into your classroom, and vice versa? What activities, lessons, assignments, readings, or actions can you take to open the transaction between home, school, and the student?

REFERENCES

Bachelard, G. (1994). *The poetics of space* (M. Jolas, Trans.). Boston, MA: Beacon Press.
Bernstein, R. J. (2000). Creative democracy—The task still before us. *American Journal of Theology & Philosophy, 21*(3), 215–228.
Davies, L. (2006). Global citizenship: Abstraction or framework for action? *Educational Review, 58*(1), 5–25.
Dewey, J. (1916/1944). *Democracy and education: An introduction to the philosophy of education*. New York, NY: The Free Press.
Dewey, J. (1927). *The later works, 1925–1953: (Vol.2)*. Carbondale, IL: SIU Press.
Dewey, J. (1940). *Creative democracy: The task before us*. New York, NY: GP Putnam's Sons.
Dimitriadis, G., & Kamberelis, G. (2006). *Theory for education*. New York, NY: Routledge.
Dimock, W. C. (2007). *Through other continents: American literature across deep time*. Princeton, NJ: Princeton University Press.
Heidegger, M. (1927/1962). *Being and time* (Trans. J. Macquarrie and E. Robinson). New York, NY: Harper Press.
hooks, b. (1990). *Yearning: Race, gender, and cultural politics*. Boston, MA: South End Press.
Jenlink, P. M., & Jenlink, K. E. (2008). Creating democratic learning communities: Transformative work as spatial practice. *Theory into Practice, 47*(4), 311–317.
Noddings, N. (2011). *Peace education: How we come to love and hate war*. Boston, MA: Cambridge University Press.

Noddings, N. (2013). *Education and democracy in the 21st century*. New York, NY: Teachers College Press.
Pinar, W. F. (2009). *The worldliness of a cosmopolitan education: Passionate lives in public service*. London: Routledge.
Ryan, F. X. (2011). *Seeing together: Mind, matter, and the experimental outlook*. Great Barrington, MA: American Institute for Economic Research.
Spivak, G. (2003). *Death of a discipline*. New York, NY: Columbia University Press.
United Nations Refugee Agency Report. (2015). *Global forced displacement hits record high*. Retrieved from http://www.unhcr.org
Waks, L. J. (2007). Rereading democracy and education today: John Dewey on globalization, multiculturalism, and democratic education. *Education and Culture, 23*(1), 27–37.
Wang, J. (2007). *John Dewey in China*. Albany, NY: SUNY Press.
Whitlock, R. U. (2005). Season of lilacs: Nostalgia of place. *Taboo, 9*(2), 7–26.
Whitlock, R. U. (2007). *This corner of Canaan: Curriculum studies of place and the reconstruction of the South*. New York, NY: Peter Lang Publishing.

CHAPTER NINE

Place

WHITNEY G. BLANKENSHIP, RHODE ISLAND COLLEGE

> Regular maps have few surprises: their contour lines reveal where the Andes are, and are reasonably clear. More precious, though, are the unpublished maps we make ourselves, of our city, our place, our daily world, our life; those maps of our private world we use every day; here I was happy, in that place I left my coat behind after a party, that is where I met my love; I cried there once, I was heartsore; but felt better round the corner once I saw the hills of Fife across the Forth, things of that sort, our personal memories, that make the private tapestry of our lives.
>
> —ALEXANDER MCCALL SMITH, *LOVE OVER SCOTLAND*

One of the first questions we ask upon meeting someone new is "where are you from?" The centrality of *place* to our understanding of our communities, our world, and ourselves is evidenced in this simple question. However, what exactly do we mean by *place*? As the quote from Alexander McCall Smith makes clear, place is much more than a location on a map with clearly defined borders, although it is most certainly that. Rather, the places that make up our lives are imbued with meaning from the memories of our visits to these spaces. What happens in a particular place, in a particular time, shapes how we respond to similar places in the future. Our place-based experiences help us to define who we are through the lens of looking at where were are from, where we have been, and where we are going. In the pages to come we will look at how the concept of "place" has been shaped over time and within the social studies disciplines, as well as unpack how those meanings shape the individuals we become.

THE MEANINGS OF PLACE

Place as Physical Location

Historically the notion of place has typically embodied the idea of a physical location. The national *Geography for Life* (Geography Implementation Project, 2012) standards defines places as having "distinctive features that give them meaning and character that differs from other locations" (Standard 4). This standard asks that students be able to describe the physical characteristics of places and to compare places across different geographic contexts. In the typical geography class, place is defined as an absolute or relative location, and I would argue that this definition is an essential starting place to understanding the pivotal role of place in our lives. Absolute location allows us to accurately pinpoint any place on earth providing a starting point for our examination of what it means to be from a specific place. Relative location contextualizes the physical address of longitude and latitude by supplying the details of the environment. Gaining knowledge of the physical characteristics of a place in the form of flora and fauna, as well as man-made features such as housing, dams, and roads, allows us to make inferences about life in this place (Geography Education Implentation Project, 2012; National Council for the Social Studies, 2010). The types of dwellings favored by the populace, such as adobe in desert areas, are intricately linked to the available resources of the location (a lot of sand and very little water, high temperatures which correlate to thicker walls to keep buildings cool). Absolute location also allows us to revisit the places we have been, returning year after year to a beloved vacation spot, or the site of important life events. Relative location allows us to choose new spaces to explore by comparing them to the places we have been that are similar. Although the Five Themes of Geography separate location and place, the way the terms are used in everyday life are often interchangeable. Therefore, as a starting point, absolute and relative location lay the groundwork for expanding our understanding of the term.

Using absolute and relative location as our starting point, we can now expand upon our definition of place as a physical location defined by its physical features. Place can also be a political entity in the form of a state defined by natural and man-made boundaries as featured on many of the maps used in social studies classes. Place as political entity is most commonly found in geography and political science courses, as well as history. Although the physical boundaries of a state delineate the extent of the state's power and control over the land and population, it is often also subdivided by the political beliefs, economic systems, and ethnic or linguistic characteristics of the people who live there. These subdivisions overlap, further complicating any description of a particular place (Center for Civic Education, 1994; Geography Education Implentation Project, 2012; National Council for the Social Studies, 2010).

An excellent example of this is the overlapping claims to the political entity of Israel. Students who are not familiar with the landscape of the Middle East in general, and Israel and her neighbors in particular, may not be aware of the proximity of cultural artifacts to one another, or how the borders impact access to commerce, and water. A number of years ago the *National Geographic Expeditions* had a feature called "Culture Goggles" which I used during the Middle East unit with my high school freshman. Using a digital "telescope" students "looked" at key places within the city of Jerusalem. In the introduction to the activity, students are told that "culture colors our perceptions of place" and that they will use the culture goggles to see how "a Christian, a Jew, or a Muslim might view the Old City of Jerusalem" (National Geographic Expeditions). Students then chose to view the Old City from the perspectives of all three religions for whom Jerusalem is sacred. Viewing Jerusalem through the lens of Christianity, students see the Via Dolorosa and the Garden of Gethsemane highlighted on the map. Switching to a Muslim point of view, the Dome of the Rock and Haram al-Sharif are the focus. The Jewish lens shows the Temple Mount and Western Wall. What becomes immediately apparent is that the Temple Mount and Western Wall occupy the same space as the Dome of the Rock and the Haram al-Sharif. For many students this is an eye-opening look into the intricacies of the Arab–Israeli conflict. Investigating these different conceptualizations of the same place set the stage for discussion of other ways that the political state and the physical location of the place called Israel were intertwined. Unfortunately, National Geographic Expeditions website is no longer being maintained. However, Google Maps would allow any teacher to create a similar and potentially much more powerful activity, by using street views to explore the area in 360 degrees. Pushing even further, students could explore how these places are framed by each group's point of view in advertisements and other media through the analysis of what is shown and what is cropped from these pictures. This kind of investigation allows for a more complex view of place by providing the opportunity to view it from multiple perspectives at the same time.

Place as a Moment in Time

Within the social studies disciplines, place also includes more abstract definitions. L.P. Hartley in his novel *The Go-Between* sets up a story centered on a man's study of a diary from 1900, the year of his thirteenth birthday, and the memories that are dredged up as a result. This leads to the observation that "The past is a foreign country; they do things differently there" (p. 17). The quote effectively describes the concept of the past as a different place from the here and now.

In history, place can be defined as a specific moment in time. The study of the past takes us to a space and a place that is significantly different from our own reality. Although history also draws on the more physical aspects of place, we might also conceive of place as an era on a timeline. The features of place, both physical and cultural, change over time, and as a result two people living in the same place in different time periods could be understood as being from two different places (Boix-Mansilla, 2000; National Center for History in the Schools, 1996; Phillips, 2004; Rosenweig, 2000; Wilschut, 2011). A key to historical thinking is understanding that people in the past acted within a specific base of knowledge and beliefs. The classic example of students' misunderstanding the issue of place within time is the declaration that the people back then must not have been very smart, why didn't they just...[fill in the blank with a contemporary solution].

Thinking of place as a particular point in time gives us the tools to contextualize the actions of historical figures, as well as make connections to our own time and place. Using the Hartley quote as a starting point, teachers can help develop students' understanding of place as a specific period in time. The most common experience is a field trip to living history museums, especially if it is local. The purpose of taking students to the museum is because we want our students to experience, as much as possible, what life was like in a particular place at a particular point in time. This is certainly one way to approach the subject. However, it often leaves out an essential element in the understanding of the past as a foreign place—the personal connections students make between their own place and time. This is where place-based teaching strategies can become powerful learning tools. Students should begin with a study of their own place and time within their communities. Beginning with more traditional ways of thinking about their communities, students can explore the resources, important landmarks and industries of their town, as well as the current demographics. But that is only the beginning.

Students should also look at the town calendar—how are holidays celebrated? What holidays are considered important enough for businesses and schools to close? Are there local festivals? Where do community members gather to share cultural experiences? As they consider these additional measures of place, students can be asked to consider *their place* within *this place*. Do they participate in local celebrations? What holidays do their families celebrate? Are these the same or different from the larger communal celebrations? Do they live in town? Or out in the country? Does this change the way they view their community? Each of these questions asks students to locate themselves within their place, whether that is physical, cultural, economic, and social spaces within their communities. Using their answers to these questions students can create an identity map of their community, showing the physical, cultural, and social spaces they inhabit and attaching them to a specific spot on a map. Students should be able to explain how each place on the map has contributed to their understanding of their community and how that has, in turn, influenced their identities. The creation of identity maps reinforces the notion that *who we are*, is shaped by *where we are*.

The next layer to add to students' understanding is that *who we are* is shaped by *where we are in time*. Students might interview older town residents to get a feel for what the town was like in the past. In their interviews students might ask about community events, social norms and mores, and important landmarks and events in the community's past. By comparing their study of the community in their own era, with the recollections of the community by older generations, students have the opportunity to see how places change over time. More importantly, the interviews give students a chance to ask elders about why things were done a certain way in an bygone era. The personal connections that allow students to see family friends and relatives as historical actors in a specific place in time aids students' development of historical empathy. Place becomes at once a physical location on a map, and a point on the timeline, each a way of thinking giving us a more nuanced understanding of our world.

PLACE ATTACHMENT, IDENTITY, AND CITIZENSHIP

Identity Development through Place Attachment

Absolute and relative location, local environments and cultures, and different eras are all important to our understanding of who we are as individuals, and as a people, at any given point in time, therefore, place has a role in our identity development (Sobel, 2004). Where we are from and the experiences we have in different places frame how we think about ourselves. We are American or English (place as physical location); we identify with rural or urban ways of thinking and doing (place as cultural artifact), we are Baby Boomers, Gen-X, or Millennials (place as a moment in time). Place is deeply ingrained in our consciousness—it defines who we are, how we think and act, the cultures into which we are assimilated, and the political philosophies we adopt (Ball & Lai, 2006; Miller, 2001; Resor, 2010; Theobold & Wood, 2010).

We cannot escape place—even when we do not have an attachment to a specific place we call "home." A lack of place attachment affects the way we view the world around us. Consider the lived experience of students whose parents are in the military, or students whose families are migrant workers. In both cases, students move often, and may only stay in one community for a limited amount of time before moving on. In the case of military families, students may never return to those places, missing opportunities to develop the deep roots needed for place attachment. Migrant families, on the other hand may return to the same areas year after year as they follow the harvest. The yearly return brings opportunities to renew attachments made in previous years. The development (or lack thereof) of place attachment in these situations influences our tolerance for change and uncertainty (Bell, 2006; Marcouyeux & Fleury-Bahi, 2011; Schuster, Sullivan, Kuehn, & Morais, 2011; Spencer, 2005; Theobold & Wood, 2010).

As social studies educators we should take note that a high tolerance for change and uncertainty is correlated with a drive to learn, making emotional connections, and the development of compassion (Stasny, 2009). Though these characteristics are central to citizenship and play a role in citizen engagement, place attachment can be a double-edged sword. Negative experiences may drive us toward civic engagement to force change, or the same experience may disengage us from the political process. The key is determining how to leverage place attachment in such a way as to encourage students to engage in the civic life of their communities, states, and nations.

This has most recently born itself out in the 2016 election cycle that culminated in the election of Donald Trump to the office of President. Postelection analysis has consistently pointed to the role of place in the outcome of the election (Badger, Bui, & Pearce, 2016; Gamio, 2016). Rural areas that have suffered long-term economic decline overwhelmingly voted in favor of Trump's promise to "Make America Great Again" by bringing back manufacturing to the United States. Urban areas were more likely to vote for Hillary Clinton, where the economic outlook is not as bleak and the population is more diverse. Nearly half of eligible voters did not vote at all. The fast pace of social change also contributed to this electoral outcome. In short, the place attachments of voters, coupled with their social and economic experiences in those places, led to Trump's surprise victory. Those whose negative experiences drove them toward civic engagement to force change, plus those whose negative experiences lead to civic disengagement, were enough to shape the outcome of the election. As social studies educators we would do well to recognize the role of place on our students' identity development and use that understanding to facilitate positive civic engagement in our youth.

Place Attachment and Civic Engagement

Downey and Levstik (1991) argue that connecting social studies content to students' personal sociocultural histories furthers student interest in the knowledge and skills needed for engaged citizenship, a key goal of social studies instruction (National Council for the Social Studies, 1992). In a similar way, culturally responsive pedagogies seek to aid students academically by building on their unique cultural experiences. These unique experiences are often found in the home and in the communities they inhabit (Au, 2009) and may include connections to communities their countries of origin, as well as in their current communities.

Civic engagement programs and curricula built around the use of local spaces and places have been around for some time. Fifty years ago a young English teacher in Appalachia, together with his students, launched the *FoxFire* magazine as a way of engaging students with the English curriculum through the creation of a student produced magazine focused on local history and culture. What started out as a local project morphed into a series of books documenting Appalachian communities (Foxfire Fund, 2016). More recently, programs such as *Generation Citizen* and *Project Citizen*, go beyond community history projects, to engage students in active inquiry, problem-solving, and informed action. Students work together to identify a problem in their community, research potential solutions, and develop a plan of action. In the course of their inquiry students interact with local government officials and experts as they formulate their solution. Throughout the process students develop critical thinking and decision-making skills as they encounter course content within the context of their lived experience within their communities. Participation in such projects not only draws on students' place attachment to engage them in learning social studies content and skills, but it may also strengthen place attachment over the long run resulting in an increased involvement in civic affairs.

There are also less traditional ways to use place attachment to leverage students' civic engagement. This would include developing an understanding of the assets of a particular place, something that is not always considered. Popular conceptions of rural and urban spaces drawn from popular culture are often negative. For example, rural areas are populated by backward, uneducated peoples who have no curiosity about the outside world; urban areas are dens of inequity with high crime rates. Students absorb these attitudes about the places they inhabit. The message many students internalize is that this place (their community) must be escaped—the only way to succeed is to leave. For students who have negative views of their communities, civic engagement takes a back seat. Why should they be involved if they are just going to leave as soon as they can?

One way of developing place attachment is to gain an understanding of what a place has to offer. This may not be readily apparent to the naked eye, but rather must be gleaned through building relationships within the community and asking residents what they value about the place. These assets may be tangible, such as access to cultural centers or natural spaces, but they also include intangibles such as communal support systems and a sense of community. When students develop an understanding of the positive assets of their communities, they may be more likely to engage in active citizenship to address needed changes within the community. Place attachment is much less likely if students believe their communities to be paths to nowhere; by emphasizing communities' positive assets, place attachment is more likely, and as a result, students are more likely to engage in active citizenship.

CONCLUSION

If active citizenship is to be an end goal of social studies instruction, we cannot afford to ignore the power of place within the social studies curriculum as an agent of effective citizenship education. Place already plays a central role within the disciplines that comprise the social studies. Whether we are teaching geography, history, government, economics or any of the social sciences, the concept of place must be addressed. Regardless of whether we teach place as a physical location, a unique point in time and space, or as the human–environment interaction in the places we inhabit, our understandings of other places are predicated on our own insight into the role of place *in* our lives and *on* our identity development. Availing ourselves of our students' natural connections to their communities in conjunction with the prominent role of place in the social studies curriculum provides another avenue by which we can connect to our students' sociocultural histories. In so doing, students are afforded the opportunity to see themselves within the curriculum, resulting in a greater sense of connection to social studies content, a renewed sense of agency (Barton & Levstik, 2004; Downey & Levstik, 1991; Epstein, 2001), and the potential for active citizenship beyond the classroom.

DISCUSSION QUESTIONS

1. Make a list of your favorite places and make a note of what you associate with each of the places on your list. Consider the role of place on your own identity development. In what ways have the places on your list influenced your identity? In what ways might these same places influence the perceptions others have of you?
2. Reflect upon your own encounters with place-based education. This might be a community service project, a field trip to a local historical site, participating in a city council meeting, or engaging in a local oral history project. To what extent did the use of local resources/topics enrich your learning? How have these experiences shaped your own attitudes about place-based pedagogies and curriculums?
3. What is the connection between place-based methodologies and culturally relevant methodologies? Where do they diverge? To what extent might culturally relevant pedagogies require a redefining of the notion of place-based education?

REFERENCES

Au, K. (2009). Isn't culturally responsive intruction just good teaching? *Social Education, 73*(4), 179–183.

Badger, E., Bui, Q., & Pearce, A. (2016). The election highlighted a growing rural-urban split. *The New York Times*. Retrieved from http://www.nytimes.com/2016/11/12/upshot/this-election-highlighted-a-growing-rural-urban-split.html

Ball, E. L., & Lai, A. (2006). Place-based pedagogy for the arts and humanities. *Pedagogy: Critical Approaches to Teaching Literature, Composition and Culture, 6*(2), 261–287.

Barton, K., & Levstik, L. (2004). *Teaching history for the common good*. Mahwah, NJ: Lawrence Erlbaum.

Bell, D. (2006). Variations on the rural idyll. In P. J. Cloke, T. Marsden, & P. H. Mooney (Eds.), *Handbook of rural studies* (pp. 149–160). Thousand Oaks, CA: Sage.

Boix-Mansilla, V. (2000). Historical understanding: Beyond the past and into the present. In P. N. Stearns, P. Sexias, & S. Wineburg (Eds.), *Knowing, teaching, & learning history: National and international perspectives* (pp. 390–418). New York, NY: New York University Press.

Center for Civic Education. (1994). *National standards for civics & government*. Calabasas, CA: Author.

Downey, M., & Levstik, L. S. (1991). Teaching and learning history. In J. P. Shaver (Ed.), *Handbook of research on social studies teaching and learning: A project of the National Council for the Social Studies* (pp. 400–410). New York, NY: Macmillan.

Epstein, T. (2001). Racial identity and young people's perspectives on social education. *Theory into Practice, 40*(1), 42–47.

Foxfire Fund. (2016). *FoxFire: Our history*. Retrieved from https://www.foxfire.org/about foxfire

Gamio, L. (2016). Urban and rural America are becoming increasingly polarized. *Washington Post*. Retrieved from https://www.washingtonpost.com/graphics/politics/2016-election/urban-rural-vote-swing/

Geography Education Implentation Project. (2012). *Geography for life: National geography standards*. Washington, DC: National Council for Geographic Education.

Hartley, L. P. (1953). *The go-between*. New York, NY: Random House.

Marcouyeux, A., & Fleury-Bahi, G. (2011). Place-identity in a school setting: Effects of the place image. *Environment and Behavior, 43*(3), 344–362.

Miller, P. (2001). Community-based education and social capital in an urban after-school program. *Education and Society, 44*(6), 35–60.

National Center for History in the Schools. (1996). *National standards for history*. Los Angeles, CA: Author.

National Council for the Social Studies. (1992). *A vision of powerful teaching and learning in the social studies: Building social understanding and civic efficacy* [Press release]. Retrieved from http://socialstudies.org/positions/powerful

National Council for the Social Studies. (2010). *National curriculum standards for social studies: A framework for teaching, learning and assessment*. Silver Spring, MD: Author.

Phillips, M. S. (2004). History, memory, and historical distance. In P. Seixas (Ed.), *Theorizing historical consciousness* (pp. 86–108). Toronto: University of Toronto Press.

Resor, C. W. (2010). Place-based education: What is its place in the social studies classroom. *The Social Studies, 101*, 185–188. doi:10.1080/00377990903493853.

Rosenweig, R. (2000). How Americans use and think about the past: Implications from a national survey for the teaching of history. In P. N. Stearns, P. Seixas, & S. Wineburg (Eds.), *Knowing,* teaching, & learning history: National and international perspectives (pp. 262–283). New York, NY: New York University Press.

Schuster, R. M., Sullivan, L. E., Kuehn, D. M., & Morais, D. B. (2011). Relationships among resident participation in nature and heritage tourism activties, place attachment, and sustainability in three Hudson River Valley communities. *Journal of Park and Recreation Administration, 29*(3), 55–69.

Sobel, D. (2004). *Place-based education: Connecting classrooms & communities.* Barrington, MA: The Orion Society.

Spencer, C. (2005). Place attachment, place identity, and the development of the child's self-identity: Searching the literature to develop an hypothesis. *International Research in Geographical and Environmental Education, 14*(4), 305–311.

Stasny, S. (2009). Uncertainty is your friend, part 1. *Psychology Today.* Retrieved from https://www.psychologytoday.com/blog/anger-in-the-age-entitlement/200902/uncertainty-is-your-friend-part-i

Theobold, P., & Wood, K. (2010). Learning to be rural: Identity lesson from history, schooling and United States corporate media (pp. 17 – 33). In K. A. Schafft & A. Y. Jackson (Eds.), *Rural education for the twenty-first century: Identity, place and community in a globalizing world.* University Park, PA: Pennsylvania State University Press.

Wilschut, A. (2011). *Images of time: The role of a historical consciousness of time in learning history.* Assen: Information Age Publishing.

CHAPTER TEN

Space

STACEY L. KERR, CENTRAL MICHIGAN UNIVERSITY

> space is a process...an ongoing product of interconnections.
>
> —Doreen Massey (2005, p. 107)

What comes to mind when you hear the word *space*? Images of the Starship Enterprise hurtling through the galaxy among vast expanses of darkness, stars, and distant planets? A wide-open field with no man-made structures as far as the eye can see? Perhaps something blank and devoid of anything—a figurative blank canvas? Conceptions of the word space abound. It is a term that spans the social and natural sciences, philosophy, and the realm of everyday life. Space can be used as both verb and noun. *Webster's Dictionary* (2016) provides 10 separate definitions of space, while Google's "define" search function gathers 17 understandings of the term. With so many definitions and usages, it is no wonder that the word space can be deployed to describe both everything and nothing.

Space is a frequently used term in educational contexts. Teachers are often encouraged to create "safe classroom spaces" for their students. Students are asked to give their desk neighbor "some space." Student teachers are taught to "space out" questions during lectures. In social studies, discussions of space tend to be most associated with the discipline of geography. But unlike the many ways space *can* be used, the teaching of geography in many social studies contexts can often lead one to believe that space can (and should for the purposes of the AP Human Geography exam, for example) be understood merely as "a portion of Earth's surface"

(Gritzner, 2002, p. 39) upon which other geographic elements like location, place, area, region, and territory are built and confined. So while there are many ways to think about space, social studies education tends to reassert a common assumption that space is simply a "container within which the world proceeds" (Thrift, 2003, p. 96). The container-like characteristics of this definition close down the possibility of what more dynamic considerations of space can offer, particularly reflections of space as a dynamic and social process that each and every individual has the ability to influence.

What I present in this chapter is the idea that spaces are continually made and remade through our relationships with each other and the world around us. This idea can be one that helps students understand their own agency and power in the shaping of the world around them. In other texts, researchers have provided excellent overviews of the various interpretations of the meaning of space and its connection to related terms like place, region, and territory (e.g., Agnew, 2011; Massey, 1993, 2005; Mazúr & Urbánek, 1983; Thrift, 1996, 2003). To gain an understanding of the multitude of ways that space has been defined, understood, and mobilized among various scholars across disciplines, I highly recommend engaging with these readings. However, the aim of this chapter is not to give a grand overview of every conception of space. I instead wish to trouble the most often used idea of space within the teaching of social studies—one in which space is understood as an empty container within which human action takes place.

SPACE AS PROCESS AND PRODUCT

Let us take a moment to engage with the quote from the introduction of this chapter by critical and feminist geographer, Doreen Massey. Massey (2005) challenges us to consider and reconsider what we assume space to be, as well as how we might think of space as an active component in our lives and the societies within which we are a part. Whereas space is often assumed to be something we simply traverse, or as I mentioned above, an empty container for human activity, Massey argues that space is less about physical locality and more about the relationships that humans form with each other, non-human beings, the material, and the immaterial. In other words, Massey takes us away from thinking about space as an empty landscape, to instead consider space as something that we make and remake through our interactions with others, the world around us, and the forces therein. I contend that it is thinking about, analyzing, and understanding these interactions with others and the world around is the crux of social studies education.

When we teach about the War of 1812, the Demographic Transition Model, or even how a bill becomes a law, we are not just teaching the most important concepts, we are teaching these concepts in the context of *why* they matter to people and their relationships with the physical world, self, and others. And all of these things happen somewhere, in spaces that we have actively created. Therefore, whenever we examine a topic within social studies, we are also analyzing the space of that topic, whether we do so with intention or not.

To provide an example of what this thinking about space looks like in practice, let's examine the idea of the "safe classroom space" I mentioned earlier. In this example, the physical expanse of the classroom might at first be understood as "the space," but it is simply the bounded territory of the space not the entirety of the safe classroom space. This physical entity defined by walls, desks, chairs, and whiteboards is perhaps the least important in the construction of a safe classroom space. More important in this creation are the interactions between members of that classroom space. A safe classroom space is built through interactions between the people within that room. It is comprised perhaps by a teacher who encourages students to feel comfortable in asking questions, and students who respect the perspectives and backgrounds of others. Other entities and forces like ideas, content and learning materials, technological devices, friendships, gender, class, power, and each individual's orientation toward those material and immaterial things are also a major part in the creation of the safe classroom space.

With these ideas in mind, take a look at the opening quote again: "Space is a process...an ongoing product of interconnections" (Massey, 2005, p. 107). Notice that Massey states the space is both a *process* and an *ongoing product*. In other words, space is both a thing (product) and the making of the thing (process). A safe classroom space is not something that simply comes to exist at random. It is built and it is maintained. For example, a teacher cannot simply announce to students, "This is a safe classroom space!" and expect it to exist as such. The idea must be supported by actions and commitments of the members therein to create that space. This is what is meant by process. It is an ongoing creation, not something that is simply said and done. Also important is the acknowledgement that as relationships between the classroom members as well as their understandings of certain ideas shift, the space changes as well. This is what Massey means by ongoing. The process continually defines and redefines the product. But what does Massey mean by production in the quote above? When we think of the word *product*, we are led to consider something that has been made. Thus, in this definition of space, it is important to recognize that everyone has an active part in creating, and thus, recreating space(s). In the context of the safe classroom space, each individual can and does influence the creation and maintenance of the space.

THE MOVING PARTS THAT MAKE SPACES

An emerging field of study within geography called *mobilities theories* extends Massey's thinking about space to investigate how various types of movement impact the process and product of creating spaces. If we were to ask students to think about spaces from a mobilities perspective, their focus would be upon analyzing, following, and understanding the consequences of physical movement as well as "potential movement, blocked movement, immobilization and forms of dwelling and place-making" (Sheller, 2011, p. 6). Movement (as well as the potential for movement, and moorings or resting points) is the main component in this rethinking of space. By looking at the relationship between the composition of space and movement, though not initially apparent, there are a number of embedded social studies topics generally studied in the curriculum—immigration, flows of capital and goods, government relations, and surveillance, to name a few.

Examinations of movement are especially important for the teaching and learning of social studies because movement is understood as an expression of the networks that make up and define spaces (Cresswell & Merriman, 2011; Sheller & Urry, 2006; Urry, 2007). How we can or cannot move through a space is deeply connected to our own identities, and those identities are connected to larger networks and structures at play. For example, consider the difficulty a refugee may have in moving across international borders. There are potential stoppages at every step: an onslaught of medical, legal, financial, and familial checkpoints that must be traversed before reaching a destination. This difficulty in movement can be put in contrast to the ease of mobility afforded to a cosmopolitan traveler armed with an American/German/British/Canadian (or other "powerful") passport. These two different experiences, and opportunities for movements, tell us a lot about the networks and structures that comprise these different spaces of the world—immigration systems, international attitudes, surveillance systems, and economic well-being, to name a few.

To expand this example, and further illustrate how mobilities theories can help us understand spaces, imagine any airport. While on the surface, airports might appear to have a singular function (a place for planes to land/depart with passengers embarking/disembarking), "airports vary in size and function, ranging from rural aerodromes to international airports and military airbases; facilitating business travel, holiday flights, amateur aviation, military bombing campaigns, and extraordinary rendition" (Cresswell & Merriman, 2011, p. 8), each airport is unique in their sizes and functions. They are unique in how they look, and where they are located, but their differences exist chiefly because of the networks present in the continuous making and remaking of their individual airport spaces. To understand this idea, consider the space of Toronto's Pearson International Airport. On a day-to-day basis, the space of this airport constantly fluctuates because of the movement present in the networks that comprise the space; networks related to passengers (where they are from, where they are going, and for what reasons, their length of time spent at the airport either for immediate departure/wait out a delay/rest during a layover), the airlines/businesses present there (what they sell, from where their products hail, where they will travel), the infrastructure of the airport (30 runways, three terminals, built for sustaining the movement of 432,800 flights moving 38.6 million passengers, and 448,000 metric tons of cargo per year (Toronto Pearson Fast Facts, 2015) and many others. Now, consider the Toronto Airport when Prime Minister Justin Trudeau and Ontario Premier Kathleen Wynne recently visited to welcome the first wave of 125 Syrian refugees to Canada. Their presence represents an adding of networks related to political movement (both explicit and implied, e.g., from a conservative and xenophobic government to a liberal and culturally pluralistic one), as well as the resulting movement of refugees (who gets to come, where in Canada will they be destined to live, will they ever get to/want to return to their homeland?). The presence of both political leaders and refugees serves as an illustration how new networks prompt new processes that in turn create new spaces, while also remaking existing ones.

The role that the networks of the built environment play in the possibility for movement in and through spaces is of particular note. All movement is connected not only to the networks that comprise spaces, but also to types of infrastructure that are present within these networks. These important non-human and immobile entities that deeply impact our movement and construction of spaces might include: "paths, railway tracks, public roads, telegraph lines, water pipes, telephone exchanges, pylons, sewerage systems, gas pipes, airports, radio and TV aerials, mobile phone masts, satellites, underground cables and so on" (Urry, 2007, p. 19). As humans, we interact with these entities on an almost constant basis—whether it's driving to school on a road, using electrical power to charge our electronic devices, or receiving a Wi-Fi signal to connect with our friends online. Thus, these immobile infrastructures are not neutral things, but are intersecting with our "social solidarities of class, gender, ethnicity, nation and age" and "orchestrating diverse mobilities, including both enforced fixity as well as coerced movement" (Urry, 2007, p. 19).

What is important to highlight in these quotes is that paying attention to the connection between infrastructure, the social world, and movement does not mean that infrastructure wholly determines the types of spaces and socialities that are possible. Rather than saying that the presence and type of infrastructure dictates movement, I instead use the above quotes to highlight that the built environment (versus the physical environment, for example) is representative of the networks of choices, ideals, predilections, and power of those who created them and is impactful and consistently interacting with social structures such as race, class, and gender. For example, oil pipelines are not neutral or natural. They represent human choices and action, particularly of where to place something and why. We could look at a map of a particular pipeline, or proposed pipeline, and ask ourselves and students questions such as "Why is the pipeline here and not there?" and "Whose interests are served in this placement?" "Whose interests are marginalized?" "Who is most affected?"

Perhaps the most useful aspect in thinking about mobilities theories and space with regards to social studies is the idea that movement and the resulting spaces are "central to how we experience the world" (Cresswell & Merriman, 2011, p. 5) and the different identities individuals can possess (Cresswell & Merriman, 2011; Fenwick, Edwards, & Sawchuck, 2011). This means that the different types of networks present (whether they be infrastructure, economic, or social structures) make possible certain type of movements as well as ways of being. In effect, the networks present in the built environment and the connected socialities and possible mobilities come together to form complex spaces that exist at a variety of scales—from the individual, to the local, to the global. There may be a number of spaces that exist at any scale, and those spaces may be interconnected with those on the same scale of others. To illustrate this idea, a teacher could simply ask students to draw a map of their classroom, school, or town which highlights the "most important" parts. What is "most important" will vary student to student, and thus, the maps will also vary. While these students will likely be in the same space, at the same time, a simple drawing of map can help illustrate differing points of view, as well as experiences with and interactions in this particular space.

THE SOCIAL WORLD IS COMPLEX, AND SO ARE SPACES

Spaces are complex. Things that are complex are different than those that are complicated (Cochran-Smith, Ell, Ludlow, Grudnoff, & Aitken, 2014; Davis & Sumara, 2006). Take a car for example. A car is comprised of individual parts that make up the whole of the machine. The car, while complicated in its composition, can be taken apart, and each individual part will wholly maintain its individual form and function. A piston removed from an engine is still a piston; it is not the engine that defines the piston's form. Entities that are complex on the other hand are not reducible in such a way. Once something complex is deconstructed or altered, the various components do not maintain the form or function they possess inside of the system. An example of something complex might be the Earth's global climate. When one factor changes (e.g., increases in precipitation, changes in temperature, sea level rise), the entirety of the system is affected in multiple ways. A mobilities approach characterizes spaces, as well as the social world they include, as complex. This is because spaces are comprised of networks that are irreducible into holistic individual parts.

Spaces are always active and undergoing constant flux. As the networks that comprise space(s) move and adjust, so do the spaces. All of these intertwining networks are important to consider because people control many of these components of the networks that comprise spaces. This means that spaces are in part authored in ways that purport certain activities, ideas, and ways of being, while simultaneously discouraging others. How spaces function is dependent upon their connections with other spaces and the networks therein. Specifically, the meaning of spaces is defined relationally; it is the "mutuality of the relationships in which they are involved constitutes what and how they are" (Urry, 2007, p. 25). Space together do not exist in entirety outside of each other. It is instead through their interconnections that they are made (Urry, 2007). In this view, "space does not exist prior to identities/entities and their relations" (Massey, 2005, p. 10) but is instead co-constituted by them. In short, space is not the "container within which the world proceeds," it is the "co-product of those proceedings" (Thrift, 2003, p. 96). Space is complex and relational.

SPACES AS TEXTS

Spaces are built through the connections of fluctuating complex networks and the entities therein. In this sense, space can also be understood as a type of text (Moore, 1986; Morrison, 2000). This is because texts have long been understood as complex systems that can be, and often are, authored in certain ways (Moore, 1986). A text is not limited solely to the written word. Many entities can also be understood as texts, such as literature, photographs, songs, maps, and even space, itself (Moore, 1986). Thus spaces, like other entities more traditionally understood as texts, are never free from bias and are seldom "natural" (Morrison, 2000, p. 87). As Werner (2000) writes:

> Texts are produced out of, and are positioned within, complex sets of relationships and processes (e.g., of publishing, marketing, consuming, reading, etc.) in particular times and places, and are not, therefore, to be read as fully self-contained and independent entities, knowable apart from their own time and the time of their recovery. (p. 194)

Thinking about texts in this way is not new in social studies education. Werner's work has been influential in encouraging educators and their students to critically examine texts they encounter in school—whether they be textbooks or maps (for an excellent example of using maps for textual interrogation in the classroom, see Segall, 2003). For example, a photograph, which is a common curricular object in social studies, might be interrogated textually. What is going on here? What makes you say that? Does this represent a point of view? Why did the photographer take the photograph in this way? What is in the frame and what is potentially outside of it? In a similar fashion, space(s) can be thought of as a text and interrogated similarly. Thinking in this way can help students see that like other texts, spaces, are also in many cases authored. They are articulations of the networks and structures present in the space, networks of relationships relating to humans, non-humans, economics, culture, and the social world. The authorship of a space can be perhaps seen most explicitly in planned spaces like a park or housing development in a suburb, but authorship of spaces also occurs in the seemingly natural.

When considering spaces as texts, it is important to remember that they are complex, and thus irreducible (as described previously). This irreducibility applies to texts of all kinds. This means, for example, that just as a literary text is not reducible to the meanings of its individual sentences, a spatial text cannot be brought down to the structure of its material parts, and history cannot be understood as a mere conglomeration of events. This is because, although the text preserves the properties of its individual elements, it produces them in such a way as to demand a particular sort of interpretation (Moore, 1986). In this way, thinking about space as a text can help someone see the ways that spaces might be open to interpretation.

For example, we might infer how (infra)structures act on spaces, and the types of implicit nods the construction of a space makes to us as people in and co-constituting it—how to act, how to move, where to be, who to speak with, and with what other entities one interacts. Further, if a space is to be understood as a text that can be interpreted, it is easier to see how a space might be imagined as a form of representation. This is not a static representation in which the essence of space can be "pin[ned] down" (Massey, 2005, p. 80) or stabilized like we might imagine a traditional map, but one instead where a space can be understood demonstrative of the attitudes, processes, and networks of people and other entities present in its composition. These representations can also be queried about what they represent; be it the social, economic, or cultural attitudes and practices of people as well as non-human entities. In other words, thinking about spaces as texts allows an easier entry into thinking about the ways that spaces and authored, and how one might begin to *read* authorship into spaces; or in other words, exhibit what we might call a critical spatial literacy.

RETHINKING SPATIAL LITERACY

If space can be thought of as a type of text, then spatial literacy becomes the study of how that text is read. Researchers in geography education assert that spatial literacy is the nexus of spatial thinking and spatial reasoning. Spatial thinking is the process of being able to "identify, explain, and find meaning in spatial patterns and relationships" (Bednarz & Kemp, 2011, p. 19) such as the dis/similarities between places, the connections between physical features and human activity, and the interconnections between communities at local, regional, and global scales. To be able to use spatial thinking, it is crucial that one develops knowledge of spatial concepts like scale and directions as well as the ability to construct and interpret spatial representations like a map (Bednarz & Kemp, 2011). Spatial reasoning, on the other hand, can be understood as putting spatial thinking to use to solve spatial problems. A spatial problem can be many things such as determining how to fit items neatly into a piece of luggage, deciding upon the best location to build a new store, or choosing the fastest route to travel home from the airport. When spatial thinking and spatial reasoning are combined then, they can be understood together as spatial literacy.

What might it mean then to think about spatial literacy with we thinking about space in the terms I have previously described? For students, it could mean identifying networks of movement and compositions of spaces and in turn, reading the authorship embedded in spaces. Reading authorship into spaces is an important part of developing a critical orientation that allows one to employ the spatial thinking and reasoning described above to question the seemingly natural, harmless, and apolitical; all things that spaces tend to be characterized as within many social studies contexts. To engage with this type of spatial literacy, students can read a space by moving in and navigating through it while using both spatial thinking and reasoning. This would be a type of spatial literacy that is utilized "on the ground" in which the student reads the authorship in spaces by assessing how their own personal movement can be encouraged, restricted, coerced, forced, or even non-existent.

Imagine asking students to walk around the space of a planned residential community, or any new type of suburb that is so common now across North America. While not immediately apparent, the networks in these communities can be read (and thus questioned) when one begins to recognize the presence of networks related to the organization of housing plots, the construction of streets and sidewalks, homeowner association (HOA) rules, housing pricing, and proximity to schools and places of business impact the ways that people and other entities can exist and behave in the space. These factors may dictate the type of people who may and do become residents (e.g., Who can afford to live there? Does public transportation service the community? Are there community service requirements or volunteering duties associated with residency?), how residents and visitors move into and through the space (e.g., Is there a gate that requires resident status or guest approval? Are there speed limits different than the county's?), and even require residents and visitors to behave in certain ways (e.g., Can you host an outdoor party? May you paint your door red? May you park your car in the driveway?). In other words, to what extent might spatial relationships constrain or enable one's freedom and what are the consequences of such a relationship for life in a democratic society? In addition to these explicit forms of spatial authorship, one might also see authorship in a space based upon more presence of more implicit cues as well as complete absences (Urry, 2007). These are important questions to ask if students (and teachers, alike) are to become more equitable producers and consumers of space.

As another example, consider the college campus. What is absent from the campus is almost as important as what is present in defining the space. What does it mean when a campus does not have a women's center? A rugby field? Adequate parking for bicycles? Accessible building entrances for those with dis/abilities? The absence of certain elements tells someone many things about the space and can encourage, discourage, coerce, or restrict their movements. By identifying absences, we can read into what is valued, what is not, what should be segregated and compartmentalized, and whose interests are regarded as important in a space (Soja, 1989). Further, if we look at implicit cues of authorship on spaces and their connections to potential movement, what does it say about a campus, for example, when faculty and students cannot use the library and academic offices during football games? Or that the names of buildings are those of affluent, white, and in many cases outwardly racist men? These are the types of questions my own students have asked of their university and questions that students at all levels might ask of their institutions because no space is immune from a particular authorship. Looking for the absences and implicit actions in the authorship of spaces can help one see that certain spaces are authored in more covert ways to advance certain ideas or mobilities while simultaneously discouraging others.

Ultimately, reading the authorship of a space is an important part of spatial literacy that can be accessed by prompting students to consider the connections between movement and the construction of spaces. In addition to adding a certain amount of criticality to traditional notions of spatial literacy, a focus on the interconnections between movement and space can also aid immensely in the problem solving process—a skill, ability, and orientation toward issues that everyone should have. If one may interpret how a space was authored, and why it was created in such a way, they might be able to better understand the processes that may happen within, and how they might solve associated problems.

CONCLUSIONS

The way we think about space matters and how we talk about it in social studies matters even more. It affects our interactions with others, understandings of global events, and individual impact upon communities. If students can be prompted to think about the way that their movement through the world is impactful upon the spaces that they experience and help create, it is possible that they might come to understand the importance of their existence, participation, movement, and analysis of all of these factors in the world. When we conceive of space not as a fixed entity but instead as a process that is always in flux, we are afforded a certain level of hopefulness, that things can change, and that what is present is not permanent. This rethinking of space is important to social studies because the world is "neither composed of atomistic individuals nor closed into an always-already completed holism. It is a world being made through relations" (Massey, 2005, p. 150). Incorporating this view into the thinking and teaching of social studies sits in opposition to the typical construction of space where something is permanent and static, but thoughts of spatiality in this way, the way that it is always changing, lends itself to an openness of the future, and in turn an optimism of what is possible, and how one might themselves affect that change. If spaces are built out of interconnections and interactions, then every single interaction, no matter how big or small, is integral to the construction and reconstruction of spaces. In short, everyone has an impact and matters in the construction of space(s). So as you can see, space can be the stuff of the Enterprise, or the home of the solar system, but it can also be so much more.

DISCUSSION QUESTIONS

1. What might it be like to think about history with a focus upon space instead of time?
2. Consider your local neighborhood—what evidence can you find that the space(s) within this neighborhood are authored? What movement is available to residents? Flora and fauna? Vehicles?
3. Why is it that different people in the same space at the same time might experience the space differently?

REFERENCES

Agnew, J. (2011). Space and place. In J. Agnew & D. Livingstone (Eds.), *Handbook of geographical knowledge* (pp. 316–330). London: Sage.
Bednarz, S. W., & Kemp, K. (2011). Understanding and nurturing spatial literacy. *Procedia-Social and Behavioral Sciences, 21*, 18–23.
Cochran-Smith, M., Ell, F., Ludlow, L., Grudnoff, L., & Aitken, G. (2014). The challenge and promise of complexity theory for teacher education research. *Teachers College Record, 116*(5), 1–38.
Cresswell, T., & Merriman, P. (2011). *Geographies of mobilities: Practices, spaces, subjects.* Farnham; Burlington, VT: Ashgate.

Davis, B., & Sumara, D. J. (2006). *Complexity and education: Inquiries into learning, teaching, and research*. New York, NY: Psychology Press.

Fenwick, T., Edwards, R., & Sawchuck, P. (2011). *Emerging approaches to educational research: Tracing the sociomaterial*. New York, NY: Routledge.

Gritzner, C. F. (2002). What is where, why there, and why care? *Journal of Geography, 101*(1), 38–40.

Massey, D. (1993). Power-geometry and a progressive sense of place. In J. Bird, B. Curtis, T. Putnam, G. Robertson, & L. Tickner (Eds.), *Mapping the futures: Local cultures, global change* (pp. 59–69). London: Routledge.

Massey, D. (2005). *For space*. Los Angeles, CA: Sage.

Mazúr, E., & Urbánek, J. (1983). Space in geography. *GeoJournal, 7*(2), 139–143.

Moore, H. (1986). *Space, text and gender: An anthropological study of the Marakwet of Kenya*. Cambridge: Cambridge University Press.

Morrison, S. S. (2000). *Women pilgrims in late medieval England: Private piety as public performance*. New York, NY: Routledge.

Segall, A. (2003). Maps as stories about the world. *Social Studies and the Young Learner, 16*(1), 21.

Sheller, M. (2011). *Mobility*. Sociopedia.isa, 1–12. Retrieved from http://www.sagepub.net/isa/resources/pdf/mobility.pdf

Sheller, M., & Urry, J. (2006). *Mobile technologies of the city*. London: Routledge.

Soja, E. W. (1989). *Postmodern geographies: The reassertion of space in critical social theory*. London: Verso.

Thrift, N. (1996). *Spatial formations*. London: Sage.

Thrift, N. (2003). Space: The fundamental stuff of human geography. In S. L. Hollaway, S. P. Rice, & G. Valentine (Eds.), *Key concepts in geography* (pp. 95–107). London: Sage.

Toronto Pearson Fast Facts. (2015). Retrieved from https://www.torontopearson.com/en/press/toronto-pearson-fast-facts/#

Urry, J. (2007). *Mobilities*. Cambridge: Polity Press.

Werner, W. (2000). Reading authorship into texts. *Theory & Research in Social Education, 28*(2), 193–219.

CHAPTER ELEVEN

Between There and Here

A Response to the People, Places, and Environments Section

JASON HARSHMAN, UNIVERSITY OF IOWA

Reflect on your recent travels so far in terms of where you are and where you were rather than what you have done. What exists in the spaces between home and work or school that are dependent upon and shaped by then and now, here and there? Have you considered that places you thought of as unchanging are actually changing? How does who you are relate to how you experience a place? Did you cross borders with ease or apprehension, without a second thought or lapse in your sense of security or belonging? When you move through spaces, do you consider the carbon footprint you leave as a well-intentioned, environmentally conscious citizen? Is there a longing for home when you are away, and if so, do you miss the physical home or the imagined sense of what home means to you?

Within the series of questions presented above are terms, concepts, and opportunities for reflection on how we approach geography education within the social studies. The theoretical turn provided by the authors featured within this section on "People, Places, and Environments" offer thoughtful readings of the diverse ways in which we construct places through our language, imagery, experiences, and curriculum, along with insights and questions to help disrupt our imagined sense of the world. Individually and collectively, the authors interrogate the conventional readings of geography education to remind readers and educators, as Edward Soja (2010) argues, that place is not a detached background to time and our experiences. Similarly, in line with the work of Raymond Williams, the critical readings of place, space, borders, home, and environment remind us that an approach to teaching about places, people, and environments that emphasize fluidity and diversity are what make for engaging lessons about experience and perspective building within geography and the social studies.

At the core of each of these chapters is our understanding of the spatial as fluid, shifting, and always becoming. Best captured in Kerr's chapter on space, the tendency to think of space as static and natural, rather than fluid and constructed, denies the reality of how diverse and subjective experiences give multiple meanings to space. As Lefebvre (1974) argues, space is simultaneously a producer and is produced by the social interactions of people. In this sense, as social relations shape one's spatial surroundings, the very same interactions are concurrently shaped by the spatial contexts within which they occur. As a result, we are actors within spaces who are simultaneously acted upon as we give new meaning to spaces. Consequently, whether it is the airport, school, university campus, or some other place, who we are is integral to how we experience and make meaning of where we are.

Practitioners can also appreciate the manner in which the authors invert questions suggested by the NCSS for teaching geography—such as "How do maps, globes, geographic tools and geospatial technologies contribute to the understanding of people, places, and environments?"—to instead highlight the limitations that are too often perpetuated. While it is important to use such tools to identify the location of a place, as Blankenship addresses in regards to *place* and Menon and Saleh for *borders*, helps instructors and students recognize how these same tools contribute to the reification and conflation of places and cultures.

Latremouille's critical reading of the type of "greenwashing" environmentalism that too often rewards well intentioned, but shortsighted actions, sounds a necessary alarm that social studies educators need to take up as part of a critically minded, place-based approach to citizenship education. When do students examine environmental racism or engage in inquiry on the extent to which a consumer, capitalist culture can coexist with an eco-minded, environmentally responsible approach to citizenship education?

Swarts' discussion of the key word "home" offers an opportunity for teachers and students to examine how we conceptualize home and the sense of security some people may associate with ownership of a home. For refugees and migrant laborers who move from place to place, what is home? Further, by examining the history of a place and the construction of race-based borders that result in red-lining in real estate, the gerrymandering of voting districts, the lines that create a school district, and more, students will come to see that access to home ownership has for too long been based on the intersection of race, class, and place. Such questions are not only provocative and complex, but they are critical to the kind of social justice oriented approach to place-based education that the authors allude to across their respective chapters.

In her 2015 TEDTalk entitled "Don't ask where I'm from, ask where I'm a local," Taiye Selasi reminds us "We can never go back to a place and find it exactly where left it. Something, somewhere will always have changed. Most of all, ourselves" (Selasi, 2015). As a person's sense of place is subjective and part of an ongoing meaning making process from which diverse experiences emerge, the opportunities to reflect, share, and then apply what was learned during those experiences is central to the kind of social studies education these and other scholars support. Further, asking students to reflect upon their own metageographies—what Lewis and Wigen (1997) define as the set of spatial structures through which people order their knowledge of the world according to continents, countries, and cities—they can then ask questions as to why they imagine a place as they do, what about a place is accurate or inaccurate, how did the borders come to be and in whose interest were they constructed, and in what ways have they contributed to a misrepresentation of people and places? By calling attention to the processes that work to construct and disrupt borders, places, cultures, and environments, social studies educators engage in teaching and learning that avoids relying on stereotypes and misrepresentations to instead teach for prejudice reduction through critical geography.

REFERENCES

Lefebvre, H. (1974). *The production of space*. Cambridge, MA: Blackwell.
Lewis, M., & Wigen, K. (1997). *The myth of continents: A critique of metageography*. Berkeley, CA: University of California Press.
Selasi, T. (2015, October 20). Don't ask me where I'm from, ask me where I'm a local. Retrieved from: https://www.youtube.com/watch?v=LYCKzpXEW6E&t=144s
Soja, E. (2010). *Seeking spatial justice*. Minneapolis, MN: University of Minnesota Press.

Section IV: Individual Development and Identity

CHAPTER TWELVE

Gender

MEGAN LIST, YOUNGSTOWN STATE UNIVERSITY

> I think the big thing to point out to people is, you know, possibly they should go and hang around with some women. And also, it's worth pointing out that people, unfortunately, misunderstand the phrase "strong women." The glory of Buffy is it was filled with strong women. Only one of those strong women had supernatural strength and an awful lot of sharpened stakes. And people sort of go "Well yes, of course Buffy was a strong woman. She could kick her way through a door." And you go "No, well that's not actually what makes her a strong woman! You're missing the point."
>
> —Neil Gaiman, BBC radio interview (December 19, 2013)

Before you continue into this chapter, stop for a moment and answer a question that may seem to have an obvious answer that you may have never considered before. Perhaps you have read books on the subject or you have given the topic a lot of consideration. The question may be three words long, but the answer is quite complex. Throughout recorded human history this question and its implications have been occasions for countless atrocities and, at the same time, honored celebrations. The question, plainly stated is: What is gender? In the case of the widely popular female vampire hunter Buffy, introduced in the epigraph above, the idea of Buffy being a "strong woman" in Gaiman's words, unhelpfully presents Buffy as simply a girl who is violent, or, to be most reductive, a girl who acts like a man. Understanding how ideas associated with strength are associated with gender, and how such ideas are in themselves *gendered*, is a goal of unsettling simplistic and traditional notions about gender and defining what gender is.

In modern western thought, people often present sex and gender as if the two concepts are the same thing: If you have physical characteristics of a man, you are a man. Others counter that not everyone is born with clearly identifiable sex characteristics, and that people often receive corrective measures to solidify a child's gender identity, such as the tragic history of David Reimer, who was born with the physical sex characteristics associated with a man, but was raised as a girl (Colapinto, 2000). Even others will be happy to discuss the fact that transgender people clearly exist, working with greater visibility in the public sphere for equal rights and public recognition. What does the historical record say about gender, and how can students engage with this question? Typically, history is presented as men are men, and women are women; therefore, they should dress and act like a man or woman to follow gender norms and societal expectations. Same sex relationships are often ignored to the point that there are almost no same-sex relationships, and everything is just about the same as it is today. Official histories sometimes spotlight a few notable biographies of people who have challenged gender rules and norms (e.g., Joan of Arc of France, Emperor Wu Zetian). However, as a teachable concept, the problem of how gender is questioned and challenged remains a significant topic in the social studies curriculum in need of unsettling.

To explore gender within your own experiences, consider the question, how many times has gender been reinforced in the past 24 hours? Have you gone to the restroom? How you engage in that act was probably related to your gender in some way, whether it was the physical process, or whether the room you used was gender specific. Have you interacted with anyone? Their responses to you were likely gendered, with, "Yes sir," or, "Certainly Ma'am!" sprinkled into casual retail conversations. When you awoke in the morning, did you perform male rituals of self-preparation, or did you go through a more feminine approach to the day? Did you shower, shave, and run out the door, or did your routine include a myriad of cosmetics and preparatory procedures common among professional women? When students confront the ways in which some of our everyday experiences are gendered and in turn shape our expressions of gender, they begin to see how gender is better thought of as a spectrum of possible expressions. According to an article for educators on the gender spectrum, Kilman (2013) helpfully clarifies that "sex exists between your legs—it's your biology, your chromosomes, your anatomy" whereas "gender exists between your ears—it's how you feel about yourself" (Kilman, 2013, n.p.). Such feelings can be complex and multilayered because the forms of which we develop a gender identity are personal, individual, and unique. A gender(ed) identity is internal to our own sense of self, giving shape to an outwardly visible array of gender expressions, which is how we present "our gender to the world through external choices" such as our style of dress and other markers of our appearance (Kilman, 2013, n.p.).

Our gender identities often influence much of what we do in a day, and much consideration has been given to these topics, but how can understanding other cultures and historical contexts help us re-think about these experiences? When students study history, they are often encounter heteronormative (i.e., everyone is straight) and cisnormative (i.e., there are only two genders) narratives. For example, teachers might encourage students to consider, in what ways did gender influence the daily actions of ancient Spartans or Mayans? Did the lowest social groups at times throughout history regard gender in ways that are similar to or different from how communities in the present regard gender? In other words, what is possible for students to consider about gender when we begin to call attention to it as a category of identity across time and across cultures in the social studies curriculum?

One way to begin the process of unsettling gender in the social studies can be exploring how heteronormative and cisgender narratives appear in the social studies curricula. Social studies educators can investigate historicized concepts of gender as a type of inquiry to assist students in developing historical empathy. Historical empathy is a type of historical thinking that helps students understand "how people from the past thought, felt, made decisions, acted, and faced consequences within a specific historical and social context" (Endacott & Brooks, 2013, p. 41). For example, to what degree can students understand and engage with the ideas from the Spartan culture without exploring their perceptions of gender? Similarly, students can investigate how Indigenous Nations of the Americas viewed and treated gender nonconforming individuals prior to colonial and Christian influences. I ask these questions and present gender nonconforming lenses as a way to enable social studies educators to consider with their students the shifting historical terrain involved in defining gender.

STUDYING GENDER THROUGH TIME

Even though the question "what is gender?" may seem simple to understand, students must use perspectives appropriate to specific historical periods in question in order to historically contextualize how people have defined gender; presentist modern perspectives will not enable students to map changes in the evolution of thought toward the concept of gender. Students may find conflicting or complex examples of defining gender depending on which aspects of gender they explore. I provide three supporting questions that will scaffold students' thinking in their pursuit of this question.

First, students should explore what it meant to be a masculine/feminine person of a specific historical time and place. This question allows students to explore gender along a spectrum of representations, customs, and laws across space and time. If students examine what it means to be feminine in 19th-century Europe, they will need to look for social markers and signifiers of femininity as a constructed characteristic in different aspects of life, such as the division between domestic or private spheres and the roles expected of men and women in these spheres of domesticity. Students would learn that in Victorian Britain expectations of feminine gendered roles included managing households, working in women's social groups to uphold specific social morals and virtues, and properly rear future generations. In contrast to this expectation, the expectations of masculine gendered roles held that men should be laboring away from home, being more visibly present in the public sphere, outside of the private or domestic sphere, where it was felt women should relegate their presence (Hughes, 2017).

Next, students should explore the many different ways expressions of gender were enforced in different historical contexts. This question allows students to apply information collected in exploring gender roles and expressions of gender and apply this knowledge to understanding complex motivations of past groups. For example, in ancient Sparta, a person could be killed for not adhering closely to the normative behavior associated with their apparent gender (Fantham, Foley, Kampen, Pomeroy, & Shapiro, 1994). Similarly, many Indigenous Nations in North America have historically treated individuals with non-normative genders as being special individuals who carried additional abilities or authority within the local councils and groups (Feinberg, 1996; Mayo & Sheppard, 2012). Indeed, within and across the many diverse Indigenous Nations of North America there are myriad ways in which the concept of gender is unsettled in Indigenous languages. For example, Brayboy (2017) points out how the Cherokee have in their language specific terms for "women who feel like men" but that the Navajo have the phrase "*Nádleehí* (one who is transformed)" and in Lakota a term is "*Winkté* (indicative of a male who has a compulsion to behave as a female)" whereas in Cheyenne *Hemaneh* is approximately translated into English as "half man, half woman" (Brayboy, 2017, n.p.). (See also Shear and Stanton's chapter *Indigenous* in this volume.)

Finally, students can extend their thinking of gender by considering how expectations of gender affected everyday lives of people during the time period under study. As students investigate concepts of gender across time and space they will see, for example, how women were affected differently in different situations, introducing students to considering gender as an intersectional issue that requires thinking about race, class, and other social markers of identity. In the curricular context of a world history course, studying Joan of Arc would reveal to students how defining gender and using normative categories of thinking about gender complicate historical narratives. As leader of the French army, Joan of Arc was an epic heroine, and yet students must analyze how the concept of gender posed a challenge for how Joan's identity and subject position as a woman was understood both in her time and in our present moment. Joan of Arc fought for France and by all historical accounts was valiant in her actions, challenging conventional and stereotypical notions of feminine gender traits as weak (Harrison, 2014). However, she was charged with heresy under controversial and specious claims of cross-dressing (Carroll, 1993). In the curricular context of a U.S. history course, students can study the biography of Albert Cashier, a Civil War solider who had the sex of a woman, but served in the military as a man and expressed her gender as masculine. Cashier was born as Jennie Irene Hodgers, and enlisted into military service with the name and identity of Albert Cashier, dressing as a man and fighting in approximately 40 different battles (Praeger, 2017). Some historians argue that Cashier's life can be analyzed as an early example of transgender history within the broader social narrative of U.S. history, and sources about Cashier's life and help illuminate the ways in which trans lives and the lives of genderqueer or nongender-conforming persons can be voices and made visible within U.S. history curriculum (Bronski, 2011).

The historical example of Joan of Arc and Albert Cashier illustrate the vexing challenges of a heteronormative framework, in which expression of gender, gender roles, and definitions of gender are placed in an oppositional binary system (i.e., men and women), forcing genders to be identified and understood through such relationships. According to Sauer (2015), before the term *heteronormativity* was created, the concept existed; male-female intercourse was the only acknowledgeable sexual relationship in premodern Western society (Sauer, 2015, p. 8). Most public schools, and many universities, teach and reinforce binary *heteronormative* and *cisnormative* gender approaches in social studies classes and subjects. However, teachers and scholars can challenge hegemonic patriarchy that marginalize not only historical figures, but the students and educators in schools. Advocating for feminism and equality or confronting toxic masculinity and gender binaries can be challenging in the face of promulgation stretching historically from Aristotle to Lawrence Summers, former president of Harvard University, who argued women were not as well represented in the sciences because they lacked the motivation and aptitude to be successful in science, thereby passing on a narrative that women are not as good as men in the sciences (Jaschik, 2005).

If we define masculine as something that is not feminine, then how do we define feminine? The same problem arises if we attempt to define any kind of meta-gender as not male or female. Breaking from these binary, static, and Western approaches, I draw inspiration in this chapter from the term used by the Bugis in India, *Bissu*. *Bissu* is an Indian word that describes a meta-gender, or gender than encompasses all genders (Graham, 2002). I will use the phrase *meta-gender*, or simply, *meta*, to refer to the possibility that cultures will reject binary gender approaches.

TWO CURRICULAR EXAMPLES FOR STUDYING GENDER IN THE SOCIAL STUDIES

I will offer two examples to help examine gender in historical contexts. Students often view history, and textbooks often reinforce these views, as part of a narrative of progress where things get better over time. Students can bring presentist and egocentric perspectives to the study of gender across places and times. They may assume that women, gay individuals, or transgender people tend to have fewer rights across time and space. Again, they view things as getting better. For example, students' present understandings of gender can shade the ways they perceive gender to exist in the Spartan culture of ancient Greece or some North American Indigenous nations. Students may be surprised to learn about the rights women hold in Sparta, Two-Spirit people in some North American Indigenous nations, and Bugis concepts in Indian communities. In these situations, gender departs from contemporary understandings and students can better understand both the present and the past through historical inquiry.

Gender in Spartan Culture

What is gender in Spartan culture? In modern popular culture, Sparta is often portrayed as being the epitome of Western gender roles. In some representations of ancient Sparta men are often presented as an ideal form of masculinity with prowess in a variety of areas, primarily in combat. In these same representations, the women of Sparta are portrayed as being passive, assenting to male power, but beguiling with certain ideals of what feminine beauty should look like. What happens, however, when we compare the historical Spartan culture with how we view them in the modern world, using the lens of gender? Table 12.1 provides an overview of gender in Spartan culture that can facilitate answering compelling and supporting questions.

In this historical context, governments regulate citizens based upon citizens' gender. Citizens are grouped as male or female with minimal private interaction between the groups and gender is enforced socially, and regionally (Assily, 2008; Fantham et al., 1994; Rubarth, 2014). Violating gender roles could result in a penalty of death, with mothers killing sons who were proven to be shameful (e.g., lacking masculinity, performing poorly in battle) (Fantham et al., 1994, p. 63). Moreover, women were expected to shave their heads and dress as men as part of the marriage ritual, as it was inappropriate for men and women to be together in public (Assily, 2008). Men kidnapped women as a means of marrying them, although this seems to be more ritualistic kidnapping than actually taking women by force, using power to regulate not only the lives of women, but to police their expressions of gender and gender identities (Fantham et al., 1994). Overall, concepts of masculinity within the ancient Greek world are configured with different regions of power and philosophical bent having different guidelines for masculinity (Rubarth, 2014).

Table 12.1. What Does It Mean to Be a Masculine/Feminine/Meta Person in Ancient Spartan Culture?

Masculine	Feminine	Meta
Non-heteronormative (Plutarch, Life of Lycurgus, 18; Talbert 1988: 30–31, quoted in Fantham et al., 1994)	Non-heteronormative (Plutarch, Life of Lycurgus, 18; Talbert 1988: 30–31, quoted in Fantham et al., 1994)	Women are expected to shave their heads and pose as men as part of the marriage ritual (Assily, 2008)
Expected to have a healthy sexual appetite (Fantham et al., 1994)	Produce strong Spartan men (Assily, 2008)	
Expected to be strong and ready for combat (Assily, 2008), effective and brave soldier (Rubarth, 2014)	Expected to be physically strong and well educated (Assily, 2008; Fantham et al., 1994).	
Expected to be courageous (Rubarth, 2014)	Expected to have a healthy sexual appetite (Assily, 2008)	
Treated harshly during training to build soldiers (Rubarth, 2014)	Able to own property and businesses (Fantham et al., 1994)	

Gender in Spartan culture is more dynamic and complex than the popular culture presentations from which many students may learn about ancient Greece. Rather than recoiling from the idea that feats of physical prowess were done either fully or partially naked, the Spartans demonstrated complex understandings of sex and gender. At first glance, contemporary audiences may view the selection of mating pairs as barbaric and crude. However, women were active participants in the ritual, shaving their own heads and changing their own clothes. While gender was heavily enforced, and specific aspects of gender were violently enforced, there is a clear differentiation between gender and sexuality. Sexuality, apart from gender, was not similarly enforced, and same-sex partnerships were often sought and maintained by both genders. Given this information about gender and sexuality, students may begin to question modern depictions of Spartan life that have more to do with the present than the past.

Social studies teachers might challenge students to confront the contradictions posed by the historical record, popular culture representations, and contemporary norms by trying to answer the question, how could a movie based in Sparta be both historically accurate with regards to gender and sexuality, while simultaneously appeal to modern Western audiences?

Two-Spirit People of Indigenous Nations

If students are to examine the idea of Two-Spirit people they must do so within the context of specific Indigenous cultures and nations. Teachers might ask students, what is gender for the many Indigenous persons of North America? Modern representations of Indigenous Nations of the Americas are historically fraught (see Shear and Stanton's *Indigenous* chapter for more). For example, popular culture representations Indigenous men as sidekicks of daring white men or the "Proud Indian Chief" do little to understand masculinity or gender in Indigenous cultures. In the 2013 *The Lone Ranger* film Tonto is presented as a sidekick and comic relief of that classical American Übermensch (i.e., German for super man). For an example of the latter, the 1954 film *Sitting Bull* demonstrates the pontificating Indian Chief, lamenting the almost helpless loss of their land to the "White Man." However, gender in Indigenous societies is far more complex than such misrepresentations.

Students can explore the ways that gender roles are enforced, or not enforced, in Indigenous communities prior to European colonization. Two-Spirit people in Indigenous cultures creates spaces for the blurring of gender lines, which in turn precluded the idealization of binary gender roles that would require enforcement. European colonization led to the external enforcement of gender roles with European settlers ascribing their gender roles and privileges to the Indigenous cultures they aimed to assimilate. Nonbinary individuals were even executed with at least one documented instance of Spanish explorers murdering Two-Spirit people with dogs (Feinberg, 1996). Table 12.2 provides an overview of Two-Spirit identities that can facilitate answering the compelling and supporting questions.

Table 12.2. What Does It Mean to Be a Masculine/Feminine/Meta Person for Indigenous American Peoples?

Masculine	Feminine	Meta
Men could end marriages they no longer felt attached to (Demos, 1995)	Women could end marriages they no longer felt attached to (Demos, 1995)	Two-Spirit people are regarded with honor in councils; "nothing can be decided without their advice." (Feinberg, 1996, p. 23)
Married men usually lived with their wife's matrilineage—Cherokee (Demos, 1995)	After divorce, women regained full support of parents, brothers and other maternal relatives—Cherokee (Demos, 1995)	Caretakers and teachers of children (Sheppard & Mayo, 2013)
Men engaged in warfare when needed (Demos, 1995)	Women prepared and processed skins for the fur trade (Demos, 1995)	Two-Spirit refers to individuals who were born with masculine and feminine spirits in one body (Sheppard & Mayo, 2013)
Often engages in hunting (Demos, 1995)	Women farmed and incorporated European tools and crops (Demos, 1995)	Could be born with male physical characteristics, but take part in women's social roles or dress as women (Sheppard & Mayo, 2013)
	Prior to colonization, women held power in the governance of their local group	

Gender and gender identity were important aspects of spirituality for many of the Indigenous Nations of the Americas. One generalizable concept across the diverse group of Indigenous First Nations is that Two-Spirit people embody both male and female, they are often given roles of teachers and leaders in the religion of the tribe (Williams, 2010). Because gender roles are not necessarily enforced, individuals can select from a variety of gender roles, including cross-gender activities.

In general, gender in many Indigenous cultures is what the spirits of the individual decide. If an individual has only a masculine spirit and a masculine body, then the individual is male. If an individual has a feminine body with a feminine spirit, then the individual is female. If they have both male and female aspects to them, then they are Two-Spirited. This is an oversimplification of the idea, but the hope here is that you will be encouraged to delve into deeper aspects of Two-Spirit history.

Social studies educators can encourage students to explore questions that consider both historical and contemporary topics. For example, after studying Two-Spirit peoples, students might consider questions like, what are the benefits of living in a culture that embraces the concept of Two-Spirit individuals? Which culture do you think is closer to the one that we live in and why?

CONCLUSION

Differences in gender are not as firm as modern Western cultures might imply. Gender reinforcement surrounds our daily experiences. For example, how often have you been in a situation where you wondered about the gender of someone? How often have you wondered, while reading fiction, why an author chose to specific gender for a character? In a recent episode of the podcast, *Writing Excuses*, Shannon Hale challenged the listeners to, "take something you've written and gender swap it. Every character that's a male, make him female. Every character that's female, make her male" (Tayler, 2016). How can such an activity allow us to better understand the gender cues, signals, and enforcements that often go unnoticed? Students can take contemporary news stories in the media and examine how the narrative or the event the narrative describes might have unfolded differently if gender roles were reversed or diverse genders are offered. Could we even characterize some characters from a social setting as Bissu? What can we learn about gender in colonial America if we asked what would have had to be different for General George Washington to be General Sandra Washington? How might she have seen the world, and what challenges would she have faced?

While gender issues can be difficult and complex, exploring gender in the curriculum can allow social studies educators to affirm gender diversity in ways that are important for students. Students can examine our underlying assumptions about how things ought to be. If you are feeling a little lost and still searching for ideas, just swap genders of famous historical figures, and see how their perception and image would be portrayed differently.

DISCUSSION QUESTIONS

1. How often during the day is your gender reinforced?
2. In what ways do you convey gender messages to individuals around you?
3. How do contemporary understandings of gender influence the ways you believe gender existed in past or far away societies?

4. How can you challenge gender assumptions when working with varieties of texts, primary sources, or textbooks?
5. How would others respond to you altering the clothing you wore to be more feminine or masculine? Why do you think people might react as they do?

REFERENCES

Assily, R. (2008, December 29). Gender in Ancient Sparta [Blog]. Retrieved from http://historianforum.blogspot.com/2008/12/gender-in-ancient-sparta.html

Brayboy, D. (2017, September 7). Two spirits, one heart, five genders. *Indian Country Today*. Retrieved from https://indiancountrymedianetwork.com/news/opinions/two-spirits-one-heart-five-genders/

Bronski, M. (2011). *A queer history of the United States*. Boston, MA: Beacon Press.

Carroll, W. H. (1993). *The glory of Christendom*. Front Royal, VA: Christendom Press.

Colapinto, J. (2000). *As nature made him: The boy who was raised as a girl*. New York, NY: Harper Collins.

Demos, J. (1995). *The tried and the true: Native American women confronting colonization (Vol. 1)*. Oxford, NY: Oxford University Press.

Endacott, J., & Brooks, S. (2013). An updated theoretical and practical model for promoting historical empathy. *Social Studies Research and Practice, 8*(1), 41–58.

Fantham, E., Foley, H. P., Kampen, N. B., Pomeroy, S. B., & Shapiro, H. A. (Eds.). (1994). *Women in the classical world: Image and text*. New York, NY: Oxford University Press.

Feinberg, L. (1996). *Transgender warriors: Making history from Joan of Arc to RuPaul*. Boston, MA: Beacon Press.

Graham, S. (2002). Sex, gender, and priests in South Sulawesi, Indonesia. *International Institute for Asian Studies, 29*, 27.

Harrison, K. (2014). *Joan of Arc: A life transfigured* (1st ed.). New York, NY: Doubleday.

Hughes, K. (2017). *Victorians undone: Tales of the flesh in the age of decorum*. Baltimore, MD: Johns Hopkins University Press.

Jaschik, S. (2005, February 18). What Larry Summers said. *Inside Higher Ed*. Retrieved from https://www.insidehighered.com/news/2005/02/18/summers2_18

Kilman, C. (2013). The gender spectrum. *Teaching Tolerance Newsletter, 44*(Summer), n.p. Retrieved from https://www.tolerance.org/magazine/summer-2013/the-gender-spectrum

Mayo Jr., J. B., & Sheppard, M. (2012). New social learning from two spirit Native Americans. *The Journal of Social Studies Research, 36*(3), 263–282.

Praeger, S. (2017). *Queer, there, and everywhere: 23 people who changed the world*. New York, NY: HarperCollins.

Rubarth, S. (2014). Competing constructions of masculinity in ancient Greece. *Athens Journal of Humanities & Arts, 1*(1), 21–32.

Sauer, M. M. (2015). *Gender in medieval culture*. London: Bloomsbury Academic.

Sheppard, M., & Mayo Jr., J. B. (2013). The social construction of gender and sexuality: Learning from two spirit traditions. *The Social Studies, 104*(6), 259–270. https://doi.org/10.1080/00377996.2013.788472.

Tayler, H. (Contributor). (2016, May 29). Writing excuses [Audio podcast]. Retrieved from http://www.writingexcuses.com/2016/05/29/11-22-examining-unconscious-biases-with-shannon-hale/

Williams, W. (2010). The "two-spirit" people of indigenous North Americans. *The Guardian*. Retrieved from https://www.theguardian.com/music/2010/oct/11/two-spirit-people-north-america

CHAPTER THIRTEEN

Race

KRISTEN E. DUNCAN, CLEMSON UNIVERSITY

> Racism, unfortunately, is part of the fabric of America's society.
>
> —GEORGIA STATE REPRESENTATIVE DAVID SCOTT, NPR, AUGUST 12, 2009

It is commonly understood that racism is deeply threaded into the history of the United States beginning with the seizing land from Native Americans, importing Africans as chattel, and legally allowing discrimination of people based on race during the Jim Crow era, Chinese Exclusion Act, and Japanese internment. There are some people, however, who believe that the race problem was solved during the Civil Rights Movement, when the Civil Rights Act of 1964 and Voting Rights Act of 1965 were passed. Additionally, many people believed that racism was eradicated with the election of President Barack Obama in 2008. Black and White people can eat lunch together in restaurants, children of different races attend the same schools, and there are no signs designating "White" and "Colored" water fountains. Racism is over and race is no longer a problem in the United States.

Not so fast, my friend. The acquittal of George Zimmerman for the murder of Trayvon Martin, along with police officers not being charged for the deaths of numerous people of color including Michael Brown, Eric Garner, and Rekia Boyd, were a clear indicator and wake up call for many people that racism is still alive and kicking in the United States. Add to this racial disparities in healthcare, education, and a successful presidential campaign that was launched by referring to Mexicans as rapists, and racism is once again front-and-center in the American psyche. The question, then, is: How do we begin to dismantle the racism that many people believed to be over? The key to tackling issues of race and racism actually lies in a concept called racial literacy (Guinier, 2004). So while this chapter is about race, my goal is to introduce social studies teachers and teacher educators to this concept so that we can begin working toward it with students.

SOCIAL STUDIES AND RACE: TRANSFORMATIVE OR STAGNANT?

Although social studies is the only subject in which teachers are explicitly charged with teaching about racism, many social studies education scholars have found the ways race and racism are presented in social studies curricula and curricular materials to be unacceptable. In fact, a number of scholars have offered critiques for the ways in which social studies textbooks and curricula present issues of race and racism (Busey, 2014; King, 2014; Ladson-Billings, 2003; Padgett, 2015; Pellegrino, Mann, & Russell, 2013; Woodson, 2015; Woyshner & Schocker, 2015). These critiques are not exclusive to the United States either, as scholars have critiqued the ways in which social studies curricula and materials address race around the world, including in Portugal (Araújo & Rodríguez Maeso, 2012), the Netherlands (Weiner, 2014), Canada (Montgomery, 2005), and South Africa (Morgan, 2010; Morgan & Henning, 2011). It appears that representations of race and racism in social studies curricula and materials is a worldwide problem, as scholars have critiqued the ways in which racially and ethnically marginalized groups are presented in curricula and textbooks, as well as the ways that curricula and texts present historical events and phenomena that involve racism.

Concerning curricula and texts utilized in social studies classrooms in the United States: many studies have found that while these materials do address race and racism, they do so in ways that leave students with an oversimplified understanding of racism and the ways in which vestiges of historical racism continue to linger in contemporary American society. For example, Alridge (2006) found that the messianic master narratives that high school U.S. history textbooks used to present Martin Luther King, Jr. offered a "sanitized, noncontroversial, oversimplified view of perhaps one of America's most radical leaders" and left students "deprived of a conceptual lens that would help them better comprehend the world around them" (p. 680). Additionally, Brown and Brown (2010a, 2010b) call attention to the issue that although elementary and middle school social studies textbooks frequently provide vivid accounts of racial violence directed toward Black people, they rarely acknowledge the larger implications of this violence, including structural and institutional racism. They also position these texts as problematic, because they leave students to understand racism as a collection of disjointed, individual actions or beliefs, as opposed to helping students understand how systems of oppression work to maintain a particular power structure based on race.

Overwhelmingly, researchers have argued that the ways that social studies curricula and textbooks address race is problematic. Textbooks and curricula that leave students with these reductive and distorted impressions regarding the historical legacy and far-reaching implications of racism contribute to students' (and Americans' at-large) impressions that racism is merely an act or set of beliefs that only those who lack morality would dare engage in. These beliefs help to support a mindset of racial liberalism, which ultimately works to maintain a racial hierarchy. In the next section, I will provide definitions for race, racism, and racial literacy, and I will also explain why it is so important that students acquire racial literacy.

MORE THAN SKIN DEEP

What Is Racism?

Omi and Winant (1986) explain that "the meaning of race is defined and contested throughout society" (p. 61), which is clear in the different ways scholars have defined and race and racism. Delgado and Stefancic (2012) define race as the "notion of a distinct biological type of human being, usually based on skin color or other physical characteristics" (p. 170), adding that race is the means by which power is distributed in the United States and throughout the world. Other scholars contend that racism is solely a social construct that exists because of the ways people think about differences in people (Appiah, 1992). Regarding racism, Scheurich and Young (1997) reference four different types, including individual, institutional, societal, and civilizational racism. Individual racism, which manifests both overtly and covertly, is the type of racism students are most familiar with. This takes place when a person exercises prejudice and discrimination against another person based on race. Institutional racism, however, presents itself when "institutions or organizations, including educational ones, have standard operating procedures (intended or unintended) that hurt members of one or more races in relation to members of the dominant race" (Scheurich & Young, 1997, p. 5). These scholars also define societal racism as societal or cultural norms that benefit one race over another, and civilizational racism as a form of racism that permeates a civilization so deeply that most members of a civilization do not understand their assumptions to be racist (Scheurich & Young, 1997). In addition to these four types of racism, structural and systemic racism also affect the daily lives of people of color in the United States. John A. Powell (2008) writes that it is important to pay close attention to structural racism, because

> Institutional racism shifts our focus from the motives of individual people to practices and procedures within an institution. Structural racism shifts our attention from the single, intra-institutional setting to inter-institutional arrangements and interactions. Efforts to identify causation at a particular moment of decision within a specific domain understate the cumulative effects of discrimination. (p. 796)

Finally, Feagin and Elias (2013) discuss the concept of systemic racism, referring to it as "the foundational, large-scale and inescapable hierarchical system of U.S. racial oppression devised and maintained by whites and directed at people of colour" (p. 936). They also note that systemic racism is deeply ingrained in American society, as racial oppression was a foundational aspect of the history of the United States. Of all the types of racism discussed here, systemic racism most explicitly ties the race to power, understanding that while institutions and networks may change, the racial hierarchy that was put in place at the founding of this nation continues to be upheld (Feagin & Elias, 2013).

What Is Racial Literacy?

As one can easily see, racism is much more than individual people discriminating against people of different races. Racism exists at the individual, institutional, societal, civilizational, structural, and systemic levels, and is explicitly linked to the power in the United States and throughout the world. Unfortunately, most students only have the opportunity to learn about individual racism in their social studies classes. While they generally learn that racism is a horrendous act, they learn that it is just that—an act, perpetuated by individual actors who are generally bad people (Brown & Brown, 2010b). This can leave students with the impression that just because they do not use racial epithets or actively discriminate, they cannot be involved or implicit in perpetuating racism. When social studies is taught through this lens, one of racial liberalism, students learn the horrors that individual and institutional acts of racism can create, but they do not learn how to recognize other forms of racism or the relationship between race and power, which does them a disservice. Teaching students only about individual and institutional racism only allows them to see the tip of the racism iceberg. In the words of Lani Guinier (2004), teaching students from a standpoint of racial liberalism is to treat the symptoms, while ignoring "the greater and more pernicious disease—white supremacy" (p. 99). Guinier, introduced the concept of racial literacy, which

> Emphasizes the relationship between race and power. Racial literacy reads race in its psychological, interpersonal, and structural dimensions. It acknowledges the importance of individual agency but refuses to lose sight of institutional and environmental forces that both shape and reflect that agency. (Guinier, 2004, p. 115)

Additionally, while racial literacy never turns its focus away from race, it does not focus exclusively on race, and instead, includes the notion of intersectionality (Crenshaw, 1988) and the ways that other aspects of identity, including gender, class, and geography among others, intersect with race to create the racialized hierarchies that mirror the distribution of power in the United States (Guinier, 2004). This is important, because these intersections allow us to see where interests converge among different racial groups, and taking advantage of these points of convergence is critical if we are working toward dismantling the racial hierarchy that has been in place for centuries. In the next section, I will discuss ways that social studies educators, teacher educators, and researchers can help the field move from a stance of racial liberalism to one of racial literacy.

SOCIAL STUDIES AS A SITE FOR RACIAL LITERACY

K–12 Students

As scholars have indicated on multiple occasions and in multiple contexts, the curricula and texts that teachers are required to use in social studies courses encourage racial liberalism and fail to challenge students to think critically about racial hierarchies and how they have managed to persist over centuries, despite the notion that racially marginalized groups supposedly acquired freedom and equal rights at various points throughout the history of the United States. The question then, is how do we move students from a stance of racial liberalism to one of racial literacy? There are several measures that those of us who work in different facets of social studies education can take in helping students become more racially literate, helping students understand the connection between race and power.

In their study of humanities teachers who practiced a culturally relevant pedagogy and taught students to become racially literate, Epstein and Gist (2015) found that each of the teachers in their study had discussions with students in which they explicitly explained race as a social construct that changed in different historical contexts. In fact, each teacher began the school year with a one- to two-week unit in which they challenged students' perceptions of the biological nature of race. It is imperative that teachers engage students in this way, because as one participant noted, "For all their talk about race, they don't have a clear view of it" (Epstein & Gist, 2015, p. 51). Teachers may be unsure of how to go about discussing race with their students could begin by taking suggestions from Hess (2011) and Woodson and Duncan (2017). Hess suggests fostering a classroom climate of respect, teaching students how to engage in civil discourse, and holding them accountable to the norms of that discourse. Woodson and Duncan discuss maintaining a psychologically safe space through the racial blunders that will likely take place in attempts to discuss race in social studies classrooms. Understanding these ideas is the very foundation for beginning to discuss a topic like race.

Beyond explicit definitions of the meaning of race and the ways it changes with historical context, there are a number of ways social studies teachers can use the content they are charged to teach to help students become racially literate. Teachers can begin by using the standards as a starting point to help students gain racial literacy. My first suggestion focuses on the points at which race is addressed in social studies curricula and courses. Typically, students learn about issues of race and racism in the United States in a historical context, which means they likely only learn about racism in history courses, or possibly, government courses. Geography, economics, and most government content are presented to students as if they are race-neutral and affect all people equally. Students need to learn about the relationship between race and power in each of these content areas, and studying topics such as redlining, the War on Drugs, and immigration law, and the ways these policies adversely and disproportionately affect people of color in the United States. Teachers could also work to make students aware of the ways that racist policies of the past continue to affect the lived experiences of racially marginalized people. This will help students understand that policies are rarely race neutral and that economic and educational disparities between races are not coincidental or due to deficits in particular racial groups.

Another suggestion for social studies teachers working toward helping students become racially literate involves having students study the plantation economy. Most states have social studies curriculum standards that require students learn about the institution of slavery and its role in colonial and Antebellum America. It is common for students learning about this historical period to learn about the role the cotton played in the plantation economy, but students rarely get a chance to delve more deeply and gain a more thorough understanding of the institution of slavery, the horrors it produced, and who benefitted from it. Instead of teaching students that only wealthy plantation owners benefitted from slavery, social studies teachers could have students research institutions and corporations that benefitted from slavery. Engaging in this research will allow students to see that many of the institutions and corporations that benefitted from the enslavement of African people are fully operational today, and many prestigious colleges and universities are among that count. After completing this research, students will better understand how the enslavement of African people laid the foundation for the current economic system of the United States.

Teacher Education

A large reason why students are not learning racial literacy in their social studies classes is because their teachers operate from a stance of racial liberalism and have not yet achieved racial literacy. Because of this, it is imperative that social studies teacher education programs help preservice teachers understand and work toward racial literacy so that they can then do the same with their students. King (2016) found that preservice teachers who had access to a Black history reader taught about race and Black history in ways that were more critical compared to the ways U.S. history has traditionally been taught. King also found, however, that participants continued to marginalize the topic of race, treating it as an addendum to the curriculum, as opposed to embedding race and racism throughout the entire social studies curriculum. As teacher educators, we have to make the invisible aspects of racism become visible to preservice teachers. We could aid preservice teachers in this journey by having them explore race not only in the context of U.S. history but all in other aspects of their education, including their universities, field placements and their own classrooms. Teacher educators could ask preservice teachers to examine why some field placements are more diverse than others, as well as the racial demographics of the students in the room and the field of teaching at-large. Students could interrogate why the teaching field is overwhelmingly White, although the majority of American public school students are children of color. They could study how this came to be, including the firing of Black teachers after schools desegregated, as well as what consequences this disproportionality may have for students. Beginning to answer questions like these can help students can help students see the role that racism plays in situations that they may have previously believed to be race neutral. Hopefully, examining these kinds of topics will help students begin to look at other situations more critically, as well.

Researchers

While it is well documented that the field of social studies education research has had a contentious relationship with the topic of race (Ladson-Billings, 2003; Howard, 2003), there has been an increase in the amount of research literature that focuses on race and racism. There is startlingly little research, however, that deals with the concept of racial literacy. If teacher educators are to help preservice teachers become racially literate in an effort to lead students to gain racial literacy, we need more research regarding how teachers go about working to help students become racially literate in addition to becoming racially literate themselves. The work of Epstein and Gist (2015) and King (2016) is a tremendous start, but it just that—a start. After finding teachers who engage in these practices, researchers need to discover what kinds of questions they are asking students to consider and how well students are able to understand the racial hierarchy of the United States as a result of this instruction. Such research will ultimately benefit teacher educators and classroom teachers, while contributing to the growing body of social studies education research that focuses on race.

CONCLUSION

It is precisely because race is such a contentious subject that social studies classrooms are the place where students should be learning about the relationship between race and power and the role that racism has played in the founding, development, and current status of the United States. If social studies classrooms are supposed to be the place where students learn about democracy, those same classrooms should be the places where students learn about the ways that racism impedes democracy. Teachers can work toward this by moving away from teaching racial liberalism—a philosophy that merely maintains the current racial hierarchy—and helping students become racially literate. Guiding students toward racial literacy helps students make explicit connections between race and power, in addition to understanding the role that structures and institutions play in creating and maintaining racial hierarchies. Helping students become racially literate also requires that they acknowledge and understand the concept of intersectionality. Hopefully, taking these steps will help students have a more comprehensive understanding of racism than current social studies curricula and texts generally allow. While racial liberalism treats only a few of the symptoms of the cancer that is racism, racial literacy allows educators the opportunity help students see the root of the problem.

REFERENCES

Alridge, D. P. (2006). The limits of master narratives in history textbooks: An analysis of representations of Martin Luther King, Jr. *Teachers College Record, 108*(4), 662–686.

Appiah, K. (1992). *In my father's house*. New York, NY: Oxford University Press.

Araújo, M., & Rodríguez Maeso, S. (2012). History textbooks, racism and the critique of Eurocentrism: Beyond rectification or compensation. *Ethnic and Racial Studies, 35*(7), 1266–1286.

Brown, A. L., & Brown, K. D. (2010a). 'A spectacular secret:' Understanding the cultural memory of racial violence in K-12 official school textbooks in the era of Obama. *Race, Gender & Class, 17*(3/4), 111–125.

Brown, K. D., & Brown, A. L. (2010b). Silenced memories: An examination of the sociocultural knowledge on race and racial violence in official school curriculum. *Equity & Excellence in Education, 43*(2), 139–154.

Busey, C. (2014). Examining race from within: Black intraracial discrimination in social studies curriculum. *Social Studies Research & Practice, 9*(2), 120–131.

Crenshaw, K. W. (1988). Race, reform, and retrenchment: Transformation and legitimation in anti-discrimination law. *Harvard Law Review, 101*(7), 1331–1387.

Delgado, R., & Stefancic, J. (2012). *Critical race theory: An introduction*. New York, NY: New York University Press.

Epstein, T., & Gist, C. (2015). Teaching racial literacy in secondary humanities classrooms: Challenging adolescents' of color concepts of race and racism. *Race, Ethnicity and Education, 18*(1), 40–60.

Feagin, J., & Elias, S. (2013). Rethinking racial formation theory: A systemic racism critique. *Ethnic and Racial Studies, 36*(6), 931–960.

Guinier, L. (2004). From racial liberalism to racial literacy: Brown v. Board of Education and the interest-divergence dilemma. *The Journal of American History, 91*(1), 92–118.

Hess, D. (2011). Discussions that drive democracy. *Educational Leadership, 69*(1), 69–73.

Howard, T. (2003). The dis(g)race of the social studies. In G. Ladson-Billings (Ed.), *Critical race perspectives on social studies: The profession, policies, and curriculum* (pp. 27–44). Greenwich, CT: Information Age Publishing.

King, L. J. (2014). When lions write history: Black history textbooks, African-American educators, & the alternative Black curriculum in social studies education, 1890–1940. *Multicultural Education, 22*(1), 2–11.

King, L. J. (2016). Teaching Black history as a racial literacy project. *Race Ethnicity and Education, 19*(6), 1303–1318.

Ladson-Billings, G. (2003). Lies my teacher still tells: Developing a critical race perspective toward the social studies. In G. Ladson-Billings (Ed.), *Critical race theory perspectives on the social studies: The profession, policies, and curriculum* (pp. 1–14). Greenwich, CT: Information Age Publishing.

Montgomery, K. (2005). Banal race-thinking: Ties of blood, Canadian history textbooks and ethnic nationalism. *Paedagogica Historica, 41*(3), 313–336.

Morgan, K. (2010). Scholarly and values-driven objectives in two South African school history textbooks: An analysis of topics of race and racism. *Historical Social Research, 35*(3), 299–322.

Morgan, K., & Henning, E. (2011). How school history textbooks position a textual community through the topic of racism / Hoe geskiedenis handboeke deur die onderwerp van rassisme 'n tekstuele gemeenskap positioneer. *Historia, 56*(2), 169–190.

Omi, M., & Winant, H. (1986). *Racial formation in the United States: From the 1960s to the 1980s.* New York, NY: Routledge & Kegan Paul.

Padgett, G. (2015). A critical case study of selected U.S. history textbooks from a tribal critical race theory perspective. *The Qualitative Report, 20*(3), 153–171.

Pellegrino, A., Mann, L., & Russell, W. I. (2013). To lift as we climb: A textbook analysis of the segregated school experience. *High School Journal, 96*(3), 209–231.

Powell, J. A. (2008). A tribute to professor John O. Calmore: Structural racism: Building upon the insights of John Calmore. *North Carolina Law Review, 86*, 791–816.

Scheurich, J. J., & Young, M. D. (1997). Coloring epistemologies: Are our research epistemologies racially biased? *Educational Researcher, 26*(4), 4–16.

Weiner, M. (2014). (E)racing slavery: Racial neoliberalism, social forgetting, and scientific colonialism in Dutch primary school history textbooks. *Du Bois Review-Social Science Research on Race, 11*(2), 329–351.

Woodson, A. N. (2015). "What you supposed to know": Black urban students' perspectives on history textbooks and civil rights leaders. *Journal of Urban Teaching, Learning and Research, 11*, 57–65.

Woodson, A. N., & Duncan, K. (2017). When keeping it real goes wrong: Race talk, racial blunders, and redemption. In C. Martell (Ed.), *Social studies teacher education: Critical issues and current perspectives.* Greenwich, CT: Information Age Publishing.

Woyshner, C., & Schocker, J. (2015). Cultural parallax and content analysis: Images of Black women in high school history textbooks. *Theory & Research in Social Education, 43*(4), 441–468.

CHAPTER FOURTEEN

Sexuality

DANIEL T. BORDWELL, UNIVERSITY OF MINNESOTA
RYAN D. OTO, UNIVERSITY OF MINNESOTA
J.B. MAYO, JR., UNIVERSITY OF MINNESOTA

[W]ords, ideas, and ideals (like "heterosexual") are among our major means of production. Our struggle over the ownership, control, and shaping of those means is key to the future of heterosexuality, the other existing sexualities, and the new sexualities to come.

—Jonathan Ned Katz (1995)

The first study that reflected national health risks for LGB (lesbian, gay, bisexual) high school students was released by the Centers for Disease Control in 2016. Looking at more than 15,000 students sampled from 25 states, the study found that when compared to their heterosexual peers, LGB students were more likely to have been physically forced to have sex, experienced physical and sexual dating violence, and bullied at school or online (CDC, 2016). Further, 40% have seriously considered suicide, with 29% reporting having attempted suicide in the past 12 months, and one in ten students reported missing school due to safety concerns (CDC, 2016). The implications of these issues "demonstrates the importance of school, community, and family support for LGB students" (CDC, 2016). It should be no surprise then to view these data as what they are a "parade of horribles" (McHaelin quoted in Tamarkin, 2007).

While laudable in its efforts to recognize the issues surrounding sexuality in schooling, the CDC report lacks a critical lens to grasp the complex power dynamics of sexuality and society. One example is the lack of inclusivity from the CDC study, solely focusing on LGB students. To acknowledge this absence, we will be using the LGBQ+ acronym for the rest of the chapter to include queerness and existence of other sexualities not yet defined, as described with our opening quotation. We also are not including the T representing transgender as that is a marker of gender identity and expression, not sexuality. Through schools' explicit, implicit, and null curricula, a clear message emerges: Sexuality is heterosexuality. Those who express a different form of sexuality are the Other. In this chapter, we first examine how sexuality is most commonly understood within the pervasive web of heteronormativity. Then we explore our collective experiences as two cis-male, straight teachers working with explicit, implicit, and null curricula in teaching sexuality to our high school students and one cis-male gay professor working within the context of a university. Finally, we report on where social studies education research has come in exposing and explicitly engaging issues of sexuality, while offering suggestions for future research. In the end, we believe social studies researchers, teachers, and graduate students interested in taking up *sexuality* within the social studies field will have a more nuanced understanding of its meaning and impact within our field.

ESTABLISHING HETERONORMATIVITY

Understanding contemporary classroom challenges linked to heteronormativity requires an overview of how homosexuality and heterosexuality have been constructed and theorized. While sexuality was present in ancient historical societies (e.g., the Greeks), its presence does not mean it existed in the same forms with analogous societal meanings to today's conceptualization. Padgug (1979) warned that "categories [such as heterosexual and homosexual] had no meaning in antiquity" (p. 13). As such, this synthesis of theorization of sexuality will intentionally focus on the formation of contemporary understandings.

Modern understandings of sexuality have precariously revolved around scientifically categorizing homosexuality through observation and medicine. Katz (1995) noted that even within the first widely published study of heterosexuality, it explicitly described homosexuality as "pathological" because same-sex desire was nonreproductive and thus, antithetical to heterosexuality as "the reproductive instinct" (p. 21–22). The normalization of heterosexuality and marginalization of homosexuality was further "stabilized, fixed, and widely distributed as the ruling sexual orthodoxy" in the early 20th century by men in the medical field, particularly Freud (Katz, 1995, p. 82). As a result, heterosexuality became equated with biological reproduction, and therefore, natural. Heteronormativity was born.

Widely considered a pillar of the study of sexuality, Foucault (1978) was one of the first contemporary philosophers to challenge heteronormative assumptions about sexuality. With precise historical research, Foucault traced the genealogy of sexuality in the medical field to demonstrate sexuality was constructed and not a natural given. Many scholars found themselves influenced by Foucault's work, proving sexuality was socially constructed and applied his approach to making sense of homosexuality (D'Emilio, 1992; Faderman, 1985; Halperin, 1990; Katz, 1976; Traub, 1995; Weeks, 1977). While ground-breaking and important theoretical shifts about homosexuality led to continual disruption of heteronormativity, heterosexuality remained relatively unexplored, often being considered an "unremarkable" sexual phenomenon (Jagose, 1996, p. 16). However, works by Cohen (1993) and Katz (1995) disrupted this normality by demonstrating heterosexuality's social and historical constructions.

Amidst the expanding discourse about heterosexuality and homosexuality emerged a new wing of sexuality scholars: queer theorists. Sedgwick (1990) critiqued the binary of homosexual and heterosexual culled from society's changing understanding of sexuality. She viewed this binary as a way to simultaneously monitor and create universal sex-norms that make sexuality easier to understand. However, Sedgwick contended this was problematic because it fixes definitions to sexuality, thereby reproducing the same oppressive normative powers that scholars have sought to disrupt in heteronormativity. Instead, Sedgwick invited people to consider sexuality a fluid and subjective part of identity where self-assignment matters more than societal conventions.

Sedgwick's work was groundbreaking, and while heavily informed by Foucault's work on sexuality, Sedgwick viewed Butler's theorizing about gender and sexuality as more influential to queer theory. In Butler's piece, *Undoing Gender* (1990), she challenged the idea that gender identities are constructed in the same manner that sexuality has been. She argued that society has come to a point wherein "certain kinds of identities cannot exist," identities in which gender does not follow from sex and those in which the practices of desire do not "follow" from either gender or sex (Butler, 1990, p. 17). Butler suggested the reason that this is so is because gender, along with sexuality, are ongoing practices that require constant performances to maintain a male/heteronormative status quo. Examples of this *performativity*, as Butler defined it, include a father telling his son to stop being such a girl because the son is crying after falling off of his bike; a mother telling her daughter to stop playing outside because she might get her shirt dirty; a coach telling his boys youth team they need to "man up" to win. Beck (2013) applied Butler's theory of performativity to sexuality in classrooms and, unsurprisingly, found that sexuality finds stable definition through analogous normative acts and language. Sayings like "that's so gay" or "no homo" define sexuality by othering homosexuality and normalizing silence around heterosexuality. As a result, discourse centered on sexuality seems inextricably linked to talk about homosexuality, when the reality is that this is another performance.

CLASSROOM EXPERIENCES WITH DIFFERENT FORMS OF CURRICULUM

When the 2002 special issue of *Theory & Research in Social Education (TRSE)* on gender and sexuality was published, same-sex marriage was illegal in the United States, *Don't Ask/Don't Tell* was military policy, anti-sodomy laws were constitutional, and many other laws and policies existed that viewed deviations from heteronormativity as wrong. Thornton (2002) noted that the social studies curriculum made the assumption that "all persons mentioned in the social studies curriculum are heterosexual until proven otherwise" (p. 179) and that this message was found loud and clear in explicit, implicit, and null curricula.

In the time that has passed since that special issue of *TRSE,* same-sex marriage has been legalized, *Don't Ask/Don't Tell* has been dismantled, and anti-sodomy laws have been deemed unconstitutional. Yet, less than a third of states have anti-discriminatory laws protecting LGBQ+ people as a class (GLAD, 2016). Additionally, the 2016 election and presidency of Donald J. Trump has led to increasing fears across the country that LGBQ+ rights will be rolled back. As we continue this chapter, we summarize existing literature and share personal experiences as classroom teachers to show that social studies classrooms, and schools more generally, are still spaces where sexuality is viewed through a binary lens as either gay or straight in the explicit, implicit, and null curricula.

Explicit Curriculum

The explicit social studies curriculum "avoids even mentioning the existence of gay people, both past and present" (Thornton, 2002, p. 179–180). I have seen this occur in my (Daniel) experience as a high school social studies teacher. Some researchers (e.g., Symcox, 2002) have examined the standards-making process as a means for promoting certain agendas (e.g., neoliberal or conservative values). Under the standards that guide my curriculum planning (the Minnesota Social Studies Standards), there is no inclusion or mentioning of LGBQ+ people, their movements, causes, or topics. The silence presented in these standards on sexuality presumes the heteronormative status quo to be the one, true way to teach.

I have seen a district take this to a new level of intolerance. In 2009, the Anoka-Hennepin School District created the "Sexual Orientation Curriculum Policy," which was commonly referred to as the "Neutrality Policy." This policy affirmed that the school board was "committed to providing a safe and respectful learning environment and to provide an education that respects the beliefs of all students and families" and then went on to say,

Teaching about sexual orientation is not a part of the District adopted curriculum; rather, such matters are best addressed within individual family homes, churches, or community organizations. Anoka-Hennepin staff, in the course of their professional duties, shall remain neutral on matters regarding sexual orientation including but not limited to student led discussions. If and when staff address sexual orientation, it is important that staff do so in a respectful manner that is age-appropriate, factual, and pertinent to the relevant curriculum. Staff are encouraged to take into consideration individual student needs and refer students to the appropriate social worker or licensed school counselor. (Anoka-Hennepin)

At the time, the District's superintendent told CNN that the district's community was diverse "and what we're trying to do, what I'm trying to do as a superintendent, is walk down the middle of the road" (Harlow, 2011). As we have shown in this chapter, "the middle of the road" isn't so middle. Fortunately, this policy was changed, but only after a settlement with the United States Department of Justice in 2012. This is one example of an explicit policy. The implication for teachers was clear: be silent or face violating the employer's policy. This double bind only perpetuated the heteronormative notions of sexuality in an explicit manner.

Implicit Curriculum

Thornton (2002) described the implicit curriculum as "loud… [and] boldly antigay. In classrooms, hallways, and lunchrooms, the boundaries of sex behavior are heavily patrolled" (p. 180). In trying to think of a time that sexuality was brought up in my own social studies learning experiences, I (Ryan) seem only capable of recalling the implicit curriculum around me, such as the off-hand remarks by peers saying, "this is so gay" or the seemingly arbitrary question a student would have for a teacher about whether or not they were married that normalized heterosexual relationships. But I cannot think of moments when sexuality was directly addressed in social studies curriculum. Even amid rising discussion about equal rights in same-sex marriage, my civics class never discussed it. The silence was normal. On occasion, a history teacher might bring up sexuality as a quirk or historic mystery to garner attention saying, "and did you know that Alexander the Great might also be gay?! Moving on…" Such acts served to implicitly reinforce the oddity of nonheterosexual behavior.

The subtle nature of implicit curriculum, how it ebbs and flows invisibly through a school is what makes it so important to understand. Reflecting on my own teaching, I see myself as a social activist, with little reservation when it comes to tackling issues of inequity in the classroom. Yet, there have been numerous occasions that I let pass into my classroom the teachings of the implicit curriculum. When a student was slow to join a group for an activity because they believed a peer was gay, I did nothing. While answering a question in economics about opportunity cost and whether a person should go on a date or work, a male student responds, "She'll wait." I challenged his misogyny that felt overt in the moment, but the opportunity to name the heteronormative power of the statement escaped. In these moments of reflection, I am aware of the danger silences like mine can do. They assist in the making of the false binary between "normal" and Other. Thinking more deeply about sexuality in my classroom, I have come to realize how little I know and how the implicit curriculum demands constant scrutiny to overcome. I wonder if asking the student who says "that's so gay" to choose different language really accomplishes the work of disrupting the implicit curriculum. Or is the lesson learned that silence precedes understanding in my classroom?

Null Curriculum

Thornton (2002) claimed the null curriculum is "what schools do not teach. Ignorance is not merely a neutral void. It has consequences for what we are able to think about and what alternatives we can consider" (p. 180). We both have the epistemological orientation that sees schools, and social studies in particular, as sites for social justice. Yet we have both have been, rightly, called out by our students for things we haven't known.

One example of this from my (Ryan) own teaching came during the unit on WWII and the rise of fascism in Germany. As we explored the texts about the growing sentiments of anti-Semitism, one student asked about Magnus Hirschfield, the man who founded the Institute for the Science of Sexuality in the 1930s. I knew nothing of this man or his work, and in this moment, the void within me grew exponentially and my stomach lurched. It was clear this student knew more than me in this instance, and this topic was of personal relevance given the passion in their voice. The fear of not knowing felt overwhelming as I weighed in the endless moments whether to feign understanding or admit ignorance. I felt ashamed and that as a teacher with a social justice frame, I was denying sexuality its place within the classroom. My not-knowing perpetuated heteronormativity, simply because I didn't know. It is this torturous moment that exemplifies the effect of the null curriculum at play.

In my (Daniel) experience, I have a hard time finding a moment when a student raised an issue of sexuality new to me. For years, I taught the Fourteenth Amendment focusing exclusively on race. Years later, when I heard legal arguments centering on same-sex marriage, I started viewing the amendment through a sexuality lens. Those intervening years were years where I did teach sexuality. It took years for me to recognize that my silence promoted the heteronormative notions we have described in this chapter. None of us can know what we do not know. This failure has impacts on all that we do and believe, all while being hidden and unrecognized.

Due to its elusive nature, we believe that the null is the most dangerous of the three curricula. How does a teacher account for their unknown unknowns? What message does the silence send? How might students recognize or fail to recognize a teacher's ignorance, intended or not? How might this implicate us as oppressors?

The unique expectation for social studies teachers to cover a wide range of topics with expertise is daunting. Our expertise is only as deep as the epistemologies that guided us to become teachers. Our schooling, teacher preparation courses, professional development, and past experiences inform our expertise. What chances then do we have to disrupt heteronormativity if sexuality remains unexplored in these sites?

WHERE WE STAND AS A FIELD OF STUDY

Daniel and Ryan have laid out compelling examples from their experience as classroom teachers about their collective understanding of sexuality within the social studies. What is striking is that while they both (now) have a nuanced *intellectual* grasp of the term and its history, their classroom teaching experience closely mirrors the limitations voiced by many of their colleagues in the social studies field. It seems clear that sexuality and sexual orientation are synonymous. Just as we stated earlier in this chapter that "sexuality is heterosexuality," sexual orientation is understood as a normalized and automatically assumed straight orientation toward the opposite sex. Linville (2009) referred to sexuality as "romantic attractions, sexual behaviors, sexual identity and desires, as well as the presumed embodied existence of these characteristics" (p. 155). This definition may potentially disrupt the field's common understanding of sexuality because it adds the layers of "attractions and behaviors," although it is highly unlikely social studies teachers will engage their students in discussions and/or classroom activities centered on queer sexual behaviors. But perhaps an overview of the research on sexuality within the social studies will uncover some spaces that will allow a more nuanced understanding of the term to surface.

Unsurprisingly, a review of the literature reveals that sexuality is commonly understood as a hidden or erased identity marker that prevents most social studies teachers from engaging the full humanity of individuals over time, effectively limiting the degree to which justice, equity, and students' acceptance of non-normative sexualities might be achieved. With an acknowledgment of the wisdom of Ladson-Billings (2003), Woodson (2016) said it best: "Whatever the reasons may be, there is a silence or a discourse of invisibility that frames our [social studies] curriculum through 'structures that continue to render many of our lived experiences invisible'" (p. 10). There is some evidence, however, that once revealed, sexuality as a human identity marker may lead to positive outcomes for present-day students in social studies classrooms. Therefore, a primary emphasis of some social studies researchers has been to highlight the sexual identities of various individuals or groups throughout history (Donahue, 2014; Hess, 2007; Mayo & Sheppard, 2012; Sheppard & Mayo, 2013; Thornton, 2003). Maguth and Taylor (2014) called upon social studies teachers to reveal more comprehensive, personal histories when talking about the worldviews, lifestyles, and advocacy of individuals like Jane Addams, Susan B. Anthony, Harvey Milk, James Baldwin and others whose sexual orientation remain hidden within the text. Pointing out that many key historical figures were lesbian, gay, bisexual, or queer disrupts the common-sense assumption (Kumashiro, 2009) that all of them were straight. It may also lead one to conclude that LGBQ+-identified people contributed to society in significant ways, which helps undo the demonized narrative that surrounds and sometimes engulfs queer people. As a result, present-day LGBQ+-identified people, and LGBQ+ youth, in particular, are provided with role models and the knowledge that they too can be contributing members of their various communities and to society writ large, despite any negative messages they might currently be receiving. The explicit naming of non-normative sexualities is by no means a panacea, but it does represent a step forward.

Sexuality is also understood as a point of connection to past and current societal issues. Many social studies teachers believe they have found a safe and appropriate way to bring (homo)sexuality into the classroom by discussing same-sex marriage, for example. Social studies researchers have joined and promoted this line of thinking as they report findings from studies that center marriage equality. Hess (2009) was clear in her belief that students should have been given the opportunity to participate in the recent national debate over same-sex marriage, calling it one of the most significant civil rights issues of our time. Further, she stressed that deliberation on this topic had "the potential to teach students essential content and skills that should be at the core of a democratic education curriculum" (p. 344). Bailey and Cruz (2013) concurred; writing that teaching about same-sex marriage increases critical thinking skills and deepens students' understanding of democratic processes and their awareness that they are "participating in history" (p. 298). Mayo (2016) offered that "marriage equality should be taught as a fundamental topic ... because it is one of many examples of themes that situate lesbian, gay, bisexual, and queer people at the center of the curriculum rather than at the periphery" (p. 85). That said, Journell (2018) strongly suggests teachers no longer treat same-sex marriage as controversial. He believes teachers have a "moral responsibility to frame marriage equality as a settled issue" (2018, n.p.).

Meanwhile, Beck (2013) noted the importance of students engaging in discussions about marriage equality, but he shows deep concern for the well-being of queer-identified students who participate in these discussions. Beck cautioned that it may be time "to consider psychological safety as the primary prerequisite in the CPI [Controversial Public Issues] discussion classroom" (p. 24). He warns that discussions that challenge dominant discourses (like heterosexuality) leave non-normative participants at some level of risk "whether speaking for or against same-sex marriage, students tend[ed] to talk as if LGBTQ students were not in the room—heterosexuality was assumed" (Beck, 2013, p. 22). Therefore, Beck reminds teachers to "be careful not to underestimate the pressure on students to enact the formula that males are masculine, females are feminine, and everyone is heterosexual" (p. 22). While issues centered on sexuality abound outside of school spaces, which make them highly relevant within the social studies classroom and for social studies research, teachers must remain consciously aware of how their lessons are impacting the diverse range of students in their classrooms. As with any number of classroom activities, there is a chance that unintended consequences may occur.

FUTURE RESEARCH

In order to deepen our understanding of sexuality and perhaps expand how it shows up in curriculum and classroom practices, we believe a queered view of the term is needed. Like gender, sexuality is not fixed, rather it is movable and contextual. How individuals identify, experience, or demonstrate their sexuality depends on context. Further, how people interpret and accept various sexualities will change over time. The critique of identity, including sexual identity, is commonly found in queer theoretical writing. Gamson (2000) wrote, "Identities are multiple, contradictory, fragmented … unstable, fluid—hardly the stuff that allows a researcher to confidently run out and study sexual objects as if they were coherent and available social types" (p. 356). In like manner, how can one possibly claim to *know* or understand the nuances surrounding the sexuality of individuals from history? Butler (1991) wrote that she is troubled by identity categories, but calls identity a "necessary error" (Butler, 1993, p. 21). Queer theory allows one to consider (and possibly accept) that blurred spaces *and* individual lived experiences exist between rigid sexual identity categories like lesbian, gay, or bisexual. When combined with the idea of "performance," sexuality may become better understood as partial and complicated, which expands the ways it will be approached by future researchers. We believe that once our collective understanding of sexuality moves beyond simplistic, dichotomous notions of heterosexual and homosexual, new questions will emerge that more fully capture the lived experiences of LGBQ+ individuals, past and present. We call upon future research to move us boldly in those directions.

DISCUSSION QUESTIONS

1. What topics or avenues exist to discuss sexuality in the social studies curriculum?
2. How might a teacher, administrator, family member, or researcher go about disrupting the perceived binaries? How might each role have different approaches to disrupting the binary?
3. Given students' performances of sexuality, gender, etc., how can one truly "know" their identities in social studies classrooms? What is the value of knowing?

REFERENCES

Anoka-Hennepin. (2009). *Sexual orientation curriculum policy.* Retrieved from http://www.edweek.org/media/720_sexorientation-blog.pdf

Bailey, R. W., & Cruz, B. C. (2013). Teaching about gay civil rights: U.S. courts and the law. *Social Education, 77*(6), 298–303.

Beck, T. A. (2013). Identity, discourse, and safety in a high school discussion of same-sex marriage. *Theory & Research in Social Education, 41*, 1–32. doi: 10.1080/00933104.2013.757759.

Butler, J. (1990). *Undoing gender.* New York, NY: Routledge.

Butler, J. (1991). Imitation and gender insubordination. In D. Fuss (Ed.), *Inside/out: Lesbian theories, gay theories* (pp. 13–31). New York, NY: Routledge.

Butler, J. (1993). Critically queer. *GLQ, 1*, 17–32.

Centers for Disease Control and Prevention. (2016). *Health risks among sexual minority youth.* Retrieved from http://www.cdc.gov/healthyyouth/disparities/smy.htm/

Cohen, E. (1993). *Talk on the Wilde side: Towards a genealogy of a discourse on male sexualities.* Hove: Psychology Press.

D'Emilio, J. (1992). *Making trouble: Essays on gay history, politics, and the university.* Hove: Psychology Press.

Donahue, D. M. (2014). Learning from Harvey Milk: The limits and opportunities of one hero to teach about LGBTQ people and issues. *The Social Studies, 105*(1), 36–44.

Faderman, L. (1985). The "New Gay" Lesbians. *Journal of Homosexuality, 10*(3–4), 85–96.

Foucault, M. (1978). *The history of sexuality volume I.* New York, NY: The New Press.

Gamson, J. (2000). Sexualities, queer theory, and qualitative research. In N. K. Denzin & Y. S. Lincoln (Eds.), *Handbook of qualitative research* (pp. 347–365). Thousand Oaks, CA: Sage Publications.

GLAD. (2016). *Anti-LGBT discrimination.* Retrieved from http://http://www.glad.org/rights/topics/c/anti-lgbt-discrimination

Halperin, D. M. (1990). *One hundred years of homosexuality: And other essays on Greek love.* Hove: Psychology Press.

Harlow, P. (2011, July 21). Minnesota school district investigated after civil rights complaint. *CNN.* Retrieved from http://www.cnn.com/2011/US/07/20/minnesota.school.civil.rights.probe/

Hess, D. (2007). From *banished* to *brother outsider, Miss Navajo* to *an inconvenient truth*: Documentary films as perspective-laden narratives. *Social Education, 71*(4), 194–199.

Hess, D. (2009). Teaching about same-sex marriage as a policy and constitutional issue. *Social Education, 73*(7), 344–349.
Jagose, A. (1996). *Queer theory: An introduction.* New York, NY: New York University Press.
Journell, W. (2018). Should marriage equality be taught as controversial post-*Obergefell v Hodges*? *Teachers College Record, 120*(8).
Katz, J. (1976). *Gay American history: Lesbians and gay men in the USA: A documentary history.* London: Plume.
Katz, J. (1995). *The invention of heterosexuality.* Chicago, IL: University of Chicago Press.
Kumashiro, K. K. (2009). *Against common sense: Teaching and learning toward social justice.* New York, NY: Routledge.
Ladson-Billings, G. (2003). Lies my teacher still tells: Developing a critical race perspective toward the social studies. In G. Ladson-Billings (Ed.), *Critical race theory perspectives on the social studies: The profession, policies, and curriculum* (pp. 1–11). Charlotte, NC: Information Age Publishing.
Linville, D. (2009). Queer theory and teen sexuality: Unclear lines. In J. Anyon (Ed.), *Theory and educational research: Toward critical social explanation* (pp. 153–177). New York, NY: Routledge.
Maguth, B. M., & Taylor, N. (2014). Bringing LGBTQ topics into the social studies classroom. *The Social Studies, 105*, 23–28.
Mayo, Jr. J. B. (2016). The imperative to teach marriage equality in the social studies classroom: A history, rationale, and classroom practice for a more inclusive democracy. In W. Journell (Ed.), *Teaching social studies in an era of divisiveness: The challenges of discussing social issues in a non-partisan way* (pp. 79–92). Lanham, MD: Roman & Littlefield.
Mayo, Jr. J. B., & Sheppard, M. G. (2012). New social learning from Two Spirit Native Americans. *The Journal of Social Studies Research, 36*(3), 263–282.
Padgug, R. A. (1979). Sexual matters: On conceptualizing sexuality in history. *Radical History Review, 20*(3), 3–23. doi:10.1215/01636545-1979-20-3.
Sedgwick, E. K. (1990). *Epistemology of the closet.* Berkeley, CA: University of California Press.
Sheppard, M. G., & Mayo, Jr. J. B. (2013). The social construction of gender and sexuality: Learning from two spirit traditions. *The Social Studies, 104*, 259–270. doi:10.1080/00377996.2013.788472.
Symcox, L. (2002). *Whose history? The struggle for national standards in American classrooms.* New York, NY: Teachers College Press.
Tamarkin, S. (2007, June 5). Queer students in search of "Safe Spaces". *New Haven Independent.* Retrieved from http://www.ct.gov/dcf/lib/dcf/latestnews/safe_spaces.pdf/
Thornton, S. J. (2002). Does everybody count as human? *Theory & Research in Social Education, 30*(2), 178–189.
Thornton, S. J. (2003). Silence on gays and lesbians in social studies curriculum. *Social Education, 67*(4), 226–230.
Traub, V. (1995). The psychomorphology of the clitoris. *GLQ: A Journal of Lesbian and Gay Studies, 2*(1 and 2), 81–113.
Weeks, J. (1977). *Coming out: Homosexual politics in Britain, from the nineteenth century to the present.* London: Quartet Books.
Woodson, A. N. (2016). "Less than a vapor": Positioning Black lesbian women in history teacher education. *Journal of Lesbian Studies*, 1–13. doi:10.1080/10894160.2016.1162545.

CHAPTER FIFTEEN

On and On

A Response to the Individual Development and Identity Section

ASHLEY N. WOODSON, UNIVERSITY OF MISSOURI

What will it take to recognize a broader spectrum of raced, sexed, and gendered bodies in social studies education? In their respective keyword entries, Kristen; Megan; and J.B., Daniel and Ryan move toward answering this question. Each chapter frames possible answers differently. Megan opens with examples of gender in history intended to draw readers' attention to shared past and present experiences with gender. Kristen begins by centering teachers; tracing how race shows up in teacher training and professional development, in curricular materials, and in educators' nightmares. J.B., Daniel, and Ryan position queer recognition as a human right, connecting our failures to engage Othered sexual bodies to violence against these bodies in our schools and communities. Though the starting places are quite different, the shared commitment to historically informed, disruptive conceptions of social identity is clear.

In making the case for historically informed conceptions of identity, the authors insist that conversations about race, sexuality, and gender remain connected to similar conversations across time and disciplinary space. Kristen's use of racial literacy is a strong example of this. She argued that racial literacy is necessarily grounded in past philosophies of race and past instantiations of racism: the plantation economy, notions of Black freedom, and structural disparities including redlining and disproportionate rates of incarceration. J.B., Daniel, and Ryan ask for a queered sexual literacy, wherein the "worldviews, lifestyles and advocacy" of those who named themselves as queer or who advanced queer theory are centered in reparative work to acknowledge and embrace LGBQ+ students. They suggest we shed light on unspoken historical sexual identities as one way to broaden conversations about queer agency in contemporary classrooms. Megan's extensive list of terms across time periods supports a similar point: historical and parallel gendered cultures are important resources for expanding the dichotomous stories of gender we tell in schools today.

These perspectives are disruptive, even revolutionary. What would it mean for racial literacy to be a prerequisite for teaching? What if we heeded the call to embrace queer bodies as factual and pertinent to the stories we tell about our past and future? Or worked to eradicate gender binaries from our curriculum and classrooms? The implications of these chapters for how we recruit, educate, and retain "good" teachers would fundamentally alter teacher preparation programs and certification exams. *What will it take to recognize a broader spectrum of raced, sexed, and gendered bodies in social studies education?* The authors suggest it takes rejecting applications that do not demonstrate racial literacy. It takes refusing epistemologies that do not challenge heteronormativity. It takes resisting standards that do not engage the complexity and dynamism of gender. In many PK–12 and college classrooms, if these are the criteria for racial, sexual, and gendered recognition then such recognition is impossible (and maybe even undesirable). If you follow the logic of these chapters through completion, however, the authors imply that these are the stakes.

In all this time and space travel, I noted the overwhelming absence of Black feminist and Black womanist philosophical thought. I was surprised by this—not because I expect much from the field of social studies in regard to Black women—but because I know some of the authors and editors. I've talked with them about the need to better and more radically represent Black women's histories, teaching and scholarship in journals, at our conferences and in our research. *What will it take to recognize a broader spectrum of raced, sexed, and gendered bodies in social studies education—particularly when critical authors, thorough editors, and left-leaning publishers accept conceptualizations of race, gender, and sexuality that minimally engage the "authorial voice of Black women?"* (Collins, 2000, p. 57). This is not a superficial call for diversity predicated on essentialist notions of identity and authority. (I appreciate the careful and reflective contributions of the Hall & Oates, Teena Maries and Amy Winehouses of social studies education to conversations about race.) Black women served as key architects of the constructs the authors argue will structure the future of our field. The omission of Black women's philosophical contributions to these conversations is a threat to any conversation about justice.

I celebrate the authors' intentional work to disrupt what we know and how we talk about race, gender, and sexuality. I encourage them (and readers) to disrupt even further. The absence of Black women theorists is sufficient cause for concern, but it is also a metaphor for all marginalized work that advances theories of identity. We undoubtedly need more expansive notions of race, gender, and sexuality. We also need more expansive understandings of the bodies of literature and actual bodies that we cite through this expansion. I also celebrate the authors' commitment to precision, and with this precision the expectation of forward social movement. They each concluded with language that anticipates the intellectual and moral maturation of our professional community: *until, when, we can begin, future, further examination*. Sadiyah Hartman or Hortense Spillers might argue that such anticipation is unfounded. The hope that the authors articulate is a privilege, and in many instances, it is a hope far removed from the lived conditions of the silenced children that the authors advocate for. Still, what inspires me about the work of Kristen and J.B. in this volume and elsewhere, and what intrigues me about the work of Megan, Daniel and Ryan, is the struggle for a future that is possibly impossible, difficult and hopeful.

REFERENCE

Collins, P. H. (2000). What's going on? Black feminist thought and the politics of postmodernism. In E. St. Pierre & W. Pillow (Eds.), *Working the ruins: Feminist poststructural theory and methods in education* (pp. 41–73). New York, NY: Routledge.

Section V: Individuals, Groups, and Institutions

CHAPTER SIXTEEN

Community

ERIK JON BYKER, UNIVERSITY NORTH CAROLINA AT CHARLOTTE
AMY J. GOOD, UNIVERSITY NORTH CAROLINA AT CHARLOTTE
NAKESHIA N. WILLIAMS, NORTH CAROLINA AGRICULTURAL &
TECHNICAL STATE UNIVERSITY

> For apart from inquiry, apart from the praxis, individuals cannot be truly human. Knowledge emerges only through invention and re-invention, through the restless, impatient, continuing, hopeful inquiry human beings pursue in the world, with the world, and with each other.
>
> —Paulo Freire (2000, p. 72)

Perhaps more than any social studies related keyword; the word "community" encapsulates the core of how the social studies curricula are organized in the United States. The word community is so commonplace in the social studies curriculum that it rarely gets analyzed (Holloway & Chiodo, 2009). Educators and teacher candidates are often content with defining community based on something akin to people who live in the same area and share similar interests. Such a definition reflects the wide variety of meanings provided in the Merriam-Webster dictionary including: (1) a unified body of individuals; (2) interacting population of various kinds of individuals in a common location; and (3) a group of people with a common characteristic or interest living together within a larger society. Indeed, community is oft associated with wholeness and harmony. Williams (1976) explains how community is "unlike other terms of social organization (i.e., state, nation) it seems never to be used unfavorably" (p. 66). Yet, the warm fuzzy associations with community lend to the irony in the word community; it is a comfortable word in thought, but a challenging word in deed. Like the Paulo Freire quote in the introduction to this chapter emphasizes, the formation of any community involves the coupling of individual identities through collective associations. Being in community inevitably means one is giving up individuality for the sake of the common good.

Conversely, being part of a community can also mean tacitly privileging the stories of those with power while silencing the stories of those without. Choi (2002) asserts how community rhetoric champions idealized notions of "others without othering" (p. 449) while at the same time neglects the divisive realities of exclusionary practices in the formation of communities. Returning to the Freire quote from above, being in a community requires an empathy and pursuit of the common good *in* and *with* the world. Community is a complicated word in society as well as in social studies and mirrors the intersectionality of what it means to be a citizen. Our chapter discusses the intersectionalities inherent in the word community by examining this keyword in social studies education.

EXPANDING COMMUNITIES

In the elementary school social studies curricula, community is organized by the notion of "expanding communities" (Hanna, 1937; McMurray, 1895). Expanding communities starts with a focus on individuals in Kindergarten, moves to investigations of the familial community in first grade, and expands to the federalist system of the local, national, and global communities throughout the elementary school curricula (Brophy, Alleman, & Halvorsen, 2012; LeRiche, 1987). Paul Robert Hanna popularized expanding communities and helped to develop it as a way to organize the social studies curriculum around geography and citizenship (Halvorsen, 2009). Hanna (1942) explains the connections between expanding communities and citizenship development as "Children will see that community life is made possible by a division of work and that only as each worker gives his best effort to carrying out his responsibility can the total community welfare be served" (p. 163). This quote reflects the Progressivist origins of expanding communities; working for the common good was part and parcel of what it means to be a citizen. Yet, as expanding communities became codified as curricula the symbolic interaction between citizens and their work toward a community's welfare was gradually replaced with identifying features of communities.

Today, the expanding communities framework continues to shape how the scope and sequence of many state standards and social studies textbooks are arranged. While there have been alternative curricula offered—like E.D. Hirsch's (2007) cultural literacy curriculum and Brophy and Alleman's (2005) cultural universals—notions about community vis-à-vis the expanding communities framework are steadfastly ingrained into much of the United States' social studies curricula. The trouble is that the word community tends to get over-romanticized

(Lamble, 2016) and rarely problematized. Social studies texts are prime examples. When discussing communities, social studies textbook publishers play it safe. Rather than nuance the word community with the inclusion of content about community conflict or the struggle for social justice within communities, publishers focus more on traditional features like the culture of communities in order to not upset folks outside educational circles (LeRiche, 1987). The trouble with a conservative vanilla retelling of the community is that it often makes the contributions of people of color invisible (Howard, 2003; Ladson-Billings, 2003); silences the history of the working class (Anyon, 1981); and marginalizes the struggle of communities (Zinn, 1995). To understand the nuance of community, one must examine the intersectionality of community when it comes to ethnicity, gender, race, sexual orientation, and socioeconomic status (SES).

COMMUNITY INTERSECTIONALITY

We critically examine community by unpacking the layers of meaning through the conceptual lens of intersectionality (Crenshaw, 1991). Our examination includes a description of a community mapping assignment that teacher candidates completed in order to investigate the intersectionality of communities where they were assigned for clinical teaching experiences. Such an assignment can also be used by practicing teachers, school administrators, and social studies teacher educators.

Intersectionality as a conceptual frame first emerged from the field of feminist studies. Traditionally situated in research about an individual's identity, intersectionality examines the interrelationship of social categories like gender, race, and SES (Hancock, 2007; Valentine, 2007). The notion is that a person is made up of many identifiers that intersect. Hancock (2007) explains that a person's intersectionality includes her or his "race, class, gender, or sexual orientation at the individual and institutional levels" (p. 64). The intersectionality of identity is not meant to privilege certain aspects of a participant's identity to the detriments of other aspects (Hancock, 2007). Rather, intersectionality sheds light on how a person's identity is interconnected and more than the sum of her parts. Intersectionality nuances identity to show the way that policies, for example, have multiplier effects in positive or detrimental ways depending on how all the way an individual identifies. Just as an individual reflects a cross-section of identity, so too does a community.

The lens of intersectionality is a helpful way to analyze and nuance community. In *Keywords for Radicals*, Sarah Lamble (2016) explains how "communities are never clearly bounded and are always changing; they have multiple, fluid, and porous boundaries...in a constant state of flow and flux" (p. 109). Given the tensions inherent in defining community, intersectionality is one way to conceptualize the crisscrossing of community aspects. Some of a community's aspects are geographic, of course, so that one can identify a community by its place, location, or region (e.g., the Carolinas). Beyond geographic coordinates, community is also an intersection of class, culture, gender, history, and socioeconomics. While the nature of a community is that it is ill-defined, we provide some definitional guidance by expanding on the earlier shared dictionary definition of community. We assert that a community is the contextual intersection of culture, economy, history, location, which reflects how groups of people associate with each other.

Community is a keyword for educators including administrators, practicing teachers, teacher candidates, and teacher educators to wrestle with and discern. The locus of the educators' work is in the communities where the school is situated. If educators are to be responsive to the needs of the children they teach and are to build their curricula to connect with their children lives, then educators need opportunities to examine the sociohistorical and sociogeography of the communities where they serve or will potentially serve. Community intersectionality illustrates how the aspects of a community are weaved together like a fabric. One way to examine and explore community intersectionality is through a community mapping exercise.

COMMUNITY MAPPING PODCAST

Community mapping exercises assist educators in engaging in the lives of their students outside the walls of the classroom. Community mapping is a mode of inquiry that requires an open mind by being alert to the strengths of a community. Rather than a deficit-model view of the community—focused solely on what a community lacks—community mapping takes a strengths-based approach to examine how the community thrives. In community mapping, some comparisons of differences can be fruitful, but examining a community does not mean taking stances of superiority or inferiority about the community. At the same time, it is critical for educators and teachers to be aware of the realities of the communities from which their students come.

There are many ways to do community mapping. One effective way is to integrate technology with a community mapping exercise through a video podcast (i.e., vodcast, videocast). The purpose of a community mapping video podcast is to capture and discuss the sociocultural and sociogeographic makeup of a school community. Such an exercise works best by walking the perimeter of the school community taking notes of the characteristics of the neighborhood including parks, community buildings, and residential and commercial retail spaces. Community mapping also includes interviewing people in the school community like bus drivers, custodial staff, media specialists, school secretaries, and school administrators to find out more about the school's history and sociocultural aspects of surrounding neighborhoods. The community mapping exercise can be published and presented as a short video podcast, which reports on and discusses: (1) the school's history; (2) school location and surrounding neighborhood environs; (3) the school's social-cultural makeup and diversity; (4) the transportation—how schools arrive to school; and (5) reflections on the school's sociogeography in relation to community mapping exercise.

We had a group of teacher candidates complete a community mapping video podcast exercise and discussed their discoveries about the school communities where they would be placed for a clinical experience. The teacher candidates reported they gained a greater awareness and familiarity with the school community after having completed the community mapping assignment. For example, in their video podcasts, teacher candidates shared similar comments, such as:

> Community mapping has helped me have a greater level of consciousness about the community where I will be practice teaching. Investigating the community allowed me to become more familiar with the cultural makeup of the school as well as the diverse races, ethnicities, cultures, and backgrounds that make up the school.

Teacher candidates also shared how community mapping taught them how their assigned school serves not only the children living in the school neighborhood, but also children from the region. In a connection to the common good, teacher candidates noticed the interaction of diverse classrooms—including race and ethnic diversity, wide range of ability levels, and socioeconomic levels. Teacher candidates developed greater familiarity with the people who support the school since they had an opportunity to interview those folks as part of the community mapping exercise. Finally, the teacher candidates shared how community mapping gave them a better picture of family involvement and community involvement within the school.

Teacher candidates commented on how the community mapping assignment influenced their own future teaching practice and developed a stronger affinity for the school community. Community mapping was instrumental in helping them better identify the environment where the students spend the majority of their time. The teacher candidates were committed to being responsive to ways that the community environment shapes how a child learns and approaches schools. For example, one teacher candidate shared how an urban garden next to her school was a way to connect with community members, while making use of land and meeting an economic need of the community. Other teacher candidates shared reflections like:

> One of the main things I learned is you will have students coming from many different backgrounds and your students should feel welcome and respected in your classroom and school and it is the teacher's responsibility to learn about the community surrounding the school and if this is where the students are living or are they bused to the school.

Community mapping stimulates sociocultural consciousness through authentic and relevant community connections. Teacher candidates explained how they gained greater understanding for the complexity of community within their students' sociogeography. For example, community spaces like nearby communal gardens allow schoolchildren to investigate their human–environmental impact within the community.

The community mapping exercise fostered a greater sense of empathy and affinity for the complexity that is reflected in the community that surround schools. Candidates' eyes were opened to the school and community connections. For example, one teacher candidate shared ideas for addressing the scarcity of important services in a community—such as safe playgrounds—through the establishment of partnerships with local businesses. It also made that same teacher candidate more committed and aware of students' need for kinesthetic learning spaces during the school day. Understanding the intersectionality of a child to the community fostered a deeper resolve among many teacher candidates to be actively involved in their clinical schools by planning and implementing lessons related to their students' everyday world.

CONCLUSION

One tension, whether spoken or silenced, seems to be between the school community and the surrounding neighborhood where a school is situated. Does the school reflect the larger neighborhood and do its bidding or is it vice-versa that the surrounding neighborhood identifies more with the school? The tension makes it compelling and brawny. Community goes beyond just the intersectionality of social studies; it is a pliable idea that people strongly identify with. At the beginning of the chapter, we started with a quote by Paulo Freire. The quote is about how knowledge is a social constructivist process, where human beings are engaged in an inquiry about the world. Freire highlights the collective and hopeful aspects of human beings—as a community engaged in inquiry—as bringing a sense of wholeness. An exercise like the community mapping video podcast highlights how the community is connected, but also quite nuanced. Connections to the community are important to the reinvention and reimagining of knowledge. Conversely, if educators and teachers ignore or silence community connections to the school; powerful learning experiences could be missed.

That is why community is such a keyword in social studies. It is a word that connects most closely with where children begin to construct their conceptions of what it means to be a member in a democratic—or even better said, a participatory citizen in the community. John Dewey (1927) related democratic activity to the heart of being part of a community, "Regarded as an idea, democracy is not an alternative to other principles of associated life. It is the idea of community life itself" (p. 148). The familiarity with the community intersectionality assists educators and teacher candidates in making connections with their learners. The familiarity with the communities that students inhabit can help educators plan lessons and learning experiences to connect students to many aspects of the community. Teacher candidates and teachers who know about the home communities of their students can begin to build meaningful home to school and community to school relationships. For example, local businesses and service-providers can become partners in school learning.

Partnerships and democratic linkages provide a certain robustness and legitimacy to the word community. Yet, community is still contentious as Lamble (2016) reminds readers, "Tensions, conflicts, controversy, and challenges are a central part of community, rather than a threat" (p. 109). The myriad of different uses for community lends to the tensions and conflicts. Today, our national community is frayed and not united. Educators make up an integral part of the community. Experiences for teachers, such as the community mapping podcast, can be a starting point to build awareness of the complexities within communities. It would be even more powerful if the podcasts were created *with* other community members and shared, revisited, and used as a springboard to more community participation, analysis, and action. As teacher educators we want to prepare teacher candidates to teach in a pluralistic community. The public school in a community is the child's first exposure to the "public community." Going to public school is where students can begin to participate in a community. Because of this, teachers assume the role of a "community leader" on their first day of teaching. If the teacher candidates can be empowered from this community mapping exercise, imagine what this simple experience could be for a faculty of experienced teachers. There are tensions in our frayed community related to inclusion, exclusion, sameness, and differences. When one observes the sense of community in an elementary classroom it provides a window into the woes and successes of society. We are not suggesting that educators can solve all of the difficulties of a community; we are simply suggesting they must become aware and participate in community complexity.

In the current milieu, another example of conflict is with the term *global community*. For some, global community is synonymous with globalization, global competencies, and 21st century skills (Friedman, 2005); for other scholars, global community is a reminder of the unbridled selfishness of neoliberalism, poverty, and a rapidly warming earth (Stiglitz, 2002). Global community is a highly contested word when one dissects it. We want to create citizens who can respond both intelligently and critically to issues in the community. Intersectionality provides a conceptual way to acknowledge and discuss the layers to community. When speaking of community it evokes *action* and *inclusion*, so for teachers, knowledge and pride in one's community will allow for the teacher, as a civic leader in the community, to help with decision-making, problem-solving, and building relationships. Teachers who see themselves in the role of community leader can help to resolve, support, and participate. This is true whether teachers are most closely situated in their school community or in the global community. Levels of critical thinking are needed to deconstruct the aspects of community. Conceptual frameworks like the critical cosmopolitan theory (Byker, 2013; Byker & Marquadt, 2016) can be instructive for developing competencies to read and rewrite the world in order to unpack the depth in the meaning of the word community.

DISCUSSION QUESTIONS

Community mapping is a way to illustrate the complexity of community by examining the intersectionality of culture, economics, geography, and history that shapes school communities. The whole exercise of community mapping shows the nuances of community as well as leads to further questions like:

1. In school communities, what community aspects are shared in common?
2. Who has the power in the school community?
3. Which community voices are silenced?
4. How does the school community evolve and change?
5. What are the effects of school community change?
6. What elements of the school community are missing in the community mapping?
7. What are the tensions in the school community?

REFERENCES

Anyon, J. (1981). Social class and school knowledge. *Curriculum Inquiry, 11*(1), 3–42.
Brophy, J., & Alleman, J. (2005). *Children's thinking about cultural universals.* New York, NY: Routledge Press.
Brophy, J., Alleman, J., & Halvorsen, A. (2012). *Powerful social studies for elementary students* (3rd ed.). Boston, MA: Cengage Learning.
Byker, E. J. (2013). Critical cosmopolitanism: Engaging students in global citizenship competencies. *English in Texas Journal, 43*(2), 18–22.
Byker, E. J., & Marquadt, S. (2016). Using critical cosmopolitanism to globally situate multicultural education in teacher preparation courses. *Journal of Social Studies Education Research, 7*(2), 30–50.
Choi, J. B. (2002). Globalization and culture. *Journal of Communication Inquiry, 26*(4), 446–450.
Crenshaw, K. (1991). Mapping the margins: Intersectionality, identity politics, and violence against women of color. *Stanford Law Review, 43*(6), 1241–1299.
Dewey, J. (1927). *The public and its problems.* Denver, CO: Swallow Press.

Freire, P. (2000). *Pedagogy of the oppressed: 30th anniversary edition*. New York, NY: Bloomsbury Publishing.
Friedman, T. L. (2005). *The world is flat: A brief history of the twenty-first century*. New York, NY: Macmillan.
Halvorsen, A. (2009). Back to the future: The expanding communities curriculum in geography education. *The Social Studies, 100*(3), 115–120.
Hancock, A. M. (2007). When multiplication doesn't equal quick addition: Examining intersectionality as a research paradigm. *Perspectives on Politics, 5*(1), 63–79.
Hanna, P. R. (1937). Social education for childhood. *Childhood Education, 14*(1), 74–77.
Hanna, P. R. (1942). Capitalizing educational resources of the community. *The National Elementary Principal, 20*(1), 162–166.
Hirsch, E. D. (2007). *The knowledge deficit: Closing the shocking education gap for American children*. New York, NY: Houghton Mifflin Harcourt.
Holloway, J. E., & Chiodo, J. J. (2009). Social studies IS being taught in the elementary school: A contrarian view. *Journal of Social Studies Research, 33*(2), 235–261.
Howard, T. (2003). The dis (g) race of the social studies. In G. Ladson-Billings (Ed.), *Critical race theory perspectives on the social studies: The profession, policies, and curriculum* (pp. 27–43). Charlotte, NC: Information Age Publishing.
Ladson-Billings, G. (2003). Lies my teachers still tell. In G. Ladson-Billings (Ed.), *Critical race theory perspectives on the social studies: The profession, policies, and curriculum* (pp. 1–14). Charlotte, NC: Information Age Publishing.
Lamble, S. (2016). Community. In K. Fritsch, C. O'Connor, & A. K. Thompson (Eds.), *Keywords for radicals: The contested vocabulary of late-Capitalist struggle* (pp. 103–109). Oakland, CA: AK Press.
LeRiche, L. W. (1987). The expanding environments sequence in elementary social studies: The origins. *Theory & Research in Social Education, 15*(3), 137–154.
McMurray, C. A. (1895). Geography as a school subject. *Educational Review, 9*(1), 459–460.
Stiglitz, J. E. (2002). *Globalization and its discontent*. New York, NY: Norton.
Valentine, G. (2007). Theorizing and researching intersectionality: A challenge for feminist geography. *The Professional Geographer, 59*(1), 10–21.
Williams, R. (1976). *Keywords: A vocabulary of culture and society*. Oxford: Oxford University Press.
Zinn, H. (1995). *A people's history of the United States 1492–Present*. New York, NY: Harper Perennial.

CHAPTER SEVENTEEN

Family

ERIN C. ADAMS, KENNESAW STATE UNIVERSITY

I find the family the most mysterious and fascinating institution in the world.

—Amos Oz

For most people, families constitute the most important institutions in their lives. They provide a source of meaning and sense of belonging and engender a loyalty and willingness to work and sacrifice unknown in other institutions, and, yet, "family" and "families" are largely left out of social studies, the very subject tasked with helping students understand the institutions they are part of. Israeli author Amos Oz (2011), in an interview about his book *The Same Sea*, articulated his fascination with families and their ability to provide endless source material for his books and stories. In the interview, Oz described his interest in why families endure and are resilient; particularly *why* people "invest in the family more than anything else in their lives" despite their potential for heartbreak, embarrassment, hurt, and their seeming lack of "socioeconomic pretext" in modern society (para. 4 & 6). Oz's quote exemplifies both the challenges and potentialities of the study of family in social studies education explored in this chapter and the contradictions they present; they do not always make sense and yet we cling to them fiercely.

This chapter will explore some ways that "family" might be rethought and reincorporated into social studies at all levels, from K–12 to preservice social studies teacher education. Here, "family" is considered a political and social *institution*, defined by the National Council for the Social Studies (2013) as "the formal and informal political, economic, and social organizations that help us carry out, or organize and manage our daily affairs" these include schools, religious groups, government agencies, courts, and families. Viewing families as institutions positions them firmly within the public, social, political and economic sphere; legitimizing their place in social studies as a topic worthy of study.

This chapter by no means a comprehensive study of families or the diversity of what counts as family; there is plenty of good work to be found on these subjects (e.g., Erera, 2002; Skott-Myhre, Gibbs, & Weima, 2012) as well as the funds of knowledge and learning that families can contribute to schools and social studies (e.g., Moll, Gonzalez, Amanti, & Neff, 1992; Shinew, 2006). The chapter provides a few starting places for the further study of "family" and "families" within social studies education and conceives of families as institutions and as sites of investment that provide endless and ever-changing subjects of social study. Moreover, it will explore how viewing families this way can be one way of doing equity and justice work in social studies education, particularly as it relates to gender and the uneven ways that families are formed and maintained along gender lines. The teaching ideas are connected to the National Council for the Social Studies' (NCSS hereafter) ten thematic standards for teaching social studies.

FINDING FAMILIES IN SOCIAL STUDIES

The study of families and family structure is a central feature of early childhood social studies education. "Family" is found in NCSS Thematic Standard #4, "individual identity development and identity" which states "in the early grades, young learners develop their personal identities in the context of families, peers, schools, and communities." This theme is about students understanding themselves in relation to others, but this learning is largely relegated to the early grades. Halvorsen (2009) noted that the study of families is rationalized in social studies education through the expanding communities model wherein "young children learn best when they study what is most familiar immediate to them and then gradually expand outward from that personal context" (p. 115). Starting this way makes sense, considering that the closest and most intimate relationships young children have are with their family members. In this approach, children start with the most personal of personal contexts—themselves and their families—in Kindergarten and work outward toward the local community, state, and ending with the nation by the end of elementary school. This approach uses "family" and specifically the discipline of geography to bring all four social studies disciplines together as it "allows children to perceive and understand the world in logical and organized steps that link everyday life to the facts and circumstances of the wider world"

(Halvorsen, 2009, p. 116). It is truly child-centered in the most literal sense as the child studies their own orientations and relationships within family and community structures that are never outside of history, government, geography, and economics.

Finding Family in Secondary Social Studies Education

As a former middle school teacher following the state standards, I taught the social studies disciplines as if families didn't matter or exist in my students' lives. In particular, I taught civics and economics units as if my students existed in the world on their own, without having to answer to anyone else or consider anyone else's preferences or needs. That is, I used language like "you would choose this product because you are motivated by price" and "you would/should be interested in this issue or vote this way because ____". It was as if the students I taught were adults living on their own, already the fully formed, informed, individuals of the future that social studies curriculum seeks to shape into ideal public citizens wholly detached from family life and the home. A look at the language used in my state's social studies standards, as well as the *C3 Framework* (NCSS, 2013) demonstrates the ways that such language presents students as individual agents. For example, economics standards address students with terms like "personal finance" and both civics and economics use terms like "personal decisions" and "citizen." Such language privileges individualism and imagines students as singular persons rather than people who are never outside of family structures and are rarely operating completely on their own. Moreover, "citizen" implies a particular social, legal status afforded to individuals and what K–12 students simultaneously are and will become. Yet, children under age 18 are not afforded full citizenship rights and are under the custodianship of adults, including teachers and parents. In other words, their individual identity is tied up in, and restricted by, their families. Students' ability to act as individual agential beings when making decisions or when taking action is always in relation to the families and other institutions they are part of.

In my past research with middle school and high school aged youth in grocery stores, I've found that their ability or desire to get certain food items hinged on their siblings and parents' desires rather than their own. For example, two siblings in high school talked about how their five-year-old brother determined what they had to eat for breakfast and lunch and how the older brother's sports schedule often determined their dinner choices. A seventeen-year-old discussed how she bought groceries for her parents and brother not because her parents couldn't afford to buy them but because Wal-Mart was on her way home from school and both of her parents worked demanding jobs. A middle schooler talked about how his parents made him choose snacks from the store's weekly buy-one-get-one-free specials and would not let him have some of the food that he wanted despite the fact that it was not expensive. This points to the influential role of families in students' lives and the ways they are able to navigate the economy in various, nuanced ways that might have little to do with them personally and might be largely out of their control.

In sum, the family as a unit of study, and the study of one's place in it, is largely left to the very earliest grades. In elementary social studies curriculum, family is recognized as a social entity worth studying early on in a child's social studies education, often in Kindergarten. The study of family, and the consideration of family, is then surpassed for contexts that are less immediate and intimate. This is based on a public/private dichotomy that relegates family to the seemingly "nonpolitical" private realm and other institutions to the public realm. Yet as I will show in this chapter, there is little about a family that is purely private. Moreover, the very reasons to study family in Kindergarten are still relevant in older grades. After all, children do not stop being close to their families or part of them as they get older. Family structures are not stable entities or institutions; they are constantly changing and developing and so the study of families, too, must be ongoing or else students will miss out understanding a key component of the social world.

Teaching Idea #1: Friends and Family

The following teaching activity challenges students to think about the rhetorical invocation of "family" by having them "find families" in media, literature and institutions. This activity relates to NCSS Theme #10, Civic Ideals and Practices. Students keep a log of the various ways they hear "family" invoked in a week. This log includes the date, time, context and imagery used. For example, students might hear a teacher refer to the students in her classroom as a "family" or a political candidate invoke "family" as a way to call for societal or institutional change. Students bring their logs to class and work in groups to sort and categorize these invocations of family. For example, students might sort by type of media (e.g., print), or by the tone of the message, or by the actions solicited (e.g., buying a certain product or behaving a certain way or sharing a certain item). Students share their categories with the class; working toward a critical examination of "family" as a discursive entity. For the second part of the activity, students explore the social and anti-social nature of families, considering what is allowable in a family that is not allowable outside of it by making a T-chart with "friends" on one side and "family" on the other and listing things that can be done with one party but not the other. For example, siblings or cousins might fight with each other, steal things from each other or borrow items in ways that would not be acceptable elsewhere. In other words, they might engage in seemingly "anti-social" behavior because in families the rules of ownership and private property may be conceived of differently. Families might provide goods and services, such as a car or a ride to the airport, for one another that they would not for someone outside of their family (however defined). Students review their lists of invocations of family alongside their lists of social practices as they consider the following questions:

- What is it we are being asked to do when people we are not legally or biologically related to call us to act as a family?
- How does exploring families in this way help us rethink the nature of labor and work?
- Who benefits from invoking "family" (e.g., capitalists, business owners, politicians, teachers, schools) and what is the purpose of these invocations?
- How might invoking "family" reinforce gender or labor inequities?
- How are friends treated differently than family? Why?
- Should our classroom have a friend or family relationship? What are the affordances and consequences of each approach? How else might we organize ourselves?

FORMING FAMILIES

Families and family formation as we know it is not a neutral or natural process. In Western society, the industrial revolution drastically changed family structures; producing the bourgeois, heteronormative, nuclear family wherein the father left the private family home to work for wages. This was a change from families centered on farms or small businesses that employed all members of the family in the upkeep of the household and family life. The reorganization of the family was a result of the reorganization of the economy, which led to the discursive function of "father as an organizing symbol" (Laurie & Stark, 2012, p.23). From this form of industrial work-family organization emerged "strategies of patriarchal domination learned in the workplace [that] creep into 'domestic' life and vice-versa" creating the notion of wage earner as the head of household (p. 24). The result was the emergence of several dominant discourses about families that are recognizable to us in education, discussed below.

The family was designated as "the exclusive site of the consumption of goods and services" (Laurie & Stark, 2012, p. 23). We can see this in economics curriculum in the form of the "household" in the circular flow diagram that is used to explain the relationship between households, government, and businesses. Households buy the goods and services businesses produce and, in return, produce new workers (children) for the businesses. Parents thus became the "trustee of the childworker" (p. 23). Because households were viewed as serving an important economic role in production and consumption (and, increasingly, consumption as children were raised by multiple caretakers), they were deemed worthy of investing in. The best way to ensure a solid investment is through governance and organization. Traces of this discourse appear when politicians talk about the importance of "investing in families" as well as efforts to fix "broken" families. Schools, as the public spaces where children spend their time (Parker, 2003) and social studies teachers as the purveyors of civic education could then be thought of as the trustees of the child-citizen-worker that is both preparing to enter society and already in it. Thus, social studies teachers, as well as families, are societally tasked with raising socioeconomic citizens that will go on to participate in democratic society and provide the labor needed to maintain the economy.

Family Formation and U.S. History

Family formation, and its governance, is an important aspect of U.S. history and conceptions of citizenship. After the Civil War imperatives were put into place that forced newly freed slaves to form (or re-form) "legal," state-recognized, and properly documented marriages between one man and one woman (Washington, 2005). These measures were part of a Reconstruction-era citizen-making processes (Franke, 1999) that sought to reestablish social and family stability by instituting a male head of household who gained independence through his care for his dependents (wife and children). These measures were undertaken, at least in part, to ensure that women and children became the legal responsibility of men and not the state. It was this sort of thinking, of men as the legal custodians of the households' citizenship, that led, at least in part, to the repression of suffrage as well as to modern day child and family custodianship issues and evolved other institutions like the juvenile and family court systems. By foregrounding family, students begin to understand how recognizing a "family" is not neutral but is forged upon civic and social recognition and governmentality, the art of government which "answers the question of how to introduce economy—that is to say, the correct manner of managing goods and wealth within the family" (Foucault, 1991, p. 92). The impetus to marry for social and economic reasons endures today and is not racially or socioeconomically neutral (Green, 2014).

These examples provide further insight into systemic economic and civic injustices toward women as well as the political, economic, and social implications and affordances of family formation today. A current example is the legalization of gay marriage, which has foregrounded the institutionalization of family in political discourse.

Sustaining Families

Families do not naturally stay together. They are constantly being re/formed; which requires *work*. Family members must continually maintain familial bonds and structures. In households, work takes the form of parents, children, and perhaps extended family members performing duties such as cleaning, cooking, childcare, and other forms of maintenance in order for it to function. Although family, and work structures, changed through time, women still have the primary responsibility of producing the worker-child, that is, raising children and maintaining the home and family. Thus, women labor twice over—working for wages to provide for families as well as caring for family (known as the second-shift).

Not only does household labor tend to fall disproportionately on women, but so does kinwork, "the conception, maintenance, and ritual celebration of cross-household kin ties, including visits, letters, telephone calls, presents, and cards to kin; the organizing of holiday gatherings" (di Leonardo, 1987, p. 442). Kinwork sustains and forms families as we know them, as "it is kinship contact across households, as much as women's work within them, that fulfills our cultural expectation of satisfying family life (p. 443). Moreover, such kinwork involves labor that is overlooked when cataloging work. In their study, de Leonardo found that men generally did not take up this kinwork in the case of divorce or death. This is not to say that men never do housework or kinwork, there are certainly examples of great strides in terms of household equity in the 21st century. New technologies such as smartphones, texting, Facebook and email have changed the way families are tied together and relate to each other. These new ways of communicating are a productive area of study in shaping the ways kinwork is distributed, that is, how is social media used to mediate family relationships? How does social media usage differ along gender lines?

Teaching Idea #2: Modern Families

For this activity, students analyze a variety of families depicted in television shows. I think that *Roseanne* and *Modern Family*, shows airing 20 years apart, produce interesting and productive comparisons, but there are probably many other shows on television that will do. Ask students to relate the shows to the ten social studies themes as well as to issues of work, labor, and family conception and production discussed in this chapter. For example, students might notice which characters in the show are doing housework and which ones are working outside the home. Then, unpack the name and designation "*Modern Family*"—what about it is "modern?" To what extent do the families in the shows reinforce or challenge normative conceptions of gender roles and family in society? To what extent do they demonstrate social progress? What roles do race and socioeconomics play in the show? Pay attention to your positionality and feelings toward the families. Which families strike you as "good" and "bad"? Why is that? Where do these feelings come from?

Analyzing sitcoms can help students begin to uncover the discursive practices that normalize certain family structures and practices. These suggestions come from my own experiences watching and discussing these television shows with preservice elementary school teachers. They dismissed *Roseanne* as outdated, pointing to the ways that men now take on household tasks such as cooking and the ways the title character appeared to be a bad mother because she yelled at her family, insulted them and told uncomfortable truths. Their comments provided an opening to discuss issues of class and gender and the comparison to *Modern Family* as promoting similar gender stereotypes, challenging the notion that *Roseanne* was outdated.

Teaching Idea #3: Technology and Family Equity

This teaching idea incorporates NCSS Themes #2 "Continuity and Change", "Theme #7 "Production, Distribution and Consumption" and Theme #8 "Science, Technology and Society." The teaching idea derives from the glossary definition of "continuity and change" found in the *College, Career, and Civic Life (C3) Framework for Social Studies State Standards* handbook. The glossary provides the following example: how electricity changed family life. The entry points to the ways doing laundry has changed over time as a result of electricity. Because people now have more clothing than ever before, the amount of time and labor needed to do a family's laundry has not changed as much for women, who still do most of the family laundry. This example provides students with a more nuanced understanding of processes, such as doing laundry, that do not affect people uniformly over time and space as well as the different relationships people have with the machines that help them do work. Social studies students can be challenged to think of other examples of how technology has affected families, and specific people within own families. This can specifically complicate rhetoric of American progress as students investigate inventions and technological developments throughout time like the automobile and mass production, the Internet, television, personal computer, and telephones and consider how these inventions have changed family life, and affected family members' lives, differently. The podcast episode "When Women Stopped Coding" (Henn, 2014) is a good starting place for considering the consequences of marketing toys to families on an entire generation of women in computer science. This leads to an inquiry into whether or not technological progress creates more or less equity in society.

FREEING FAMILIES

This section is inspired by Deleuze and Guattari (1972/2009), who warned against the psychoanalyzing and psychologizing of families and who drew attention to the revolutionary potential within families. This section attempts to "free" families from damaging discourses and the burdens heaped upon it by neoliberal capitalism that pathologizes families, particularly mothers; "the family is indeed the delegated agent of this psychic repression, insofar as it ensures 'a mass psychological reproduction of the economic system of a society'" (p. 118). The job of economic reproduction was put upon the family (and then the family and school) so that they could be blamed when things went wrong. Idealizing the nuclear family and then blaming it for societal ills allows capitalism to remain hidden "the problem becomes less whether to be 'for' or 'against' the family than what sorts of social services, working conditions and legal frameworks are most needed to curb the inequities and deprivations existing across the whole spectrum of private households" (Laurie & Stark, 2012, p. 28). In other words, it can be easier to blame parents or family for being in poverty rather than the austerity measures that have diminished many social safety nets and services for families limit the degree to which many parents are able to provide for their children. Historical policies such as FHA loans under the New Deal led to housing segregation and the ability for white families to build generational wealth black families were not afforded. Capitalists and politicians delegate to parents and the teacher, acting in loco parentis, responsibility for a functional society in which they are only a part of a greater whole. Family ought to occupy a prominent place of study within social studies, but should not do so to the exclusion of other influential institutions and government programs and policies that act on families.

Moreover, Deleuze and Guattari (1972/2009) warned that psychology and psychoanalysis focus too closely on family structure and position and that by determining who and what went wrong, delegates to the family the source of individuality and subjectivity. This shows up in classrooms and teacher education with rhetoric about parenting, students' "good" and "bad" parents/families, broken families, and children's stages of development in educational psychology. Studying families and the ways they are impacted by other institutions (court system, legal system, social services, etc.) or lack thereof, helps to break this cycle of blame and create more informed citizens who are not so easily swayed by rhetoric and who can work for the good *of* families rather than the problematic and damaging creation of *good families*.

Finally, Deleuze and Guattari (1972/2009) point to ways that "family" can serve as a place of revolutionary action and civic learning generally assign to social studies teachers; "the child does not wait until he is an adult before grasping-underneath father-mother-the economic, financial, social, and cultural problems that cross through a family…with which he is already planning his ruptures and his conformities" (p. 276). It is first within their own families that children begin their social studies; testing boundaries and experiment with obeying or resisting authority, starting with their parents. Thus, within families we not only see the social studies disciplines, but also early signs of conformity and rebellion to authority and governance. Radically, it might be within families, not schools, where children learn activism and rebellion needed to change society—and that should get social studies teachers' attention! Hence, "family" should not be thought of as outside of civics, economics, history and geography, but as a consequence, or product of, these disciplines.

Teaching Idea #4: Families and Political Action in Children's Books

Several children's books can be used to demonstrate the role of families in fostering children's political agency. I've used the following in my courses; *My Brother Martin* by Christine King Farris (2003); *I Dissent: Ruth Bader Ginsberg Makes her Mark* by Debbie Levy (2016) and *¡Si, Se Puede!/Yes, We Can!: Janitor Strike in L.A.* by Diana Cohn (2002). All three books show parents planting the seeds of activism and change in their children by pointing out injustices in society. These books relate to NCSS Theme #1, "Culture" and Theme #3 "Individual Development and Identity" as students investigate the roles family life can play in fostering civic and historical agency. Moreover, these books highlight the ways that families, in addition to social studies teachers, are integral in the citizen-making process.

CONCLUSION: FOCUSING ON FAMILIES

Studying families serves to remind us as social studies teachers to be cautious; in the ways that we talk about students' families, in the ways that we teach about families, and the ways that we may attempt to separate family life from the social world of social studies. On one hand we can say family is an intimate relationship among people that his highly influential and on the other hand remain cognizant that families are not the explanation for all social ills. What social studies educators might do is help students consider how families are produced in social and educational discourses. Families are not stable entities, but shift and change over time. The ways these shifts happen is often indicative of larger societal shifts. Moreover, the idea of "family" shifts with changes in social, political, and economic practices over time and in different places.

Finally, I respectfully challenge the idea taken up by Walter Parker via Vivian Paley that [children] "are just emerging from life's deep wells of private perspective: babyhood and family. Then, along comes school. It is the first real exposure to the public arena" (Paley, quoted in Parker, 2003, p. 252). As I have demonstrated in this chapter, families, and children, are always engaged in the public sphere and families are tasked with the creation of a public good (socioeconomic citizens). School might be a formal introduction into a pluralistic society/classroom but a child's life pre-school is not devoid of governmentality or exposure to public life.

The teaching ideas demonstrated how the study of family could be used to investigate the social studies disciplines as well as concepts like authority and rebellion. Moreover, as I have demonstrated, family is not only an appropriate topic of study with many areas of interest conversion; it is necessary for the creation of more democratic, just, and equitable societies. However, there would be little in secondary social studies curriculum, when taught in isolation from families, that would help students navigate these nuanced ways dealing with the political, economic, civic and historical forces that impact their lives and the ways that parental authority and family and household expectations might even be at odds with social studies teaching that is too focused on individualism and personal agency and responsibility.

DISCUSSION QUESTIONS

1. What does invoking "family" to define nonfamilial relationships, such as teachers and students in a classroom, constrain or enable?
2. Consider a family (real or fictional). Who has the authority? How is it gained or earned? How does it circulate among family members?
3. How do economic and political relationships and circumstances affect familial relationships? What role does capitalism play in these economic relationships?
4. How are family values similar to values promoted in social studies curriculum? How are they different?
5. Are families a private or public entity?

REFERENCES

Cohn, D. (2002). ¡Si, se puede! / Yes, we can!: Janitor strike in L.A. El Paso, TX: Cinco Puntos Press.
Deleuze, G., & Guattari, F. (1972/2009). *Anti-Oedipus: Capitalism and schizophrenia* (R. Hurley, M. Seem, & H.R. Lane, Trans.). New York, NY: Penguin Books.
Di Leonardo, M. (1987). The female world of cards and holidays: Women, families, and the work of kinship. *Signs, 12*(3), 440–453.
Erera, P. I. (2002). *Family diversity: Continuity and change in the contemporary family*. Thousand Oaks, CA: Sage.

Farris, C. K. (2003). *My brother Martin: A sister remembers growing up with the Rev. Dr. Martin Luther King, Jr.* New York, NY: Simon and Schuster.

Foucault, M. (1991). Governmentality. In G. Burchell, C. Gordon & P. Miller (Eds.), *The Foucault effect: Studies in governmentality: With two lectures and an interview with Michel Foucault* (pp. 87–104). Chicago, IL: University of Chicago Press.

Franke, K. M. (1999). Becoming a citizen: Reconstruction era regulation of African American marriages. *Yale Journal of Law, 11*(2), 251–309.

Green, E. (2014, January 15). Wealthy women can afford to reject marriage, but poor women can't. *The Atlantic.* Retrieved from: https://www.theatlantic.com/business/archive/2014/01/wealthy-women-can-afford-to-reject-marriage-but-poor-women-cant/283097/?utm_source=atlfb

Halvorsen, A. (2009). Back to the future: The expanding communities curriculum in geography education. *The Social Studies, 100*(3), 115–120.

Henn, S. (2014, October 21). When women stopped coding. *Planet Money.* Retrieved from: http://www.npr.org/sections/money/2014/10/21/357629765/when-women-stopped-coding

Laurie, T., & Stark, H. (2012). Reconsidering kinship: Beyond the nuclear family with Deleuze and Guattari. *Cultural Studies Review, 18*(1), 19.

Levy, D. (2016). *I dissent! Ruth Bader Ginsberg makes her mark.* New York, NY: Simon and Schuster.

Moll, L. C., Gonzalez, N., Amanti, C., & Neff, D. (1992). Funds of knowledge for teaching: Using a qualitative approach to connect homes and classrooms. *Theory into Practice, 31*(2), 132–141.

National Council for Social Studies. (2013). *College, career, and civic life (C3) framework for social studies state standards.* Silver Spring, MD: Author.

Oz, A. (2011). Erasing the line between fiction and confession (G. Robinson, interviewer). Retrieved from: http://www.jbooks.com/interviews/IP_ROBINSON.htm

Parker, W. (2003). *Teaching democracy: Unity and diversity in public life.* New York, NY: Teachers College Press.

Shinew, D. (2006). Citizenship and belonging: Constructing "a sense of place and a place that makes sense." In A. Segall, E. Heilman, & C. Cherryholmes (Eds.), *Social studies—The next generation: Re-searching in the postmodern* (pp. 77–93). New York, NY: Peter Lang.

Skott-Myhre, K., Gibbs, H., & Weima, K. (2012). *Writing the family: Women, auto ethnography, and family work.* Rotterdam: Sense Publishers.

Washington, R. (2005). Sealing the sacred bonds of holy matrimony: Freedmen's Bureau marriage records. *Prologue-Quarterly of the National Archives and Records Administration, 37*(1), 58–65.

CHAPTER EIGHTEEN

Religion

COLLEEN FITZPATRICK, WAKE FOREST UNIVERSITY
STEPHANIE VAN HOVER, UNIVERSITY OF VIRGINIA

> We cannot teach history without teaching about religion any more than we could prepare beer without using yeast. Something crucial would be missing.
>
> —Passe and Willox, 2009, p. 103

> This is religion. This is not what actually happened. This is not what actually happens to you.
>
> —Michael, classroom teacher

Burgett and Hendler (2014) assert that a keyword is "a term that marks a site of significant contestation and disagreement, not consensus. If it can be defined in a stable and agreed-upon way, the term is not a keyword" (p. 10). An important keyword in social studies, one that certainly meets the criteria of contestation and disagreement, is *religion*. We argue that religion is a concept that has taken on new meanings over time, place, space, and political context. Since the events of 9/11, research (and any nightly news program) indicates that religious illiteracy—and religious intolerance—is growing in the United States (Nash & Bishop, 2009; Prothero, 2007) and that Americans do not understand the impact religion has, and has had, on society and individuals. In fact, scholars question if people understand what *religion* as a concept actually is (Hall, 1997; McGreevy, 2011). How is this keyword defined?

As Schultz and Harvey (2010) observe, religion is "everywhere and nowhere" in mainstream discussions about history and modern society; religion is ever present, but rarely discussed or defined in the larger narrative of American history. Over the past few decades, interpretations and conversations over the meaning of the concept *religion* have shifted. Oman (2013) traces how the definition of religion has changed over the centuries and observes that *religion* entered our lexicon as an all-encompassing term that included denominations and individual belief but more recently has been divided into religion and spirituality. That is, while the terms *religion* and *spirituality* are used frequently in civic discourse, it is evident that very little agreement or specificity about the definitions exist. More Americans are claiming they are "spiritual, but not religious," usually citing attendance at a religious service or membership to an organization as the difference. Is religion simply the established and organized places of worship? Does simply attending services make an individual religious? Separating religion from spirituality could lead to confusion over the role religion has played and should play in society. Treating religions as only organizations and buildings ignores the "social, psychological impact" personal belief has on society (Barton, 2015). It separates the two and leads to confusion over the role religion has played and should play in society. In addition, treating religion only as institutions ignores personal choice and how individuals enact established religion in their daily lives. Debates in the field of religious studies continue about whether the study of religion should focus on denominational studies or the study of lived religion by its adherents (Hall, 1997). In effect, is religion the established organizations, the people within these organizations, or something much more personal? The lack of understanding of what religion is only increases religious intolerance and illiteracy. One common approach discussed by scholars to combat religious illiteracy is to ensure schools teach about religion. However, what *religion* should be taught, and how should it be taught? When scholars argue students should learn about religion to combat religious illiteracy, what is it they want students to learn?

LESSONS LEARNED FROM MICHAEL

In 2014, a position statement on teaching religion in public schools published by the National Council for the Social Studies' (NCSS) stated:

> Study about religions should be an essential part of the social studies curriculum. Knowledge about religions is not only a characteristic of an educated person but is necessary for effective and engaged citizenship in a diverse nation and world. Religious literacy dispels stereotypes, promotes cross-cultural understanding, and encourages respect for the rights of others to religious liberty. (NCSS Position Statement, n. p., 2014)

The position statement goes on to cite Justice Tom Clark in the 1963 *Abington v. Schempp* decision that, "[o]ne's education is not complete without a study of comparative religion or the history of religion and the relationship to the advancement of civilization." If the goal of social studies education (and history education) is to prepare students for a democratic society (Hess & McAvoy, 2015), then both the NCSS position statement and the quote cited above by Passe and Willox (2009) are vital to consider—that "teaching history without religion" is like "beer without yeast. Something crucial would be missing" (p. 103). Students must learn about religion as a central component of informed citizenship as participants in a diverse society. Many states tacitly recognize this as attention to world religions is included in nearly all social studies state standards (Douglass, 2000). But what does the teaching of religion look like in practice?

Diane Moore (2007) outlines approaches public schools typically take toward teaching about religion. The two approaches most frequently used—the phenomenological approach and the historical approach—each approach religion from a value neutral perspective and, as Moore argues, ignore the impact religion has on political, intellectual, and cultural aspects of life. In a phenomenological approach, the topic of religion is approached from a non-sectarian perspective. Religions are usually compared using distinct categories (e.g., holy days, places of celebration). Students are implicitly or explicitly expected to "suspend judgment and approach the study of religion in a spirit of empathy" (Moore, 2007, p. 68). In a historical approach, religion is included as a topic in ancient history through attention to the development of religious traditions, as well as any time religion exerted a significant impact on the politics of the time. Religion is treated as "fundamentally separate from other dimensions of human life" (Moore, 2007, p. 71). These ways of teaching about religion, as Moore argues, deemphasizes the importance and implications of religion in modern society. Moore argues for a cultural studies approach to teaching religion where it is assumed "religion is deeply imbedded in all dimensions of human experience" (2007, p. 79) and that in teaching about religion, it is crucial to situate the religion and understand the context the religion occurs in (i.e., time, country etc.) instead of treating religious traditions as universal beliefs (Moore, 2007).

Yet, as Kilman (2007) observes "for decades, educators have wrestled with how to handle the increasing diverse religions of an increasingly diverse student body" and that "teaching religion has become a subject one high school teacher calls even more controversial than teaching sex-ed" (Kilman, 2007, para. 3). Research supports Kilman's assertion and indicates that many teachers choose to avoid teaching about religion in their classrooms for a number of reasons (Ayers & Reid, 2005; James, 2015; Passe & Willox, 2009) including confusion over the legality of doing so, discomfort with the topic, and fear that the line between teaching religion and teaching about religion would blur (Passe & Willox, 2009). Teachers (and schools) who avoid teaching about religion can contribute to students' misconceptions about religious groups and can, as a result, potentially diminish the significant role religion plays in society (James, 2015; National Council for the Social Studies, 2014). At the same time, Keith Barton (2015) argues that simply "increasing the amount of attention given to religion may not lead to a better understanding of people and society" (p. 61). Barton continues by noting "some of the most problematic aspects of developing students' understanding of religion occur when schools most directly address the topic" (p. 64).

Barton identifies and explores three problems that frequently arise when teachers teach about religion in the classroom: (1) teaching from an ethnocentric perspective, (2) static portrayals of religion, and (3) ignoring the social, political, and psychological implications of religion and religious belief (2015, p. 62). Barton theorizes that while curriculum might include topics related to religion, "religious ideas are so deeply ingrained in our thinking…[that] as a result, we interpret other religions in light of our own backgrounds" (2015, p. 69). Barton refers to this as "ethnocentrism" and asserts that until teachers recognize their identity and recognize diversity within religions, little movement will be made. The curriculum, as it is now, Barton observes, presents an incomplete, static picture of religion. Despite the impact religion has on society, students "have few opportunities to consider what religion means for individual identity or in society at large" (Barton, 2015, p. 73). Requiring students to learn the "basic facts about the beliefs of selected world religions is not adequate for understanding such a complex feature of human life" (p. 76).

THE CASE OF MICHAEL

As researchers and teacher educators who spend much time watching teachers teach, what we see and hear emphasizes the importance of critically (re)considering the way the teaching of religion and the way the keyword *religion* is attended to by social studies educators. We use two examples from the classroom of Michael, the world history teacher quoted at the beginning of this chapter, as a lens through which to highlight and problematize some of the questions and issues when we see religion taught in schools. These lessons, on Ancient Egypt and the development of Islam, actualize some of the issues outlined by Moore and Barton that arise when teachers discuss religion in their classroom.

In a lesson taught early in the year on ancient Egypt, standing in front of a PowerPoint, Michael talked about Egyptian religion:

> Michael: Egyptian religion. It was polytheistic. Can anybody tell me what polytheistic is?
> Student: Belief in more than one god.
> Michael: Good, belief in more than one god. We're looking at pictures at the Egyptian Book of the Dead…. This is Osiris. What was he god of?
> Student: The afterlife.

Michael referenced the Book of the Dead again and stated that this book described the Egyptian belief that:

> ...when you passed away, your body and soul would go to Osiris' hall and this is where you would be judged. Your heart would be placed on a balance with a feather of truth. If the heart was heavier, you would be fed to a crocodile. If it was lighter you would be released into open wheat fields.

A student immediately asked, "Wouldn't the heart always be heavier than a feather?" Michael answered this by saying "the feather has magical power." A different student followed up by asking, "Where did the magic come from?" Michael responded, "It's their belief." A few more students asked questions about the relationship between the feather and magic. In response, Michael compared the weighing of the feather to the Christian belief in judgment at the gates:

> Michael: In Christianity today, what do most people believe is going to happen when you die?
> Class responds (in unison): Heaven or hell.
> Michael: You go to heaven or hell. When you're at the gates, you're judged are you not? And if you've led a good life and done things you're supposed to do, you'll go to heaven. And if not, you're released to where?
> Class: Hell
> Michael: Good. When you go to the gates, you're judged and then released. If you don't believe in Christianity, this doesn't happen. Today most people in Egypt are Islamic. That's another monotheistic religion that we will talk about later.

After this analogy, many students were still expressing their confusion. The class was talking at once, but a few students were audible above the rest. A student asked again "How can a feather weigh more than a heart?" Michael threw his hands in the air and claimed "It's religion. It's not something that actually happened. When you die, as an ancient Egyptian, you believe in this. Religion. This ain't something that actually happened. This is not what actually happens to you." Michael then said, "If you believe in Christianity, this doesn't happen. I don't think it happens at all cause I'm Christian." He asked the other adult in the room if there was a better way to explain it. The other adult affirmed Michael's teaching and Michael moved onto another topic. At the end of this conversation one student asked "Do Egyptians still get eaten by a crocodile today?" but Michael continued with his PowerPoint without addressing the students question.

Later in the year, Michael addressed the topic of Islam. As part of class, Michael showed a 2010 ABC news-Diane Sawyer film "Muslim in America." The film placed Islam in relation to Christianity by referring to Islamic schools as "Sunday schools" and focused on how the Five Pillars of Islam were similar to the basic tenets of Christianity. During the brief 10-minute film, Sawyer interviewed self-identified moderate Muslims in America and asked them about their religion.

The video showed images of mosques in America as well as Muslims praying at various locations (i.e., home, work). One of the interviewees in the film stated, "[g]et to know us. We're just like everybody else."

After viewing the video, Michael asked students to identify some of the things they learned. At least two students immediately commented that they did not know Jesus played a role in Islam. Michael responded by saying that before watching the film he "didn't know that" about Muslims' view of Jesus and that "that also stood out to me." A student asked whether "all Muslims go to hell," Michael responded "it's not up to me" and "it depends on your ideology." He then added that he did believe that "not all Muslims are suicide bombers." After that statement, Michael shifted to talking about Muslim women—that "scarf wearing" was a tradition, not a religious belief, that "just radical ones" insist on scarves, that the oppressive context of Saudi Arabia meant that women "did not have free will" and wore head-scarves "because [they had] been raised that way." A student then asked, "Isn't Obama a Muslim?" Michael responded by saying "even if [Obama] was born a Muslim, how is Obama converting a bad thing? And [Obama] says he has always been Christian." After a few minutes of off-topic conversation about politics, Michael redirected students by asking, "Did this [video] change your view on Islam?" Another student mentioned that they had learned how similar Islam is to Christianity and "how Jesus plays a role in Islam." One student quickly responded, "Extremists give Islam a bad name." Michael nodded and then stated "if you see a Muslim on a plane, you don't have to be worried." As we analyzed this lesson, we debated whether he was attempting to promote a theme of tolerance, or intending to be funny, as the comment was jokingly stated. However, one student clearly misinterpreted this comment and asked, "Why don't we just blow it [the Dome of the Rock] up?" Another student responded to Michael's quip by stating, "but those towel things are so weird." Michael either did not hear these comments or chose to ignore them, moving on to a PowerPoint lecture that covered the Five Pillars of Islam. Michael, admirably, attempted to teach his students to approach Islam with tolerance and understanding by promoting similarities between the two religions. However, Michael disassociated religious beliefs from an individual's action. Similar to Michael's lesson on Egypt, religion was dissociated with everyday life.

LESSONS LEARNED FROM MICHAEL

These very brief excerpts are not meant to overly criticize Michael or to generate sweeping generalizations about whether he is a "good" or "bad" teacher. Rather, we offer them as one lens through which to explore complex issues surrounding religion in the public sphere. Questions abound about what *is* happening and what *should* happen when we teach about religion. Does Michael's portrayal of religion accurately depict what religion is? Is religion bounded by an organized community? Does religion require membership in an organization? Are there certain rules and expectations that need to be followed and met? What role does faith play in religion? What role do individuals and individual belief play in religion? How does one thoughtfully teach the social, political, and psychological implications of religion and religious belief? Michael taught in a very specific teaching context, with state standards that treated religion as a list of facts to be presented, and his students shared similar religious beliefs and worldviews. If religion is defined by a set of facts, or described only as belief or series of events in the unobservable world, it misses the impact religion has on society, in the observable world. Michael's class may be able to recite facts about religion on end of the year tests, but are they able to fully understand what religion is and the impact it has on society? Knowledge of these facts is not sufficient to understand the complex meanings and implications of religions.

Students' ability to recite facts about religions, such as holidays, does not get to the core of what a religion is. In addition, this seeking of commonality between religions can be superficial and over exaggerate similarities, ignoring any true differences between religions. Wars, social movements, political campaigns have been driven by religious belief. Not recognizing and valuing the differences between religions leads to confusion and an increase in religious intolerance and illiteracy. Schools are supposed to be "parliaments of religion" (Bender & Klassen, 2010, p. 1) where students of all different faiths interact and discuss issues central to their diverse faith. But what happens when there is no diversity? How do students learn, in meaningful and thoughtful ways, about religion?

If, as Schweber (2006) asserts, "history and religion are one and the same," what is it that students are learning about religion (p. 408)? Moreover, what is it that students need to know to understand what religion is? If we claim that religion is necessary to understand to become an "educated person" (National Council for the Social Studies, 2014), we need to understand what religion is and ensure our students do as well. As religion is taught in standards-based classroom settings and pervades civic discourse, we must examine what religion is being taught and what best helps students understand the issues surrounding religion in the public sphere. Religion is often currently defined as institutions that are unchanging and untouched by individuals outside of their leaders or sets of facts to be memorized. Do these definitions of religion provide students with a clear picture of the intricacies of religious organizations and the people that make up the organizations? The controversy around the keyword *religion*—and the vital need to unpack and explore the contested understandings of this concept—is heightened daily. From the current presidential campaign in which politicians are using religion as a central part of campaigning, to controversy across the country about what excerpts from religious texts are appropriate to teach (versus indoctrinate) Islam, the keyword *religion* is certainly a vital one for the field of social studies to grapple with and unpack.

DISCUSSION QUESTIONS

1. What happens when students are in schools and communities where there are a limited number of students from diverse religions or students do not feel comfortable enough at school to voice their religious beliefs?
2. How can we teach students who are not in religiously diverse contexts to be able to understand and engage in productive dialogue with people of different faiths?
3. How can teachers understand how their religious backgrounds influence their own teaching of religion?

REFERENCES

Ayers, S. J., & Reid, S. (2005). Teaching about religion in elementary school: The experience of one Texas district. *The Social Studies, 96*(1), 14–17. doi:10.3200/TSSS.96.1.14-17.

Barton, K. C. (2015). Reconsidering religion in the curriculum. In J. H. James (Ed.), *Religion in the classroom* (pp. 61–78). New York, NY: Routledge.

Bender, C., & Klassen, P. E. (2010). *After pluralism: Reimagining religious engagement.* New York, NY: Columbia University Press.

Burgett, B., & Hendler, G. (Eds.). (2014). *Keywords for American cultural studies* (2nd ed.). New York, NY: New York University Press.

Douglass, S. (2000). Teaching about religion in national and state social studies standards. Fountain Valley, CA: Council on Islamic Education/Nashville, TN: First Amendment Center.

Hall, D. (1997). Introduction. In D. Hall (Ed.), *Lived religion in America: Toward a history of practice* (pp. 1–13). Princeton, NJ: Princeton University Press.

Hess, D. E., & McAvoy, P. (2015). *The political classroom: Evidence and ethics in democratic education.* New York, NY: Routledge.

James, J. H. (2015). *Religion in the classroom.* New York, NY: Routledge.

Kilman, C. (2007, Fall). One nation, many gods. *Teaching Tolerance, 32.* Retrieved from http://www.tolerance.org/magazine/number-32-fall-2007/feature/one-nation-many-gods

McGreevy, J. (2011). American religion. In E. Foner & L. McGirr (Eds.), *American history now* (pp. 242–261). Philadelphia, PA: Temple University Press.

Moore, D. L. (2007). *Overcoming religious illiteracy: A cultural studies approach to the study of religion in secondary education.* New York, NY: Macmillan.

Nash, R., & Bishop, P. (2009). *Teaching adolescents religious literacy in a post-9/11 world.* Charlotte, NC: Information Age Publishing.

National Council for the Social Studies. (2014). Study about religion in the social studies curriculum. *Social Education, 78*(4), 202–204.

Oman, D. (2013). Defining religion and spirituality. In R. F. Paloutzian & C. L. Park (Eds.), *Handbook of the psychology of religion and spirituality* (pp. 23–47). New York, NY: Guilford Press.

Passe, J., & Willox, L. (2009). Teaching religion in America's public schools: A necessary disruption. *The Social Studies, 100*(3), 102–106. doi.org/10.3200/TSSS.100.3.100.3.102-106.

Prothero, S. R. (2007). *Religious literacy: What every American needs to know—And doesn't*. New York, NY: Harper Collins.

Schultz, K. M., & Harvey, P. (2010). Everywhere and nowhere: Recent trends in American religious history and historiography. *Journal of the American Academy of Religion, 78*(1), 129–162. doi.org/10.1093/jaarel/lfp087.

Schweber, S. (2006). Fundamentally 9/11: The fashioning of collective memory in a Christian school. *American Journal of Education, 112*(3), 392–417. doi.org/10.1086/500714.

CHAPTER NINETEEN

Embracing Complexity in the Social Studies

A Response to the Individuals, Groups, and Institutions Section

SARA A. LEVY, WELLS COLLEGE

Religion, community, and family are common topics in the social studies classroom, but their purpose and meaning within the curriculum are not often interrogated. For many students, studying these topics presents an opportunity to examine intimate parts of their own lives from multiple perspectives and within a diverse classroom setting. While democratic society benefits from students developing understandings of these topics beyond their own religious, community, and family experiences, the study of these personal topics in the public space of the classroom may lead to pedagogical challenges for which teachers may not feel prepared. These are issues unique to social studies teaching and the three chapters in this section illustrate the complexity of teaching about seemingly simple, everyday topics.

In Byker, Good, and Williams' examination of a community mapping exercise for preservice teachers, the authors demonstrate how communities are dynamic, shifting entities developed within complicated cultural, economic, historical, and geographic contexts. They demonstrate the power this exercise can have in fostering asset-based attitudes toward the school communities in which the preservice teachers will be working. The exercise works because the preservice teachers focus not on whether a school is in a *good* neighborhood or the number of students who qualify for free and reduced lunch, but instead on the experiences and opinions of community members such as local businesspeople and school staff. As I read through the authors' description of this work, I was struck by the potential power the same activity might have for K–12 students. Particularly for students whose communities are misunderstood by larger institutions, giving students this level of agency in the study of community structure, institutions, and knowledge could be a powerful way to help them analyze what it means to belong to a community and how community members can work to support, change, and advocate for their communities.

In their chapter, Fitzpatrick and Van Hover examine the contexts in which religion is constructed and taught in social studies classrooms. Their in-depth description of one teacher's struggle to teach about religion in a way that was honest and accurate points to the challenging nature of this task. As they note, teachers often shy away from, or choose not to, teach about religion for many reasons, including their own and their students' identities and beliefs within national and local contexts. As I read their account of Michael's teaching of Islam, the comments made by students provided me a vivid picture of the context in which Michael was teaching as he "attempted to teach his students to approach Islam with tolerance and understanding" (p. 186). In order to teach religion in a way that is not disjointed from everyday life, as the authors compellingly argue should be the case, teachers must develop a deep understanding of their own identities and their students' identities. Additionally, they must consider local and national narratives about the superiority and/or inferiority of certain religions when teaching about religion in a way that is meaningful and authentic. Doing this preparatory work would allow for a more honest, if complicated, approach to this often controversial topic.

Adams' examination of the family as an institution worthy of study in social studies classes throughout students' K–12 experiences focuses on the myriad ways in which families must be considered within the social studies disciplines. In particular, as she astutely notes, the family as an institution is shaped not only by the individuals who call themselves "a family," but also by other institutions such as government and religion. Throughout her chapter, Adams exhorts teachers and teacher educators to have students interrogate the ways in which students are members of the family as an institution and how that membership is impacted by the interaction of families and government and economies, for example. Her critical look at family reminds us that students are not islands, and therefore that their understanding of history or economic decision-making processes will necessarily be filtered through their own experiences as members of a family. Additionally, her "teaching ideas" provide concrete examples of powerful connections between students, their families, and important social studies concepts and content.

All three chapters provide strong support for a more robust and authentic teaching of social studies that uses the complexity of modern life to engage students in critical thinking about topics that are often used to support specific political agendas and around which media are developed and promoted, but which are rarely interrogated from the perspective of the *common good*. Importantly, doing this work necessitates teachers who know their students and their students' families and communities. Developing these understandings will allow teachers to guide their students in meaningful and active learning that asks students to think about *why* religious traditions often generate powerful myths about the afterlife and how those myths shape students' own lives as well as the lives of others around the globe. Teachers will be able to have students interrogate how governments use law and infrastructure to shape and narrate family life, from debates around subsidized child care and family leave to examining the impact of mass incarceration on the lives of students and their families. Teachers can help students study, critique, participate in, and define their own communities, which would necessitate the examination of culture, ethnicity, race, socioeconomic class in relation to their own and outside communities.

By guiding students in this type of meaningful, active, powerful learning, teachers can help their students lift the curtains that often appear to shroud the most powerful institutions in our society. In order for students to become active, informed citizens who can carefully consider multiple perspectives and think through complicated problems, they must be allowed to critically examine the institutions that shape and govern every aspect of their lives. All students, in one way or another, come into contact with religion, community, and family. It is our duty as social studies educators to help them think critically about how all of these pieces work together to generate the worlds in which they live.

Section VI:
Power, Authority, and Governance

CHAPTER TWENTY

Democracy

JANE C. LO, FLORIDA STATE UNIVERSITY
AMANDA GEIGER, LEON HIGH SCHOOL

> Democracy cannot succeed unless those who express their choice are prepared to choose wisely. The real safeguard of democracy, therefore, is education. It has been well said that no system of government gives so much to the individual or exacts so much as a democracy. Upon our educational system must largely depend the perpetuity of those institutions upon which our freedom and our security rest. To prepare each citizen to choose wisely and to enable him to choose freely are paramount functions of the schools in a democracy.
>
> —FRANKLIN D. ROOSEVELT, MESSAGE FOR AMERICAN EDUCATION WEEK, 1938

From the FDR quote above, it is easy to see how democracy goes hand-in-hand with education. Because of its complexity, democracy requires due diligence from its people. A quick Internet search of the term "democracy" yields this definition: "a system of government by the whole population or all the eligible members of a state, typically through elected representatives." Even though this is a simplified description of democracy, most students generally accept it without question; similarly, "free and open elections" seems an important outcry for all democratic movements. While the notion of being able to freely elect one's leader may intuitively be at the heart of democracy, why is it such an important part of democracy? And why is democracy such an important aspect of the social studies? This chapter explores these questions and provides some insights into what makes democracy both a challenge and a worthwhile endeavor.

As social studies educators and researchers, we often teach democracy and about democracy without necessarily considering its intricacies and improbability. We know students ought to understand the democratic system and its importance, but we may not always appreciate how difficult a form of government it is, and how much faith and power it places into the hands of its citizens. This chapter is divided into two major sections: one details the challenges of democracy (historic and modern); the other provides some solutions to the challenges. The goal of this chapter is to help readers appreciate the complexities of democracy and what it means to teach students about democracy in social studies courses.

THE CHALLENGES

Historical Context

Even though the idea of democracy has been around since ancient times, its history is anything but straightforward and successful. As a mostly western concept, this section of the chapter will deal with democracy's Western European origins. In *First Democracy*, Woodruff (2006) outlines the difficulties faced by the world's first recorded experiment with a formalized democracy in Athens during the 5th century BCE. People who have ever attempted to make a definitive decision about where to go for lunch with more than five people can begin to appreciate the difficulties of incorporating everyone's input. It is often easier and much quicker for one individual (a dictator) or a small group of individuals (an oligarchy) to decide on a course of action rather than to allow everyone a voice in the decision. Yet a democracy, by definition (in Greek, *demo* means commoners and *cracy* means rule: rule of the commoners), takes all of its citizens' voices into account. Ancient Athenians attempted a model of direct democracy, but eventually went through various periods of oligarchies and different iterations before collapsing under Roman rule. Of course, the Romans also dabbled with democracy, when they overthrew the monarchy in 509 BCE.[1] Eventually, competing political factions and military powers led the Roman democratic experiment through oligarchical phases. Ultimately, the rise of a series of Caesars as emperors ended large-scale democracies in the West until modern times.

Throughout the Middle Ages in Western Europe, many dalliances with democracy existed mostly on a smaller scale, but it was not until the writing of the Magna Carta in 1215 that powers of the monarch were restricted and transferred into individual freedoms in what became known as the English Writ of Habeas Corpus.[2] It is not a coincidence that limits on monarchical rule came with the rise of the written law, since rule of law dictates that no one shall be above the law, not even monarchs and members of the ruling party (Bingham, 2011). These written laws gave commoners new hope for gaining rights and a foothold in deciding their own fates. With the rise of the Enlightenment, writers like John Locke (1980), Rousseau (2014), and Montesquieu (1989) began arguing for equal rights and equality for individuals under the law. While these writers and historical events shaped the formation of democratic systems that we see today, it took a few more democratic experiments and centuries before the idea of democracy took hold.

Even though various modern systems of democracy differ in their emphasis and structures, at the heart of democracy still sits this principle—giving people a voice in governing themselves. Unlike the divine rules, dictatorships, or aristocratic oligarchies of the past, democracies give individuals an opportunity in deciding how they want to be governed in society. However, giving people a voice may be the easiest part of democracy, because this multitude of voices makes governance tricky and delicate, sometime even impractical. Furthermore, being rooted in western ideology, democracy may underrepresent other ways of understanding the world. And yet, as Churchill is often quoted as saying, "Many forms of Government have been tried, and will be tried in this world of sin and woe. No one pretends that democracy is perfect or all wise. Indeed it has been said that democracy is the worst form of Government except for all those other forms have been tried from time to time" (Churchill, 2008, p. 574). With these thoughts in mind, the next sections of this chapter will explore some challenges of democracy.

Liberal versus Illiberal Democracy

So far, this chapter has argued that a central tenet of democracy is the existence of free and open elections so that people may voice their will. While this is true, other complementary attributes are needed for democracies to function practically and adhere to the principles of "rule by the people." Specifically, there are key differences between two major views of democracy: liberal versus illiberal. Key attributes of liberal democracies include: "Popular sovereignty, majority will, civil rights and liberties, rule of law (constitutionalism), beyond free and fair elections" (Parker, 2012, p. 613). On the other hand, illiberal democracies do not require these checks and simply use majority votes to justify governing decisions.[3] The distinction between liberal and illiberal democracies is an important one, since illiberal democracies allow for the tyranny to arise through popular vote, while liberal democracies attempt to disallow tyranny of any kind.

Consider for a moment a classroom of 30 students that need to decide what the class will do with their free time by voting. If 12 students agree to play a game, whereas 10 students decide to nap, and eight students decide to read, allowing them all to do what they want will lead to chaos and inequality, since the gaming students might disturb the napping/reading students. In an illiberal democracy, the teacher might arbitrarily decide that 12 votes are enough of a plurality to show that more students want to play a game than the other choices, and force everyone to play a game. Similarly, the teacher can decide that 18 students want a quiet environment, making up a majority, and then force the 12 students to nap or read. By contrast, in a liberal democracy, where rights and liberty matter, the teacher might consider helping the 12 students come up with a game that they can play quietly so as to not disturb the students who are reading or napping. And of course, the rule of law becomes especially important, because whatever compromise the students come up with, they need to adhere to it as a contract or agreement. For example, if it's agreed on that the 12 students can only play a game if it does not disturb the students who wish to nap and read, then the rule must be enforced. Whereas illiberal democracies only care about determining what the majority wants (or using the majority vote to justify what one faction wants), liberal democracies care also about what happens to the minority if the majority gets their way. With liberal democracies, the written rules apply to everyone, and no one is above these agreed upon rules. There are always ways to amend or change the rules, but the process requires compromise among the stakeholders involved—this is at the heart of the social contract in obtaining citizens' consent to be governed. This process also requires citizens to choose wisely, and to have the wisdom to choose, which as FDR reminded us in the quote above, is an important purpose of education.

It is worth noting to students that processes meant to avoid the "tyranny of the majority" (Hamilton, Madison, Jay, & Kessler, 2000), in this case the establishment of a compromise led by the teacher, slow down the decision-making process. At the same time, democracy in the classroom may end up taking up illiberal qualities, where minority voices are either ignored or silenced. Therefore, it is important to help students understand the importance of liberal democratic ideals, so that unpopular (or marginalized) voices do not become squashed in the name of majority rule. However, the process might be slow and arduous. Liberal democratic governments often purposefully create frameworks for the operation of government that may seem inefficient. On further examination, they are designed this way to establish and protect the rule of law for both the minority and majority. Similarly, it is important to point out that liberal democracies are rare and fragile (Diamond, 2016), and since a major goal of democracy is to create a fair system for all, the rest of this chapter will deal mostly with the liberal form of democracy—both its challenges and its importance.

Sense of Community and Citizenship

Touraine (2008) claims, "there can be no democracy without a sense of belonging to a political collectivity" (p. 64). This sentiment is true in that democracy is about collective governance, and for one to be involved in governing another, one must feel some sense of responsibility toward another. This is especially true if we expect everyone to collectively partake in deciding what rules will apply to everyone. In a sense, people must have a stake in the process, or they will either not be involved, or not care about the process. At the same time, this sentiment rings false as globalization continues to defy our understanding of citizenship, both legally and philosophically. Yet, just because our ideas of citizenship are changing does not mean that belonging to a political collectivity is any less important. For example, cosmopolitanism seeks to promote and sustain democratic values in a world less restricted by borders and walls. But the democratic values continue to ring true through people's desires and dispositions for a more free and equal world, even as political entities shift and change (Hansen, 2009). The political entity in cosmopolitanism is less bound by nation-states and more bound by humanity as a whole.[4] Therefore, Touraine's sentiment continues to hold true: democracy can only exist when individuals care and feel responsible for the realm under which democracy hopes to prevail.

So to recap, democracy is all about (1) giving people a voice in governance, but it only works if (2) people have a collective sense of what they are governing, which leads us to the biggest challenge of liberal democracies: Pluralism and differences of opinions.

Pluralism and Differences of Opinions

Pluralism is the concept that people have different views about the world, and these views, while different, are all valid as long as they do not cause harm to others. As democracies continue to allow for people's voices to dictate governance, they will inevitably elicit different opinions, causing pluralism to arise. In other words, pluralism embodies the coexistence of diverse and competing understandings of the world and what it means to live well in it. On a small scale, pluralism can be seen as people's choices to be vegetarian, pescatarian, or omnivore. All are valid ways of engaging with the world and they can all coexist. On a large scale, pluralism arises in disagreements about political, religious, or existential beliefs. While all are potentially valid, their peaceful coexistence is less guaranteed. The goal of pluralism is to have these differences of opinions exist peaceably together.

Pluralism and democracy have a symbiotic relationship. In order for people to govern themselves, they must take pluralism into account, because other people's opinions can potentially dictate the laws that affect you. At the same time, in order for these different opinions to not devolve into chaos or war, individuals must abide by the rule of law created under democracy. One cannot exist without the other. Pluralism is a major challenge for liberal democracies, but it is also an important tenet. One can imagine democracies may run much more smoothly if everyone involved agreed on the same tenets of what it means to live well in the world. But generally speaking, people often disagree, and a goal of liberal democracy is to take all these voices into account so as to come up with a solution that is viable for all involved. The goal is to preserve pluralism while making sure the louder voices do not squelch the lesser voices. Again, tyranny of the majority is still tyranny to be avoided.

It may be worth mentioning in this section that pluralism (or differences of opinion on controversial topics) is a challenging concept for social studies teachers to teach (Hess, 2009). Since students often need to interact or have an experience with the concept before really learning it, it is imperative to students to experience pluralism firsthand in a classroom setting.

POTENTIAL SOLUTIONS

So how do democracies work with pluralism and the challenges of ruling with people who disagree with you? Some of the solutions come in practical or systemic ways. The United States utilizes a democratic republic system of representation that distills many voices into a more manageable two party system. Many other democracies utilize a parliamentarian system where people's voices are distilled into a multi-party system that brings forth the major issues at hand. Notice that both of these systems avoid a direct democratic representation. Creators of these modern democratic systems have learned from the failures of ancient democracies and their inability to keep factions at check. This is why modern democratic systems often have some form of representation, rather than direct democratic systems. In fact, James Madison argued that representation is a much stronger form of democracy when he said that the effect of representation is

> …to refine and enlarge the public views by passing them through the medium of a chosen body of citizens, whose wisdom may best discern the true interest of their country and whose patriotism and love of justice will be least likely to sacrifice it to temporary or partial considerations. (Hamilton et al., 2000, p. 76)

In a sense, if we are able to elect individuals who we trust to discern the interests of the people and keep the larger goal of democracy in mind, their representation of our voices would be much more beneficial to the longevity of democratic values.

In that same *Federalist No. 10*, Madison warned against the rise of factions in all systems where individuals disagree. Representation was his suggestions for how to fend off dangerous factions that may oppress others with different interests. The idea is that self-interest would necessarily have to be toned down or filtered through the process of electing a representative, so that the representative will always have to hold multiple interests in balance in order to best serve all of the various factions within his/her constituency. But as we know from modern day politics, this only works if different interests all have an equal voice in the election process, which makes individual participation such an important part of the democratic process. If only some people are involved in electing their members of Congress, then only their voices and views would be represented. And yet, we know that people are generally inattentive to processes of democracy and politics (Soroka & Wlezien, 2010, p. vii). For example, in the 2012 presidential election, only 64% of eligible voters participated (Enten, 2014). This conundrum brings us to the importance of democracy in social studies education.

Democracy and Social Studies Education

Many social studies educators teach democracy as an important concept situated around one person-one vote or the right to self-govern. But as this chapter points out, democracy is much more complex and much more important than those simple ideas. Some educators might be leery of teaching about pluralism or liberal ideas because they do not want to impose their own political understandings and leanings on students. While this caution is valid, it is important to point out there is a difference between teaching for democracy and teaching for partisanship. Teaching for partisanship means promoting one's own beliefs so that students take on those ideas. On the other hand, teaching for democracy means teaching students about the ideals of democracy, its complexities, challenges, and necessity in protecting everyone's freedoms, regardless of their political opinions. Teaching for partisanship is about squelching dissent, whereas teaching for democracy is about preserving pluralism, despite inevitable dissent. Teaching for democracy helps students see and understand a system of governance that ultimately tries to fight for everyone's voices. This is true if we hope to teach about the liberal democratic ideals, especially rule of law and civil rights and civil liberties. While complicated, these ideals are worthy of maintaining by future generations. So how might teachers accomplish this without alienating students to a system that they are a part of?

The pluralistic nature of society is evident in public schools, where students learn to interact with people who are different from them. School is often the first place where students experience things that are different from their homes and communities. Even in communities that are homogenous, students recognize differences among themselves. A key part of teaching for democracy is to help students begin to view these differences in a new light. Rather than dismiss people who are different from us, we can teach students to respect, embrace, and engage with those who are different. Specifically, social studies, as a subject in K–12 schooling, give students a chance to learn about historical and modern perspectives and differences of opinions. There are numerous occasions for social studies classes to offer students opportunities to practice respectful dialogue on issues where plurality of opinions exists. One way to achieve this in a classroom is through simulations and role-play, where students can safely take on positions that are different from their own (Lo & Parker, 2016). Providing a safe space in classrooms where students can express their views and listening to others may help them feel more confident in their ability to do so in the real world (Parker, 2010).

Democratic governing schemes in schools and classrooms can also help students experience democracy firsthand. Many teachers often begin the school year by having students agree on a set of classroom rules or norms—this is an example of liberal democracy. Rather than simply using this technique to get student buy-in, teachers might explain to students their responsibility for coming up with rules that will work for everyone and not just a small percentage of students. Having rules that we all can abide by and agree with is an important part of civil society. Similarly, this process might help students see they can have an impact on their day-to-day existence, even before they are able to vote. The key is helping students see that their involvement matters, in class, in school, in community, in society—these are all various political collectives students experience every day. Let us help them learn to not only participate in them, but feel like their voice matters in the process. At the same time, it is important for them to recognize that other people's voices matter just as much as their own; that we are all in this together.

FINAL THOUGHTS

The definition of democracy is simple enough—rule by the people—but its manifestation and success is anything but simple. As this chapter points out, the aims of democracy are lofty and the process difficult, but the rewards are worthwhile. Besides, the alternatives—as history reminds us—are not appealing. At the same time, democracy only works when people are willing to involve themselves in the process. It is a true collective effort. As the quote at the beginning of this chapter suggests, democracy is hard work for its people, and it requires a lot from its people. This is the ultimate challenge that democracy poses for social studies educators everywhere. How will we take up the baton of democracy and pass it onto the next generation of decision makers, liberty protectors, and injustice fighters? Luckily, history shows us as long as people continue to fight for freedom, equality, and justice, democracy will prevail, until something better comes along.

DISCUSSION QUESTIONS

1. How does education influence/impact our democratic processes?
2. Should schools promote democratic values? If so, which ones?
3. Why is it important for students to understand the differences between liberal and illiberal democracies?

4. What strategies can social studies teachers use to promote tenets of democracy?
5. How should social studies educators teach about democracy and its complexities?

NOTES

1. See Bringmann (2007) for a definitive account of the rise and fall of the Roman Republic.
2. To find out more about habeas corpus see Halliday's (2012) book on the topic.
3. Examples of this include some authoritarian regimes that hold elections, or even the demagogical rule that occurred in Ancient Greece.
4. See Brock and Brighouse (2005) or Nussbaum (2002) for more on cosmopolitan ideologies.

REFERENCES

Bingham, T. (2011). *The rule of law* (Reprint edition). London: Penguin UK.
Bringmann, K. (2007). *A history of the Roman Republic* (1st ed.). Cambridge; Malden, MA: Polity.
Brock, G., & Brighouse, H. (Eds.). (2005). *The political philosophy of cosmopolitanism*. Cambridge, MA: Cambridge University Press.
Churchill, W. (2008). *Churchill by himself: The definitive collection of quotations* (R. Langworth, Ed., 1st ed.). New York, NY: Public Affairs.
Diamond, L. (2016). *In search of democracy*. New York, NY: Routledge.
Enten, H. (2014, May 8). Midterm election turnout isn't so different from presidential year turnout. Retrieved from http://fivethirtyeight.com/features/midterm-election-turnout-isnt-so-different-from-presidential-year-turnout/
Halliday, P. D. (2012). *Habeas corpus: From England to empire* (Reprint edition). Cambridge, MA: Belknap Press.
Hamilton, A., Madison, J., Jay, J., & Kessler, C. R. (2000). *The federalist: A commentary on the constitution of the United States* (R. Scigliano, Ed.). New York, NY: Modern Library.
Hansen, D. T. (2009). Chasing butterflies without a net: Interpreting cosmopolitanism. *Studies in Philosophy and Education, 29*(2), 151–166. http://doi.org/10.1007/s11217-009-9166-y
Hess, D. E. (2009). *Controversy in the classroom: The democratic power of discussion*. New York, NY: Routledge.
Lo, J. C., & Parker, W. C. (2016). Role-playing and role-dropping: Political simulations as portals to pluralism in a contentious era. In W. Journell (Ed.), *Reassessing the social studies curriculum: Promoting critical civic engagement in a politically polarized, post-9/11 world* (Reprint edition, pp. 95–108). Lanham, MD: Rowman & Littlefield Publishers.
Locke, J. (1980). *Second treatise of government*. (C. B. Macpherson, Ed.). Indianapolis, IN: Hackett Publishing Company, Inc.
Montesquieu, C. de. (1989). *Montesquieu: The spirit of the laws*. (A. M. Cohler, B. C. Miller, & H. S. Stone, Eds.). Cambridge, MA: Cambridge University Press.
Nussbaum, M. C. (2002). Patriotism and cosmopolitanism. In J. Cohen (Ed.), *For love of country?* Boston, MA: Beacon Press.

Parker, W. C. (2010). Listening to strangers: Classroom discussion in democratic education. *Teachers College Record, 112*(11), 2815–2832.

Parker, W. C. (2012). Democracy, diversity, and schooling. In J. A. Banks (Ed.), *The encyclopedia of diversity in education* (pp. 613–620). New York, NY: Sage.

Rousseau, J. (2014). *The major political writings of Jean-Jacques Rousseau: The two "Discourses" and the "Social Contract."* (J. T. Scott, Ed., Reprint edition). Chicago, IL: University of Chicago Press.

Soroka, S. N., & Wlezien, C. (2010). *Degrees of democracy: Politics, public opinion, and policy.* Cambridge, NY: Cambridge University Press.

Touraine, A. (2008). *What is democracy?* Boulder, CO: Westview Press.

Woodruff, P. (2006). *First democracy: The challenge of an ancient idea.* London; New York, NY: Oxford University Press.

CHAPTER TWENTY-ONE

Freedom

ELI KEAN, MICHIGAN STATE UNIVERSITY
JEFFREY CRAIG, UNIVERSITY OF ARIZONA

> For to be free is not merely to cast off one's chains, but to live in a way that respects and enhances the freedom of others.
>
> —Nelson Mandela

Freedoms are at the core of our national identity as Americans. Yet, freedoms have a troubling history. Who gets what freedoms and what precisely are they free to do? Although seemingly ubiquitous in social and political discourse in the United States, the disparate enactment and protection of various freedoms makes it clear that people do not share similar conceptualizations of this fundamental democratic value. Social studies classrooms are ideal spaces for investigating and gaining a more complex understanding of freedom. In this chapter, we offer two lenses through which educators can consider freedom. First is freedom's relationship with restriction; that is, how freedoms are used or called upon to restrict individual's rights and opportunities. Second is freedom's relationship with resistance; that is, how individuals, groups and communities have utilized resistance as a means to reassert or gain freedoms.

FREEDOM AND RESTRICTION

Freedom has always been an essential characteristic of U.S. culture, defining our brand of democracy and guaranteed to its citizens through the Constitution. However, dominant narratives in the social studies tend to ignore the fact that the freedoms provided to some have always been restricted from others. In this sense, the presence of freedom often aligns with the presence of other kinds of privilege; these privileged characteristics have shifted and expanded somewhat through time, but the restriction of people's freedoms is a defining characteristic of almost every era of U.S. history, including the current day. In this section, we focus our attention in this section on three historic and contemporary attempts to limit people's freedoms.

Restrictions and the Exercise of Religion

Under the U.S. Constitution, citizens have a right to express any religious belief—or, presumably, none at all—without government sanction or prohibition. However, the privileging of Judeo-Christian beliefs over others is prevalent in every U.S. social institution. In the 114th U.S. Congress, nearly 92% of its members were Christian (Pew Research Center, 2015); compare this to the 73% of American adults who identify as Christian. On the other hand, almost all other religious identities are underrepresented in Congress, including Buddhists, Muslims, and Hindus. Though the implication of the First Amendment is that the government should not have a preference for one religion over others, atheists are legally banned from running for office in seven states, and voters often question the morality and ethics of atheist politicians. Indeed, both major political parties invoke Judeo-Christian beliefs as a foundation for certain political actions.

While state legislators are privileging Christianity within its ranks and advancing their own version of Christian beliefs in their bills, they are also attempting to codify Islamophobia. Recent world events have made the United States extremely hostile to Muslims or others who may be mistaken for Muslims, such as Sikhs. Since the attacks of September 11, 2001, Muslims have been the target of fear-based hate crimes and bigoted political rhetoric, finding their mosques vandalized and firebombed. Since Donald Trump assumed the presidency, he has signed several Executive Orders—later deemed unconstitutional by the courts—aimed at obstructing immigrants, refugees and other international travelers from predominantly Muslim countries in the Middle East (Reinl, 2017). Although Islam is the second largest religion in the world, politically charged rhetoric would like to make us believe that Muslims' very existence is a threat. In 2010, a Gallup poll reported that almost half of all U.S. Muslims reported that they had personally experienced racial or religious discrimination in the past year (Gallup, 2010). Strickland (2016) reports that there were more than six bills introduced in various state legislatures in 2015 that intended to bar foreign law, specifically Sharia law, from state's courts—even though courts are already obligated to follow U.S. law.

Bans on Sharia law are just one example of legislators attempting to restrict individual freedoms. For the past several decades, lawmakers have put forth hundreds of so-called Religious Freedom bills, which allow states to make exceptions to preexisting antidiscrimination laws. These bills are largely based on the Religious Freedoms Restoration Act signed by President Clinton in 1993, which applies only to the federal government. More than twenty states have passed religious freedom laws that allow private and/or public employees to refuse service due to their deeply held religious beliefs without legal or disciplinary consequence. Primarily, these beliefs stand in opposition to a customer's sexual orientation, gender identity or gender expression. Proponents of religion freedom laws claim that they are protecting business owners' First Amendment rights. In this instance, we come to the intersection of two freedoms: freedom of the employee to express and uphold their own religious beliefs, and the freedom of LGBTQ customers to patronize any business of their choosing without discrimination.

Restrictions on the Freedoms of Transgender People

Transgender people's freedoms are restricted in numerous ways. The presumption of a gender binary is woven into every institutional policy and practice. For example, it is exceedingly difficult for many transgender Americans to obtain ID that matches their gender. The medical field—and by proxy health insurance—is restrictive to transgender people who often need medical care that is not covered for their designated sex (Spade, 2015). For example, transgender men often struggle to have insurance companies pay for gynecological care. In addition, hate speech is routinely used to inhibit transgender people's freedom of expression. In this way, many of the everyday freedoms that cisgender people take for granted are restricted for transgender people.

When Laverne Cox graced the cover of Time in 2014 and the magazine declared transgender rights the "new civil rights frontier," some transgender people were simultaneously delighted and worried. For all the positive effects of having the first openly transgender person on the cover of Time, that kind of visibility can also spur attempts to restrict and silence. Hate speech and microaggressions against transgender people continue to have negative and serious consequences, including trans* people's ability to freely express themselves. Julia Serano (2017) offers this reflection:

> As a child, I saw how gender-variant people were openly and relentlessly mocked, so I decided not to tell anyone about what I was experiencing. As a young adult, I continued to remain quiet about my identity. Colloquially, we call this being "in the closet," but that's just a fancy way of saying "hiding from hate speech and harassment." Of course, I

technically had free speech, but that doesn't count for much if speaking your mind is likely to result in you being bombarded with epithets, losing your job, being ostracized by your community, and possibly other forms of retribution. When I attended my first transgender support group in the early '90s, we held our meetings in a secret location because, despite our First Amendment right to peaceably assemble, it was simply not safe for us to meet in public or be discovered by others.

One of the dominant ways that policymakers have recently attempted to restrict transgender people's freedoms is through so-called "bathroom bills", which require transgender people to use the restroom that aligns with their sex assigned at birth (Griffin & Keisling, 2015). Logistically speaking, this means that every public facility must employ some kind of gender verification system—a serious invasion into people's personal and medical privacy. The reason provided by supporters of these bills is to stop male sexual predators from gaining easy access to women's restrooms. However, the factual basis for this concern is dubious. In fact, there are examples of harassment and assault in public restrooms from cisgender (non-transgender) people, including reports of cisgender people harassing transgender people whom they believe to be in the "wrong" restroom and reports of cisgender men assaulting women in restrooms, dressing rooms and locker rooms—including the current President of the United States, Donald Trump. The effect of these bills—even if they are only proposed and do not become law—is widespread fear and ignorance about transgender people, which further restricts transgender people's freedoms.

Restrictions on the Freedom of Speech

The spirit of freedom of speech is protection for full citizens from state action restricting their speech. Nevertheless, the U.S. Congress and Judicial system have limited freedom of speech by restricting speech that is considered obscene or inciting lawless action. These exceptions help represent the Court's typical perspective on freedom of speech: that is, speech is protected by default and only suppressed or punishable under exceptional circumstances.

This default stance toward freedom of speech resulted in a decision Citizens United v. Federal Election Committee (2010) wherein the Supreme Court ruled in a 5–4 decision that corporations and unions could not have their political contributions restricted; the majority opinion invoked freedom of speech as their primary reasoning, arguing that restrictions on political contributions amount to a fine on political speech. At its heart, the Citizens United v. FEC (2010) decision hinges on what actions are protected by freedom of speech and its print-focused neighbor, freedom of the press.

In 2017, lawmakers in multiple states have proposed laws that "would make it a serious crime to assemble in groups and express political dissent" (Jackman,

2017, n.p.). In Washington state, for example, "a lawmaker termed some protests 'economic terrorism'...in Minnesota, a person convicted of participating in an 'unlawful assembly' could be held liable for costs incurred by police and other public agencies" (Jackman, 2017, n.p.). Legislators in Indiana proposed a law that would "direct police encountering a mass traffic obstruction to clear the road by 'any means necessary,' echoing a phrase made famous by Malcolm X during the 1960s civil rights movement" (Jackman, 2017, n.p.). In response to recent large-scale public protests against police brutality and other threats to the lives of marginalized people, state legislatures have proposed bills that would further restrict protestors' freedom of speech and assembly, astoundingly attempting to criminalize actions that should be constitutionally protected.

The protest by the Sioux tribes of North and South Dakota against the construction of the Dakota Access pipeline spurred just such a response from the North Dakota legislature. The Sioux tribes and their supporters raised legitimate concerns about the proposed route, which intersects with the Missouri River, potentially destroying their main source of agricultural and drinking water for the area, in addition to disturbing ancient burial grounds. Protesters created an encampment at Standing Rock Reservation and remained in place from April 2016 through February 2017, when the National Guard and other law enforcement officers forcibly cleared the area through the use of water cannons, concussion grenades, and other militarized weapons (Wong, 2016). Soon after, the North Dakota legislature introduced a bill that would essentially decriminalize vehicular manslaughter, if the victim was a protester and the driver claims it was an accident. These kinds of bills are incredibly dangerous to the freedoms of all individuals, especially considering the recent death of Heather Heyer, who was killed when an individual intentionally drove his car through an anti-white supremacy protest in Charlottesville, Virginia (Carissimo, 2017).

The fuller struggle to realize freedom of speech must include a discussion of silencing the voices of marginalized voices through the exertion of power physically and through dominant discursive moves and histories. The struggle against silencing is visible during the current debate about "political correctness." Those who invoke their freedom of speech by arguing that political correctness is trespassing on their speech do so contradictorily. The argument goes: you are fighting for space to voice your nondominant ideas instead of my dominant ideas, so you are restricting my freedom of speech. What those who argue against political correctness do not realize is when people construct safe and brave spaces they do so precisely because in dominant spaces their speech is silenced. Spaces where different speech and ideas are spoken is not censorship of dominant speech, it is the exercising of free speech and resistance.

FREEDOM AND RESISTANCE

The most prevalent method of resistance in our history is nonviolent resistance. The use of social media by marginalized communities has become a powerful tool in resisting injustice and the restrictions on freedoms. In addition, large-scale nonviolent resistance such as labor union strikes and more recent protests against police brutality often utilize their own bodies in order to physically resist inequity and injustice.

Social Media as a Form of Resistance

Social media allows anyone with access to the Internet the ability to reach a wide audience with their speech with near immediacy. Historically marginalized groups are utilizing social media in powerful ways to actualize their freedom of speech and organize nonviolent resistance. Shirky (2011) cited how social media can act as a tool for citizens to rally each other to pursue collective goals and demand changes of corporations and social institutions. Meanwhile, hateful and bigoted people are free to express their opinions as well, and are doing so with abandon in nearly every comments section. Numerous news stories feature an individual who has been disciplined or fired from their place of employment due to discriminatory comments posted on social media. In addition, women are routinely the recipient of vicious, demeaning and sexist comments which they can do little to stop, other than avoiding social media altogether. Clearly this hateful speech does not enhance the freedom of others; in fact, it detracts from others' freedoms through pain and fear.

Some of our experiences teaching students who may have grown up as digital natives suggests to us that they are more prepared to engage social media with literate practices that are more likely to enhance the freedom of others; they understand "trolling" and clickbait headlines, for example. We suggest that Thurgood Marshall's advocacy of freedom of speech as critical to the open debate of ideas is a role that classroom teachers should take. Navigating the complex, layered speech on social media around #blacklivesmatter, for instance, to engage students in nuanced discussions of the grievances and responses could be a great role for teachers.

Social media also provides people a space to enact their freedom of speech in ways that enhance the freedoms of others. In particular, social media is a space where counternarratives to dominant discourses survive and thrive. Despite the oft-discussed terrible backlash against those who openly resist supremacist structures through their speech acts on social media, the backlash only happens because people are forced to struggle with ideas that are counter to their own. We argue that these counternarratives enhance the freedoms of all others who read them, by freeing their thought and speech from the power of dominant discourses, however temporarily. Resistance through speech occurs whenever a person speaks their truths out loud to confront and disrupt the re-circulation of incomplete narratives.

Large-Scale Acts of Nonviolent Resistance

In the past few years, people have utilized public protest to resist everything from schooling conditions to police brutality to election results. The importance and purpose of protests as acts of resistance cannot be understated. Protest redefines and interrupts public space as a location of connection instead of isolation. Protests are a form of collective communication and visual solidarity. Most importantly, it is a method through which everyday citizens can exert power and pressure on decision-makers to improve oppressive and unjust practices.

Historically, the most notable means through which freedom of assembly has been historically invoked to display resistance is through the actions of labor unions. Indeed, other than the Civil Rights Movement, labor union strikes are the most common example of free assembly in U.S. history texts. Even though this freedom to publicly resist is supposedly a fiercely protected freedom, educational scholars have found that textbooks largely present neutral or negative portrayals of organized labor (Kean & Schmitt, 2015). For example, a middle school U.S. history textbook ends its description of the Haymarket Affair by saying that "following the Haymarket Riot, many middle class Americans associated the labor movement with terrorism and disorder" (Appleby, Brinkley, Broussard, Ritchie, & McPherson, 2009, p. 567–568). Instead of treating demonstrators with reverence for utilizing a constitutionally guaranteed right, the dominant reaction to protesters continues to be one of confusion, disdain, or fear.

The NCSS C3 Framework (2013) does not speak specifically about the freedom of assembly or the ways in which this freedom has been utilized historically. However, some state standards specifically reference actions of public resistance such as the Pullman Strike or the Haymarket Affair. In many states, these standards are written in a way that places the protesters and strikers in a negative light. For example, Arkansas expects its 12th graders to "Investigate the sources of national fear and violence in post World War I" (Arkansas Department of Education, 2006); the examples of "sources of national fear" provided include xenophobia, communism, anarchists, the Ku Klux Klan, and labor strikes. How is it possible that a constitutionally sanctioned freedom such as striking could be considered a source of national fear? Taken together with the textbook excerpt described above, it is clear that the dominant social studies narrative perceives strikes and other public assemblies as disruptions rather than enactments of freedom in order to resist injustice.

When considering the question of who has the freedom to peaceably assemble, or who is freedom of assembly for, looking across the nation we find that nearly two-thirds of all U.S. states have limitations on, or outright prohibit, public employees from striking (Kerrigan, 2012). When situations become dire, such as in the Detroit Public School system, teachers have resorted to widespread "sick-outs" to call attention to the decrepit state of their schools and inadequate teacher compensation (Felton, 2016). A common rationale used by state legislators for prohibiting public employees from exercising their constitutionally guaranteed freedom is that they provide an "essential service" that should not be interrupted. Being so limited in their freedom to peaceably assemble, teachers have few avenues through which to call public attention to and garner support for much needed improvements.

Outside of the public sector, backlash against the Black Lives Matter (BLM) movement protests is an example that one's freedoms are limited based on one's ideological message. The response, for example, to white college students violently rioting after a sports game is markedly different from the primarily peaceful protests against police brutality. Since 1997, the Department of Defense has supplied local police departments with more than $5 billion worth of military-grade vehicles, weapons and other equipment (Apuzzo, 2014), which get deployed regularly against BLM protesters.

CONCLUSION

We suggest that teachers can center alternative humanizing and counter-narrative pedagogies that try to engage speech as a creative act as attempts to speak to issues that are not mainstream curricular topics. A multitude of amazing resources have been created by scholars in the past few years that are galvanized around a particular event or issue, such as the Black Lives Matter Syllabus (Roberts, 2016), the Trans* Justice Syllabus (Committee for Advancing Trans Studies in Sociology, 2017), the Standing Rock Syllabus (NYC Stands with Standing Rock Collective, 2016), and the Intersectional Crip Syllabus (Leibowitz, 2016). We argue that practicing freedom of speech to enhance the freedom of others involves three considerations: (1) the intentional use of silence as a means both to avoid oppressive speech and to counter oppressive speech, (2) the use of speech as creative acts meant to humanize self and others, and (3) using privilege to speak against oppression. Although the freedoms inscribed in the First Amendment to the Constitution of the United States are stated in ways that make most explicit that they are freedoms from laws, the freedoms are all nonetheless comprised of freedoms for particular people, from specific interference, to act in certain ways. These freedoms implicitly extend only for those people considered to be citizens under the law; there is no shortage of contemporary issues regarding who freedoms are for, with, for example, undocumented immigrants and people convicted of crimes.

In the spirit of the Nelson Mandela quote offered at the beginning of this chapter, we look to a future where freedom is less of an individual characteristic, pitting one's freedoms against another, to a society where we enact our freedoms in ways that builds community and lifts everyone up. Mandela's quote insists upon a particular strategy of gaining and maintaining freedoms—this strategy being the development of alliances, being each other's allies and accomplices (Indigenous Action Media, 2013) in this journey toward freedom for all.

DISCUSSION QUESTIONS

1. Can freedoms be guaranteed? If so, by whom and for whom? If not, why not?
2. What is the relationship between oppression and freedom? What is the relationship between privilege and freedom?
3. What should happen when two freedoms appear to clash, such as when one person's freedom of speech is used to suppress other people's freedom of religion?
4. How is the word freedom used in political and social discourse? In what ways do people who hold drastically different political ideologies utilize the idea of freedom(s)?
5. What is challenging about discussing freedoms such as freedom from terror or freedom from want?

REFERENCES

Appleby, J., Brinkley, A., Broussard, A., Ritchie, D., & McPherson, J. (2009). *The American journey.* Columbus, OH: McGraw-Hill.

Apuzzo, M. (June 8, 2014). War gear flows to police departments. *New York Times.* Retrieved from http://www.nytimes.com/2014/06/09/us/war-gear-flows-to-police-departments.html

Arkansas Department of Education. (2006). *American History (United States History) social studies curriculum framework.* Retrieved from http://www.arkansased.gov/public/userfiles/Learning_Services/Curriculum%20and%20Instruction/Frameworks/Social%20Studies/amer_hist_2006.doc

Carissimo, J. (2017, August 13). Woman killed in Charlottesville, Virginia car attack identified. *CBS News.* Retrieved from https://www.cbsnews.com/news/heather-heyer-charlottesville-virginia-car-attack/

Citizens United v. Federal Election Commission, No. 08-205, 558 U.S. 310 (2010).

Committee for Advancing Trans Studies in Sociology. (2017). *Trans justice syllabus.* Retrieved from http://www.transjusticesyllabus.com/category/syllabus/

Felton, R. (2016). How Detroit's teacher 'sickout' cast a spotlight on unsafe school conditions. *The Guardian*. Retrieved from https://www.theguardian.com/us-news/2016/may/07/detroit-public-schools-sickout-lawmakers-plan

Gallup Poll. (2010). Retrieved from http://www.gallup.com/poll/157082/islamophobia-understanding-anti-muslim-sentiment-west.aspx

Griffin, C., & Keisling, M. (2015, April 24). Op-ed: We must stop the legislative war on transgender people. *The Advocate*. Retrieved from http://www.advocate.com/commentary/2015/04/24/op-ed-we-must-stop-legislative-war-transgender-people

Indigenous Action Media. (2013, August 14). *Accomplices not allies: Abolishing the ally industrial complex*. Retrieved from http://www.indigenousaction.org/accomplices-not-allies-abolishing-the-ally-industrial-complex/

Jackman, T. (2017, February 4). How far can protesters go before the government steps in? *The Washington Post*. Retrieved from https://www.washingtonpost.com/local/public-safety/how-far-can-protesters-go-before-the-government-steps-in/2017/02/04/bd96357e-e8b8-11e6-bf6f-301b6b443624_story.html?utm_term=.ad3aa688cf12

Kean, E., & Schmitt, A. J. (2015). What's missing from the textbook?: An inquiry-based lesson plan on the untold histories of labor unions. *The Georgia Social Studies Journal, 5*(1), 15–27.

Kerrigan, H. (2012). *Why public-sector strikes are so rare*. Retrieved from http://www.governing.com/topics/public-workforce/col-why-public-sector-strikes-are-rare.html

Leibowitz, T. (2016). Crip lit: Toward an intersectional crip syllabus. *Autostraddle.com*. Retrieved from https://www.autostraddle.com/crip-lit-an-intersectional-queer-crip-syllabus-333400/

National Council for the Social Studies. (2013). *The college, career, and civic life (C3) framework for social studies state standards: Guidance for enhancing the rigor of K-12 civics, economics, geography, and history*. Silver Spring, MD: Author.

NYC Stands with Standing Rock Collective. (2016). *#StandingRockSyllabus*. Retrieved from https://nycstandswithstandingrock.wordpress.com/standingrocksyllabus/

Pew Research Center. (2015). *Faith on the hill: The religious composition of the 114th Congress*. Retrieved from http://www.pewforum.org/2015/01/05/faith-on-the-hill/

Reinl, J. (2017, June 29). Trump's Muslim ban comes into effect. *Al Jazeera*. Retrieved from http://www.aljazeera.com/news/2017/06/trump-muslim-ban-redefining-family-170629193344749.html

Roberts, F. L. (2016). *Black lives matter: Race, resistance, and populist protest*. [Syllabus]. New York, NY: Gallatin School of Individualized Study, New York University.

Serano, J. (2017, February 6). Free speech and the paradox of tolerance. *Medium.com*. Retrieved from https://medium.com/@juliaserano/free-speech-and-the-paradox-of-tolerance-e0547aefe538#.xlc7kz4g6

Shirky, C. (2011). The political power of social media: Technology, the public sphere, and political change. *Foreign Affairs, (90)*1, 28–41.

Spade, D. (2015). *Normal life*. Durham, NC: Duke University Press.

Strickland, P. (2016, January 30). US anti-Islamic bills create 'environment of fear'. *Al Jazeera*. Retrieved from http://www.aljazeera.com/news/2016/01/anti-islamic-bills-create-environment-fear-160129195330843.html

Wong, J. C. (2016, November 21). Dakota Access pipeline: 300 protesters injured after police use water cannons. *The Guardian*. Retrieved from https://www.theguardian.com/us-news/2016/nov/21/dakota-access-pipeline-water-cannon-police-standing-rock-protest

CHAPTER TWENTY-TWO

Terrorism

WAYNE JOURNELL, UNIVERSITY OF NORTH CAROLINA AT GREENSBORO

Not all Muslims are terrorists, but all terrorists are Muslim.

—BRIAN KILMEADE, *FOX & FRIENDS* HOST, 10/15/10

Living with a persistent threat of terrorism has become the "new normal" for citizens of the United States and many nations throughout the world. Since the attacks on September 11, 2001, terrorism has become an accepted reality of life in the 21st century, and many of our everyday routines have likely been irreparably altered. These changes range from the pragmatic, such as increased security at airports, to more controversial measures, such as government surveillance of personal data (Garrett, 2016).

Our students only know of life in a post-9/11 world, which makes teaching about terrorism both challenging and necessary. As terrorism and its associated phrases (e.g., "War on Terror") have become part of the cultural lexicon, it has come at a cost. For most Americans, terrorism conjures specific, and I would argue simplistic, images of Muslim jihadists seeking to kill innocent people in Western nations, as evidenced by the quotation by *Fox & Friends* host Brian Kilmeade that prefaces this chapter. The idea of using violence or fear to achieve political goals did not start with the 9/11 attacks, nor does Islam hold a monopoly on contemporary acts of terrorism.

The formal social studies curriculum, however, does little to combat these stereotypes. Recent analyses of social studies textbooks and state curriculum standards have found that terrorism is rarely mentioned within the formal curriculum of K–12 schooling, and when it is, it is rarely discussed in a nuanced way that moves beyond Islamic extremism (Bellows, 2016; Stoddard & Hess, 2016). Not only does this treatment of terrorism minimize its influence on global affairs, but it also does little to combat the stereotype of Arabs and Muslims as terrorists that is pervasive in American society (Saleem & Thomas, 2011; Yoder, Johnson, & Karam, 2016).

In this chapter, I attempt to complicate this post-9/11 definition of terrorism by looking at the historical evolution of terrorism, as well as acts of violence in recent years that I argue should fall within a more complex definition of terrorism used within the social studies curriculum. I conclude the chapter by discussing how teachers can engage in critical discussions of terrorism with their students that move beyond simplistic and stereotypical definitions.

A (BRIEF) HISTORY OF TERRORISM

An understanding of the history of terrorism can help debunk students' preconceived notions about who terrorists are and why they engage in such acts. Space constraints prohibit a comprehensive chronology of terrorism here (for a more extensive discussion, see Law, 2015); however, acts of violence carried out as a form of political intimidation can be traced to antiquity. Even if teachers do not want to extend this discussion to ancient Greece and Rome, they could start at the French Revolution and the origins of the word *terrorism* in its modern context. During the Reign of Terror, a period of time in which the Jacobins publicly executed thousands of "enemies of the revolution" via the guillotine, the Jacobins referred to themselves as "terrorists" and openly touted executions as a way to intimidate their enemies and force compliance to their rule.

This type of state-sanctioned terrorism, in which acts of violence are used by governments to control their citizenry, has been a centerpiece of every authoritarian regime in human history. Historical examples include the fascist dictatorships in Germany and Italy prior to World War II and Cambodia under Pol Pot, but contemporary examples exist in North Korea and in many nations located in what is colloquially termed the "Third World." Even the histories of democratic nations often are blemished by state-sanctioned terrorism; the use of fire hoses, police dogs, and beatings by police officers as a way to enforce Jim Crow policies in the United States during the first half of the 20th century could meet this definition, and some have argued that the disproportionate number of African-Americans killed at the hands of police in recent years does as well (King, Warren, Bender, & Finley, 2016).

Contemporary use of the term terrorism, however, is rarely used in conjunction with state-sanctioned violence. Rather, it is used to describe violence carried out by nongovernmental groups, often groups in the political minority or on the extreme ends of the political spectrum. Even after narrowing the definition in this way, the history of terrorism extends well beyond September 11th and Muslim extremists.

As early as the mid-19th century, political groups across Europe began using terrorism as a form of activism. Perhaps the most well-known was the Irish Republican Brotherhood that engaged in a series of bombings in Britain in the 1880s to generate fear and help sway public opinion toward Ireland's independence. Other groups across the continent carried out assassinations and other violent acts in an attempt to overthrow governments or push radical agendas.

The 20th century saw more of the same; however, the perceived successes of European terrorists led to the spread of terrorism across the globe. Also, increased technology made attacks deadlier. Although it is around the mid-20th century that Islamic groups began to use terrorism as a tool for political influence, it is important to note that 20th-century terrorism was not confined to a single religion or ideology. The Northern Ireland Conflict, for example, was a thirty-year guerrilla war between the largely Catholic Irish nationalists and the predominately Protestant British loyalists in which both sides engaged in numerous terrorist attacks.

The creation of Israel as a Jewish state within the Palestine region in 1948 led to the rise of Islamic extremism as we know it today. Groups such as Fatah and the Palestine Liberation Organization (PLO) carried out guerrilla warfare tactics against Israel in the 1970s and 1980s, including the hijacking of planes, the murdering of Israeli schoolchildren, and the capture and subsequent murder of Israeli athletes at the 1972 Olympic Games. Israel condemned such actions as terrorism; however, the PLO described them as part of a war for liberation.

Although Israel rescinded its terrorist rhetoric against the PLO in 1993 after the latter agreed to recognize Israel's existence and cease armed conflict, other Islamic extremist groups were coming to power at the same time. These new organizations, most notably Al-Qaeda and the Taliban, broadened their scope beyond Israel to include all Western-controlled Arab nations and their allies, with the goal of instilling Islamic fundamentalist regimes throughout the region. For the first time, these groups began targeting American interests; in 1993, Al-Qaeda-trained terrorists bombed the World Trade Center in New York City, killing six people and wounding more than a thousand. Other Al-Qaeda attacks on Americans included the bombing of two U.S. embassies in Africa in 1998, killing 224 people, and the USS Cole in 2000, killing 17 American sailors.

The pinnacle of Islamic extremist terrorism occurred on September 11, 2001 when Al-Qaeda operatives hijacked commercial airliners and flew them into the World Trade Center and the Pentagon, killing nearly 3,000 people. In the years since, the organizations have changed—Al-Qaeda's influence, for example, has waned, leading to the rise of the Islamic State of Iraq and the Levant (ISIL)—but the use of terrorism as a political weapon has not. Islamic extremists have attacked civilians across the globe, and in many ways, they have been successful in their goal of disrupting the Western world's way of life.

Finally, lest students think that terrorism is a practice that is unique to "others," they should be made aware of the history of terrorism in the United States. Perhaps the best example of American terrorism is the Ku Klux Klan, which engaged in lynchings, bombings, and other forms of violence in the name of White supremacy. Although the Klan's apex was the late 19th and early 20th centuries, factions of the organization still exist today. During the 1960s, organizations such as the Weather Underground engaged in domestic terrorism in opposition to the Vietnam War, bombing government facilities. Finally, prior to 9/11, the deadliest terrorist attack on American soil was carried out in 1995 by Timothy McVeigh, a right-wing extremist, who bombed a federal government building in Oklahoma City, killing 168 people.

As already noted, a nuanced history of terrorism is unlikely to be found within state standards or other aspects of the formal curriculum. Therefore, it is likely that teachers will have to make space for this historical understanding within the context of other topics. For example, world history teachers could draw parallels to modern terrorism when they cover the French Revolution, and U.S. history teachers could compare the acts of the Klan to contemporary acts of terror when they cover Reconstruction, as well as discuss state-sanctioned terrorism when discussing the Civil Rights Movement. Civics and government teachers could engage in discussions of historical terrorism as a means of contextualizing acts of terror that permeate into the classroom under the guise of current events.

Such information need not be presented as lectures or dissemination of facts. Rather, teachers might use YouTube to find news reports of terrorist acts from the 20th century that break from the typical post-9/11 narrative and engage their students in critical discussions of how those acts compare with modern conceptions of terrorism. Popular culture offers other options for teachers; for example, the television series *The West Wing* aired a special episode less than a month after the 9/11 attacks entitled "Isaac and Ishmael" in which they cautioned against Islamophobia and drew parallels between Muslim extremists and other extremist groups, such as the Klan (Jones & Dionisopoulous, 2004), and other filmic depictions of historical acts of terror could be used to start similar discussions. Similarly, popular music often converges with politics and can be used to engage students in critical explorations of sensitive topics (Soden & Castro, 2013); U2's "Sunday, Bloody Sunday," for example, describes one of the more violent acts during the Northern Ireland conflict, and another example can be found in Billie Holliday's 1939 song "Strange Fruit," which describes systemic violence against African-Americans. Although a nuanced discussion of the evolution of terrorism is beyond the scope of elementary-aged students, many scholars have argued that young children can grapple with difficult topics (e.g., Bickmore, 1999; Libresco & Balantic, 2016), and teachers can use tools such as trade books to raise questions about why people might be compelled to engage in acts of terrorism and draw comparisons among different groups who engage in such acts (Bellows, 2016; Libresco & Balantic, 2016).

CONTEMPORARY TERRORISM

Five events occurring over a three-month period at the end of 2015 and beginning of 2016 illustrate the complexity and ambiguity in defining terrorism in contemporary society. On November 13, 2015, the world's attention turned to Paris, France where a series of coordinated attacks by suicide bombers and gunmen outside of the Stade de France, inside the Bataclan theatre, and throughout crowded cafes in downtown Paris resulted in 130 deaths and hundreds more injured. ISIL claimed responsibility for the attacks, proclaiming that they were in retaliation for French airstrikes on ISIL military targets in Syria and Iraq (*British Broadcasting Corporation*, 2015).

Two weeks later, on November 27, a 57-year-old White male named Robert Dear killed three people and injured nine others when he opened fire at a Colorado Springs Planned Parenthood facility (Turkewitz & Healy, 2015). Dear, who as of this writing has been declared mentally incompetent and unfit to stand trial, admitted that his actions were politically motivated. He intimated to police that the shootings were in response to a video produced by the antiabortion group Center for Medical Progress that accused Planned Parenthood of making profits from fetal organ sales. The video went viral on social media and became a talking point in early Republican presidential primary debates, although subsequent investigations of Planned Parenthood by twelve states and three congressional committees found that the organization had not engaged in any wrongdoing (*Huffington Post*, 2015; Legum, 2015).

Five days later, Syed Farook and Tashfeen Malik, a married couple of Middle Eastern descent and practicing Muslims, killed 14 individuals and wounded 22 more when they opened fire at Farook's place of employment in San Bernardino, California. What was initially believed to be a workplace dispute was later determined to be an act of domestic terrorism after stockpiles of assault weapons and bomb-making materials were found at the couple's home. A subsequent investigation of the couple's digital footprints indicated that they had been radicalized by Islamic extremists several years earlier and were actively planning to carry out an attack within the United States (*Los Angeles Times*, 2015).

Shortly after the new year, a group of armed anti-government militants led by Ammon Bundy, son of noted anti-government protestor Cliven Bundy, seized the Malheur National Wildlife Refuge in Oregon. The occupation reportedly began in response to the federal government's conviction of two Oregon ranchers for arson on federal land; however, as the occupation progressed, Bundy demanded that the federal government relinquish control of the Malheur National Forest in addition to overturning the ranchers' convictions. For over three weeks, over 25 gunmen engaged in a standoff with state and federal authorities. On January 26, 2016, Bundy and other leaders of the movement were arrested, and one militia member was killed by police. When the standoff finally ended in mid-February, 27 people were arrested for their part in the occupation (*The Oregonian*, 2016).

The final event occurred on January 30th in Nigeria. Militants from the Islamic extremist group Boko Haram firebombed huts and proceeded to kill over 80 residents of the Dalori village in a siege that lasted over four hours. Three suicide bombers then targeted the neighboring village of Gamori, killing and injuring even more people. The attack was part of Boko Haram's quest to establish Islamist rule in Nigeria which has claimed over 20,000 lives and displaced 2.3 million Nigerians from their homes since 2009 (*British Broadcasting Corporation*, 2016).

Based on the technical definition of terrorism, which is "the use of violent acts to frighten the people in an area as a way of trying to achieve a political goal" (Merriam-Webster, 2016), it would seem that all five events should be classified as such. The Paris, Colorado Springs, San Bernardino, and Nigeria attacks were obviously violent in that people were killed; however, the Oregon standoff used the threat of violence as a way of inciting fear, as evidenced by the closing of schools in districts surrounding the occupied site. Moreover, all of these acts were carried out in the hopes of achieving a political outcome which separates them from other high-profile acts of violence, such as the 2012 Sandy Hook Elementary School and 2017 Las Vegas shootings, that had no apparent political motive, at least at the time of this writing.

Yet, each of these events were treated differently within American social and political discourse. Only the Paris and San Bernardino killings, both perpetrated by Muslim extremists with clear disdain for Western culture, were widely deemed as terrorist acts. Robert Dear, the Planned Parenthood shooter, was widely derided as a misguided crazy person and not a domestic terrorist (Paul, 2015; Young, 2015), and the Oregon anti-government militants were viewed in some political circles as heroes for standing up to the federal government (Asa, 2016).

As already noted, within American society the word terrorism is often exclusive to acts of violence by Muslim extremists. However, the American response to the Nigeria attack complicates this definition slightly. Following the Paris attacks, Americans of every political stripe were glued to television and social media seeking updates, and Facebook and other social media sites created an option for users to update their profile pictures with the colors of the French flag to show support for the people of Paris. Yet, the Nigerian attacks two months later did not generate anywhere close to the same level of response; Facebook, for example, has never offered the option of changing one's profile picture to show support for the victims of Boko Haram even though they have killed over 150 times the number of Nigerians as were killed by ISIL in the Paris attacks. A more precise definition of terrorism within American society, then, appears to be acts of violence by Muslims on Western nations. Sadly, the majority of Americans appear to view acts of violence like what has occurred in Nigeria over the past five years as simply "business as usual" for West African countries.

The Facebook reactions to the Paris and Nigeria attacks highlight another important aspect of how terrorism is defined in contemporary society. Media plays a major role in how acts of terror are depicted and which groups of people are described as terrorists. Conservative media outlets are more likely to make explicit ties between Islam and acts of terror, whereas liberal outlets are more likely to treat acts of terror by Muslims as actions by radicalized individuals as opposed to an indictment on an entire religion. Similarly, the ideological leanings of media outlets likely determine whether non-Muslims who engage in acts of political violence are labeled terrorists or simply extreme partisans. Media literacy is an essential aspect of civic education (Masyada & Washington, 2016), one that has taken on increased importance in an age of social media in which news is shared more broadly than ever before. Having students analyze how different media sources respond to acts of political violence and the labels that they use to describe those involved can contribute to critical media literacy and help unpack contemporary definitions of terrorism.

As the events described in this section illustrate, terrorism has become an increasingly utilized form of political activism in the 21st century. Restricting the definition of terrorism to violent acts by Muslims against Western nations limits a contemporary understanding of the term. It is also important to note that this definition is likely to evolve as would-be terrorists find new ways to instill fear to achieve political goals. Cyberterrorism, for example, appears poised to be the next evolution in the history of terrorism (Hayward, 2015). Given the reliance on technology among most Western countries, cyber attacks that steal data, interfere with democratic functions, or disrupt normal ways of life have the potential to affect more people than random acts of violence.

RATIONALIZING THE EVIL OF TERRORISM

A final element of understanding terrorism in K–12 education is attempting to understand why terrorism exists. Simply framing terrorists as "evil" individuals who kill "innocent" victims does little to encourage students to think critically about terrorism, the reasons why individuals and groups use terror tactics to achieve political goals, and who should be considered terrorists in contemporary society.

Since 9/11 it has been commonplace in the United States to describe terrorism as "evil"; in his first State of the Union address following the attacks, President George W. Bush, for example, famously described Iraq, Iran, and North Korea as an "axis of evil" that promoted terrorism. However, as den Heyer and van Kessel (2015) have noted, "the concept of evil can be detrimental to the development of good citizens when it is used as a political and educational shibboleth to shut down critical thought about traumatic historical and contemporary events" (p. 79). Framing terrorism as an evil enterprise can be problematic when it encourages people to ignore the political underpinnings of terrorist acts. Evil conjures up images of serial killers and other psychopaths who murder people for no other reason than the joy of killing; for terrorists, violent acts are a means to a political end, and ignoring the political aspect of terrorism prohibits a true understanding of why it occurs in contemporary society.

That said, teachers should not conflate political outcomes with moral justification. Engaging in violent acts against defenseless citizens is never justified, regardless of the political motivation behind it. Even in the cases where extremists have employed a skewed interpretation of a certain culture or religion to justify their violent deeds, we have a responsibility as democratic citizens to disavow cultural practices that "violate anyone's right to civic equality" (Gutmann, 2004, p. 78).

Seeking to understand motives, however, is different than justifying actions. For most Americans, the idea of carrying out a suicide bombing is an irrational behavior; therefore, it is easy for Americans to default back into the overly simplistic "evil" narrative when describing terrorism. For the suicide bomber, however, the act is a rational, calculated risk. As economist Claude Berrebi (2009) has argued, "it is not so much that terrorists are victims of some external pressures but rather that they are acting in sensible ways given their preferences and surrounding state of the world (whether perceived or accurate)" (p. 151). Whether the benefit is future monetary support for one's family, the promise of a favorable afterlife, or simply the knowledge that one is making the ultimate sacrifice to a political cause, the cost associated with such an act is outweighed by the perceived benefits.

The same argument could be extended to contemporary non-Islamic terrorism. Consider, for example, the Oregon militants. It is unlikely that they actually believed that the federal government would surrender the Malheur National Forest to them, and they probably recognized that, at the very least, they would be arrested at the conclusion of the standoff. Yet, the national publicity the standoff received, to them, outweighed any potential jail sentence that may have resulted from their actions.

While one can rationalize singular acts of terrorism, the question becomes, then, whether the collective effort of terrorist acts is rational. Again, attempting to look at terrorism from the perspective of the terrorists is helpful here. In the case of Islamic terrorism, Islamic extremists perceive themselves to be in a war against the Western world, whereas the Western World is more concerned with protecting itself from terrorism as opposed to attempting to destroy a certain way of life. So, even though American politicians say that we are engaged in a "War on Terror," it does not mean the same as when we were in wars against Japan or Germany in World War II where the military objective was to conquer an entire group of people.

That distinction is important to understanding contemporary Islamic terrorism. Americans decry terrorism as evil; however, the idea of war, in which innocent civilians are often collateral damage, is generally accepted as an inevitable outcome of human nature. The question, then, is whether terrorism is the way in which war will be waged in the 21st century. Had a country claimed responsibility for the 9/11 attacks, it is likely that Congress would have officially declared war for the first time since World War II. Instead, we are militarily engaged with an enemy that identifies by ideology, not nationality, and spans multiple continents. Islamic extremists will likely never possess traditional weapons of war; therefore, terrorism may be the most effective method they have in waging war against the Western World.

Framing terrorism as an act of war complicates its definition. Where is the distinction between war and terrorism in the 21st century, and what implications does that distinction (or lack thereof) have for U.S. foreign policy? Is contemporary terrorism simply the byproduct of new geopolitical boundaries created by social media and digital technologies, making the idea of waging war against a specific nation-state an outdated proposition? Does it mean that in order to win the "War on Terror" the United States and its allies will have to go on the offensive and fight terrorism in a similar manner?

Clear answers for those questions do not yet exist; however, they raise a final way in which the definition of terrorism can be problematized. If Americans have been conditioned to view acts of Islamic terrorism as evil and not part of a larger political struggle, then one must question how our counterterrorism efforts have been perceived by our enemies and whether the violent acts that we commit on behalf of protecting the homeland (e.g., drone strikes on Muslim nations in which innocent civilians are often killed) should be considered a form of terrorism as well.

Certainly, the United States, like all nations, holds a responsibility to protect its citizens' safety and has the right to defend itself from foreign attacks. Yet, it is unclear where the line between military protection ends and terrorism begins. During the 2016 Republican presidential primary, for example, candidates used language that illustrated how this distinction has become murky. U.S. Senator Ted Cruz claimed that if he were elected president, he would "carpet bomb" ISIL, which would result in massive civilian casualties given the terror organization's propensity to situate themselves within densely populated areas (Salhani, 2016, para. 1). Donald Trump, the Republican nominee and eventual winner of the general election, went even further, stating that he would "take out [terrorists'] families" as a way of dismantling ISIL (Atkin, 2015, para. 3). Targeting innocent civilians and the family members of combatants have been deemed international war crimes; however, depending on how terrorism is defined, such measures may be considered acceptable. As the "War on Terror" continues to evolve, we can expect the line between war and terror and, ultimately, Americans' views on acceptable and unacceptable military conduct, to evolve as well.

CONCLUSION

It seems safe to contend that the informal, post-9/11 definition of terrorism as acts of violence by Islamic extremists on Western nations is both inaccurate and archaic. The purpose of this chapter, however, was not to posit a new definition of terrorism to take its place. Doing so would be a futile endeavor; even if one could accurately define terrorism, that definition would be specific to a certain time and context. If history is any indication, terrorism will only continue to gain strength as a political weapon, and any definition of the term will likely need to be refined over time.

The purpose of this chapter, then, is to encourage teachers to critically analyze contemporary terrorism as part of the social studies curriculum. Simply characterizing terrorists as evil or as exclusive to one group or religion does little to prepare students for 21st-century citizenship. By situating contemporary terrorism within a historical backdrop and forcing students to think critically about who qualifies as a terrorist and what distinguishes terrorism from other violent means to political ends, teachers can make students more literate about the increasingly interconnected world in which they live.

While troubling the definition of terrorism within the social studies curriculum is necessary, it will likely not be easy to enact. In times of war or in the immediate aftermath of tragedy, public education often becomes insulated within a shroud of nationalism defined by racism and xenophobia (Ben-Porath, 2011; Gilbert, 2016). Moreover, the political polarization that has that has occurred since 9/11 only seems to intensify, making discussions of anything smacking of anti-American sentiment challenging and potentially risky for teachers (Journell, 2011; McAvoy & Hess, 2013). Given the recent uproar in conservative media over a course on 9/11 at the University of North Carolina at Chapel-Hill in which students were asked to read texts from the perspectives of the terrorists as well as the victims of the attacks (Chiaramonte, 2015), having students rationalize the actions of terrorists, question American military policies, and equate the actions of individuals like Robert Dear and the Oregon militants with Islamic extremists is likely to anger some parents and school administrators. Yet, as long as the mission of social studies education is to equip future citizens with the knowledge and dispositions needed for active and informed citizenship, then engaging in courageous conversations that complicate socially constructed, simplistic definitions of complex phenomena is worth the risk.

DISCUSSION QUESTIONS

1. In politics, do the ends ever justify the means?
2. In this chapter, the Oregon militants are labeled as terrorists for the armed occupation of a federal wildlife reserve even though they did not kill or injure anyone during the standoff. Should, then, #BlackLivesMatter activists, some of whom have engaged in rhetoric suggesting violence against police officers, be considered terrorists as well? What are the differences and similarities in the two groups?
3. What should be the American response to terrorist acts by Islamic extremist organizations against American interests and allies? Should the United States intervene against acts of terror that do not directly affect us or our allies, such as the case of Boko Haram in Nigeria?
4. How can K–12 teachers effectively engage their students in discussions that complicate the definition of terrorism? What could this look like in elementary, middle, and secondary classrooms?
5. Research has shown that despite more media outlets available to individuals than at any other point in history, most Americans tend to gravitate to outlets that reinforce their preexisting ideological beliefs. How does media selectivity influence Americans' understanding of terrorism? How might teachers unpack the influence of media on societal definitions of terrorists and acts of terror?

REFERENCES

Asa, J. (2016, February 12). Never forget: The Oregon occupiers are true American heroes. *Copblock.org*. Retrieved from http://www.copblock.org/153858/never-forget-oregon-occupiers-are-true-american-heroes/

Atkin, E. (2015, December 3). To defeat ISIS, Trump openly suggests committing war crimes. *Think Progress*. Retrieved from http://thinkprogress.org/world/2015/12/03/3727303/donald-trump-kill-isis-family-members/

Bellows, E. (2016). Including 9/11 in the elementary grades: State standards, digital resources, and children's books. In W. Journell (Ed.), *Reassessing the social studies curriculum: Promoting critical civic engagement in a politically polarized, post-9/11 world* (pp. 29–40). Lanham, MD: Rowman & Littlefield.

Ben-Porath, S. (2011). Wartime citizenship: An argument for shared fate. *Ethnicities, 11*, 313–325.

Berrebi, C. (2009). The economics of terrorism and counterterrorism: What matters and is rational-choice theory helpful? In P. K. Davis & K. Cragin (Eds.), *Social science for counterterrorism: Putting the pieces together* (pp. 151–208). Santa Monica, CA: RAND Corporation.

Bickmore, K. (1999). Elementary curriculum about conflict resolution: Can children handle global politics? *Theory & Research in Social Education, 27*, 45–69.

British Broadcasting Corporation. (2015, December 9). Paris attacks: What happened on the night. Retrieved from http://www.bbc.com/news/world-europe-34818994

British Broadcasting Corporation. (2016, January 31). Boko Haram blamed for deadly attack on Nigeria village. Retrieved from http://www.bbc.com/news/world-africa-35454652

Chiaramonte, P. (2015, August 31). Skewed view: UNC's 'literature of 9/11' course blames America, says critics. *Fox News.* Retrieved from http://www.foxnews.com/us/2015/08/31/skewed-view-unc-literature-11-course-blames-america-say-critics.html

den Heyer, K., & van Kessel, C. (2015). Evil, agency, and citizenship education. *McGill Journal of Education, 50*, 79–96.

Garrett, H. J. (2016). Big data, surveillance, and the unprecedented conditions of citizenship. In W. Journell (Ed.), *Teaching social studies in an era of divisiveness: The challenges of discussing social issues in a non-partisan way* (pp. 127–142). Lanham, MD: Rowman & Littlefield.

Gilbert, L. (2016). National identity and citizenship in a pluralistic society: Educators' messages following 9/11 and *Charlie Hebdo*. In W. Journell (Ed.), *Reassessing the social studies curriculum: Promoting critical civic engagement in a politically polarized, post-9/11 world* (pp. 55–68). Lanham, MD: Rowman & Littlefield.

Gutmann, A. (2004). Unity and diversity in democratic multicultural education: Creative and destructive tensions. In J. A. Banks (Ed.), *Diversity and citizenship education: Global perspectives* (pp. 71–96). New York, NY: Jossey-Bass.

Hayward, J. (2015, May 20). Cyberterrorism is the next 'big threat,' says former CIA chief. *Breitbart.* Retrieved from http://www.breitbart.com/national-security/2015/05/20/cyberterrorism-is-the-next-big-threat-says-former-cia-chief/

Huffington Post. (2015, November 28). Planned parenthood shooting appears to have been politically motivated. Retrieved from http://www.huffingtonpost.com/entry/planned-parenthood-shooting-appears-to-have-been-politically-motivated_us_565a60cfe4b079b2818a98ab

Jones, R., & Dionisopoulous, G. N. (2004). Scripting a tragedy: The "Isaac and Ishmael" episode of *The West Wing* as parable. *Popular Communication, 2*, 21–40.

Journell, W. (2011). The challenges of political instruction in a post-9/11 United States. *The High School Journal, 95*, 3–14.

King, L. J., Warren, C. A., Bender, M., & Finley, S. Y. (2016). #Black Lives Matter as critical patriotism. In W. Journell (Ed.), *Teaching social studies in an era of divisiveness: The challenges of discussing social issues in a non-partisan way* (pp. 93–110). Lanham, MD: Rowman & Littlefield.

Law, R. D. (Ed.). (2015). *The Routledge history of terrorism.* New York, NY: Routledge.

Legum, J. (2015, November 28). The political motivations of the planned parenthood shooting suspect, revealed. *Think Progress.* Retrieved from https://thinkprogress.org/the-political-motivations-of-the-planned-parenthood-shooting-suspect-revealed-c12d91823855#.dgu7zfsyb

Libresco, A. S., & Balantic, J. (2016). Every issue is a social studies issue: Strategies for rich discussion in the upper elementary classroom. In W. Journell (Ed.), *Teaching social studies in an era of divisiveness: The challenges of discussing social issues in a non-partisan way* (pp. 13–30). Lanham, MD: Rowman & Littlefield.

Los Angeles Times. (2015, December 14). Everything we know about the San Bernardino terror attack investigation so far. Retrieved from http://www.latimes.com/local/california/la-me-san-bernardino-shooting-terror-investigation-htmlstory.html

Masyada, S. S., & Washington, E. Y. (2016). Civil liberties, media literacy, and civic education in the post-9/11 era: Helping students think conceptually in order to act civically. In W. Journell (Ed.), *Reassessing the social studies curriculum: Promoting critical civic engagement in a politically polarized, post-9/11 world* (pp. 83–94). Lanham, MD: Rowman & Littlefield.

McAvoy, P., & Hess, D. (2013). Classroom deliberation in an era of political polarization. *Curriculum Inquiry, 43,* 14–47.

Merriam-Webster. (2016). Terrorism. Retrieved from http://www.merriam-webster.com/dictionary/terrorism

Paul, D. (2015, December 2). Why Robert Lewis Dear is terrifying but not a terrorist. *Huffington Post.* Retrieved from http://www.huffingtonpost.com/david-paul/robert-lewis-dear-is-terr_b_8697202.html

Saleem, M. M., & Thomas, M. K. (2011). The reporting of the September 11th terrorist attacks in American social studies textbooks: A Muslim perspective. *The High School Journal, 95,* 15–33.

Salhani, J. (2016, March 22). Cruz reiterates proposal to 'carpet bomb' ISIS after Brussels attack. *Think Progress.* Retrieved from http://thinkprogress.org/world/2016/03/22/3762335/cruz-carpet-bomb-isis/

Soden, G. J., & Castro, A. J. (2013). Using contemporary music to teach critical perspectives of war. *Social Studies Research and Practice, 8,* 55–67.

Stoddard, J., & Hess, D. (2016). 9/11 and the war on terror in American secondary curriculum, fifteen years later. In W. Journell (Ed.), *Reassessing the social studies curriculum: Promoting critical civic engagement in a politically polarized, post-9/11 world* (pp. 15–28). Lanham, MD: Rowman & Littlefield.

The Oregonian. (2016, March 8). Oregon standoff timeline: How the occupation unfolded. Retrieved from http://www.oregonlive.com/oregon-standoff/2016/03/oregon_standoff_timeline_how_t.html

Turkewitz, J., & Healy, J. (2015, November 27). 3 are dead in Colorado Springs shootout at Planned Parenthood center. *New York Times.* Retrieved from http://www.nytimes.com/2015/11/28/us/colorado-planned-parenthood-shooting.html?_r=0

Yoder, P. J., Johnson, A. P., & Karam, F. J. (2016). (Mis)perceptions of Arabs and Arab Americans: How can social studies teachers disrupt the stereotypes? In W. Journell (Ed.), *Teaching social studies in an era of divisiveness: The challenges of discussing social issues in a non-partisan way* (pp. 63–78). Lanham, MD: Rowman & Littlefield.

Young, C. (2015, November 30). Extremist violence brings out the broad brushes. *Newsday.* Retrieved from http://www.newsday.com/opinion/columnists/cathy-young/is-robert-lewis-dear-a-radical-christian-terrorist-not-by-a-long-shot-1.11178152

CHAPTER TWENTY-THREE

Passwords to Citizenship?

A Response to the Power, Authority, and Governance Section

CATHRYN VAN KESSEL, UNIVERSITY OF ALBERTA

There is unique power in words like *democracy*, *freedom*, and *terrorism* that cannot be replicated. These words are like computer passwords—they both give power and take it away. There is nothing inherently wrong with those words; democracy, freedom, and terrorism describe specific phenomena. What can become troubling is how these words are taken up by those with the power and influence to shape meanings and implications.

Jane Lo and Amanda Geiger's chapter traces tensions about *democracy* over time. Who counts as the people who comprise democracy? In what ways can their voices be heard? Lo and Geiger deftly illuminate how illiberal democracies can invoke the word *democracy* in ways that shut down the possibility of plurality. As social studies educators, we have an opportunity to forgo tyrannies of the majority by modeling democratic spaces that provide for negotiation, compromise, and attend to minority perspectives.

In their chapter, Eli Kean and Jeffrey Craig cast a light on the darker side of *freedom*. Freedom is a ubiquitous word that sounds lovely, but it can be employed to restrict others' rights. Although religious freedom was a founding principle of the United States, Christian privilege pervades U.S. politics and society, and permeates education (Burke & Segall, 2017). Freedom of religion, then, can morph into the freedom to discriminate (e.g., denying services to LGBTQ+ customers). Similarly, freedom of speech can suppress voices. Social media provides opportunities for multiple perspectives, and yet marginalized voices can remain as such because of fear of backlash, as illustrated by Gamergate, when some men harassed women who identified sexism in the video game industry (Sanghani, 2014). Freedom of assembly also plays a double role—it can protect workers advocating for labor rights or people demonstrating for Black Lives Matter, but the freedom of assembly when applied to armed groups, like the white supremacists in Charlottesville in August 2017, can subsume freedom of speech (Lithwick & Stern, 2017). The presence of weapons forecloses possibilities for freedom of speech by those with opposing perspectives, and has also led to murderous acts of what ought to be labelled as terrorism.

This example leads to the question of who earns the label "terrorist." In this section's final chapter, Wayne Journell sparks discussion about how the definition of *terrorism* has moved beyond any violent act to scare a population for political means; rather, it has become associated almost exclusively with Muslim extremists. This limited definition of terrorism fails to account for the myriad of terrorists in a variety of time periods and places. Journell traces terrorism throughout a range of historical and geographical locations, aptly pointing out that simplifying terrorists as "evil" can prevent critical thinking about the roots and various manifestations of terrorism. Who is called a terrorist instead of an extremist or a person with a mental illness? And, what are the implications of naming people as such?

These chapters speak powerfully to the issue of how keywords can operate in ways that can harm underserved and oppressed groups. *Freedom* can counterintuitively limit freedoms, particularly the freedom of religions other than Christianity in the United States. Furthermore, people espousing hate and/or fear of Islamic terrorism have exacerbated violent attacks on Muslims (and those misunderstood to be Muslims, like Sikhs), which then violates other fundamental rights. Lo and Geiger's chapter in many ways provides a solution to such a problem: how democracies have potential to foster plurality, so that otherwise marginalized voices can be not only tolerated, but also nurtured.

Politicians and pundits can dazzle us with loaded terms, thus sparking our bodies and minds to respond in ways that shut down our thoughtfulness about complex topics. A student once said to me: "it's not that there's evil and then there's the other people, there's evil and then there's *us*" (van Kessel, 2017, p. 593). We are on the side of *democracy* and *freedom*, and others are the evil *terrorists*. As such, those labeled as terrorists become subject to the "politics of evil," and thus discussions from a place of empathy, or even inquiries into root causes, can be met with scorn. This situation stifles freedom of speech, and thus the potential for a pluralistic society. In social studies, teachers are tasked with developing students' political literacy, and part of that literacy needs to include broader understandings of these powerful keywords that shape popular discourse. Although as educators we wish to light a fire in our students, we do not want that fire to turn into a blaze of hatred and bigotry.

We can invoke the words discussed in this section—*democracy*, *freedom*, and *terrorism*—in ways that help or harm. The authors of these chapters have given us flashes of insight to approach those keywords with appropriate thoughtfulness, and thus open up possibilities for students/citizens who think independently from authority, while remaining interconnected with society. If we wish for democracy to be an ethos regarding all aspects of social and political life, instead of merely one type of political decision-making (Biesta & Lawy, 2006), then it is vital to put careful thought into how these keywords can operate contextually in both helpful and harmful ways.

REFERENCES

Biesta, G., & Lawy, R. (2006). From teaching citizenship to learning democracy: Overcoming individualism in research, policy and practice. *Cambridge Journal of Education, 36*, 63–79.

Burke, K. J., & Segall, A. (2017). *Christian privilege in U.S. education: Legacies and current issues.* New York, NY: Routledge.

Lithwick, D., & Stern, M. J. (2017, August 14). The guns won: Charlottesville showed that our first amendment jurisprudence hasn't reckoned with our second amendment reality. *Slate.* Retrieved from http://www.slate.com/articles/news_and_politics/jurisprudence/2017/08/the_first_and_second_amendments_clashed_in_charlottesville_the_guns_won.html

Sanghani, R. (2014, September 10). Misogyny, death threats and a mob of trolls: Inside the dark world of video games with Zoe Quinn—target of #GamerGate. *The Daily Telegraph.* Retrieved from http://www.telegraph.co.uk/women/womens-life/11082629/Gamergate-Misogyny-death-threats-and-a-mob-of-angry-trolls-Inside-the-dark-world-of-video-games.html

van Kessel, C. (2017). A phenomenographic study of youth conceptualizations of evil: Order-words and the politics of evil. *Canadian Journal of Education, 40*, 576–602.

Section VII:
Production, Distribution, and Consumption

CHAPTER TWENTY-FOUR

Consumption

KIM PENNINGTON, UNIVERSITY OF CENTRAL OKLAHOMA

> ...for most Americans, history unfolds against a stable environmental backdrop. Nature is taken for granted, and passed over in the rush to discuss what really mattered—wars, elections, and the other mainstays of political and intellectual history.
>
> —TED STEINBERG, DOWN TO EARTH: NATURE'S ROLE IN AMERICAN HISTORY (P. IX)

Humans consume. Like all animals on planet Earth, our consumption of food, water, and natural resources are necessary to sustain life. Unlike other animals on planet Earth, humans consume resources in incredible quantities (Grooten, Almond, & McLellan, 2012). In *Down to Earth: Nature's Role in American History* (2002), environmental historian Ted Steinberg examines U.S. history from an environmental perspective from the first European settlements through the 20th century. Steinberg's environmental approach to U.S. history is a powerful reminder that while we are accustomed to the idea of multiple perspectives in social studies discourse, we rarely consider the perspective of the environment and how habits of consumption impact it. In the interests of a safe and prosperous future, social studies educators must introduce the environment as an entity that is more than just scenery for human action.

Multiple analyses of consumption patterns indicate that human consumption is so excessive that the survival of countless species is now at risk (Turner, 2014). For example, by 2050, humans are on track to consume 140 billion tons of natural resources per year, an increase of 30% from current consumption rates (Giljum et al., 2009; Hertwich, 2010). Water is a particularly significant concern as consumption of this precious resource has been rising steadily for decades. The United Nations reports that 663 million people currently live without water security and this number is projected to rise as population centers in developing states continue to grow (UNICEF, 2017).

It is no coincidence that as human consumption of resources has grown, biodiversity has rapidly declined. Since 1988 the United Nations has been evaluating the impact of human activity on global biodiversity and releasing increasingly alarming reports. In the Global Diversity Outlook Report (Leadley, 2010), the UN noted that between 1970 and 2000 vertebrate species fell by nearly one third on average and that threats to a variety of habitats remained constant or continued to rise. Despite the fact that global conversations about overconsumption have grown more urgent, consumption patterns show no signs of slowing.

Undeterred by decades of warnings from every corner of the globe, the human species continues its voracious consumption of the very resources that sustain life. Our unsustainable consumption places us on a collision course with ecological disaster and perhaps our own extinction. This stark reality begs many questions: what is the responsibility of the social studies educator in light of these pressing environmental issues? How is the topic of consumption related to or embedded within the social studies curriculum? If the aim of social studies is to create and support informed and active citizens, how can social studies educators teach about human consumption and overconsumption in the classroom?

This chapter first considers the ways in which overconsumption has become normalized human behavior despite the fact that it has increasingly negative consequences. Practitioners are then encouraged to uncover hidden assumptions about consumption that exist in curriculum and texts through an exploration of Eisner's (1985) explicit, implicit, and null curriculum lens. Finally, theoretical and practical suggestions for educators are provided who are interested in disrupting a normalized consumption narrative.

THE NORMALIZATION OF OVERCONSUMPTION

In *Keywords* (2014), Williams tells us that until the mid-20th century, to consume meant to "take up completely, devour, waste or spend" (p. 78). Tellingly, for decades the deadly illness of tuberculosis carried the dark nickname "consumption" because tuberculosis bacteria literally consumed the lungs, almost always terminally. Williams' contended that in the 20th century, the word consume has been shaped by capitalism and advertising. He explains that the need to predict consumption levels of manufactured goods in order to plan for profitable production "implies, ironically as in the earliest senses, the using-up of what is going to be produced" (p. 79). Today, students are likely to associate the word consume(r) in regard to their freedom of choice in the market place. In the latter half of the 20th century, consumer has become synonymous with customer, though historically consumption has carried a far more negative connotation.

It's hard to pinpoint a time in modern history when human consumption was not excessive. In fact, a long view of the issue takes us all the way back to the Agricultural Revolution, circa 10,000 BCE. In the novel *My Ishmael* (2009), Daniel Quinn recounts this event through the parable of Leavers and Takers. In Quinn's story, hunter-gatherers are known as *Leavers* because they "thought of themselves as living in the hands of the gods" (p. 51), thereby leaving their fate to the gods. Leavers demonstrated their trust in the gods through living a hunter-gatherer lifestyle and only consuming resources to sustain life, instead of stockpiling surpluses. Not content with leaving their fate in the hands of the gods, some tribal groups, known as Takers in Quinn's parable, adopted permanent settled agriculture and began to lock-up food surpluses. Growing powerful from these resources, Takers deliberately and systematically conquered Leaver tribes one at a time, requiring them to convert to settled agriculture in order to obtain food and avoid war. Quinn writes that settled agriculture became "the pattern not only for years ahead but for the centuries and millennia ahead. Food production increased relentlessly and the Taker population increased endlessly, impelling them to expand into one land after another" (p. 57). This parable of the Agricultural Revolution concludes with Taker tribes instituting a totalitarian agriculture whereby the life ways of Leavers were erased and collectively forgotten (see Krutka's *Technology* chapter for more on agriculture).

Even though most people do not actively participate in the act of producing agricultural products today, our inability to even consider an alternative to the Taker lifestyle is proof of its powerful cultural impact. When the Agricultural Revolution is taught in history courses (which is not often), it is characterized as a triumph of man over environment, while the costs of the revolution remain unquestioned. Quinn refers to this erasure of alternatives as the Great Forgetting and summarizes the typical story of the Agricultural Revolution like this:

> The human race was born just a few thousand years ago in the vicinity of the Fertile Crescent. It was born dependent on crops, and planted them as instinctively as bees build hives. It also had an instinct for civilization. So as soon as it was born, the human race began planning crops and building civilization. There was of course, utterly no memory left of humanity's tribal past, extending back hundreds of thousands of years. That had disappeared without a trace in…the Great Forgetting. (p. 114)

Similarly, in most social studies curricula the consumptive tradition of settled agriculture is told as a wonderful and progressive development. The evolutionarily stable and sustainable lifestyles of hunter-gatherers, whose life ways are nearly extinct in the 21st century, are not recognized as a source of knowledge or wisdom.

Quinn's fictionalized explanation of this early struggle for resources during the Agricultural Revolution illustrates the fundamental shift from sustainable consumption to consumption for consumption's sake. This shift has cast a long shadow that shapes the way we engage in and view the act of consumption in the 21st century.

Consumption is so ingrained into modern human existence that it barely registers when we engage in it. In fact, for millennia the act of consumption has moved increasingly toward rampant overconsumption, especially in the wealthiest areas of the world. As individuals and societies increasingly consumed, their choices became habitual and reinforced through countless cultural and media messages. Today, the habit of consumption has become an expectation. For many living with affluence, what we purchase and consume are representations of who we are and where we sit within a complex array of societal positions, both within micro (local) and macro (global or dominant) cultural groups. Overconsumption has become so enculturated that many people, including our students, see no other possible way to exist.

It follows that we must carefully ask questions about how our patterns of consumption are influenced, directed, and perhaps controlled by those who benefit. *Whose interests are served through the overconsumption of resources and products? And, why might they resist movements or policies that challenge these patterns?* These questions, though uncomfortable and certainly unwelcome to some, must be asked if we intend to interrupt the powerful habits and dangerous consequences of overconsumption that exist within social studies narratives.

IDENTIFYING UNDERLYING ASSUMPTIONS THAT PROMOTE CONSUMPTION

The idea that curricula and classroom texts are not value neutral, and that they communicate powerful explicit and implicit messages to students, has been extensively theorized in the field and remains incredibly important for practitioners to consider (Anyon, 1978; Apple, 2004; Schiro, 2012; Waters, 2007). One helpful tool that can help practitioners uncover hidden messages within curricula and texts is Eisner's (1985) explicit, implicit and null curriculum theory.

The Explicit Curriculum: All Growth Is Good

Students are commonly instructed in what Eisner calls the "explicit" curriculum (Eisner, 1985; Parker, 2010). The explicit curriculum tells normative stories, promotes and reinforces dominant voices, and legitimizes them in ways that perpetuate an established and dominant social order (Anyon, 1978). There are many moments in the wide span of social studies subject-area curriculum that the normative aspects of overconsumption are explicitly taught. The overvaluation of concepts and topics closely tied to consumption, such as unlimited (economic, geographic, military, and political) growth and consumerism within a capitalist market structure, reinforce and normalize consumption. Rarely, if ever, do students learn the corollary and unheard stories of the costs, both human and environmental, of unchecked growth and consumption.

In a U.S. history course, for example, students learn explicitly that more is always better—more land, more people, more buildings, more military, more energy, and more consumer goods. They learn that all territorial growth is good; it should have no limits and that ultimately it is beneficial to the people who are subsumed into U.S. borders. This pervasive message is echoed in traditional narratives about the triumphant Westward march of the United States from 1492 to the final formation of the 50 U.S. states and the acquisition of overseas territories (see Shear and Stanton's *Indigenous* chapter for related critiques). The absence of any historical story before 1492, which would include the lifestyles of pre-agriculturalists, is an excellent example of the victory of Quinn's Great Forgetting. The traditional, nearly mythological story of Manifest Destiny has been contested in recent decades within social studies discourses (Shear, Knowles, Soden, & Castro, 2015), specifically with regard to the human cost however, the environmental costs of Westward Expansion has been largely ignored.

Another example of the explicit normalization of consumption can be found when students learn about the Cold War. Students explicitly learn a victorious story of United States over the U.S.S.R. during the Cold War arms race, without mention of the environmental costs of the arms race and proxy wars around the world (Steinberg, 2002). The race to build more and bigger nuclear weapons throughout the latter half of the 20th century fueled a surge in nuclear testing that spanned the globe. Domestically, the clean up from underground nuclear weapons testing in Nevada is rarely discussed, nor are the short and long-term global impacts of nuclear testing. For example, students learn that in our efforts to outgun the Soviets, certain environmental tolls were inevitable and necessary, particularly in the Pacific Ocean. They are rarely asked to consider the devastating damage done to the Bikini Atoll where the United States dropped 23 separate nuclear bombs during the 1960s, leaving the atoll radiated and uninhabitable (Davis, 2005). "Winning" the Cold War arms race came at a precious environmental cost as Steinberg (2002) described:

> The biological consequences of the nuclear arms race were (and are) simply staggering. It seems hopelessly inadequate and crude to put a price tag on such far-reaching destruction. But according to one estimate, in the United States alone, it will take three-quarters of a

century to achieve just a partial cleanup of defense-related contamination at a cost of anywhere from 100 billion to 1 trillion dollars. Globally, the fact that U.S. military installations remained, for the most part, exempt from environmental regulations has left many parts of the world profoundly contaminated and with little prospect of redemption. (Steinberg, 2002, p. 264)

The arms race occurred decades before their birth but our students and more importantly, the direct victims of ecological devastation, will be dealing with the long-term environmental consequences for centuries. When we fail to teach students about the consequences of military consumption and unchecked growth, we hinder their ability to deal with the residual effects as citizens. Examining curriculum and texts for explicit messages that normalize and promote consumption is an important first step.

The Implicit Curriculum: Bigger Is Better

Eisner (1985) also offers that an implicit curriculum exists in the hallways and corridors of schools and its function is to inculcate the dominant norms and values of society. The implicit curriculum has no connection to "core" courses, but nonetheless it is enacted every day. For example, students implicitly learn to obey authority, be on time, and reach maximum productivity at school from an early age. Many argue that the powerful implicit curriculum, which often reflects an economic imperative, is actually the primary aim of schooling as a societal institution (Anyon, 1980). While students spend hours, days and years learning prescriptive curriculum only to forget most of it after their exams, the lessons of the implicit curriculum last a lifetime and ripple through society.

What are students learning implicitly at school about consumption? Is there a culture that "more is better" on school campuses? At the large, suburban high school where I taught for a dozen years, there were many ways the campus culture encouraged and normalized unhealthy consumption. The best example of this could be seen in the design and footprint of our campus.

As is typical of suburban campuses across the nation, the school exemplified sprawl, with an enormous floor plan and even larger parking lots. Travel to and from school was essentially only possible by driving a car onto campus. Located on an always-busy suburban street, there were no pedestrian friendly sidewalks or bicycle lanes that provided ingress to our campus. Those who were brave enough to walk or bike to campus had to share the road with busy commuter traffic, an incredibly dangerous situation. Once on campus, bikers found precious few places to secure a bicycle during the school day. Implicitly, the built campus environment encouraged consumption of natural resources by restricting access to walkers and bikers and by only facilitating the movement of automobiles onto the campus.

What did this signal to students about transportation choices? I believe they learned that the only way to travel to and from school is enter into a "car culture" and to leave their environmentally friendly bicycle at home.

More generally, and definitely seen beyond my own campus, U.S. students have witnessed the increasing consumption of standardized tests and test preparation materials within their schools. Sadly, teachers and students from coast to coast are familiar with the "more is better" testing mentality that has permeated our federal and state education policies since the mid-1990s. The notion that schools must pursue "Adequate Yearly Progress" on standardized tests, as directed in federal education policy, is itself an implicit message that growth in the form of test scores is the highest priority. What are students implicitly learning about the role of testing in their education? I believe they learn that more testing is better and that learning is only measured through the consumption of traditional high stakes assessments.

The Null Curriculum: Where Is Sustainability?

A close and critical examination of explicit curriculum often reveals glaring absences. The people, places and events that are not in the explicit curriculum constitute the null curriculum, which is a "… giant absence, a foreclosure consisting of all the subject matter that is not included in the taught curriculum. Here are whole topics (e.g., the agricultural revolution), whole peoples (e.g., gays and lesbians in history), and whole courses (e.g., anthropology)…" (Parker, 2010, p. 7). Consumption is explicitly and implicitly promoted within much of the social studies, while alternative approaches or competing ideas, such as sustainability, are largely absent. Outside of courses that have a focus on human–environmental interaction, such as geography, the concept of sustainability sits primarily in the social studies null bin (Hadjichambis, Paraskeva-Hadjichambi, Ioannou, Georgiou, & Manoli, 2015). Retrieving the concept of sustainability from the null bin and introducing it as an alternative is essential for those who aim to counter the consumption narrative.

Those who make curricular decisions determine what is "worth knowing" and often, their choices reveal ideological positions, in this case the promotion of a consumption narrative that serves the status quo (Flinders, Noddings, & Thornton, 1986). For example, in the National Council for the Social Studies (NCSS) National Curriculum Standards for Social Studies (2010), consumption explicitly appears as an economic term in "Theme Seven: Production, Distribution and Consumption", but limits to consumption are not mentioned at all. Consumption is treated as part and parcel of a market economy without mention of negative consequences. In "Theme Three: People Places and Environments", the document recommends that students examine how people interact with the environment, but it fails to link the concept of consumption and the environment together, treating them as separate and unrelated concepts.

Eisner's (1985) framework can help educators to evaluate the degree to which students explicitly and implicitly learn that consumption is necessary, ideal, and inevitable, and the degree to which alternatives to consumption, such as sustainability, reside in the null curriculum.

TAKING SUSTAINABILITY OUT OF THE NULL BIN

While it is true that sustainability and other related concepts are almost always in the null bin, it is also important to recognize that teachers do possess the agency to change this. Thornton (1989) reminds us that teachers often act as "curricular gatekeepers" enabling them to take concepts like sustainability from the null curriculum and elevate them in the classroom.

What does it mean to be sustainable? To think or act sustainably means to thoughtfully measure the needs of the present against those of the future. It requires an understanding of balance in order to ensure a prosperous future for subsequent generations. The U.N. defines sustainability as "the use of services and related products, which respond to basic needs and bring a better quality of life while minimizing the use of natural resources and toxic materials as well as the emissions of waste and pollutants over the life cycle of the service or product so as not to jeopardize the needs of further generations" (ABCs Sustainable Consumption/Production, 2010, p. 12). Our levels of consumption today are directly related to the potential sustainability of our future (see Latremouille's *Environment* chapter for more on sustainability).

Theoretically, teachers may find the idea of ecological democracy useful in their efforts to integrate sustainability into social studies classrooms. In comparison to traditional conceptions of democracy such as liberal democracy and multicultural democracy, ecological democracy makes explicit the relationship between individuals, governments, policies and the natural world. Houser (2009) writes that ecological democracy,

> ...would acknowledge the transactional nature of organism-environment relationships between humans and non human life. Students of ecological democracy would contemplate the proposition that humanity is not located outside, beyond or above but within the environmental matrix that supports and contains it. Informed members of an ecological democracy would reflect on the proposal that the health of the environment is central to the health of the organism just as the health of the organism is central to the health of the environment. Since each organism constitutes the environment of other organisms, the ecological democrat would seriously consider the proposition that to care for life is to care for one's self and that to care for oneself is to care for life. (p. 208)

A theory like ecological democracy can be enacted in classroom practice through the inclusion of environmental education programs (EEPs). There is a wealth of EEP educational materials, in print or online that can help a teacher introduce the concept of sustainability or limits to growth in the classroom (Wheeler, 2013). Not surprisingly, most EEPs are situated in the science and STEM curricular fields, which may require social studies practitioners to creatively adapt them into a social studies course. The lack of EEPs with a distinct social studies focus is a reflection of its omission as a key concept within the field.

Within the social studies specifically, it is crucial for teachers to recognize how pervasive the concept of consumption is throughout the span of a course. Once those assumptions are revealed, teachers can shift classroom conversations by asking students to consider alternatives to historical trends of consumption. For example, students can examine the lifestyles and patterns of less-consumptive societies. When studying Westward expansion, students can evaluate whether or not territorial growth was ultimately beneficial from an environmental perspective by analyzing the township and range system that was utilized to divide up territories. When studying the rise an automobile culture, students can explore and critique the massive expansion of highways and roads across the country that led to suburban sprawl. They could investigate moments in American history when the public prioritized recycling and conservation such as during World War II and the early environmentalist movement. The environmental connections embedded within these historical events are often left unconsidered across much of the social studies curriculum but require a fresh examination.

Our environment is more than just a static backdrop against which we live our lives and against which history unfolds. As social studies teachers it is our responsibility to question the causes and consequences of consumption by making the environment a key player in our curricular story and by explicitly teaching for a more sustainable world.

DISCUSSION QUESTIONS

1. What assumptions exist in curricula, textbooks, or other materials that economic, political, military, or geographic growth is an unquestioned good, regardless of the human or environmental consequences?
2. Who benefits from unchecked and unconsidered growth and is this addressed in curricula/texts? Is a limit-to-growth ever considered?
3. Is the environment depicted as simply a backdrop against which human activity happens or is it considered alongside human action?

4. How and when are natural resources discussed in curricula/text? Is the conversation centered on exploitation of natural resources for the sake of profit or for conservation?
5. How does your campus climate encourage consumption, either implicitly or explicitly? Is there a "more is better" attitude in the school culture?

REFERENCES

ABC of SCP: Clarifying concepts on sustainable consumption and production. (2010). United Nations Environmental Prgram.

Anyon, J. (1978). Elementary social studies textbooks and legitimating knowledge. *Theory & Research in Social Education, 6*(3), 40–55.

Anyon, J. (1980). Social class and the hidden curriculum of work. Journal of Education, 162 (1), 67–92.

Apple, M. W. (2004). *Ideology and curriculum.* London: Routledge.

Davis, J. S. (2005). Representing place: "Deserted isles" and the reproduction of Bikini Atoll. . *Annals of the Association of American Geographers, 95*(3), 607–625.

Eisner, E. W. (1985). *The educational imagination.* New York, NY: Macmillan.

Flinders, D. J., Noddings, N., & Thornton, S. J. (1986). The null curriculum – its theoretical basis and practical implications. *Curriculum Inquiry, 16*(1), 33–42.

Giljum, S., Hinterberger, F., Bruckner, M., Burger, E., Frühmann, J., Lutter, S., ... Kernegger, L. (2009). Overconsumption? Our use of the world's natural resources, *Friends of the Earth Europe; Brussels (Belgium), 41 (50).*

Grooten, M., Almond, R., & McLellan, R. (2012). *Living planet report 2012: Biodiversity, biocapacity and better choices*: =Gland, Switzerland: World Wide Fund for Nature.

Hadjichambis, A. Ch., Paraskeva-Hadjichambi, D., Ioannou, H., Georgiou, Y., & Manoli, C. C. (2015). Integrating sustainable sonsumption into environmental education: A case study on environmental representations, decision making and intention to act. *International Journal of Environmental & Science Education, 10*(1), 67–86.

Hertwich, E. (2010). *Assessing the environmental impacts of consumption and production: priority products and materials*: UNEP/Earthprint. Paris, France.

Houser, N. O. (2009). Ecological democracy: An environmental approach to citizenship education. *Theory & Research in Social Education, 37*(2), 192–214.

Leadley, P. (2010). *Biodiversity scenarios: Projections of 21st century change in biodiversity, and associated ecosystem services: A technical report for the global biodiversity outlook 3.* UNEP/Earthprint. Paris, France.

National Curriculum Standards for Social Studies: A framework for teaching, learning, and assessment. (2010). National Council for the Social Studies, Silver Springs, MD.

Parker, W.C. (2010) *Social Studies today: Research and practice.* Routledge.

Quinn, D. (2009). *My ishmael.* New York, NY: Random House.

Schiro, M. S. (2012). *Curriculum theory: Conflicting visions and enduring concerns.* Thousand Oaks, CA: Sage.

Shear, S. B., Knowles, R. T., Soden, G. J., & Castro, A. J. (2015). Manifesting destiny: Re/presentations of indigenous peoples in K–12 US history standards. *Theory & Research in Social Education*, *43*(1), 68–101.

Steinberg, T. (2002). *Down to earth: Nature's role in American history*. Oxford: Oxford University Press.

Thornton, S. J. (1989, March). Aspiration and practice: Teacher as curricular-instructional gatekeeper in social studies, presented at annual meeting of the American Educational Research Association, San Francisco, CA.

Turner, G. (2014). Is global collapse imminent? An updated comparison of the limits to growth with historical data. *MSSI Research Paper* No. 4, Melbourne Sustainable Society Institute.

United Nations International Childrens Emergency Fund (2017). UNICEF Annual report. New York, NY.

Waters, T. (2007). The sacred and the profane in american history curriuclum. *The Social Studies*, *98*(6), 246–250.

Wheeler, G. (2013). Integrating education for sustainability into the K-12 system: A model from washington state. In *Schooling for sustainable development in Canada and the United States* (pp. 109–122). Springer, Dordrect.

Williams, R. (2014). *Keywords: A vocabulary of culture and society*. Oxford: Oxford University Press.

CHAPTER TWENTY-FIVE

Class[1]

E. WAYNE ROSS, UNIVERSITY OF BRITISH COLUMBIA

> In North America, discussions of social class are considered to be in questionable taste, indeed are surrounded by formidable taboos. It is less outré to converse graphically about kinky sex than to suggest that social classes exist, or that their existence has important consequences.
>
> —James Laxer, *The Undeclared War*

This chapter is about you-know-what ... the dark concept, the concept that-must-not-be-named. Well, to be fair, the concept can be named, but only as a passing reference to an identity category and only in combination with other identity categories such as race, gender, and sexual orientation, which will be seriously explored. You may use the homonym for you-know-what when referring to a group of students, a course, or a learning space. Under certain circumstances (e.g., reports of neo-positivist research) you may employ bland, inoffensive euphemisms, such as socioeconomic status or social stratification, to downplay the existence of the dark concept. It is important to remember the concept that-must-not-be-named should never be seriously discussed in the textbooks or research literature, except in reference to the distant past or unpatriotic ideologies.

It is difficult to dispute the existence of these guidelines for social studies education after examining curriculum and scholarship in the field.

INVISIBILITY OF CLASS IN SOCIAL STUDIES

Class is undeniably important in understanding the human enterprise over time and space. It is perhaps the single most important variable in society. Class affects individuals and society across the spectrum of social issues including health, social mobility, education, crime, who fights in wars, economy, as well as trust, social and civic participation, attitudes, and happiness. Despite its importance, in every practical sense, class is not a keyword in social studies curriculum. Social class historian Howard Zinn observed the "history of working people and the labor movement is not taught ... It's not in the school books and it's not in the mass media. So workers are unaware of past labor struggles, and this can have a debilitating effect" (Peterson, 1999, p. 73). A school textbook editor told James Loewen, author of *Lies My Teacher Told Me*, "there are three great taboos in textbook publishing, sex, religion, and social class" (Loewen, 1995 p. 24).

Loewen's (1995) analysis of textbooks remains the most fulsome description of class as a null curriculum in social studies; Orlowski's (2008) investigation of the social studies curriculum in British Columbia concludes that class remains a forgotten identity marker in 21st-century social studies. While textbooks cover certain events of labor history (e.g., 1894 Pullman Strike and 1911 Triangle Shirtwaist Factory fire) most are in the distant past and never connected to analysis of social class. Half of the textbooks Loewen analyzed contain no index entries for *social class, social stratification, class structure, income distribution, inequality* or related ideas; none of the books included reference to *upper class* or *working class*. Loewen found only four textbooks provided analysis of social stratification in the United States, and "even these fragmentary analyses are set mostly in colonial America" (1995, p. 203).

Government and democracy are key elements of the social studies curriculum, but upper class founders who emphasized government as a protector of the propertied classes are remade in textbooks as champions of rule of the people. Madison was keenly aware of the threat the lower classes posed to a capitalist democracy,

> An increase of population will of necessity increase the proportion of those who will labour under all the hardships of life, & secretly sigh for a more equal distribution of its blessings. These may in time outnumber those who are placed above the feelings of indigence ... symptoms of a leveling spirit, as we have understood, have sufficiently appeared in a certain quarters to give notice of the future danger. How is this danger to be guarded agst. on republican principles? How is the danger in all cases of interested coalitions to oppress the minority to be guarded agst.? (Kurland & Lerner, 1987, p. 544)

Madison's questions reflect a key principle of the founders, voiced by the president of the Continental Congress, John Jay, "the people who own the country ought to govern it" (Monaghan, 1935, p. 323). The role of class (and class war from above) in the founding of the United States appears in no textbooks.

One of the key messages of social studies is that we live in a democracy, despite the fact that the United States behaves nothing a like a democracy. As Chomsky (2013) explains,

> ... the lower 70% on the wealth/income scale—have no influence on policy whatsoever. They're effectively disenfranchised. As you move up the wealth/income ladder, you get a little bit more influence on policy. When you get to the top, which is maybe a tenth of one percent, people essentially get what they want, i.e. they determine the policy. So the proper term for that is not democracy; it's plutocracy. (para. 5)

Gilens and Page (2014) conducted an empirical study that attempts to answer the questions: Who governs? Who really rules? To what extent is the broad body of the U.S. citizenry sovereign, semi-sovereign, or largely powerless? The results categorized the U.S. political system as Economic Elite Domination and Biased Pluralism (that is where corporations, business associations and professional groups dominate), but there was little evidence to support descriptions of the United States as a Majoritarian Electoral Democracy. These findings contradict the central tenet of the social studies curriculum in North America. The evidence confirms the United States not a functioning democracy, rather it is a plutocracy as Chomsky has claimed.

Why do social studies textbooks omit (and distort) such an important construct and present inaccurate history? Loewen says to ask that question is to ask what the purpose of history courses and textbooks is. For Loewen (1992), ethnocentrism, fear (of poor sales figures; offending influential people), and laziness contribute to the textbook publishing mantra that "it's safer to repeat what everyone else says, even though everyone else is wrong" (p. 28). And, of course, textbooks purposefully omit and lie because their aim is to provide "feel good" nationalist history that promotes a conformist view of "good citizenship." Besides, teaching about class runs the risk of destroying (or at least contesting) illusions of equality, meritocracy, and a fair social and economic playing field, which are key messages of the social studies curriculum.

For different reasons, which I describe below, class is also virtually absent from the scholarly literature in social studies. Issues of class and education, while not the mainstream of educational research, have received significant attention from critical educational researchers over the years, but social studies education has remained largely isolated from this work, despite relevant applications (e.g., Allman, 2010; Anyon, 1980; Bernstein, 1971; Bowles & Gintis, 1976; Finn, 1999; Willis, 1977).

In the 43-year run of *Theory and Research in Social Education* (*TRSE*), the premier scholarly journal of social studies education, there have been only two articles whose primary focus included social class (Holmes, 1982; Tupper, Cappello, & Sevigny, 2010). *TRSE* regularly published articles examining social studies from critical social theory perspectives, particularly in its early years under the editorship of Jack Nelson, and again from the mid-1990s to the turn of the century, but these studies rarely if ever used class as a central organizer or engaged in class-based analysis. Class is a missing concept in the nearly 50 articles on economics education published in *TRSE*. Searches beyond *TRSE* turn up less than a handful of articles that specifically focus on social studies and class (e.g., Anyon, 1979; Orlowski, 2008; Queen, 2014; Ross & Queen, 2013).

What Is Class?

Class is a somewhat complex notion, used in various ways, both descriptively and theoretically (particularly in Marxist thought). The modern sense of class, with fixed names for particular social classes (lower, middle, upper), belongs to the era between late 1700s and mid-1800s, "the period of the Industrial Revolution and its decisive reorganization of society" (Williams, 1983, p. 61). But as Williams and Brenner (2016) point out, despite common usage, what exactly the tripartite divisions reference is remains unclear.

According to Williams, the introduction of the concept of class is linked to increased consciousness—as a result of newly experienced individual mobility—that social position was made, not merely inherited. This changing consciousness also resulted in a new understanding of society as a particular social system that created social divisions. Williams points out one of the early uses of class in this sense, by James Madison in The Federalist No. 10,

> A landed interest, a manufacturing interest, a mercantile interest, a moneyed interest, with many lesser interests, grow up of necessity in civilized nations, and divide them into different classes, actuated by different sentiments and views. (Madison, 1787, para. 7)

Ambiguity and confusion abound in discussions of class because, as Williams points out, the two modern senses of the concept rest on different models: (a) class as a general, descriptive term for social grouping (e.g., upper, middle, lower class status groups) and (b) class as a specific description of a economic-relationship (wage-laborers, capitalists and landlords; bourgeoisie or proletariat). A term such as socioeconomic status, which attempts to merge these two models, muddies these distinctions.

A further complexity is that class may be understood as an economic category (wage-laborers) and as a formation (the working class). Marxist theory focuses on the idea of class as a formation, but even for Marx class is sometimes an economic category and sometimes a formation or consciousness of class. Marxist class consciousness is an achievement—as opposed to the liberal notion of consciousness as an origin (e.g., consciousness as the basis of individual freedom). For historical reasons consciousness or subjective awareness of economic rank, class structure, and shared interests of a class is developed and then class-based organization to respond to the situation develops, with an aim to actively pursue its own interests. Marx (1932) made the distinction between "class in itself" (that is a category of people with common relations to production) and "class for itself" (a class organized in pursuit of its own interests, the key to sparking a revolution).

The complexities of social ranking or stratification in relation to the "basic classes" have been present from the beginning for Marxists. Marx noted the existence of classes apart from the Owners of the Means of Production and the Producers that may be intermediate between the basic classes or dependent upon one or the other. As Bottomore (1985) notes, at the end of *Capital* (Vol. 3) Marx observes that in England "intermediate and transitional strata obscure the class boundaries," and in *Theories of Surplus Value*, Marx writes he is disregarding for the purpose of preliminary analysis "the real constitution of society, which by no means consists only of the class of workers and the class of industrial capitalists."

Class consciousness and class action are dialectically constructed out of everyday life experience and interpretations of its meaning. Marx argued, *economic* conditions transformed the mass of the people into workers; capital created a common situation and interests for them. "This mass is thus already a class as against capital, but not yet for itself." Workers become united and constitute itself as class for itself and the interests it defends become class interests. "But the struggle of class against class is a *political* struggle" (Marx, 1885, Chapter 2, Part 5, para. 24, emphasis added).

Despite the centrality of class to Marxist thought, Marx never presented his ideas on class in a systematic form (Bottomore, 1983). Ollman (1968) provides a useful survey of how Marx employed the concept, and notes "the plurality of criteria Marx uses in constructing classes is reminiscent of present day confusion on this subject" (para. 12). For example,

> Even where the basis for distinguishing classes appears to be a group's relations to the prevailing mode of production the question is not the simple one of whether there are two or three classes, for Marx applies this label to several other economic units. Two outstanding examples are the petty bourgeoisie and the peasants. The former are small shopkeepers who own no means of production or, sometimes, a very tiny morsel, and employ at most a few workers; and the latter are the owners of small plots of land which they farm themselves. Their respective relations to the prevailing mode of production in capitalism are not those of the capitalists, the proletariat, or the landowners. Where, then, does Marx place small businessmen and peasants when he talks of society being made up of three classes. At what point does a small businessman stop being petty bourgeois and become a capitalist? How much land does a peasant have to own before he becomes a landowner? (Ollman, 1968, para. 2)

Marx also encountered problems in a discussing a straight economic division of society when attempting to categorize the intelligentsia, which he described as "the ideological representatives and spokesmen" of the bourgeoisie "who make the perfecting of the illusion of the class about itself their chief sources of livelihood." Ollman argues Marx saw the intelligentsia and capitalists as siblings, "similar at the core" and "merely specializing in different areas of capitalist 'work'" (para. 6). In the *Communist Manifesto*, the intelligentsia are referred to as the "paid wage-laborers" of the bourgeoisie (Marx & Engels, 1848, para. 15). But at other times Marx applies different criteria and allows for the independence of the "ideological classes" (e.g., cultural or political classes, including educators) from the capitalist class.

So, where does this examination of the complexity of class leave us when considering it as a keyword in social studies? "Class conflict" in social studies education appears to be the circumstance created by *de facto* denial of class in North American society, a claim made in the face of the existential reality of class inequality and in tandem with a grand narrative that erroneously claims that our society is one where equality and meritocracy are the hallmarks of life.

There are at least two takeaway messages. First, the absence of class from social studies curriculum and research, contributes to the poverty of both. At the very least, it leaves little or no room for consideration of class-based identity as a social, cultural, or economic subjectivity—an irony in an age of hegemonic identity politics. (Why is classism rarely, if ever, part of the social studies discourse?) And because class issues intersect and interact with cultural and psychological processes (e.g., identity) as well as relations of power (e.g., subjectivities) our understandings and explorations of the full range of human experience are impoverished. The failure to think and learn about social issues without reference to class weakens efforts to understand the nature of social problems and distorts our conceptions of and inquiry into possible responses and solutions.

Secondly, when explaining the absence of class from social studies discourse, we need look no further than Marx's characterization of the intelligentsia (here applied to social studies educators at all levels) as paid wage-laborers of the bourgeoisie, whose work has provided a foundation for schools as factories of illusion where the core issue of our time—color-coded social and economic inequality—is met with lessons that teach this is a multicultural society, democracy trumps inequality, and we can all be president (Gibson & Ross, 2015). When it comes to thinking and teaching about class in social studies, as Pogo said to Porky Pine, "we have met the enemy and he is us."

What Are the Obstacles That Prevent Social Studies from Taking Class Seriously?

While there are assuredly more, below I examine four issues we must consider in taking class more seriously in our work as social studies educators: fear of embarrassing students, individuals' class positions, the ideology of neutrality, and failing to attend to the larger contexts when teaching social issues.

First, the most common excuse for ignoring class in social studies is teachers do not want to embarrass their students. As teachers we want to create a safe learning environment, where students are not threatened or embarrassed, but this excuse is merely an appeal to emotion that obscures reasoning. Social studies education should seek to create conditions in which students can develop personally meaningful understandings of the world and recognize they have agency to act on the world, to make change. Students already know a lot about social privilege or the lack thereof, but usually do not know how class structure works. Loewen describes his experience teaching about social class this way,

> When my students from nonaffluent backgrounds learn about the class system, they find the experiences liberating. Once they see the social process that helped keep their families poor, they can let go of their negative self-image about being poor. If to understand is to pardon, for working-class children to understand how stratification works is to pardon *themselves* and their families. Knowledge of the social-class system also reduces the tendency of Americans from other social classes to blame the victim for being poor. (1995, p. 205)

Finn (1999) elaborates on this idea, drawing on work of John Dewey and Paulo Freire to develop a rationale and strategies for educating working-class students in their individual and collective self-interest as well as preparing teachers to do so.

Secondly, class affects the way people think about class, this explains in part why some (primarily middle class) teachers believe teaching class might embarrass poor and working-class students. Others believe that teaching about class promotes divisiveness, even class war. But the war against the poor and working class has long be underway, *Time* magazine journalists Donald Bartlett and James Steele declared the United States now has a "government for the few at the expense of the many."

Thirdly, an ideology of neutrality is often at the heart of arguments that social studies should avoid potentially controversial topics, such as class. Schools and teacher education program encourage teachers to be "neutral" and avoiding "politicizing" the classroom. The rebuttal is that education is inherently political and teaching that does not reinforce the status quo is usually seen as politicization. Striving for neutrality is problematic, instead we should attempt to teach objectively, an approach that requires knowledge claims to be exposed to the fullest range of criticism. Achieving objectivity requires that we take seriously alternative perspectives and criticisms of any particular knowledge claim. The objective teacher considers the most persuasive arguments for different points of view on a given issue; demonstrates even-handedness; focuses on positions that are supported by evidence, etc. But it is impossible to achieve objectivity in teaching if political discourse is circumscribed and neutrality is demanded (Ross & Queen, 2013).

Lastly, the reality of class is more than appearances. As with all social phenomena, focusing exclusively on appearances—on the evidence that strikes us immediately and directly—can be misleading. Trying to understand the world via what we see, hear, or touch in our immediate surroundings can lead us to conclusions that are distorted or false. Understanding anything in our everyday experience requires that we know something about how it arose, developed, and fits into the larger context or system of which it is a part (Ollman, 2003). Ollman points out, for example, people of various political persuasions have pointed out the paradox of the growing wealth of the few and the increasing poverty of the many, as well as connections among interests of corporations, actions of governments, and of being powerless and poor. Despite awareness of these relations, most people do not take such observations seriously. Lacking a theory to make sense of what they are seeing, people do not know what importance to give it; forget what they have just seen, or exorcise the contradictions by labeling them a paradox.

The problem is socialization we experience (in social studies, school, and beyond) encourages us to focus on the particulars of our circumstances and to ignore interconnections. Thus, we miss the patterns that emerge from relations. Dialectics, on the other hand, is an effort to understand the world in terms of interconnections—the ties among things as they are right now, their own preconditions, and future possibilities. Dialectics takes change as the given and treats apparent stability as that which needs to be explained and provides specialized concepts and frameworks to explain it (Dialectics for Kids, 2013; Gibson, 1993; Ollman, 2003; Ross, 2016). Dialectics is an approach to understanding the world that requires not only a lot of facts that are usually hidden from view, but a more interconnected grasp of the facts we already know.

What Would Social Studies Education Look Like if Class Were a Keyword in the Field?

Surprisingly this is not a merely a rhetorical question, because we have historical, conceptual, and contemporary practice examples. While not specifically examples of social studies education in the contemporary sense, we have historical examples of schools and programs that sprang from socialist, anarchist, labor, and counter-cultural movements that focused on educating working-class students. These include Socialist Sunday Schools (Teitelbaum, 1993) and the Modern School

Movement (Avrich, 2005 as well as many free schools (Miller, 2002). In addition, we can look for clues in the mid-20th-century teaching and textbooks of Harold Rugg (Evans, 2007).

The conceptual development of revolutionary Marxist social studies has grown out of work originally labeled Critical Multicultural Social Studies (Malott & Ford, 2015). Malott and Ford expose attacks on critical thinking and social studies and illustrate processes that lead to working-class students experiencing standardized curriculum that serves the interest of capital, while bourgeois students are taught critical thinking and creativity. Their analysis poses a major challenge to notions of social justice education within capitalism, which suggests exploitation is the result of greed, prejudice, and bias. Less radical thinkers have concluded that the influence of social class characteristics are so powerful that schools cannot be overcome it (e.g., Rothstein, 2004).

Surface appearances of unequal outcomes have led to belief that "social justice can be achieved by tinkering with distributions, ensuring equal educational opportunities or equal rights for democratic citizenship" (Malott & Ford, 2015, p. 115). Malott and Ford contend that Marxist social studies begins with the insight that to capital all people are equal, capital strives to accumulate as much surplus value as possible, working workers to death. In this context, the capitalist state relies on intensified ideological management to devalue producers and justify exploitation, which also suppresses social unrest of laborers. Malott and Ford are conceptualizing a social studies that bends toward communism, while responding to its capitalist context.

Finally, the most elaborated example of contemporary class-based social studies education can be found in the teaching and writing of Greg Queen, a social studies teacher in Detroit, MI (Queen, 2014; Ross & Queen, 2013). Queen has for years used class as the organizing principle for his American Studies course, which interweaves five themes (inequality, capitalism, racism, globalization, and war) and fits within National Council for Social Studies curriculum standards.

If class were a keyword in social studies education, curriculum, teaching, and scholarship in the field would not be what it is today. The challenge we face as social studies educators is to make our work relevant to broader efforts to achieve freedom and equality in society. Taking class seriously is a step in the right direction.

DISCUSSION QUESTIONS

1. Why is classism rarely if ever a part of the social studies discourse? How might this deficiency be addressed in schools and in teacher education? For some ideas see organizations such as Class Action (classism.org) and What About Classism? (whataboutclassism.org).

2. What academic and popular culture sources might social studies educators use to bring working class history and culture into the classroom? For some ideas see the bibliographies of working-class literature and cinema at libcom.org
3. In his book *Class and Schools*, Rothstein (2004) presents evidence that in nearly every statistic used to describe the racial achievement gap, social class explains almost all the difference in test scores between majority and minority students. Racial prejudice, discrimination, and white supremacy are real and produce devastating effects, but when poor students are at the bottom of achievement rankings regardless of race, what are the implications for the discourse on and responses to the "achievement gap?"
4. How does ignoring class affect the education students receive (in schools and universities)? For some ideas listen to John Lennon's song "Working Class Hero."

NOTE

1. This chapter is adapted from "Why Teaching Class Matters" by E. Wayne Ross with Greg Queen as published in E. W. Ross, *Rethinking Social Studies: Critical Pedagogy in Pursuit of Dangerous Citizenship* published in 2017 by Information Age Publishing.

REFERENCES

Allman, P. (2010). *Critical education against global capitalism: Karl Marx and revolutionary critical education*. Rotterdam: Sense Publishers.

Anyon, J. (1979). Ideology and United States history textbooks. *Harvard Educational Review, 49*(3), 361–386.

Anyon, J. (1980). Social class and the hidden curriculum of work. *Journal of Education, 162*(1), 7–92.

Avrich, P. (2005). *The modern school movement: Anarchism and education in the United States*. Oakland, CA: AK Press.

Bernstein, B. (1971). *Theoretical studies towards a sociology of education*. London: Routledge and Kegan Paul.

Bottomore, T. (1983). Class. In T. Bottomore (Ed.), *A dictionary of Marxist thought* (pp. 74–77). Cambridge, MA: Harvard University Press.

Bottomore, T. (1985). *Theories of modern capitalism*. London: Unwin Hyman.

Bowles, S., & Gintis, H. (1976). *Schooling in capitalist America: Educational reform and the contradiction of economic life*. New York, NY: Basic Books.

Brenner, J. (2016). Class. In K. Fritsch, C. O'Connor, & A. K. Thompson (Eds.), *Keywords for radicals: The contested vocabulary of late-capitalist struggle* (pp. 79–86). Chico, CA: AK Press.

Chomsky, N. (2013, August 17). The U.S. behaves nothing like a democracy. *Salon*. Retrieved from http://www.salon.com/2013/08/17/chomsky_the_u_s_behaves

Dialectics for kids. (2013). Retrieved from http://home.igc.org/~venceremos/
Evans, R. W. (2007). *This happened in America: Harold Rugg and the censure of social studies*. Charlotte, NC: Information Age Publishing.
Finn, P. J. (1999). *Literacy with an attitude: Educating working class children in their own self-interest*. Albany, NY: State University of New York Press.
Gibson, R. (1993). Dialectic materialism for the earnest: A very short course. Retrieved from http://www.richgibson.com/diamata.html
Gibson, R., & Ross, E. W. (2015). Education and empire: Education for class consciousness. In P. R. Carr & B. J. Porfilio (Eds.), *The phenomenon of Obama and the agenda for education: Can hope (still) audaciously trump neoliberalism?* (2nd ed., pp. 249–276). Charlotte, NC: Information Age Press.
Gilens, M., & Page, B. I. (2014). Testing theories of American politics: Elites, interest groups, and average citizens. *Perspectives on Politics, 12*, 564–581.
Holmes, M. (1982). The new middle class and the organization of curricular knowledge. *Theory & Research in Social Education, 10*(2), 33–44.
Kurland, P. B., & Lerner, R. (1987). *The founders' constitution*. Chicago, IL: University of Chicago Press. Retrieved from http://press-pubs.uchicago.edu/founders/print_documents/v1ch15s35.html
Laxer, J. (1998). *The undeclared war: Class conflict in the age of cyber capitalism*. Toronto, Canada: Penguin.
Loewen, J. W. (1992). *Lies my teacher told me about Christopher Columbus*. New York, NY: New Press.
Loewen, J. W. (1995). *Lies my teacher told me: Everything your American history textbook got wrong*. New York, NY: Touchstone.
Madison, J. (1787, November 22). Federalist No. 10. The same subject continued (The union as a safeguard against domestic faction and insurrection). Retrieved from http://www.gutenberg.org/files/1404/1404-h/1404-h.htm#link2H_4_0010
Malott, C. S., & Ford, D. R. (2015). *Marx, capital, and education: Towards a critical pedagogy of becoming*. New York, NY: Peter Lang.
Marx, K. (1885). *The poverty of philosophy*. Retrieved from https://www.marxists.org/archive/marx/works/1847/poverty-philosophy/ch02e.htm
Marx, K. (1932). *The German ideology*. Retrieved from https://www.marxists.org/archive/marx/works/1845/german-ideology/ch01d.htm
Marx, K., & Engels, F. (1848). *Manifesto of the communist party*. Retrieved from https://www.marxists.org/archive/marx/works/1848/communist-manifesto/
Miller, R. (2002). *Free schools, free people: Education and democracy after the 1960s*. Albany, NY: State University of New York Press.
Monaghan, F. (1935). *John Jay*. New York, NY: Bobbs-Merrill.
Ollman, B. (1968). Marx's use of "class." *American Journal of Sociology, 73*(5), 573–580. Retrieved from https://www.nyu.edu/projects/ollman/docs/class.php
Ollman, B. (2003). *Dance of the dialectic: Steps in Marx's method*. Urbana, IL: University of Illinois Press. Retrieved from https://www.nyu.edu/projects/ollman/books/dd.php
Orlowski, P. (2008). Social class: The forgotten identity marker in social studies education. *New Proposals: Journal of Marxism and Interdisciplinary Inquiry, 1*(2). Retrieved from http://ojs.library.ubc.ca/index.php/newproposals/article/view/118

Peterson, R. (1999). Why teachers should know history: An interview with Howard Zinn. In R. Peterson & M. Charney (Eds.), *Transforming teachers unions: Fighting for better schools and social justice* (pp. 73–76). Milwaukee, WI: Rethinking Schools.

Queen, G. (2014). Class struggle in the classroom. In E. W. Ross (Ed.), *The social studies curriculum: Purposes, problems, and possibilities* (4th ed., pp. 313–334). Albany, NY: State University of New York Press.

Ross, E. W. (2016). Broadening the circle of critical pedagogy. In N. McCrary & E. W. Ross (Eds.), *Working for social justice inside and outside the classroom: A community of teachers, researchers, and activists* (pp. 206–218). New York, NY: Peter Lang.

Ross, E. W., & Queen, G. (2013). "Shut up. He might hear you!" Teaching Marx in social studies education. In C. S. Malott & M. Cole (Eds.), *Teaching Marx across the curriculum: The socialist challenge* (pp. 203–228). Charlotte, NC: Information Age Publishing.

Rothstein, R. (2004). *Class and schools: Using social, economic and education reform to close the black-white achievement gap*. New York, NY: Teachers College, Columbia.

Teitelbaum, K. (1993). *Schooling for "good rebels": Socialist education for children in the United States, 1900–1920*. Philadelphia, PA: Temple University Press.

Tupper, J. A., Cappello, M. P., & Sevigny, P. R. (2010). Locating citizenship: Curriculum, social class, and the "good" citizen. *Theory and Research in Social Education, 38*(3), 336–365.

Williams, R. (1983). *Keywords: A vocabulary of culture and society*. New York, NY: Oxford University Press.

Willis, P. (1977). *Learning to labour: How working-class kids get working-class jobs*. Westmead: Saxon House.

CHAPTER TWENTY-SIX

Entrepreneurship

MATTHEW T. MISSIAS, CULTIVATED LEARNING, LLC
KRISTY BRUGAR, UNIVERSITY OF OKLAHOMA

> ... learning community engagement practices while in school may actually support responsible entrepreneurship. When we teach collective action and organizing skills for community improvement, we also teach an ethics of responsibility to the community and to the public good. In our capitalist economy, responsible entrepreneurs can assist community activists and support resources for programs and projects that work toward the common good. It is wise to acknowledge that many young people are motivated to create socially just, environmentally sound businesses, and teachers committed to community-action projects may want to support these more individualistic leanings while simultaneously cultivating a commitment to the public good.
>
> —OYLER, 2012, P. 159

We have a confession: as deeply ensconced as the concept of entrepreneurship is in the social studies, and while it is an endeavor that is not only admirable but worth celebrating, entrepreneurship lacks, well, flair. Preparing to write this chapter conjured up images of motivational posters extolling the virtues of teamwork, excellence, or leadership under an image of a beautiful landscape or an impossibly perfect array of smiling businesspeople. We dusted off an old copy of *Atlas Shrugged* (Rand, 1957), laughed a little bit at its assumptions, shuddered a little bit at its continued popularity, and then put it away again. We dug into our history books and found examples of great entrepreneurs in American history. We Googled quotations about entrepreneurship and waded through the thousands of platitudes that business people assembled to quickly drop very meaningfully into their Powerpoints—like, "be a doer, not a dreamer!" We may or may not have binge watched *Office Space* (Judge et al., 2005) and other office-related tv shows and films for inspiration, noting that common reality of office work and making money in popular culture is so often conflated with entrepreneurship. We read articles about maximizing your resources as a small business, and all of the ways that you can learn from entrepreneurs like Richard Branson, Mark Cuban, and Mark Zuckerberg. It didn't escape our attention how many white men were extolled as the pinnacle of what it means to be an entrepreneur—more on this later.

While there is an element of pleasure in surveying the landscape of entrepreneurship, and how popular media shapes and is shaped by it, we were left with an overwhelming feeling of indifference. We were searching for a brand of entrepreneurship that was as socially conscious as it was economically conscious. We sought the kind of entrepreneurship that is rooted in the fundamental elements of making our communities stronger in all ways, not just those that would benefit the bottom line (Yunus, 2010). As teacher educators and education researchers, we approach our work with both an understanding of the realities of our social institutions as well as a belief that preparing teachers to realize the possibilities within their practice will foster opportunities to engage others in the practice of making their communities better. For us, the project of social education is as much about developing strategies that work across boundaries to affect a more just world as it is about strengthening that practice through rigorous work in and with social studies curricular content. Entrepreneurship in and of itself isn't strictly antithetical to that project, but too often the connotations and ethical considerations associated with the capitalistic endeavors appropriated by the term entrepreneurship requires that, as teacher educators, our pedagogical acts require a challenging level of nuance. Put another way, in order to understand entrepreneurship as a cornerstone in social studies education as we see it, its application to the social studies curriculum must be constructed precisely, lest we slide down the slippery slope into the world of motivational posters.

Our primary focus here is to conceive of a way of approaching entrepreneurship as a pedagogical act—not simply a function of the social studies curriculum—but as one where students are invited to actively participate as citizens, for themselves, their families, and the communities in which they participate. For all of the benefits of high quality social studies curricula that address elements of entrepreneurship (e.g., Junior Achievement, the Stock Market Game), entrepreneurship as it is exercised in the social studies curriculum celebrates individual and monetary accomplishments. Forging a sense of entrepreneurship as a pedagogical act for community engagement seeks to transgress traditional notions of the term, and instead embrace the commitment of scholars to challenge notions of what is and can be entrepreneurial based social studies curriculum (Whitlock, 2015).

ENTREPRENEURSHIP IN THE SOCIAL STUDIES CONTEXT

Entrepreneurship is as inexorably a part of the American psyche as it is inexorably about business. During his final State of the Union Address (The White House, 2016), President Obama devoted approximately a third of the speech exploring how we can face our collective challenges, stating in part, "America is every immigrant and entrepreneur from Boston to Austin to Silicon Valley, racing to shape a better world. That's who we are." History books have long participated in the heroification of business leaders from Eli Whitney to Henry Ford and Bill Gates (Lindaman & Ward, 2004; Loewen, 1995; Roberts, 2014) and the course of American history is closely tied to our economic successes and failures (e.g., The California Gold Rush, Stock Market Crash of 1929). Civics curricula routinely describes democratic citizenship not just in terms of understanding our democratic republic but in broader contributions to society (Westheimer & Kahne, 2004) and, in some critical examinations of social studies, the effects of inequities and oppression, both political and economic, on both nationalist and global elements of citizenship (Vinson, 2006). In all cases, what it means to be American is very much about the ability of Americans to be entrepreneurs. In popular parlance, it might be referred to as pursuing the American Dream or the American Ideal.

Conciliation between the American Ideal and its relationship to entrepreneurship is elusive at best. The American Ideal is best construed as the embracing of individual and cultural differences so as to strengthen and unify American society (Lintner, 2005). Yet, underlying that ideal is the assumption that all Americans have equal opportunity and ability to both participate in society and to pursue their desired vision of happiness. It is the belief in a pluralistic America, where diverse peoples and ideas converge to produce the best in all of us.

As is true of most things ascribed with the word "ideal," the idyllic often gives way to a much more problematic reality. Scholars, journalists, and cultural critics across the continuum have devoted much energy over the course of American history describing ways in which the American Ideal is complicated and troubled. It is beyond the scope of this chapter to examine those, so here we want to rely on a colloquialism: there is a trend throughout American history of Americans who love America but hate other Americans. In addition, the American Ideal, like entrepreneurship, is couched in economic terms—success defined by the fame and money we can acquire. Because of the ubiquity of the notions like Americanism, the American Ideal, and the American Dream across the social studies curriculum, the practice of teaching social studies becomes imbued with individualistic notions of entrepreneurship and privileges the false notion that entrepreneurship is limited to economic indicators.

ENTREPRENEURSHIP, INNOVATION, AND COMMUNITY

Despite, or perhaps because of, the nearly interchangeable relationship between entrepreneurship and economics in social studies curricula, we believe that practitioners of social studies pedagogy might re-appropriate the language used in social studies curricula to engage learners with community-oriented versions of entrepreneurship. One term strongly associated with the American Ideal is innovation. Innovation seems to be often connected to dispositions like invention, change, and creativity, and is seen as often in conversations about the arts as it is in business. Shane and Venkataraman (2000) argue that entrepreneurship comprises both "enterprising individuals" and "entrepreneurial opportunities". Deploying a broader interpretation of innovation is one example of entrepreneurship that includes not only economic interests but political and social interests which serve the larger society. We argue that it is incumbent on social studies educators to further develop our understanding of what it means to be an entrepreneur well beyond individuals and any economic interests, and instead focus on how those interests support and develop an understanding of responsible citizenship and support of the public good.

If part of being a responsible citizen is participating in society with respect to civic virtues (National Council for the Social Studies [NCSS], 2013), then being a good entrepreneur must be more than maximizing profits. Entrepreneurship for the public good in that context is less about advocating for individual economic interests through democratic participation, and instead advocating for business practices that support the communities in which democratically minded entrepreneurs inhabit. The public good is neither a static nor necessarily economic concept, but when associated with entrepreneurship, the effects of the public good become more about participating in citizenry that is both economically viable but socially responsible (Westheimer & Kahne, 2004). Citizenship education challenges us to foster socially just practices in our communities (Westheimer & Kahne, 2004), and as Oyler (2012) suggests those practices can be extended to entrepreneurs and to classroom teachers. As teachers of social studies, our challenge is not to just foster the dispositions that would create socially responsible entrepreneurs, but to embed those dispositions within our pedagogy such that we are challenging the assumptions that are made in and about our curriculum.

There may be no greater challenge to that project than in addressing the standards that underlie the curriculum social studies teachers bring to life every day. *The C3 Framework for Social Studies State Standards* (NCSS, 2013) is a document to guide the development of social studies standards with a focus on the use of inquiry-based instruction and students' uses of disciplinary concepts. The *C3 Framework* envisions entrepreneurs and entrepreneurship as:

Entrepreneurs: Individuals who are willing to take risks in order to develop new products and start new businesses. They recognize opportunities, enjoy working for themselves, and accept challenges. Example: A person who opens a new restaurant, dry cleaning store, or other business in the community is an entrepreneur. People who have already started businesses, such as Bill Gates, are also entrepreneurs (NCSS, 2013, p. 99).

Entrepreneurship: A characteristic of people who assume the risk of organizing productive resources to produce goods and services. Example: People who own and operate local businesses in the community (e.g., auto body repair shops, or restaurants) demonstrate entrepreneurship. (NCSS, 2013, p. 99)

What we notice in each of these definitions is the identification of risk toward the growth and development of business or economic pursuits. However, we believe this is somewhat limiting and we can expand our notion of entrepreneur/entrepreneurship to be inclusive of other aspects of life (and the social studies curriculum), and in turn the American Ideal, beyond simply economics. Fundamentally absent from this more technical definition of entrepreneurship is the role that community engagement and improvement plays in innovation of entrepreneurial endeavors.

The term entrepreneur is rarely critically questioned, but rather used as an assumption of goodness and prosperity. In other words, in social studies, too often when entrepreneurship is presented in our curriculum, it assumes that to be an entrepreneur is fundamental to the American experience. Whether through entrepreneur fairs or in ascribing entrepreneurship as a characteristic of empowered women/minorities, in the way that we treat it within the curriculum, the very essence of entrepreneur is taken for granted. It is an end goal rather than a process or set of characteristics an individual (or group of individuals) demonstrates—and that goal is unequivocally positioned as beneficial to society. It may be true that in opening a restaurant, a dry cleaner, or an auto body repair shop the owner assumes financial and legal risks to produce a good or service. But such a definition is entirely too technical and fails to consider the range of mitigating factors that would help determine whether the entrepreneurial endeavor was a benefit to the community, the nation, or the world. For example, what of the entrepreneur who doesn't pay her employees a livable wage, or the entrepreneur who cuts corners to save money and pollutes the local watershed, or the entrepreneur who sexually harasses his employees? Each example is rooted in the realities and complexities of being an entrepreneur in an increasingly globalized and interconnected world. On the most basic philosophical level the concern is if the goal of the business created by the entrepreneur designed to improve the condition of society. For us, it illustrates is that entrepreneurship as it is deployed in our everyday vernacular about what it means to be an American, is entirely insufficient.

Entrepreneurship demands a qualifier. To simply say that someone has taken on the risk of ownership and production is a reductionist argument about both what entrepreneurism is and the consequences of being an entrepreneur. Positioning entrepreneurship in the social studies curriculum in that way points to, even privileges, particular groups of people, most obviously white, upper class men. The reality however is that what comprises the entrepreneurial spirit, and its role in shaping the American Ideal, is that it embodies a set of dispositions that in fact highlight the contributions of those who are rarely seen as entrepreneurial: social entrepreneurs, political entrepreneurs, community activists, and notably women and people of color. Further, those dispositions enable social studies educators to challenge the idea of what an entrepreneur is, and can be, and that the social consequences of operating as an entrepreneur are significant. This is nexus of entrepreneurship, innovation, and the American Ideal. Moving beyond the capitalist assumptions of what constitutes entrepreneurship to a reality of the entrepreneur situated within a social context; one where the entrepreneur believes in her responsibility to the communities of which she is a part as a function of citizenship, and one where innovation is driven by that responsibility.

SHIFTING LENSES: A MODEL

Social studies educators might then think of an entrepreneur as someone trying to solve a social problem for the public good. In that context, entrepreneurs are people who do more than start and operate businesses, but instead embody a set of characteristics that can be more broadly applied to social studies writ large. We argue here that there are five characteristics of entrepreneurs across various aspects of society (business, culture and the arts, politics, etc.) that can be readily applied to social studies curricula. These five characteristics are (1) a need for change, (2) innovative thinking, (3) seizing opportunity/opportunities, (4) risk-taking, and (5) a desire to lead. There are both opportunities and drawbacks for the entrepreneurs/innovators as well as the societies/communities in which these are happening. Put another way, for however it means to be an entrepreneur, through example, demonstrating how to apply this framework to inquiry in social studies might foster more nuanced and thoughtful conversations about what constitutes entrepreneurship.

No matter how powerful an impact these characteristics have on rethinking entrepreneurship, there remains the reality that these must be attended to consciously with respect to the common good, such that students are invited to become engaged more holistically in their communities. Our goal here is not to provide an exhaustive list of American entrepreneurs who either exemplify or problematize the concept of entrepreneurship. Rather, for K-12 social studies teachers, it is essential to explore the possibilities embedded in the curriculum to better engage in the complexities of entrepreneurship as a public good and not simply regard it as an economic inevitability.

Need for Change

To begin, entrepreneurs identify a need for change within society. The necessity for change may be in business and industry or politics or the arts. In many ways, Steve Jobs serves as the entrepreneurial archetype. He encouraged people to "think differently" as he helped to revolutionize technology in our everyday lives. Further, in the last several years there have been several adolescent and young adult biographies about Steve Jobs. At least one was identified as "notable" on the National Council for the Social Studies Notable Book List (*Steve Jobs: Insanely Great*, Hartland, 2015). K–12 social studies students whose everyday actions and interactions are a result of Jobs' innovations and entrepreneurial efforts, we might engage them in conversation about the ways in which his efforts have changed society for the good as well as the unintended consequences of these technological advances.

When we explore the need for change, this idea is certainly not confined to economics or the business world. As we think about our social studies curricula, it is replete with examples of individuals who "thought differently" and identified a need for change. From Susan B. Anthony to Cesar Chavez, Americans have been challenging the notion of the status quo and constructing an entrepreneurial spirit on both economic and socially just successes. George Washington Carver is a prime example of an American who used innovation and entrepreneurship to affect a better society. Carver was intent on diversifying U.S. Southern agricultural interests, not simply for a more stable economic environment, but because doing so would demonstrably improve the lives of the poor.

In each of these cases, the need for change doesn't operate in a vacuum, but in a social reality wherein the entrepreneur makes choices to affect change for based on ethical as well as financial interests. We might shift our ideas about the "need for change" as one where there are consequences that serve the public good.

Innovative Thinking

The American Ideal, rightfully, celebrates individuals (or groups of individuals) who attempt to change business and society through innovative thinking. Social studies teachers and students may traditionally learn about Henry Ford and the assembly line through the lens of innovation. In our history/social studies textbooks, Ford is credited for developing an industrial process that is faster and more efficient. Thus, American industry becomes an example for countries around the world. However, this example of the American Ideal and innovation is touted for its efficiency has not always served the public good. Shifting our thinking, we might consider Franklin D. Roosevelt as an entrepreneur, a political entrepreneur. In the midst of The Great Depression, FDR used his political position and innovative thinking in the development of the myriad of programs for the public good.

Seizing Opportunity

In this dimension, an individual or individuals capitalize on a moment in time. Many may recognize the need for change and have innovative ways to address these needs for change, which they share around a dinner table or in social media posts. Typical examples are those noted above individuals like FDR, Ford, or Carver that take advantage of the particular time and place in which they lived to make a significant difference on society.

However, there are other examples of individuals "seizing opportunity." For example, Jesse Owens demonstrated his athletic prowess in the 1936 Olympic Games in Berlin as Hitler flooded the airwaves with hate speech of ethnic superiority. Thinking about Owens not only as an athlete who showed strength in a time(s) of adversity, but as an entrepreneur may help social studies students and teachers understand the moments at which one needs to act for the betterment of the public good.

Risk-taking

Inherent in this characteristic of entrepreneurship is an element of danger—danger to one's financial, or possibly social well-being. The idea of risk-taking is more than simply risking capital or money; it is also risking one's well-being for the greater good. In the vernacular of social studies curricula, individuals like Carnegie and Walton are risk-takers in the sense that they are incalculably focused on economic and personal achievement. To obtain the kind of entrepreneurial success that made them wealthy, that transformed the world, and indeed, made them fixtures throughout social studies texts, each had to assume great personal and financial risks that precariously had the potential to be either ruinous or laudatory—nothing in between. Consequently, the narratives about Carnegie serve as an example of both risk-taking and The American Ideal. Being born to poor parents and emigrating to the United States, he makes his fortune in the steel industry and gives generously to various philanthropies. He espouses the "Gospel of Wealth" and encourages others to do the same.

Yet, we might also consider Harriet Tubman as a risk-taking entrepreneur. As a conductor of the Underground Railroad, she risked her life and (potentially) the lives of others in order for individuals live more freely. These risks for the public good are identified but might be more thoroughly discussed with social studies students. How did Tubman's risks benefit and challenge society in her lifetime? Beyond her lifetime? The risks she took were literally life and death, and the effect she had society resonates even now. In our view, she is more similar to traditional entrepreneurs than not, however rarely being considered as such.

Desire to Lead

Social studies textbooks and curricula are filled with examples of leaders, who are so often depicted through the superficial, and conveniently unproblematic, dichotomy of "good" or "bad." The desire to lead is a characteristic that encompasses individuals who are involved in various aspects of our society from economics and politics to social and military examples; those who embody the entrepreneurial spirit of the American Ideal are "good." George Washington, for example, is presented as the quintessential American leader. During the American Revolution, he led the Continental Army through challenging conditions and onto victory against the British. In many ways the narrative of Washington establishes the American Ideal—uniting the nation toward a public goal of independence. Yet we know his life and times were far more complex than that simple narrative; perhaps it's the tensions caused by the complexity of his individualism and the times in which he lived that make him a compelling figure rather than the outmoded notions of Washington being pure.

Both similar to and different from Washington, Susan B. Anthony exemplifies a less traditional leader. In her efforts for women's suffrage, she risked her life and the lives of others for a cause to benefit the public good. Anthony was innovative in her use of various strategies to convey her message from speeches and petitions to voting in defiance of the law. In her efforts to lead, she identified a need for change, utilized innovative thinking, seized opportunities, and was willing to take risks for the betterment of society. All of this is accurate, and yet, to truly illustrate the entrepreneurial reality that demonstrated her desire to lead, one must confront the social complexity of the time in which she lived and worked.

CONCLUSION

These examples are not meant to serve as a map to follow. Rather, they serve as a starting point for which one might begin to explore entrepreneur/ship within the categories we describe here. These examples across social studies curricula provide opportunities for students and teachers to think more broadly about this concept and possible associations to the American Ideal. We are hopeful about the role that social studies teachers will have in shaping new ideas about entrepreneurs. It is precisely the complications outlined here that make being a social studies educator that much more important to preserving, or perhaps persevering, the American Ideal and the capacity we have to support our students as entrepreneurs who see their role as building the public good, not only in developing economic sustainability. To raise questions about what constitutes the terms discussed here (e.g., the American Ideal, entrepreneurship, innovation) and for whom these terms are designed, and what the consequences of that vision are for engendering a more just world isn't just our privilege, but a pedagogical imperative to further the scope of social studies and social education.

DISCUSSION QUESTIONS

1. What are the common dispositions you would describe as being entrepreneurial and what effect do those dispositions have on our understanding of social studies?
2. What constitutes the "American Ideal" and how is it shaped by assumptions of innovation? Whose voices are predominant in the "American Ideal?"
3. How can we teach of elements of social studies differently by developing alternative orientations of entrepreneurship?
4. How does exploring the relationship between entrepreneurs and those that build on their innovation help us understand the concept of "public good" and how it might be bolstered or undermined across time and place?
5. Who else could we study who aren't typically thought of as entrepreneurs? Who in your life could be an entrepreneur based on these qualities?

REFERENCES

Hartland, J. (2015). *Steve Jobs: Insanely great*. New York, NY: Schwartz & Wade.
Judge, M., Rotenberg, M., Rapaport, D., Livingston, R., Aniston, J., Root, S., ... Twentieth Century Fox Home Entertainment, Inc. (2005). *Office space*. Beverly Hills, CA: 20th Century Fox Home Entertainment.
Lindaman, D., & Ward, K. R. (2004). *History lessons: How textbooks from around the world portray U.S. history*. New York, NY: The New Press.
Lintner, T. (2005). A world of difference: Teaching tolerance through photographs in elementary school. *Social Studies, 96*(1), 45.
Loewen, J. (1995). *Lies my teacher told me: Everything your American history textbook got wrong*. New York, NY: The New Press.
National Council for the Social Studies. (2013). *The college, career, and civic life (C3) framework for social studies state standards*. Silver Spring, MD: Author.
Oyler, C. (2012). *Actions speak louder than words: Community activism as curriculum*. New York, NY: Taylor & Francis.
Rand, A. (1957). *Atlas shrugged*. New York, NY: Random House.
Roberts. S. L. (2014). Effectively using social studies textbooks in historical inquiry. *Social Studies Research and Practice, 9*(1), 119–128.

Shane, S., & Venkataraman, S. (2000). The promise of entrepreneurship as a field of research. *The Academy of Management Review, 25*(1), 217–226.

Vinson, K. D. (2006). Oppression, anti-oppression, and citizenship education. In E. W. Ross (Ed.), *The social studies curriculum: Purposes, problems, and possibilities* (3rd ed., pp. 51–76). Albany, NY: SUNY Press.

Westheimer, J., & Kahne, J. (2004). Educating the "good" citizen: Political choices and pedagogical goals. *American Educational Research Journal, 41*(2), 1–7.

The White House, Office of the Press Secretary. (2016). Remarks of President Barack Obama—State of the Union as delivered [Press release]. Retrieved from https://www.whitehouse.gov/the-press-office/2016/01/12/remarks-president-barack-obama-prepared-delivery-state-union-address

Whitlock, A. M. (2015). Economics through inquiry: Creating social businesses in fifth grade. *The Social Studies, 106*(3), 117–125.

Yunus, M. (2010). *Building social business: The new kind of capitalism that serves humanity's most pressing needs*. New York, NY: Public Affairs.

CHAPTER TWENTY-SEVEN

How Should We Teach the Children?

A Response to the Production, Distribution, and Consumption Section

MARY BETH HENNING, NORTHERN ILLINOIS UNIVERSITY

Pennington, Ross, and Missias and Brugar write compelling chapters problematizing economic concepts that are little taught or often mistaught in American schools. They add to a burgeoning literature base advocating for critical and compassionate approaches to economic education and financial literacy (Carr, 2012; Lucey, Agnello, & Laney, 2015; Pinto & Chan, 2010; Willis, 2008). In my response to their chapters, I suggest more practical applications of these keywords to curriculum and instruction, particularly emphasizing the elementary and middle level.

Pennington's well-founded criticism of concentrating on consumers and overconsumption of goods and services was popularized by Loewen's (2007) best-selling book *Lies My Teacher Told Me* questioning the way progress is portrayed in high school history texts. Holst (1999) offers many other practical ideas to elementary teachers who want to explore how "less is more." The classic concept of conspicuous consumption is one that can be taught through analysis of popular television series or movies (see Henning & Batson, 2017 for instructional suggestions). Students and teachers may connect with the slow movement, minimalism, and buying local/small business movements. Laney (2008, 2017; Laney & Moseley, 1994; Lucey & Laney, 2009) has published numerous lesson plans using the arts to help students of all ages question the values underlying consumption and capitalism. Finally, there is a growing body of literature that promotes stewardship of resources and explorations of the spiritual dimensions of financial and economic decisions which may be relevant to teachers wishing to combat the overemphasis on consumerism (Lewis & Potter, 2011; Lucey, 2008; Wilkinson & Pickett, 2011).

At the end of his essay and in the accompanying questions, Ross suggests several resources that might be appropriate to share with high school students and teachers who want to investigate classism. Besides reading descriptions of Greg Queen's high school teaching in Warren, Michigan (Ross, 2017), those looking for specific lesson ideas to teach about class might turn to Lucey and Laney's (2012) lesson plan which uses Dorothea Lang's photographs and Bob Miller's 1932 protest song "The Rich Man and the Poor Man" to teach 4th–8th graders about class. Sensoy (2011) described seventh graders' creating their own photo essays illustrating classism, racism, and sexism. Fox (2010) has published a unit for elementary students to explicitly learn about poverty and social action to alleviate poverty. Lucey and Giannangelo (2017) provide two simulations that guide elementary and middle school students to consider the effects of classism in legal proceedings and in manufacturing industry.

I applaud Missias and Brugar's practical focus on identifying entrepreneurs who illuminate a deeper conceptual understanding of entrepreneurship. However, the authors' characteristics of entrepreneurs seem to better define good leadership in general. While profit does not need to be the primary goal of every business, it is still central to the definition of entrepreneur, so exemplars of entrepreneurship should have some profit motive. I would like to suggest that readers consider some excellent examples of international entrepreneurship documented in award-winning children's and young adult literature. Besides George Washington Carver as a strong case study of entrepreneurship, I recommend case studies of Dave Drake (Hill & Collier, 2010), Juan Quezada (Goebel & Diaz, 2011), Isatou Ceesay (Paul & Zunon, 2015), William Kamkwamba (Kamkwamba & Mealer, 2010; Kamkwamba, Mealer & Zunon, 2012) and Kwabena Darko (Milway & Fernandes, 2008). All of these entrepreneurs exemplified a need for change, innovative thinking, seizing opportunities, risk-taking, and leadership. They also recognized the need to make a financial profit while improving their communities.

Because social studies has been defined as "the social sciences adapted and simplified for pedagogical purposes," it is essential that after defining and defending the importance of key words in the social sciences, pedagogical resources be identified for teachers and students (Wesley, 1937, p. 4). Whether through contemporary media, children's literature, young adult literature, photos, art, or music, this response challenges social studies educators to share more of their ideas for vigorous student inquiry into key economic concepts.

REFERENCES

Carr, P. R. (2012). Connecting financial literacy and political literacy through critical pedagogy. In T. A. Lucey & J. D. Laney (Eds.), *Reframing financial literacy: Exploring the value of social currency* (pp. 3–25). Charlotte, NC: Information Age.

Fox, K. R. (2010). Children making a difference: Developing awareness of poverty through service learning. *The Social Studies, 101*(1), 1–9.

Goebel, N. A., & Diaz, D. (2011). *The pot that Juan built*. New York, NY: Lee & Low Books.

Henning, M. B., & Batson, T. (2017). Leonardo DiCaprio: The "Economic Man" and key economic concepts in his movies. In W. B. Russell III & S. Waters (Eds.), *Cinematic social studies: A resource for teaching and learning social studies with film* (pp. 495–512). Charlotte, NC: Information Age.

Hill, L. C., & Collier, B. (2010). *Dave the potter: Artist, poet, slave*. New York, NY: Little Brown.

Holst, C. B. (1999). Buying more can give children less. *Young Children, 54*(5), 19–23.

Kamkwamba, W., & Mealer, B. (2010). *The boy who harnessed the wind: Creating currents of electricity and hope*. New York, NY: HarperCollins.

Kamkwamba, W., Mealer, B., & Zunon, E. (2012). *The boy who harnessed the wind*. New York, NY: Dial Books for Young Readers.

Laney, J. D. (2008). Teaching financial literacy through the arts: Theoretical underpinnings and guidelines for lesson development. In T. A. Lucey & K. S. Cooter (Eds.), *Financial literacy for children and youth* (pp. 237–257). Atlanta, GA: Digitaltextbooks.biz.

Laney, J. D. (with Willerson, A.). (2017). Teaching for economic literacy and economic justice with and through the arts. In M. B. Henning (Ed.), *Innovations in economic education: Promising practices for teachers and students in grades K-16* (pp. 46–65). New York, NY: Routledge.

Laney, J. D., & Moseley, P. A. (1994). Images of American business: Integrating art and economics. *The Social Studies, 85*(6), 245–249.

Lewis, T., & Potter, E. (2011). *Ethical consumption: A critical introduction*. New York: NY: Routledge.

Loewen, J. W. (2007). *Lies my teacher told me: Everything your American history textbook got wrong*. New York, NY: Touchstone.

Lucey, T. A. (2008). Economics, religion, spirituality, and education: Encouraging understanding of the dimensions. In T. A. Lucey & K. S. Cooter (Eds.), *Financial literacy for children and youth* (pp. 558–577). Atlanta, GA: Digitaltextbooks.biz.

Lucey, T. A., Agnello, M. F., & Laney, J. D. (2015). *A critically compassionate approach to financial literacy*. Rotterdam: Sense Publishers.

Lucey, T. A., & Giannangelo, D. M. (2017). Simulations to promote economics and citizenship in elementary education. In M. Henning (Ed.), *Innovations in economic education: Promising practices for teachers and students K-16*. (pp. 22–45). New York, NY: Routledge.

Lucey, T. A., & Laney, J. D. (2009). This land was made for you and me: Teaching the concept of economic justice in the elementary and middle school grades. *The Social Studies, 100*(6), 260–272.

Lucey, T. A., & Laney, J. D. (2012). Using art and community investigation to motivate preservice teachers' learning and teaching of social and economic/financial justice issues. In T. A. Lucey & J. D. Laney (Eds.), *Reframing financial literacy: Exploring the value of social currency* (pp. 253–277). Charlotte, NC: Information Age.

Milway, K. S., & Fernandes, E. (2008). *One hen: How one small loan made a big difference*. Toronto: Kids Can Press.

Paul, M., & Zunon, E. (2015). *One plastic bag: Isatou Ceesay and the recycling women of the Gambia*. Minneapolis, MN: Millbrook.

Pinto, L. E., & Chan, H. (2010). Social justice and financial literacy: Are gender and socio-cultural equity missing from the discussion? *Our Schools, Our Selves, 19*(2), 61–77.

Ross, E. W. (with McQueen, G.). (2017). Why teaching class matters. In E. Wayne Ross (Ed.), *Rethinking social studies: Critical pedagogy in pursuit of dangerous citizenship* (pp. 97–121). Charlotte, NC: Information Age.

Sensoy, O. (2011). Picturing oppression: Seventh graders' photo essays on racism, classism, and sexism. *International Journal of Qualitative Studies in Education, 24*(3), 323–342.

Wesley, E. B. (1937). *Teaching the social studies: Theory and practice*. Boston, MA: DC Heath.

Wilkinson, R., & Pickett, K. (2011). *The spirit level: Why greater equality makes societies stronger*. New York, NY: Bloomsbury Press.

Willis, L. E. (2008). Against financial literacy education, Faculty Scholarship, Paper 199 Retrieved from http://scholarship.law.upenn.edu/faculty_scholarship/1999

Section VIII:
Science, Technology, and Society

CHAPTER TWENTY-EIGHT

Technology

DANIEL G. KRUTKA, UNIVERSITY OF NORTH TEXAS

For a list of all the ways technology has failed to improve the quality of life, please press three.

—Alice Kahn[1]

Of all my technologies, my smartphone probably brings with it the most blessings. I am ever appreciative that its map applications can guide me and my car to my destination with suggested routes if traffic piles up. It streams whatever music I choose and pulls up e-mails so I can be productive even at red lights. The apps, sites, and programs allow me to explore cities around the world within seconds. It delivers to me online gifs and memes that make me laugh, and I have even built meaningful professional relationships through its social media platforms. In my classes, the collaborative, digital, and virtual capabilities allow me and my students to transform our learning in innovative ways. Sometimes I sit back in admiration and warmly think, *thank you for being there, right in my pocket, whenever I need you.*

But, as in some relationships, the burdens—individual and social—become evident with time and reflection. I rely on my smartphone and when things are not working, I get frustrated quickly, particularly if a room full of students are waiting on me to fix the problem. At times, the array of apps can be distracting when I am trying to listen to someone else, fall asleep for the night, or read something longer than a tweet. The ways in which my smartphone beeps at me can cause anxieties when I want calm. And, I know my smartphone sends all my data to a variety of companies who then sell my information off for a tidy profit. I also know that my smartphone was likely created at a monstrous factory in Zhengzhou, China by workers who make under two dollars an hour with components shipped from around the globe, which upon completion, were then shipped in a Boeing 747 to the United States (Barboza, 2016). At times, I want to technofast and *turn off, find zen, sign out.*

I guess I would describe my relationship with technology, in the lingo of Facebook, as: *it's complicated.* In 2018, our affairs with technologies are some combination of incredible, complicated, and troubling, but too often in the social studies, we approach the topic with a dispassion that accepts technologies on their terms, not ours. In this chapter, I am hoping to start a conversation about how social studies teachers might teach with and about *technology* so our students might make its uses and effects more compatible for democracy.

CH-CH-CH-CH-CHANGES (TURN AND FACE THE STRANGE)

Just like the apps on my smartphone, the word *technology* requires periodic updates. The term is rooted in the Greek *tekhnologia* and Latin *technologia* to "describe a systematic study of the arts or the terminology of a particular art" (Williams, 1976/1983, p. 316). This definition may seem strange when contrasted with the ways technology is often talked about in education today: "My technology isn't working"; "Our district needs to keep up with changing technology"; "I learned about new technology at the conference." The contrast between classical and contemporary uses of the term suggest changes across peoples, places, and points in time. Raymond Williams outlined at least three historical variations of *technology.*

The first variation dates to the 1st century and relates to the definition I just shared: *techno-* as a useful art (i.e., *technics*), systematic study of a topic, or the terminology of an art or craft that uses *technical* language. In describing craft or manufacturing skills, the term was often used in contrast to the fine or performing arts. Technology and art may seem to make strange bedfellows to us today, but the past is a foreign country (Lowenthal, 2015). For example, people of medieval societies did not view the world through binary or mathematical lenses that divorced technology and art as contrasting ways of seeing the world. Instead,

> ...the Earth was considered a living being, and the human artisan was an assistant or midwife to nature. Metals grew in the womb of the Earth. The miner, smelter, metalworkers and goldsmith engaged in the sacred tasks of helping nature reach perfection.... (Briggs & Peat, 1999, p. 148)

The objectivity of the scientific revolution and the efficiency of the industrial revolutions ushered in modernist worldviews and, consequently, uses of technology of which are more familiar today. Prior to the 19th century the term was lightly used in English, but this era saw technology represented as the practical application of sciences like medical *technology*. Just as the printing press divorced words from their speaker, *technology* shifted from skilled method or jargon toward invented objects that exist separate from ourselves. Finally, the 20th century saw the rise of *technocracy* where government is run not by elected officials but specialized experts solving disjointed *technical* problems (see Postman, 1992 for more). Educators are intimately familiar with top-down directives of technocratic "experts" (rarely educators themselves) who aim to settle the social studies certification requirements, state standards and tests, and curricular frameworks and structures.

DEEP IN THE TEKS OF TEXAS

As these shifting and intertwined definitions suggest, the history of this keyword is about much more than the newest gadgets and gizmos. While students in some social studies classes may learn the *techniques* of historians or research *techniques*, they primarily learn technologies as objects from the past (e.g., cotton gin, telegraph) and present (e.g., tablets, interactive whiteboards). Take the official high school standards known as the Texas Essential Knowledge and Skills for Social Studies, (un)affectionately TEKS, that make mention of the prefix *techno-* in some form sixty-seven times (Texas Education Agency, 2010). Of these sixty-seven uses of *techno-*, I coded[2] forty-eight as pertaining to technologies (definition 2), three as techniques (definition 1), and none that touched upon technocracy (definition 3). Taken together, the TEKS tell a story not only of technologies as inventions and objects, but they convey a narrative of technological progress.

These standards primarily present technologies as positive by directly pairing *technology* with *innovation* (14 times[3]) or discussing technologies in terms of advancements, developments, or improvements to standard of living or quality of life. In 19 instances, references resided in what I considered neutral sentences that asked for descriptions, impacts, or effects of technology, or mentioned the term as part of a laundry list of considerations. There is not a single reference in the high school standards that specifically encourage students to critically consider negative effects and uses of technologies in the past or present. The TEKS for sociology and financial literacy do not even make reference to the term. The former is probably the discipline most inclined to ask critical questions about the effects of technologies on society and the latter is a field with digital banking, hacking, and currency. Students who study technologies as the TEKS present them will have little preparation in asking important questions about technologies in the present.

The narrative of technological progress presented in the TEKS is a familiar one that I have seen in my years as a social studies classroom teacher and teacher educator. While some teachers and students may abstain from using specific emerging technologies, they usually give in if others use them, a department adopts them, or their institution buys them. The textbooks, educational technology conferences, and tweets I have viewed within and beyond the social studies collectively tend to look back into the past with a sense of nostalgia for the inventors, inventions, and associated benefits. And, the nostalgia is understandable. These technological innovations contribute to quality of life amenities many of us can hardly imagine living without (and others can hardly imagine living with). Technologies have unquestionably led to progress in some areas for some people. The problem with narratives of technological progress is not what is included, but what is excluded.

In an effort not to maintain a narrative of technological progress, the authors of the TEKS were forced to bend the wording of the standards in strange ways. There are no cases in the TEKS where students are asked to consider a negative aspect of technology even when such effects are obvious and important. For example, students are expected to learn "of significant technological innovations in World War I such as machine guns, airplanes, tanks, poison gas, and trench warfare that resulted in the stalemate on the Western Front" (n.p.). This standard takes dubious historical and moral stances. First, the standard directs our historical gaze on the military outcome of the Western Front with no mention of the impact of these "innovations" on soldiers, civilians, and societies. Second, by labeling these technologies simply as "innovations," the standard authors do not seem to want us to deliberate on the technoethics of using such technologies in warfare. Asking such historical questions might cause students to ask similar contemporary questions about the use of unmanned drones or other technologies administered by their governments in the present. Instead, the message seems to be, *Invent things. Use them. Move forward.* Don't stop to ask questions.

Do we not think the soldiers who battled in trench warfare as bullets whizzed by their heads asked ethical questions both during and after the war? Are we supposed to believe that soldiers and civilians subject to the horrors of poison gas would describe these technologies simply as "innovations"? How would the narrative change if students were asked whether the use of poison gas constituted a war crime? These questions encourage historical empathy about what is gained and lost with new technologies in the lives of people in the past (Davis, Yeager, & Foster, 2001). They are also questions students are likely to find interesting and valuable. The story the TEKS tell of technological advances and innovations from only positive or neutral places is a boring one where the outcome is determined and human drama, decisions, and intrigue are sucked from history.

That these vital historical and ethical questions are ignored is troubling considering the narrative of technological progress is not a story social studies educators even need to tell. *Invent things. Use them. Move forward.* Our Western culture whispers this story to us relentlessly. It is evident in the planned obsolescence of smartphones and cars; Once iPhone X is released your iPhone 8 Plus suddenly appears dated or your perfectly running car seems inadequate when compared to newer models. The refrain in schools for more Smart Boards and iPads often lacks evidence, rationale, or plans for how they might improve educational experiences (see Cuban, 1986, 2001). And the ways in which we focus on the immediate benefits of technologies at the expense of associated problems is evident as schools adopt Google tools without consideration of the invasiveness of the corporate collection of students' data (Singer, 2017). This all begs the question, when are students afforded opportunities to question narratives of technological progress?

TROUBLING TECHNOLOGIES: CLONED DINOSAURS, HUMANOID CYBORGS, AND PRECOGS

For better and worse, students gain large quantities of social studies knowledge outside of the classroom. Making connections between teacher lessons and the outside world can help students find, make, and enhance meanings. When it comes to asking ethical questions about technologies, the social studies has much to learn from science fiction. Even though there are plenty of contemporary and historical examples of technological conundrums, science fiction—a genre grounded in assumptions of technological advances—is far more effective at asking moral questions about the role of technologies in our lives. Michael Crichton's chaos scientist Ian Malcolm from *Jurassic Park* (1990) offers a particularly useful model of techno-skepticism[4]. When presented with a theme park of cloned dinosaurs, Malcolm argued that while gaining expertise in most fields requires years of discipline, "scientific power is like inherited wealth: attained without discipline. You read what others have done, and you take the next step ... You can make progress very fast ... There is no humility before nature" (p. 306).

What might it mean to show "humility before nature?" Answering this question requires educators and students to step back from the immediate benefits of technologies, particularly those with means, and consider their downside and unintended consequences. Returning to the language of war, *collateral damage* is not a term that shows up next to "military technologies" in the TEKS. It is a *technical* term used in the military to avoid describing, and thus humanizing, innocent civilians who are injured or die due to imperfect technologies or human error. Of course, technologies and the humans who use them are imperfect, but for those affected, such technical language is likely unpalatable. Instead of engaging in these important ethical dilemmas, the TEKS authors chose a framing where the only effect of poison gas is maintaining a strategic military stalemate.

My point is not to cast judgment on the morality of these technologies or the people using them. The effects around technologies, like my smartphone, are undoubtedly complex, but we must ask the questions. Students and teachers should take a break from the forward march of technological progress that often defines the social studies and ask questions as science fiction authors do. When I consider the ethics of artificial intelligence (AI) or nuclear war, I vividly recall the ethical conversations between the Terminator, Sarah and John Connor, and Cyberdyne Systems engineer Miles Bennett Dyson (Cameron, 1991). When I hear of preventive crime efforts (e.g., the war on drugs), I consider lessons learned from the case of accused Chief of PreCrime John Anderton from *Minority Report* (Molen, Curtis, Parkes, de Bont, & Spielberg, 2002). All of these science fiction examples—cloned dinosaurs, humanoid cyborgs, and precogs—prompt the same ethical question that should be central to social studies discussions of technoethics, *even if we can, should we?* And if we do accept technologies in our societies, *how* should we use them as individuals and communities?

FOREGROUNDING TECH: TEACHING WITH *AND* ABOUT TECHNOLOGIES

The overarching question for the remainder of this chapter is, *how can social studies educators teach with and about technologies?* Teaching with *and* about technologies requires social studies educators and their students to first consider, what *is* technology? Just asking this question can foreground the technologies that surround us and spur us to interrogate our complicated relationships with them. Students and teachers should be awakened to see the array of Google tools, computer tablets, lighting, air conditioning and heating systems, beams and girders (that hold up the school), chalk or white boards, cars and pavement outside, and pencils, paper, and books as objects of study worthy of analysis.

When used well, technologies can allow us to amplify or transform educational activities, but they are almost always accompanied by a downside. Technologies like Google Earth or Expeditions offer obvious transformative benefits as they allow classes to digitally explore much of the world in ways that were impossible until recently, but they also threaten privacy and support unwanted surveillance. Similar to the TEKS, educators can tend to skip over important technoethic questions like, *should anyone in the world be able to see in your backyard by pulling up Google Earth on their smartphone or computer?* Yet, emerging technologies can be exciting. I love exploring street views of cities from around the globe during geography lessons with students. Students often need help understanding the excitement that surrounded emerging technologies of the past because they seem commonplace now. For example, Roberts and Butler (2014) explain how teachers are often surprised to read the following 1827 evaluation of the newest school invention, the chalkboard:

It is surprising and delightful to see the interest which it kindles in even the dullest scholar. By rousing the curiosity and holding the attention beyond all other means, it would almost completely banish that weariness which makes a schoolhouse a place hated to so many children and that *listlessness* and *idleness* which renders that time spent there so often worse than lost.... (As cited in Schechter, 2010, p. 32)

When we think of technologies in terms of their affordances (what a technology allows us to do) and drawbacks, we become less susceptible to educational fads. The chalkboard extended the visual field of students and teachers to include a shared place to write and read. Instead of solely relying on orality to convey ideas with each other, the chalkboard allowed teachers and students to easily display symbols, figures, and drawings to the entire class. However, as technologies give, they also take away.

An interesting corollary for today's chalkboard is Google documents, a web-based Word processor program that allows for multiple users to edit text synchronously or asynchronously. Like the chalkboard, Google docs can afford a shared learning experience, but it can come at the expense of the physical presence of sharing a common space or field of vision. Particularly in a one-to-one classroom where students all have individual computer tablets, students can narrow their gaze to the Google doc without looking at their fellow collaborators. In an age with nearly ubiquitous devices, where, why, and when students focus their attention should be an educational priority (Rheingold, 2012). Teachers can develop mindful policies with students for how and when class participants should focus on their devices and when they should turn and give attention to those with whom they share a physical space (Levy, 2016).

Teaching *about* technologies is challenging because if technologies are familiar, common, or relatively old (like the chalkboard), we tend to take them for granted. Teachers and students can often have vastly different experiences with technologies, particularly as they reflect on the technologies introduced during their lifetime or those which defined their youth (e.g., portable CD players and Nintendo Entertainment System in my case). Understanding what life was like before a particular technology or the role a technology played in youth culture can offer rich content for investigation. The NCSS (2010) Themes, which include numerous provocative questions in the "Science, Technology, and Society" section asks, *is new technology always better than that which it replaces?* Educators are wise to open the floor to students' questions, concerns, and ideas about technologies and their effects in the past and present. Social studies educators can encourage investigations of the various technologies present in their school and consider: *Who invented it? When and why did they do so? For what purposes is it used and how have they changed over time? What are its intended and unintended consequences? Who has access to this technology and does it privilege any particular group?*

Similar to the TEKS, students can passively view technologies as neutral, especially those invented in the distant past. To see a technology as mundane as the chalkboard as once innovative requires students to practice historical perspective and consider why an invention was disruptive at the time of its introduction. Considering what would be different in the absence of familiar technologies can be an effective and creative way to interrogate them. This might be accomplished by technofasting from commonly used technologies like social media and taking stock of how it changes our days (Damico & Krutka, 2018). Students can also examine obsolete technologies within their school, at local museums or via online exhibits, or bring them from home. Educators can assign students to create a classroom museum of technologies accompanied by information that answers the questions I offered at the end of the previous paragraph. Foregrounding the technologies around us and our experiences with them offers one way toward preparing students to ask important and ethical questions about *technology* as citizens in a democracy.

DISCERNING TECHNOLOGIES: BURDENS, BLESSINGS, AND CONTROL

Discerning among technologies, their effects, and whether and how they might serve the common good has never been more important than in the present because technologies have never arrived, spread, and shifted cultural practices with more speed than in the present era (Thomas & Brown, 2011). People and cultures used to be afforded generations to adjust to major technological innovations, but that is not the case now. As Mark Helmsing and Annie Whitlock point out in addressing *time* in this volume, we even rush to name generations, which can lead to mythical concepts that describe youth as *multitaskers* and *digital natives* without much evidence (Kirschner & De Bruyckere, 2017). Technological pessimist Neil Postman (1992) argued that when evaluating technologies, we are better off to err toward Ian Malcolm's type of skepticism. However, Postman stated, "it is a mistake to suppose that any technological innovation has a one-sided effect. Every technology is both a burden and a blessing; not either-or, but this-and-that" (pp. 4–5). Two questions will guide our efforts going forward: *What are the burdens and blessings of technologies?* And, *in what ways do we control our technologies or in what ways do they control us?* Attempting to answer these questions require us to challenge assumptions of technological neutrality and illustrate how technologies, often unbeknownst to their inventors and users, change *us* in unforeseen ways.

Discerning the effects of technologies is a challenging task because we cannot view them from afar as objects separate from our uses of them. Individuals and groups can each have different and unique relationships with technologies that lead to different effects and meanings. Still, we must develop some point of departure for discerning among technologies and their effects. If we consider *how* different technologies change what we can do in the world then we might begin to assign value as to whether, and for whom, technological benefits are worthwhile. Nicholas Carr (2010) categorized technologies in terms of their physical (the first three) or intellectual (the last one) effects:

1. Increase physical attributes: For example, the plow can increase strength, the car can increase speed, or the shield can increase resistance.
2. Enhance senses: For example, the microscope or telescope can increase vision and the microphone can increase sound.
3. Reshape nature: For example, a reservoir can prevent floods and provide water and birth control can reduce unwanted pregnancies.
4. Increase intellect: For example, a clock can change the way people conceive of time and organize their day.

Social studies educators can help students think about the different ways our technologies change our physical and mental capacities. These are important considerations because once a technology enters our culture, we often have little choice as individuals to participate and feel the effects.

A long-standing debate regarding the influence of technologies on human societies centers on the degree to which we control our technologies or they control us. Instrumentalists hold the former position and argue that our technologies are essentially value-neutral and in using them, humans control whether they are used for good or evil. This is the view that tends to be continually reaffirmed by a larger Western culture where almost any new technology passes into society with little resistance. Technological determinists stand at the other end of the spectrum in contending that our technologies are embedded with values that change us. Neil Postman (1992) argued that the United States has adopted the ethics of machines, namely efficiency, objectivity, and the rejection of human judgment. He cites as an example the late 18th-century *technical* invention of grading. He points out how this quantification of human thoughts took hold because of its technical nature and people are now unable to conceive of education without it. This perspective, whether ultimately right or wrong, allows us to step back and reconsider the trajectory upon which technologies take us. In Lance Mason's unsettling of the keyword *media*, he raises similar issues concerning media forms like books, televisions, and social media where he reconsiders *media as environments*.

This theoretical debate has played out throughout history as new technologies supported, challenged, or overthrew existing values and social structures. The famously maligned Luddites were 19th-century English textile workers who challenged the ways that weaving machinery undermined their bargaining power as skilled workers. Luddites were not anti-technology, but as machines and de-skilled labor replaced their work and marginalized their social roles, smashing those machines became a method to preserve their livelihoods and dignity (Postman, 1992). While the embodied craftsmanship of Luddites was developed through years of sacrifice, the invention of machines to replace that work represented, as Ian Malcolm would put it, the "next step." While instrumentalists would argue that humans had a choice in how these machines were used, determinists maintain that decisions concerning how to use weaving machineries were already made because, in the long run, our tools control us. We abide by *their* ethics. The English, and other peoples, reorganized themselves around the values of efficiency and profit inherent in the weaving machinery, not the other way around. Moreover, the Luddites offer a rare example of people rejecting the effects of a technology, and in doing so, their name has become synonymous with foolish resistance to technological progress. Social studies educators might ask students, how does the plight of the Luddites compare to contemporary debates about automation technologies, artificial intelligence, or driverless cars? Inventors and early adopters rarely pause to reflect upon the assumptions built into technologies. Social studies teachers might address the ways in which the rise of agricultural techniques and the invention of cars have yielded burdens, blessings, and control which merit interrogation.

An Agriculture of Control

Agricultural "advances," as the TEKS refer to them, made way for a Neolithic Revolution that occurred, and is still occurring, gradually around the globe and did much more than produce crops; these new techniques carried within them an ethic of human control over the environment. Until approximately 11,000 years ago, all humans lived in nomadic gathering and hunting societies that generally abided by natural principles that governed all species on earth. Like all other species, bands of humans traveled in various geographic regions and succeeded or failed within the opportunities and constraints of the available food sources. However, through advancements in agricultural techniques, agriculturalists took control over nature (e.g., plant crops, domesticate animals) as they built cities with the necessary food surpluses to transcend nature's limits. The ethic of control inherent in these innovations gave rise to social hierarchies and unchecked population growth as "civilized" agriculturalists assimilated or eliminated "primitive" hunting and gathering "savages" across the globe. Daniel Quinn (1996) argued that agriculturalists invoked a form of "totalitarian agriculture" in which the entire world is viewed as a source for unrestrained and and ecologically unsustainable human expansion. Our narrative of technological progress reminds us to skip over questions about the short and long term downsides of agriculture or what was lost from those nomadic societies which dominated most of human history. *Invent things. Use them. Move forward.*

A Sprawling Automobile

While new techniques charged agriculturalists with control over their environment, automobiles followed by bringing about more control over more space. The built environment of human cities had always been built around the original form of transportation—walking. Walkable cities and communities have long been defined by density, shared public spaces, and mixed-use neighborhoods where exercise and interaction were inherent in daily living. Daily activities regarding food, work, and play often kept people within walking distance of home. However, the rise of the automobile enabled a restructuring of the human built environment into what Jeff Speck (2013) called America's worst invention, suburban sprawl. With the help of significant highway investment, the car enabled people to separate from those different from themselves (e.g., white flight, redlining), exacted a larger per person toll on the environment, and contributed to a variety of health maladies. Building cities around cars created a reliance on driving to accomplish daily activities and alienated people from their surroundings. With increased driving and decreased walking, Americans have seen incredible spikes in obesity, diabetes, asthma, car crash deaths, and a lowering of overall lower life expectancies for the first time in centuries (Speck, 2013). If the ethic of the automobile was the individual conquering geographic space then sprawl was the enactment of that ethic. Yet, even though this issue is one of public debate, it is often invisible in official U.S. history curricula that either ignores, or treats as neutral, the urban organization of the first U.S. cities along with the rise of "innovations" like cars, highways, and sprawl without consideration of the intended and unintended consequences.

Both of these cases offer examples of historic technologies in the social studies curriculum that might be further troubled. They are both interesting because imagining life without agriculture or cars yields very different worlds. They are informative because gathering and hunting societies and walkable communities offer lessons about sustainable and healthy communal living that are relevant for the present. They are both relevant because many of us are born into a society dependent on agriculture and cars to the point that most of us have no choice but to participate in the systems that resulted from these technological innovations. Yet, our standards and textbooks often present each of these developments as either positive or neutral whispering to us to accept blessings of each "innovation," but bypassing burdens or questions of who is really in control. *Invent things. Use them. Move forward.*

LOGGING OFF

In an era of rapid technological change, social studies teachers should help students foreground, discern, and trouble the effects of technologies in the past and present. As technologies become ever more powerful, active and engaged citizens who are able to assess the burdens and benefits of *technology* may be our last line of defense against cloned dinosaurs, humanoid cyborgs, and precogs. By discerning technologies and their effects in the present, past, and future, students might initiate dialogues, habits, and even laws to mitigate the downsides of our beloved smartphones. While I often see my smartphone for the immediate benefits and burdens it brings, I hope we can begin to see our smartphones as a social studies investigation waiting to happen. If our students are to disrupt the drumbeat of *Invent things. Use them. Move forward* long enough to ask questions about where technology is taking us, then social studies educators might need to act a little more like a chaos scientist in a dinosaur theme park and ask: *Even if we can, should we?*

DISCUSSION QUESTIONS

1. How has the term *technology* and related terms changed over time and place, and what can that tell us about the technoethics of societies in the past and present?
2. Identify technologies present in your school, home, or community and answer, what are possible burdens of this technology?
3. Choose several major technological inventions in your curriculum and ask, in what ways do these technologies enhance or diminish our physical or intellectual abilities?
4. Identify historical or contemporary technologies and explore, in what ways would we and our societies be different if these technologies were never invented? What are the blessings and burdens for different technologies? And, in what ways do we control technologies and in what ways do they control us?

NOTES

1. Of the many gifts of the Internet, the endless array of unattributed and misattributed quotes is one I wish I could return. When searching for a possible epigraph I came across this quote, supposedly attributed to Alice Kahn, but I could not verify it. Still, I liked the quote and decided to keep it.

2. Due to the size of the codebook and the nature of this chapter (i.e., theoretical, not empirical), I did not include it in this volume as the TEKS are only meant as an illustrative example. Contact me via electronic mail if you would like to see my data analysis.
3. In the high school TEKS, the term *technology* was directly paired with another word 34 times: innovation 14 times; electronic 6 times; transportation 3 times; communication, computer, current, and military 2 times; information and medical 1 time each.
4. As skeptical scientists, paleobotanist Dr. Ellie Sattler and paleontologist Dr. Alan Grant are also excellent exemplars.

REFERENCES

Barboza, D. (2016, December, 29). An iPhone's journey, from the factory floor to the retail store. *New York Times*. Retrieved from https://www.nytimes.com/2016/12/29/technology/iphone-china-apple-stores.html

Briggs, J., & Peat, F. D. (1999). *Seven life lessons of chaos: Spiritual wisdom from the science of change*. New York, NY: HarperCollins.

Cameron, J. (Producer & Director). (1991). *Terminator 2: Judgment day*. Culver City, CA: TriStar Pictures.

Carr, N. (2010). *The shallows: What the Internet is doing to our brains*. New York, NY: W. W. Norton & Company.

Crichton, M. (1990). *Jurassic Park*. New York, NY: Ballantine.

Cuban, L. (1986). *Teachers and machines: The classroom use of technology since 1920*. New York, NY: Teachers College Press.

Cuban, L. (2001). *Oversold and underused: Computers in the classroom*. Cambridge, MA: Harvard University Press.

Damico, N. & Krutka, D. G. (2018). Social media diaries and fasts: Educating for digital mindfulness with pre-service teachers. *Teaching and Teacher Education, 73*, 109–119.

Davis, O. L., Yeager, E. A., & Foster, S. J. (Eds.). (2001). *Historical empathy and perspective taking in the social studies*. Lanham, MD: Rowman & Littlefield.

Kirschner, P. A., & De Bruyckere, P. (2017). The myths of the digital native and the multitasker. *Teaching and Teacher Education, 67*, 135–142.

Levy, D. M. (2016). *Mindful tech: How to bring balance to our digital lives*. New Haven, CT: Yale University Press.

Lowenthal, D. (2015). *The past is a foreign country – revisited*. New York, NY: Cambridge University Press.

Molen, G. R., Curtis, B, Parkes, W. F., de Bont, J. (Producers) & Spielberg, S. (2002). *Minority report*. Los Angeles, CA: 20th Century Fox.

National Council for the Social Studies (NCSS). (2010). *The revised standards, National curriculum standards for social studies: A framework for teaching, learning, and assessment*. Silver Spring, MD: Author. Retrieved from https://www.socialstudies.org/standards/strands

Postman, N. (1992). *Technopoly: The surrender of culture to technology*. New York, NY: Knopf.

Quinn, D. (1996). *Story of B*. New York, NY: Bantam.

Rheingold, H. (2012). *Net smart: How to thrive online*. Cambridge, MA: MIT Press.

Roberts, S. L., & Butler, B. M. (2014). Consumers and producers in the social studies classroom: How Web 2.0 technology can break the cycle of "teachers and machines." In W. B. Russell (Ed.), *Digital social studies* (pp. 147–166). Charlotte, NC: Information Age Publishing.

Schechter, H. (2010). *Killer Colt: Murder, disgrace, and the making of an American legend*. New York, NY: Ballantine Books.

Singer, N. (2017, May 13). How Google took over the classroom. *New York Times*. Retrieved from https://www.nytimes.com/2017/05/13/technology/google-education-chromebooks-schools.html

Speck, J. (2013). *Walkable city: How downtown can save America, one step at a time*. New York, NY: Farrar, Straus, & Giroux.

Texas Education Agency. (2010). *Chapter 113. Texas essential knowledge and skills for social studies subchapter C. High school*. Retrieved from http://ritter.tea.state.tx.us/rules/tac/chapter113/ch113c.html

Thomas, D., & Brown, J. S. (2011). *A new culture of learning: Cultivating the imagination for a world of constant change*. Lexington, KY: CreateSpace.

Williams, R. (1976/1983). *Keywords: A vocabulary of culture and society*. Oxford: Oxford University Press.

CHAPTER TWENTY-NINE

Media

LANCE E. MASON, UNIVERSITY OF INDIANA, KOKOMO

> A medium is a technology within which a culture grows; that is to say, it gives form to a culture's politics, social organization, and habitual ways of thinking.
>
> —Neil Postman

Dictionary.com defines the word *media* as the plural of medium, a noun that indicates "the means of communication, as radio and television, newspapers, and magazines that reach or influence people widely: *The media are covering the speech tonight.*" When looking up the singular form, *medium*, one encounters several definitions centered on the idea of transmitting something between two things. When media is conceived as a message transmitter, it follows that media education would primarily involve analyzing the content of media messages.

In social studies education, content analysis is currently the dominant focus of media education. In their updated position statement on media literacy, the National Council for the Social Studies (NCSS, 2016) asserts that social studies "has an opportunity to lead the way in teaching students to both analyze and produce rich, complex, diverse, and engaging mediated messages" (p. 183). The NCSS argues that the participatory features of new media create an expectation of involvement from students, leading to possibilities for students to create their own media. However, their primary focus is having students critically analyze the content of messages:

> Through the decoding of content-rich media texts in the social studies classroom, students learn and practice the habits of asking key questions, applying historical analysis,

identifying perspectives, assessing credibility, providing text-based evidence, drawing conclusions, and reflecting on their own process of reasoning. (NCSS, 2016, p. 183)

They also provide a series of questions designed to assist educators in investigating media messages. This focus on message content represents the vast majority of media education in the social studies. The NCSS position statement rightfully cites the close involvement of newer media, but gives no indication of how new ways of engaging with media might affect participants. Thus, they effectively treat media forms as simply being useful for more efficiently transmitting messages and content.

A focus on media as a vehicle for content delivery has also dominated conceptions in the field of communications and only began to be challenged with Marshall McLuhan's (1964) assertion that "the medium is the message" (p. 24), or that the medium itself is ultimately of greater societal consequence than the particular messages that it may carry. Media scholar Lance Strate (2012) explains:

> models of communication…typically present the medium (or channel) as an afterthought, suggesting that first we have a message, and then we decide on which medium to send it through. Based on this view, it is only natural to assume that messages exist in some ideal form, independent of the media, and unaffected by them. The *medium is the message* is intended to correct this mistaken view by also conveying the idea that the medium precedes the message. We begin with a medium, for example, a language, and compose a message by selecting and combining elements of the medium, or in this instance the code, according to the rules of grammar…there is no information independent of form. (p. 11)

If messages do not exist in isolation from the medium in which they were crafted, then the idea of media as merely a delivery device for content is inadequate for understanding the impact of media on society.

RETHINKING MEDIA

There is another way to conceive of media beyond it merely serving as a message transmitter. Consistent with McLuhan's arguments, Neil Postman (2006) explains that "a medium is a technology within which a culture grows; that is to say, it gives form to a culture's politics, social organization, and habitual ways of thinking" (p. 62). When considered through the biological metaphor of bacterial cultures, media no longer appear to be simple transmitters of messages, as they are also the environments that provide contexts for social behavior. Though underdeveloped, this basic conception is not entirely absent from the discourse of media education in the social studies. For example, the idea of *participatory cultures*, or the claim that new media spaces like YouTube and Facebook allow users to become producers as well as consumers (Jenkins, 2006), could be understood from this perspective as the development of new cultural forms made possible by digital media technologies. However, these new cultural forms are often studied as mere additions to the existing culture, as is the case when new media enthusiasts tout advances in media that now afford multi-directional (consumers/producers to each other) instead of merely unidirectional (mass media to consumers) experiences, allowing users to disrupt mass media by creating their own media content and connecting with others via new media technologies. Such optimistic accounts about digital media and their potential to affect positive social change (see Jenkins, 2006, 2009; Rheingold, 2008) hold insights, but ultimately underplay the vast cultural changes—many of which are problematic—that emerge in the wake of new media technologies. Reconsidering *media as environments* could allow social studies educators and researchers to more effectively study both the positive and negative individual and social consequences due to media changes.

John Dewey (1916/2009, 1938) argued that educational environments were a crucial factor in the learning process that deeply influenced students' attitudes and behaviors. In many ways, a Deweyian approach to education requires attending closely to classroom dynamics and their habitual influences on students (Mason, 2013, 2016a). Recognizing media as environments would help social studies teachers identify the unique features of new media forms. It would also allow them to consider how students' changing media practices will ultimately impact how they conceive of themselves both as individuals and members of social groups, while also affecting their ideas about citizenship and social action.

Presently, there is concern both inside and outside education about the effects of new media environments on youth. Sociologist Zygmunt Bauman (2010) highlights the individualization of online environments, with simplified interactions lacking ambiguity or complexity, "Unlike its offline alternative, the online world renders an infinite multiplication of contacts conceivable—both plausible and feasible. It does this through reducing their duration and, consequently, by *weakening* such bonds as call for, and often enforce duration" (p. 15).

Bauman argues that a strong sense of self and a deep understanding of difference are fostered by the quality and depth of human interactions, and online environments are negatively affecting these developments. For example, think of a local coffee shop. Such a place invites a mix of various groups in one public space (which is often connected to other public places inextricably linked to their physical location). The shop facilitates casual interactions while also connecting to social and political events within the community. Social media may provide some of these variables, yet tends to simplify these dynamics because it allows individuals to control the manner, degree, and duration of interactions with less worry about constraints from others. Simply put, the physical environment weaves a thicker web of community interaction that ultimately holds civic significance.

Part of the distinction between physical and virtual environments can be understood by the orientation needed to negotiate each respective space. The coffee shop may be privately owned, but is essentially a public space where one at least accepts the possibility of unexpected social engagement. By contrast, Internet spaces are engaged at the convenience of individuals who are in individualized, if not privatized, spaces, which do not preclude but also do not require social commitment in order to participate.

This aligns with Sherry Turkle's (2011) research into youth and social networking sites, which suggests that people have lower expectations for each other in online environments. Turkle describes vulnerable youth who anxiously craft their social networking profiles in the hope of earning the approval of their peers (p. 177). Many of the youth interviewed by Turkle find face-to-face interaction disconcerting because they cannot carefully control their responses. While social awkwardness may be a long-standing feature for American youth, because of new media environments, society must now contend with heightened influence from peer groups along with technologies that allow youth to more effectively retreat behind their online personas. Turkle's (2015) later research connects this research to the conception of empathy, or the ability to understand and share other's feelings. She cites a wealth of research that connects the use of social media and digital technologies to decreased ability to read and respond to others' emotional cues. Similar concerns have been articulated in education (Gardner & Davis, 2013) and in quantitative research into empathy (Konrath, O'Brien, & Hsing, 2011) and narcissism (Twenge, 2013; Twenge, Konrath, Campbell, Foster, & Bushman, 2008a, 2008b). All of this suggests that the practices associated with new media technologies often foster interactions that inhibit the development of deeper forms of empathy and more robust senses of self.

If Dewey (1939/1976) is correct in asserting that democracy depends on a personal way of life connected to the depth of interpersonal engagement, then these developments should be a central concern for citizenship and democratic education (Mason, 2015a). A conception of media as simply transporters of content provides no avenues for understanding or investigating the media forms themselves. With the current way media is described in education, these concerns are often obscured behind the idea that new media make for better, faster transmitters of content, rather than as creators of new environments that help shape the attitudes and behaviors of both individuals and social groups in ways that social studies teachers should understand.

Some may be quick to dismiss such concerns by citing the many advantages that new media technologies afford users. These points also deserve consideration, but from the perspective of media as environments, it is the disadvantages or problems associated with media technologies that tend to be ignored because the advantages are often immediately apparent, whereas the problems often emerge only after new media technologies become commonplace. Whatever one's stance on digital media, reconsidering how media is understood may help clarify the connections between the complex dynamics of personal growth, social relationships, and the media technologies that impact these matters. I do not call for a rejection of new media. Rather, I suggest that a new curriculum is needed that can help social studies teachers, teacher educators, and students attain greater awareness of the effects of media technologies.

HOW MEDIA ENVIRONMENTS STRUCTURE INTERACTION

When envisioning media as environments, it becomes easier to see how such environments structure interactions in particular ways. Marshall McLuhan (1964) argues that media extend human senses, yet because human senses function in balance with one another, this also creates amputations. Put simply, each form of media heightens certain senses while diminishing others.

Consider the physical experience of reading a book. One typically sits or lies down. The reader may notice the sensation of holding the book or smelling its pages, but the sense of vision is generally the dominant, active sense when reading. People usually hold their head steady in order to track the words from left to right on the page, while often isolating themselves to avoid outside stimuli. Compare this to verbal communication. Sound, as opposed to sight, comes at us from every direction and cannot be turned off. While people must turn their heads in a particular direction to view something, hearing pours into their ears whether they want it to or not. When listening, people tend to orient their entire body toward the speaker. In Western culture, physical gestures such as head nodding, eye contact, and brief speech utterances such as "uh-huh" are part of what can be called active listening.

When writing became widespread, words were at least partially transformed from participatory events into things that could be captured, studied, and reflected upon. When one writes a book, they become separated from what they have written, unlike in spoken language. This encourages the understanding that ideas can exist independently of people, making it easier for readers to objectify the world by perceiving themselves as removed from it (Constantineau & McLuhan, 2012, p. 51).

The television viewing experience is profoundly different from the visual emphasis of print literacy, as screen viewing offers an in-depth sensory experience that McLuhan (1964) contends is closer to the sense of touch than vision. Screen experiences are based primarily on what Peirce (1958) called iconic symbols that closely resemble what they represent. Reading requires learning vast combinations of abstract symbols that takes years to master. By contrast, the iconic symbols of television and video are instantly perceived as an immediate, "felt" experience, which provokes a tendency to respond emotionally, as opposed to an analytic response like that encouraged by the experience of reading.

Experientially, new media are best understood as extensions of television in that they tend to encourage immediate felt experiences as opposed to reflective ones (Strate, 2014). Facebook updates and "tweets" require clipped, abrupt statements that resemble a television commercial, although in this case the individual plays the role of both marketer and consumer. New media make interpersonal communication easier and allow users to receive more sources of information, but they also extend the emotional impression bias of television and this has both individual and social consequences that should be examined as part of media education.

For example, political communication through Twitter is strictly limited to 280 characters per "tweet." Yet even political interaction through Facebook, which does not have the same degree of restrictions as Twitter, still encourages speedy consumption over depth. This may be due to privileges of the form itself, which is designed for rapid scanning of vast amounts of information. Also, when not mediated by the physical body, many seem to respond in a more emotive, less analytical way when receiving political news through social media, while having less patience for prolonged deliberative political encounters.

EXPANDING THE DEFINITION OF MEDIA

Within the idea of media as environments is not only a revised conception of media, but an expanded one. If media are seen as environments, then anything that can alter the environment becomes something to analyze. This could include traditional mass media, newer digital media, physical objects, and even language, which is the primary means of communication in most human interactions. McLuhan (1964) demonstrates this expanded idea of media with his example of railways as a medium:

> The railway did not introduce movement or transportation or wheel or road into human society, but it accelerated and enlarged the scale of previous human functions, creating totally new kinds of cities and new kinds of work and leisure. This happened whether the railway functioned in a tropical area or a northern environment, and is independent of the freight or content of the railway medium. (p. 24)

From this perspective, the things that mediate social experiences influence how people make meaning of those experiences. Marshall and Eric McLuhan (2011) explain how human meaning-making is filtered through the objects we use around us: "We are the content of anything we use, if only because these things are extensions of ourselves. The meaning of the pencil, or chair I use is the interplay between me and these things" (p. 6). In other words, changes in the objects that facilitate our interactions in the world alter both cultural dynamics and individual attitudes and behaviors. As Walter Ong (1982) states, "technologies are not mere exterior aids but also interior transformations of consciousness" (p. 81). From this point of view, what is typically identified as media should be considered along with other tools and technologies as being mediating factors in human experiences. As these variables change, so does one's understanding of social experiences and one's sense of self.

Consider the example of President Trump and Twitter. Many have criticized his use of the social media platform to express his frustrations over policy matters. In traditional media terms, Twitter is merely a venue that Trump uses to transmit ideas that express his volatile personality. However, if we follow McLuhan and Ong and take the media as environments perspective seriously, Trump's use of Twitter, which allows him to get instant gratification from his reactions, may contribute to his volatile personality by both providing a medium of immediate expression and offering rapid social validation of it. It may also stoke more volatile reactions from both supporters and critics, thereby contributing to an already polarized political landscape.

TOWARD A NEW PARADIGM FOR MEDIA EDUCATION: FIGURE/GROUND ANALYSIS

Figure/ground analysis was first applied to media by Marshall McLuhan as a way to perceive changes in media environments that might otherwise remain invisible for users. Simply put, a figure is what one consciously identifies in their environment; ground is composed of the things they ignore. Put another way, the figure is what is foregrounded; the ground is synonymous with the background. Ground provides the conditions under which a figure emerges and as such helps to shape perception of that figure. In terms of media, "the medium forms a ground for the content that it transmits and as such changes the message" (Logan, 2011, p. 2). In other words, the reader or viewer notices the foregrounded content, while ignoring the medium in the background that is an integral part of the message. Kawasaki and McLuhan (2010) elaborate:

> Media are ground in two ways. Watching a film on TV, one ignores the TV. In a cinema, one ignores the theatre, the screen, and other patrons while attending to the film. Reading a book, one ignores the page, the book itself, the room, even the actual printed words and letters while one's mind looks at meanings and images. (p. 4)

The prevailing tendency for Western media users is to ignore the ground of the media form and focus on the figure of the content. The standard notion of media education follows from this tendency. Reconsidering media education from the perspective of figure/ground analysis requires creating a perception-based curriculum that reveals the hidden ground of various media environments, leaving them open for critical inspection. The way to achieve this is for teachers to create anti-environments that allow what is typically perceived as background, or ground, to emerge as figure in the foreground (McLuhan & McLuhan, 2011).

One technique for moving items from ground to figure is to imagine what society would be like without them (McLuhan & McLuhan, 2011). This could be done for both historical and contemporary media technologies depending upon the subject and purpose of the teacher. For example, given an expanded conception of media, one can consider the automobile, which was a crucial invention that mediated culture in numerous ways throughout the 20th century and continues to do so today. In an American History class, imagining life without the automobile would bring the field of services and changes that automobiles have facilitated from ground to figure for students; increasing their ability to make connections between technological and social change. Students could imagine how they would get to school without a car, or how the size and location of schools may be different without automobiles. The entire service environment around cars would not exist as it does today, from roads and gas stations to repair shops, nor would many technical jobs. Without automobiles, the expansion of the suburbs would not have occurred in the mid-20th century, while cities would never have suffered from car congestion. Similarly, interstate and international commerce would be fundamentally different, possibly making our economic system less centralized. Such imaginings could lead into inquiries regarding ways that the automobile culture transformed life for Americans and fostered the rise of consumer culture beginning in the 1920s, or considering the role of oil consumption in decisions for the United States to enter into numerous armed conflicts in the second half of the 20th century up to the present day. Undertaking such exercises, students would acquire a deeper understanding of subject matter while simultaneously becoming more aware of how the tools they use help to construct their world in particular ways.

McLuhan (1964) observes that as users become accustomed to a media technology, they become numb to its effects. Today's students are likely to be numb to the effects of social media and mobile devices. A powerful example of the above exercise would be to have students imagine how life would change if social media or mobile digital devices did not exist (Mason, 2016b). Considering the absence of both simultaneously, students could consider how they would interact with others without such tools. How would their relationships with friends, family, and the rest of the world change? How would they share their consumer tastes and preferences with others? How would they meet others who share similar interests? In what other ways would their lives change? Such questions would help bring the environments created by these tools from ground to figure for students to critically explore.

An extension of imagining life without a technology would be to actually live without a technology for a short period of time (Mason, 2015b). Teachers could ask students to conduct media blackouts of particular technologies such as social media or mobile devices for an evening or for one 24-hour period. If this is difficult for teachers to enforce, students could merely keep an inventory of media use for one day to one week. Many students will likely find that they spend more time with media or felt more reliant on media than they expected. Either exercise would move students' personal media use from ground to figure, which would engender opportunities for reflective examination.

Figure/ground analysis can also be used to explore screen media. For example, political commercials are a common item for analysis in social studies classrooms. Typical questioning frameworks such as that provided by NCSS (2016) focus mostly on media content, although they sometimes ask students to consider what persuasive techniques are used. Content is always important, but as noted earlier, content cannot be entirely separated from its medium. Following this, understanding more about the medium will help students gain greater command of media content. The immediacy of screens can overwhelm viewers' perceptual capabilities and leave them with mere impressions of what they viewed (Mason, 2015c). This is especially true for commercials and music videos, which tend to include particularly fast cuts and dense imagery. This is also crucial to understand for political advertisements, because campaigns use the screen form to craft subtle images about their candidate or their opponent in ways that are difficult to fully comprehend through analytic content exercises alone (Mason, 2015d).

Using figure/ground analysis, images will generally be foregrounded on a fast moving screen (McLuhan & McLuhan, 2011), with other material fading to the background. Isolating the other sensory features such as the spoken language or music will help bring this material to the foreground, or figure, for students to analyze. This could be achieved by shutting off the screen while listening to the commercial's music and spoken words to consider these aspects in isolation. Teachers can also mute the sound and ask students to focus only on the changing images in the ad or the written text.

Another powerful technique for bringing material from ground to figure is to transpose it into another medium. A teacher could type out the spoken words from a political commercial or other advertisement on a piece of paper. Often, such words amount to little substance, a point that can be cleverly obscured through the dense imagery of the screen but becomes clearer through this exercise. Larger segments of the commercial could also be transposed into a written narrative for a comparative examination of media forms (for a detailed layout of this approach, see Mason 2015c, 2015d).

CONCLUSION

The standard idea of media as a transmitter of content is useful for basic analysis, although it does not allow teachers and students to explore how their own relationships with media impact their conceptions of the world, each other, and themselves. Recognizing media as environments can help address this deficiency, while a curriculum centered on figure/ground analysis could not only assist students in exploring their media environments, but could also lead to more robust understandings of existing subject matter in the social studies. Given the rapid pace of change in media technologies and the unpredictable consequences of those changes, a move to this broader understanding of media is needed.

DISCUSSION QUESTIONS

1. What is the significance of recognizing media as environments?
2. In what ways is it important for students to understand how their use of media technologies influences their lives?
3. In what ways do new media practices alter conventional ways of communicating? What might be some of the positive and negative consequences of these changes for society and for individuals?

REFERENCES

Bauman, Z. (2010). *44 letters from the liquid modern world.* Malden, MA: Polity Press.
Constantineau, W., & McLuhan, E. (2012). *The science of investigation: Working with equations. Book 2: The human equation toolkit.* Toronto, ON: BPS Books.
Dewey, J. (1916/2009). *Democracy and education.* Greensboro, NC: WLC Books.
Dewey, J. (1938). *Experience and education.* New York, NY: Touchstone Books.
Dewey, J. (1939/1976). Creative democracy—the task before us. In J. Boydston (Ed.), *John Dewey: The later works, 1925–1953, 14* (pp. 224–230). Carbondale, IL: Southern Illinois University Press.
Gardner, H., & Davis, K. (2013). *The app generation: How today's youth navigate identity, intimacy, and imagination in a digital world.* New Haven, CT: Yale University Press.
Jenkins, H. (2006). *Convergence culture: Where old and new media collide.* New York, NY: New York University Press.

Jenkins, H. (2009). *Confronting the challenges of participatory culture: Media education for the 21st century*. Chicago, IL: MacArthur Foundation Press.

Kawasaki, K., & McLuhan, E. (2010). Critical thinking and the learning commons. *Leading journeys: Papers of treasure mountain Canada research retreat*. Retrieved from tmcanada.pbworks.com/f/Final+edit+article+for+TM+Canada+May+5+2010sz.pdf

Konrath, S. H., O'Brien, E. H., & Hsing, C. (2011). Changes in dispositional empathy in American college students over time: A meta-analysis. *Personality and Social Psychology Review, 15*(2), 180–198. doi:10.1177/1088868310377395.

Logan, R. K. (2011). Figure/ground: Cracking the McLuhan code. *E-Compos, Brasilia, 14*(3). Retrieved from http://www.e-compos.org.br

Mason, L. E. (2013). Locating Dewey's "lost individual" through 21st century education. *Philosophical Studies in Education, 44*, 75–87.

Mason, L. E. (2015a). Media and democracy. *Democracy and Education, 23*(1), Article 14. Retrieved from http://democracyeducationjournal.org/home/vol23/iss1/14

Mason, L. E. (2015b). Commentary: Science, technology, and society in guidelines for using technology to prepare social studies teachers: A reply to Hicks et al. and Crocco and Leo. *Contemporary Issues in Technology and Teacher Education, 15*(3). Retrieved from http://www.citejournal.org/vol15/iss3/socialstudies/article2.cfm

Mason, L. E. (2015c). Analyzing the hidden curriculum of screen media advertising. *The Social Studies, 106*(3), 104–111. doi:10.1080/00377996.2015.1005284.

Mason, L. E. (2015d). Media literacy: Analyzing political commercials. *Social Studies Research and Practice, 10*(2), 73–83.

Mason, L. E. (2016a). Cultivating civic habits: A Deweyan analysis of the National Council for the Social Studies position statement on guidelines for social studies teaching and learning. *Education & Culture: The Journal of the John Dewey Society, 32*(1), 87–110.

Mason, L. E. (2016b). McLuhan's challenge to critical media literacy: The *City as Classroom* textbook. *Curriculum Inquiry, 46*(1), 79–97. http://dx.doi.org/10.1080/03626784.2015.1113511

McLuhan, M. (1964). *Understanding media: The extensions of man*. New York, NY: A Signet Book.

McLuhan, M., & McLuhan, E. (2011). *Media and formal cause*. Houston, TX: NeoPoiesis Press, LLC.

National Council for the Social Studies. (2016). NCSS position statement: Media literacy. *Social Education, 80*(3), 183–185.

Ong, W. (1982). *Orality and literacy: The technologizing of the word*. New York, NY: Routledge.

Peirce, C. (1958). *Selected writings*. New York, NY: Dover Publications.

Postman, N. (2006). The humanism of media ecology. In C. M. K. Lum (Ed.), *Perspectives on culture, technology and communication: The media ecology tradition* (pp. 61–69). Cresskill, NJ: Hampton Press.

Rheingold, H. (2008). Using participatory media and public voice to encourage civic engagement. In W. L. Bennett (Ed.), *Civic life online: Learning how digital media can engage youth* (pp. 97–118). Cambridge, MA: The MIT Press.

Strate, L. (2012). The medium and McLuhan's message. *Razon Y Palabra, 80, 1–23.*

Strate, L. (2014). *Amazing ourselves to death: Neil Postman's brave new world revisited*. New York, NY: Peter Lang.

Turkle, S. (2011). *Alone together: Why we expect more from technology and less from each other*. New York, NY: Basic Books.

Turkle, S. (2015). *Reclaiming conversation: The power of talk in a digital age*. New York, NY: Penguin Press.

Twenge, J. M. (2013). The evidence for generation me and against generation we. *Emerging Adulthood*, 1(1), 11–16. doi:10.1177/2167696812466548.

Twenge, J., Konrath, S., Campbell, W. K., Foster, J., & Bushman, B. J. (2008a). Egos inflating over time: A cross-temporal meta-analysis of the Narcissistic Personality Inventory. *Journal of Personality*, 76(4), 875–902. doi:10.1111/j.1467-6494.2008.00507.x.

Twenge, J., Konrath, S., Campbell, W. K., Foster, J., & Bushman, B. J. (2008b). Further evidence of an increase in narcissism among college students. *Journal of Personality*, 76(4), 919–928. doi:10.1111/j.1467-6494.2008.00509.x.

CHAPTER THIRTY

Cyber Salvation and the Necessity of Questioning

A Response to the Science, Technology, and Society Section

SCOTT ALAN METZGER, PENN STATE UNIVERSITY

Lance Mason's chapter opens with a pointed example for considering how technology and media affect society. The Dictionary.com definition of "media" is made possible by a recent technology—the World Wide Web. I still remember the print dictionary my parents bought me in the 1980s, bound in dark (faux) leather with (faux) gilded page edges, the cool smoothness of its cover and smell of its paper—what Mason calls the "physical experience" of reading. I don't know what happened to this lovely old dictionary. A more convenient (not necessarily more informative) technology has long since replaced it.

Dan Krutka's chapter on Technology and Lance Mason's on Media are provocative and important at a historical moment when technological transformations and ubiquitous mass media engagement are being invited into virtually every political, educational, social, and economic facet of life. Krutka and Mason remind us that these transformations are both creative and destructive. As technology and media communication enable new ways of living, other ways are disrupted. Such shifts, while produced through the accumulation of millions of individual choices, often seem to end up precluding individual choice. When powerful institutions buy in to a new technological paradigm, individuals who must interface with the institution have no choice but to adapt to some degree.

Popkewitz (2004) in his analysis of mathematics education observed that modern school subjects were designed to "save the soul through the works of science" (p. 7) and that pedagogy and curriculum are a "modern salvation story that prepares the child for an uncertain future" with readiness for ubiquitous "change" as the chief goal (p. 8). He concluded that conflation of scientific discourses with discourses for social change yields pedagogy inadequate, even tangential, for academic learning. I wonder if schools inscribe on teachers and learners similar mental predispositions toward digital media and technology as secular salvation—generating social and economic progress that will save democratic equality if everyone can learn to accept change into their lives.

Krutka and Mason challenge a master narrative of "progress" that runs through school and society when it comes to new media and technology. We shouldn't be surprised by prevailing assumptions of progress because, as Mason points out, advantages are often immediately apparent but problems emerge more gradually. Krutka reminds us that the "march of technological progress" usually favors particular economic interests. Media outlets responsive to these interests frame technological innovation as an unalloyed good.

Yet consider how the U.S. government and most states have shifted many citizen services entirely online. Internet service isn't a public utility in most places—it is a for-profit concession parceled out by government boards to an oligopoly of corporate interests. Recent efforts to end net neutrality and allow this oligopoly to sell high-speed web traffic to websites that pay and slow down traffic to those that don't pay—or potentially with political orientations they don't like—are just one reason to interrogate the too-easy narrative of progress. Another is how mass reliance on the Internet has enabled the U.S. government to quickly (and largely secretly) expand its power of surveillance over communications, foreign and domestic.

Wright-Maley, Lee, and Friedman (2018) observed that seismic shifts brought on by the personal computer and Internet reshape ways of thinking about schooling. Children are connected to information and each other through digital tools and virtual platforms that can provide powerful new learning opportunities, including educational games and simulations of visual richness hardly imaginable in the past. The risk, as Mason points out, is that constant immersion in digital technology and media can shape the perceptions of young people. It can be difficult to ask them to imagine doing without technology and kinds of media that have become patterns of daily life.

How much immersion is too much? Bolick (2017) has argued for an inclusive diffusion model of technology integration in education that supports a "technoculture" in which people can "live and learn in ways that are better than they could before they had the technology" (p. 514), though the field needs to value pedagogical plurality that includes the consequences of technology. I find this a helpful starting point because it asks educators to attend both to the affordances gained from a technology as well as drawbacks or limitations. Of course, what makes a way of living "better" is often a difficult value judgment.

Mason's chapter unsettles assumptions about media as merely conveying content that people need to learn to consume. The field of social studies has seen an upsurge of scholarly interest in media, especially for history teaching and learning. Paxton and Marcus (2018) have noted that research interest in film and history goes back to the early days of the motion picture industry in the 1920s. Why so much interest for so long? According to Paxton and Marcus, the concern is uniquely important to societies saturated by an ever-growing assortment of historical media to consume. A consumption mentality reinforced in schools may led to a future in which most of what the public thinks it knows about the past comes from commercial media saturation rather than academic learning.

Stoddard and Marcus (2017) have pointed out that all media—film, games, online sites—are "designed experiences" reflecting "ideological worlds" through what perspectives or choices are included or excluded (p. 493). They see a need for more reflection on the decisions and processes that occur in media production: "Too often media education and technologies are separated out, but there are many strong and compelling reasons for this bifurcation to end and for media and technology to be viewed as interconnected" (p. 494). As Mason explains, the form of the medium shapes the message and content. Media are designed by *people* for *purposes*, which unavoidably have ideological repercussions. A videogame's design reflects an "ideological world" through choices it allows to the player—where you can go, what outcomes win or lose, and (as is the case for so many games) whom you are allowed to kill or not kill. Look online at SJW ("social justice warrior") arguments over videogames to see heated public debate on ideological ramifications of game design.

While Krutka raises attention to the historical patterns and consequences of technology, Mason similarly calls the field to attend to the forms of media and their social consequences. The global expansion of new social media has already had considerable impact on political discourse. We see less distanced, long-form political analysis and more instant hot reactions. The headlines "trending" on social media are managed by the owning corporate entity. Reductionist news updates ignore complexity and nuance to appeal to short attention spans. Digital discourse between individuals is intimate (Facebook "friend") yet at the same time impersonal (separated from the visual and spoken cues that facilitate human empathy). The result seems to be a cycle of volatility—increasingly knee-jerk, uncivil, and extreme—that President Trump's Twitter account is, sadly, far from alone in representing.

Krutka crucially challenges educators to keep in mind that technological change is not new. While certainly there is a marked acceleration in the Western world since 1800, the diffusion of labor-modifying (and removing) technology is a historical process since the Neolithic Revolution. Krutka shows teachers how to view technology as a force in historical causation that connects to our present day.

Mason's figure/ground paradigm of "media as environments" harnesses attention to both content and form for considering media effects broadly, even historically. Without wider historical consideration, people can become "numb" to how ubiquitous mass media cause change individually and socially. Numbed citizens will sooner or later find themselves living in a perplexing world not altogether certain how it came to be.

Recognizing this historical process while it is ongoing through essential questions raised by Krutka and Mason is a powerful way teachers can prepare youth not to become numb to the social, political, and economic effects of media and technology. Without citizens ready to ask critical questions, unbridled technological automation combined with centralized mass media could lead to an undemocratic future—with corporate-controlled, for-profit digital sites becoming what passes for the new public square, as physical town centers (Mason's "coffee shop") vanish. YouTube is already providing a glimpse into possible undemocratic effects, using automated algorithms to sort submitted content by what speech is "advertiser friendly" and should be promoted to wider audiences. Krutka and Mason offer perspectives for how media education can teach students how to question media and technology effects as they emerge. Where in the school curriculum will these critical perspectives be examined if not in social studies?

REFERENCES

Bolick, C. M. (2017). The diffusion of technology into the social studies. In M. M. Manfra & C. M. Bolick (Eds.), *The Wiley handbook of social studies research* (pp. 499–517). Malden, MA: Wiley Blackwell.

Paxton, R. J., & Marcus, A. S. (2018). Film media in history teaching and learning. In S. A. Metzger & L. M. Harris (Eds.), *The Wiley international handbook of history teaching and learning* (pp. 579–601). New York, NY: Wiley Blackwell.

Popkewitz, T. (2004). The alchemy of the mathematics curriculum: Inscriptions and the fabrication of the child. *American Educational Research Journal, 41*(1), 3–34.

Stoddard, J. D., & Marcus, A. S. (2017). Media and social studies education. In M. M. Manfra & C. M. Bolick (Eds.), *The Wiley handbook of social studies research* (pp. 477–498). Malden, MA: Wiley Blackwell.

Wright-Maley, C., Lee, J. K., & Friedman, A. (2018). Digital simulations and games in history education. In S. A. Metzger & L. M. Harris (Eds.), *The Wiley international handbook of history teaching and learning* (pp. 603–629). New York, NY: Wiley Blackwell.

Section IX:
Global Connections

CHAPTER THIRTY-ONE

Global

KENNETH T. CARANO, WESTERN OREGON UNIVERSITY
ROBERT W. BAILEY, SOUTH PLANTATION HIGH SCHOOL (FL)

> Whether the borders that divide us are picket fences or national boundaries, we are all neighbors in a global community.
>
> —Jimmy Carter

Ah, the word *global*. It has become ubiquitous. Used in textbooks, news media, a keyword of book titles; but what does it actually mean? We think we know, but do we? For example, a reader may find the above quote a relatively straightforward statement. Is it, though? What exactly do we mean by global? A cursory look through *global's* synonyms includes the following words: universal, worldwide, comprehensive, total, inclusive, overall, large-scale, international, blanket, cosmic, cosmopolitan, earthly, ecumenical, encyclopedic, general, grand, mundane, and planetary.

Clearly, these words do not all have the same meaning. Depending on one's perspective of *global* the conceptualization may shift significantly. Using the term's synonyms, we examine a couple of the possible interpretations.

Statement A: Whether the borders that divide us are picket fences or national boundaries, we are all neighbors in an inclusive community.

Statement B: Whether the borders that divide us are picket fences or national boundaries, we are all neighbors in a grand community.

The initial example conceives *global* as a term encompassing all services, facilities, or items. Statement B implies looking at an issue from a large, magnificent, or imposing point of view. While some may argue the two meanings could have some similarities, in no way do they imply the same thing. Statement A implies itemized relationships while statement B implies a spatial relationship.

Classroom teachers appear to have different views of *global's* meaning and its classroom application, as the following examples from former colleagues attest. Jennifer, a secondary educator who teaches AP Psychology and AP Human Geography defines *global* as being "able to see through a plethora of cultural lenses." Jennifer's effort to include multiple perspectives becomes evident when stating, "My students learn how to empathize with how the other half live. I always play Devil's Advocate, so my students are forced to critically analyze their personal beliefs and question how those beliefs came to fruition." Jennifer stated, "I do not only teach from a Western ideology, but a *global* one." Robert, who teaches a law and government high school curriculum, defined *global* a little differently than Jennifer, stating "*global* means developing an understanding of an interconnected and interdependent life coupled with responsible choice."

The conceptualization of a word's meaning is critical to understanding, particularly in the case of buzzwords such as *global*. During this chapter we explore where the word has been taught in the social studies disciplines, the overarching iterations associated with *global* in the literature, and demonstrate how minute differences in the concept can be troubling. Additionally, we explore four themes most associated with social studies education, each shifting *global's* meaning.

GLOBAL: WHERE DOES IT BEGIN, WHERE DOES IT END?

Chances are you've heard the phrase, "Think global, act local," a slogan popularized in the 1970s. The expression epitomizes the confusion surrounding perceptions of *global*. *Global* is defined or characterized by both local and global considerations. Yet, is there a significant difference between *local* and *global*? Hall (1991) says the following about the global and local relationship,

> What we usually call the global, far from being something which, in a systematic fashion, rolls over everything, creating similarity, in fact works through particularity, negotiates particular spaces, and works through mobilizing particular identities and so on, so there is always a dialectic between the local and the global. (p. 62)

Merryfield and Wilson (2005) claim the *local* and *global* divide centers on people coming to understand their own connections to the larger world. Within the literature, there appears to be two schools of thought on how the *local* and *global* relationship should be addressed in social studies. In the first, curricula often treat these dimensions in isolation rather than as an active relationship (Myers, 2006). One problem with teaching this way is that education focused on local perspectives does not serve students entering an increasingly interconnected world in which they will be competing for and partnering with people, institutions, and economies on an international scale (Kapur & McHale, 2005).

The second school of thought, which is often not taught, is that *local* and *global* are interconnected. In this conceptualization, a person learns how actions and beliefs of people throughout the world influence her and her local community and in turn how her own community impacts the rest of the world. Zhao (2010) argues that *global* is a place and it is everywhere; therefore, the idea of a local community is extinct. Instead, we all live in an interconnected *global* world. For example, issues such as global food production, global warming, global economy, global cultures, global entertainment, and global migration are addressed in a manner that explores how each affects every community (Kenreich, 2010). Bodle (2013) states that through education, local spaces provide students the experiences that allow them to make sense of just how these local interconnections relate to global issues. Waterson and Moffa (2015) also promote local and global connections by suggesting that local community life be used to foster global citizenship in rural school environments. One teacher we interviewed said, "*Global* means the whole wide world, but taking hyper-local steps can be *global*."

One aspect of this local and global gray area is the Internet. Increasingly, scholars argue that technological advances via the Internet, such as social media, have allowed "others" in distant lands to become neighbors and friends, as human as those in local communities (e.g., Appiah, 2006; Carano & Stuckart, 2013; Krutka & Carano, 2016). While we remain physically distant from "others," such distances are regularly bridged with rapid transit or instantaneous communication. What happens on one side of the world increasingly ripples across the planet, impacting people on the other side. Unfortunately, just as this has blurred the *global* and *local*, the increasing interconnection is further complicated by a couple of factors. First, there is a case to be made that this is the exception and not the rule, as often these connections are dependent on people having common languages. Also, the digital divide is an obstacle. The U.S. Department of Education (2018) shows that children without or with limited access to technology lack opportunities to experience these global and local interconnections. Therefore, used wisely, social media in the social studies classroom has the potential to lead to increased equity and understandings among students of different racial and socioeconomic backgrounds by providing access to information and information technology (Darling-Hammond, Zielezinski, & Goldman, 2014; Grinager, 2006).

GLOBAL USE IN SOCIAL STUDIES TEXTBOOKS

During our exploration of *global* we reviewed eight U.S. secondary social studies textbooks used in History, Economics, Geography, and Civics. While no *global* definition was articulated, the term was often paired with vocabulary, assisting the term's meaning. The most frequently identified topic, global economy, was represented in four textbooks. On each occasion a discussion of economic interdependence of resource and trade was a central topic. Global warming was the only other global issue mentioned in multiple textbooks. In *Civics: Participating in Government*, global warming refers to the greenhouse effect. However, when defining the term *global* itself, no reference to size, space, or citizenship is provided (Davis & Fernlund, 2001). In *Social Studies: The World*, global warming refers to a gradual increase in the Earth's temperature and the potential for human impact and references Kyoto and international concern or law (Addison-Wesley, 2003). Other *global* subjects worth noting are globalization and global connections. In *Economics: Principles in Action*, globalization is used to discuss economic trends producing shifts from local to world markets and impacting employment. Global connections looks at the interconnecting systems across world countries (Sullivan & Sheffrin, 2001).

So, what does this all mean? Unfortunately, neither academic articles nor textbook publications provided a definition for the term *global*. This may or may not prove troubling as the word is employed within several textbooks when addressing issues such as trade and climate change and a concept left ambiguous allows for interpretations with often unintended consequences.

GOING *GLOBAL* IN THE SOCIAL STUDIES CLASSROOM

The social studies course traditionally using *global* in its title is Global Studies. Even this course has different conceptualizations of course curricula and the word *global*. Unlike traditional social studies courses (e.g., American History, World History, Economics, Government), in which similarly structured curriculum exists across country, Global Studies courses often espouse differing curricula within states.

In conversations with teachers from three states, we found Global Studies courses taking four forms:

1. Global Studies as World History 2: Age of Exploration to the Current World
2. Global Studies as Teaching 20th- and 21st-Century World History
3. Global Studies as Thematic approach (e.g., Terrorism, Climate Change)
4. Global Studies as World Geography

While teaching a Global Studies course in Florida, one of the authors taught this course with a thematic approach, focusing on what his district deemed as 21st-century global issues, such as global terrorism, climate change, and human rights.

In Oregon, the three other approaches have been observed. For example, Global Studies is sometimes offered as a geography course by high schools not offering world geography courses. One teacher stated, "we find it necessary to have students take a global studies course, so they can learn geography as freshman and at least know where places are and people come from when they are taking World History."

In separate Oregon districts not more than an hour apart, schools take a different approach. For instance, both employ Global Studies as a second World History course, but with varied objectives. One district has it as a Teaching 20th- and 21st-Century World History course while the other district does World History 2: Age of Exploration to the Current World. Mike, a teacher in the latter district stated, "by teaching world history this way, we can go more in depth in both World History and Global Studies."

Cameron, a teacher transferring to a new district within Washington State, spoke to the course's ambiguity. When describing his curriculum in Global Studies for the forthcoming academic year he stated "I'm really not sure. In the past when I taught Global Studies it was a geography course but I am moving to a new district and I haven't found out if that is the content of their school's Global Studies course."

GLOBAL'S UNDERLYING THEMES

Global appears to be used in a variety of ways, but we still have not gotten to its root, epistemologically. Establishing a consensus for the word *global* is no easy task, as it is difficult to find a conceptualization of the word when it is used in the academic literature. In fact, Scheunpflug and Asbrand (2006) argue that *global* has never been well established. Eville Lo (2001) states *global* can be used interchangeably with international and transcultural, but a look through international and transcultural definitions finds the definitions, at times, incompatible. Scholte (2000) identifies *international* as being embedded in territorial space, while Tamcke (2013) points out that *transcultural* transcends territorial space as being a person's existence of living and interacting within and across multiple cultural realities. Scholte (2000) further complicates matters by assuming readers have a uniform conceptualization of *global* when defining globalization as "the process of becoming more global" and globality as the "condition of being global" (p. 42). Yet, Scholte never addresses *global's* actual definition. This failure of discussing *global's* core elements should not be taken lightly.

One's understanding of *global* can have political as well as intellectual implications. Every conceptualization reflects a specific historical context, a given theoretical perspective, certain normative commitments, and particular political interests. For example, a colleague once stated that he is uncomfortable with the term "global citizen," but is fine with the term "citizen in a global world." To him, the former implies allegiance to a sinister one-world order attempting to undermine personal liberty. In his explanation, the latter phrase allows one to retain patriotic citizenship while acknowledging living in an interconnected world.

When used alone, *global* may not be conceptualized in the academic literature, however its iteration has frequently been used as an adjective (e.g., global education, global awareness, global citizenship). By investigating underlying meanings of these phrases, it appears that a general conceptualization of global is *whole earth*, a meaning popularized in the 1890s. Prior to that, in the popular English lexicon, the adjective appeared to commonly refer to *spherical* (Scholte, 2000). But what are the intricacies of whole earth? Does whole earth mean the same thing to everyone when discussing the word *global*? The answer becomes difficult due to the lack of an epistemological exploration and unpacking of *global*.

While *global's* exact meaning remains unsettled, we have identified four common themes most associated with *global* as a concept within social studies academia: spatial, standardized, multiple perceptions, and interconnectedness. These themes can be quite different from one another, yet, at times, synonymous.

Spatial

Some use *global* in the spatial sense to describe arrangements around the earth. For example, when defining global education, Merryfield (2001) uses *global* as a spatial conceptualization while discussing the need to understand both mainstream and marginalized perspectives in different parts of the world, and the effects of historical imperialism on the decolonized mind, which refers to examining subconscious biases that result from growing up in a culture of entitlement. Garii (2000) argues a *global* view focuses on understanding perspectives of other places and cultures, implying a *spatial* sense. Myers (2006) also appears to view *global* spatially when saying, "Similar to the way that U.S. citizenship is built on rights guaranteed in the Constitution, universal human rights are the foundation of global citizenship within the world community" (p. 376).

Carano and Stuckart (2013) conceptualize *global* as space when using social media to teach global literacy and cross-cultural awareness. Additionally, when Bodle (2013) discusses *global* and *local* connections, he refers to *global* in the spatial sense, as the following quotation attests: "All spaces, according to Doreen Massey, are both *local* and *global*" (p. 207). Ho and Seow (2013) further this assumption of spatial undertones when discussing a social studies lesson comparing the history and geography of Chinatowns around the world and argue that Chinatowns are influenced by *global* and *local* environments. In the classroom, *global* as spatial appears to be most associated with geography curricula. For example, among teachers interviewed, when speaking of *global* in these terms, they spoke of it being used in reference to instruction on locales, aspects, and peoples, in different world places.

Standardized

Another underlying theme is that *global* is used to identify similarities everywhere in the world. In this sense, the word is synonymous to standardizing at the world level (Veseth, 2006). This meaning is inspired by companies such as McDonald's, Coke, or Visa. Most associated with an economics curriculum, it comes from the concept *global market*, which by definition is a market of one (same) product everywhere as opposed to a set of national markets, each one with a local variation of the product and different terms of trade. In this interpretation, *local* and *global* are analogous.

Myers (2006) acknowledges that some people are concerned that *global* and its elements are tantamount to *Americanization*, where American culture overwhelms local cultures through a form of popular cultural hegemony (Barber, 1996). Some academics and pundits imply that the word is code for support of a unified world governance (e.g., Buehrer, 1990; Cunningham, 1986). Others define *global* as standardized when debating whether globalization means countries should move from national to global curricula (Parker, Ninomiya, & Cogan, 1999; Pike & Selby, 1995).

Multiple Perspectives

Blanks (2015) appears to be discussing *global* through a multiple perspectives lens when stating global education provides students exposure to differing religious, social, and cultural values. Additionally, when discussing global education in social studies classrooms, Moffa (2016) does not define *global*, but discusses nationalism in a manner that contrasts with *global* as a perspective.

This theme can be seen in economics, history, and geography curricula. If we examine a global phenomenon from multiple perspectives, what is the commonality? The central matter that underscores both the event and the perspective is entirety or whole. For instance, looking at global economics, we might consider an American worker who has had her manufacturing job shipped off to Southeast

Asia; perspective will certainly matter to both the American who lost the job and the Asian who gained a job. Perspective also matters to the international corporation and stockholders who decided to send work abroad and reap greater profits. While objections to teaching the global event are doubtful, objections to the inclusion of multiple perspectives may very well generate resistance, perhaps by American families who lost a job.

What is the purpose for teaching in such a manner? How are students, and society-at-large, served by teaching from a *global* perspective? In theory, this form of teaching empowers and enables students to see a bigger picture, and as a result, encourages informed civic choices.

Interconnectedness

In this instance *global* references the impact an individual event in one locale has on another locale and people living there. Hanvey (1976) references the assumption of interconnectedness when developing global dimensions focused on interactions, developing cultural understandings, and an individual's impact on others. Anderson (1990) alludes to *global* as interconnectedness when stating that globalism leads to an erosion of Western dominance and decline in American power and influence, and that those factors are globalizing the culture and economy of the United States, bringing them closer with others.

Interconnectedness is found in multiple social studies disciplines. For example, in economics it can be used when looking at how the U.S. economy is impacted by world markets and vice versa. In both history and geography global as interconnectedness is addressed when discussing trade, the spread of ideas, and push/pull factors.

Teachers' Global Themes

Since teachers are on education's front lines, we asked fourteen secondary school social studies teachers for their definitions of *global*. The most preferred theme was interconnected with spatial a close second. Two respondents referred to global as cultural relativism or multiple perspectives, providing further credence to the word's lack of consistent interpretation (see Table 31.1). Interestingly, the standardized theme was not named. This may not be that surprising since it is also social studies academics' least noted underlying theme.

Table 31.1. Teachers' Definitions of Global

Theme	Examples
Interconnectedness—7	"I use the term frequently when I am trying to get my students to understand how much the economy in the U.S. is impacted by the other markets around the world."
	"I equate global with transoceanic network of sustained contact, communication, and most importantly trade."
	"The interconnections between continents and travel."
	"Anything from a good, religion, idea to a disease than can be spread."
Spatial—5	"All aspects or places in the world."
	"I think of the community outside of the U.S."
	"All the places and people around the world."
Multiple perspectives—2	"Global means thinking with cultural relativism."
	"Able to see through a plethora of cultural lenses."

Source: Authors.

SIGNIFICANCE OF DIFFERING GLOBAL THEMES

The phrase, "Climate change is a global issue" clearly evokes different reactions depending on the person's perspective of *global's* meaning. For example, in the first theme, spatial, it loosely translates to climate change being everywhere. A person who sees *global* from the standardized theme could interpret the sentence to mean climate change is the same everywhere. Someone interpreting *global* as multiple perspectives may interpret the issue as a topic that is culturally relative and; therefore, perhaps, not a serious issue. The interconnected theme implies climate change impacts all of us, regardless of origin.

It should be noted that within uses of *global* in the academic literature, the meaning of the word infrequently changes. For example, James Becker, a preeminent early global educator regularly employs *global* as a spatial issue (1979). However, within this conceptualization of global education, he also includes the other three themes as important aspects to teach. This is common among global educators (e.g., Carano & Stuckart, 2013; Gaudelli, 2003; Merryfield & Wilson, 2005).

Defining a Global Citizen

Another critical reason for understanding the term *global* is because global educators often cite global citizenship as a central purpose when educating students (e.g., Kirkwood-Tucker, 2012; Merryfield & Wilson, 2005; Zong, 2009). While the exact nature of global citizenship is contested, its meanings and implications can become further complicated when perceptions of *global* differ. Leading scholars on cosmopolitanism articulate the term as belonging to the world as a whole within the ideals of universal concerns for others and respect for legitimate differences (e.g., Appiah, 2006; Schueth & O'Loughlin, 2007). In Appiah's discussion of cosmopolitanism he uses *global* in the spatial context when contrasting it with nationalism, but within that context he discusses the importance of other *global* themes as, essentially, sub-themes of the primary spatial theme. Similarly, Schueth and O'Loughlin assume the spatial context for *global* when framing cosmopolitanism in a local/global discussion and bring in another theme (interconnected) as a sub-theme when stating "…cosmopolitans occupy ethical spaces of encounter in the intensifying human interdependence accompanying material processes of globalization" (p. 927).

Assuming spatial acts as an umbrella for *global* and including other themes under that umbrella, arguably provides a broader set of knowledge and skills of producing a global citizen. On the other hand, many teachers define *global* as only one of these sub-themes. Therefore, are teachers failing to provide students opportunities of being well-rounded global citizens? As previously mentioned, one's understanding of *global* can have political as well as intellectual implications. For example, *global* as standardized appears to dismiss our rich diversity and may be an underlying reason for some peoples' hostility to the term global citizen being synonymous with being unpatriotic or having one worldwide government, as Burack (2003) alludes to both of these when discussing teaching for a global citizen ideology by saying, "Transnational progressives endorse a concept of post-national (global) citizenship and seek to shift authority to an institutional network of international organizations and sub-national political actors not bound within any clear democratic, constitutional framework" (p. 48). On the other hand, *global* as multiple perspectives often encourages examination of this rich diversity in order to build critical analysis skills. These various conceptualizations may present a politically contentious climate for teachers seeking to foster global citizenship dispositions.

CONCLUSION

As the chapter ends we return to former president Jimmy Carter's quote from our chapter's beginning. By looking at this quote from the lens of the four varying *global* themes, one sees how *global* fits each, yet defies any one definition. He could have been talking about the global community being neighbors in a spatial sense. The border dividing us may have been a metaphor for a community not realizing how similar, or standard, we are as a people. It may have been referring to all of us living in an interconnected world and its unique perspectives. At the same time, reviewing this quote from the various lenses also provides *global* as a word of connections. Maybe putting all the themes together Jimmy Carter is referring to living in a world that we all share, at both the *local* and *global* scale, bringing rich perspectives, in which we are becoming increasingly interconnected through a rapidly changing spatial nature precipitated by digital technology.

Ultimately, given the contentious air surrounding the word, the term is deserving of proper consideration within the social studies field. In conclusion, we recommend *global* be employed similarly to other key social studies concepts that regularly cause confusion. Terms such as *liberal* mean very different things depending on whether the reader finds herself reading an economics or politics text. The term *global* may find itself in a similar need for clarification. Due to language differences that exist, publishers, authors, and teachers should provide an operational definition when employing the term *global* or unnecessary debates and objections will continue.

DISCUSSION QUESTIONS

It is your turn to wrestle with the paradox that is *global*. To jumpstart your discussion, consider the following questions.

1. What is your definition of *global*?
2. What is the relationship between *global* and *local* in social studies education?
3. Which of the four global themes identified in this chapter most easily dovetail with existing social studies curricula, and why might that be the easiest to integrate on a regular basis?
4. When trying to provide multiple perspectives, show the interconnected nature of things, discuss examples of how the world is becoming more standardized, or include spatial elements in a lesson, some resistance may be encountered. What strategies might a teacher employ when attempting to circumvent such barriers and successfully include such global elements?
5. Some teachers may be more or less inclined to include the four themes identified in this chapter into their daily lessons. For instance, if one travelled while growing up, they might have developed a personality that is more prone to including multiple perspectives. What other personal life circumstances might motivate a teacher toward the inclusion of the four global themes?

REFERENCES

Addison-Wesley Educational Publishers. (2003). *Social studies: The world.* Boston, MA: Author.
Anderson, L. F. (1990). A rationale for global education. In K. A. Tye (Ed.), *Global education: From thought to action* (pp. 13–34). Alexandria, VA: Association for Supervision and Curriculum Development.
Appiah, A. (2006). *Cosmopolitanism: Ethics in a world of strangers.* New York, NY: W.W. Norton.
Barber, B. (1996). *Jihad vs. McWorld: How globalism and tribalism are reshaping the world.* New York, NY: Ballantine Books.
Becker, J. M. (1979). The world and the school: A case for world-centered education. In J. M. Becker (Ed.), *Schooling for a global age* (pp. 33–57). New York, NY: McGraw-Hill.
Blanks, D. E. (2015). Building global citizens through the common core. In T. Turner, J. Clabough, & W. Cole (Eds.), *Social studies and the common core* (pp. 65–76). Charlotte, NC: Information Age Publishing.
Bodle, A. T. (2013). World tour by bus: Teaching and learning about globalization by exploring local places in search of global connections. In L. Nganga, J. Kambutu, & W. B. Russell III (Eds.), *Exploring globalization opportunities and challenges in social studies: Effective instructional approaches* (pp. 207–216). New York, NY: Peter Lang.
Buehrer, E. (1990). *The new age masquerade: The hidden agenda in your child's classroom.* Brentwood, TN: Wolgemuth and Hyatt.
Burack, J. (2003). The student, the world, and the global education ideology. In J. Leming, L. Ellington, & K. Porter (Eds.), *Where did social studies go wrong?* (pp. 40–69). Washington, DC: Thomas B. Fordham Foundation.
Carano, K. T., & Stuckart, D. W. (2013). Blogging for global literacy and cross-cultural awareness. In L. Nganga, J. Kambutu, & W. B. Russell III (Eds.), *Exploring globalization opportunities and challenges in social studies: Effective instructional approaches* (pp. 179–196). New York, NY: Peter Lang.
Cunningham, G. L. (1986). *Blowing the whistle on global education* (Unpublished report). Denver, CO: U.S. Department of Education, Region VIII.
Darling-Hammond, L., Zielezinski, M. B., & Goldman, S. (2014). *Using technology to support at-risk students' learning.* Alliance for Excellence in Education. Retrieved from https://edpolicy.stanford.edu/sites/default/files/scope-pub-using-technology-report.pdf
Davis, J. E., & Fernlund, P. M. (2001). *Civics: Participating in government.* New York, NY: Prentice Hall.
Eville Lo, D. (2001). Borrowed voices: Using literature to teach global perspectives to middle school students. *The Clearing House, 75*(2), 84–87.
Garii, B. (2000). U.S. social studies in the 21st century: Internationalizing the curriculum for global citizens. *The Social Studies, 91,* 257–264.
Gaudelli, W. (2003). *World class: Teaching and learning in global times.* Mahwah, NJ: Erlbaum.
Grinager, H. (2006). How education technology leads to improved student achievement. *Education Issues.* National Conference of State Legislatures. Retrieved from http://www.ncsl.org/portals/1/documents/educ/item013161.pdf
Hall, S. (1991). Old and new identities; Old and new ethnicities. In A. Smith (Ed.), *Culture, globalization and the world-system* (pp. 41–68). London: Macmillan.

Hanvey, R. G. (1976). *An attainable global perspective*. New York, NY: American Forum for Global Education.
Ho, L., & Seow, T. (2013). Teaching geography through "Chinatowns": Global connections and local spaces. *Social Education, 77*(1), 36–41.
Kapur, D., & McHale, J. (2005). *Give us your best and brightest: The global hunt for talent and its impact on the developing world*. Washington, DC: Center for Global Development.
Kenreich, T. W. (2010). Power, space, and geographies of difference: Mapping the world with a critical global perspective. In B. Subedi (Ed.), *Critical global perspectives: Rethinking knowledge about global societies* (pp. 57–75). Charlotte, NC: Information Age Press.
Kirkwood-Tucker, T. F. (2012). Preparing global citizens through the study of human rights. *Social Education, 76*(5), 244–246.
Krutka, D. G., & Carano, K. T. (2016). "As long as I see you on Facebook I know you are safe": Social media experiences as humanizing pedagogy. In A. Crowe & A. Cuenca (Eds.), *Rethinking social studies education in the twenty-first century* (pp. 207–222). New York, NY: Springer International Publishing.
Merryfield, M. M. (2001). Moving the center of global education: From imperial world views that divide the world to double consciousness, contrapuntal pedagogy, hybridity, and cross-cultural competence. In W. B. Stanley (Ed.), *Critical issues in social studies research for the 21st century* (pp. 179–207). Greenwich, CT: Information Age.
Merryfield, M. M., & Wilson, A. (2005). *Social studies and the world: Teaching global perspectives*. Silver Spring, MD: National Council for the Social Studies.
Moffa, E. D. (2016). Fostering global citizenship dispositions: The longterm impact of participating in a high school global service club. *The Social Studies, 107*(4), 145–152.
Myers, J. P. (2006). Rethinking the social studies curriculum in the context of globalization: Education for global citizenship in the U.S. *Theory and Research in Social Education, 34*(3), 370–394.
Parker, W. C., Ninomiya, A., & Cogan, J. (1999). Educating world citizens: Multinational curriculum development. *American Educational Research Journal, 36*(2), 117–145.
Pike, G., & Selby, D. (1995). *Reconnecting from national to global curriculum*. Toronto: International Institute for Global Education, University of Toronto.
Scheunpflug, A., & Asbrand, B. (2006). Global education and education for sustainability. *Environmental Education Research, 12*(1), 33–46.
Scholte, J. A. (2000). *Globalization: A critical introduction*. New York, NY: St. Martin's Press.
Schueth, S., & O'Loughlin, J. (2007). Belonging in the world: Cosmopolitanism in geographical contexts. *Geoforum, 39*(2), 926–941.
Sullivan, A., & Sheffrin, S. M. (2001). *Economics: Principles in action*. Boston, MA: Prentice Hall.
Tamcke, M. (2013). On the path to transculturality. In M. Tamcke, J. de Jong, L. Klein, & M. van der Waal (Eds.), *Europe—space for transcultural existence* (pp. 143–150). Göttingen: Universitätsverlag Göttingen.
U.S. Department of Education. Institute of Education Sciences, National Center for Education Statistics. (2018). *Student access to digital learning resources outside of the classroom*. (NCES 2017098). Retrieved April 21, 2018 from https://nces.ed.gov/pubs2017/2017098.pdf
Veseth, M. (2006). *Globalony: Unraveling the myths of globalization*. Lanham, MD: Rowman & Littlefield Publishers.
Waterson, R. A., & Moffa, E. D. (2015). Applying Deweyan principles to global citizenship education in a rural context. *Journal of International Social Studies, 5*(1), 129–139.

Zhao, Y. (2010). Preparing globally competent teachers: A new imperative for teacher education. *Journal of Teacher Education, 61*(5), 422–431.

Zong, G. (2009). Global perspectives in teacher education research and practice. In T. F. Kirkwood-Tucker (Ed.), *Visions in global education: The globalization of curriculum and pedagogy in teacher education and schools* (pp. 71–89). New York, NY: Peter Lang.

CHAPTER THIRTY-TWO

Immigration

DILYS SCHOORMAN, FLORIDA ATLANTIC UNIVERSITY
RINA BOUSALIS, FLORIDA ATLANTIC UNIVERSITY

> We've had times throughout our history where anti-immigration sentiment is exploited by demagogues. The language is identical… America is a nation of immigrants. That's our strength. Unless you are a Native American, somebody, somewhere in your past showed up from someplace else, and they didn't always have papers. And the genius of America has been to define ourselves not by what we look like or what our last name is or our faith but our adherence to a common creed.
>
> —President Barack Obama, whose father was an immigrant, addressing anti-immigrant attitudes in the United States, June 2016 (Scott & Chason, 2016)

> I would build a great wall, and nobody builds walls better than me, believe me, and I'll build them very inexpensively. I will build a great, great wall on our southern border. And I will have Mexico pay for that wall.
>
> —Donald Trump, whose paternal grandparents were immigrants, candidacy announcement speech, June 2015 (CBS News, 2015)

IMMIGRATION IN A CONTEMPORARY CONTEXT

"Immigration" has become a keyword on the global political stage, likely to dominate headlines and generate controversy in local, national, and international arenas (Anderson, 2011). Although countries such as Canada have been successful in embracing cultural pluralism and openness to immigration (Jones, 2016), immigration has also emerged as a point of national tension as evident in Britain's decision to exit from the European Union (EU). Immigration has become a central facet of the political platforms of world leaders. The burgeoning humanitarian crisis in the context of Syrian refugees reveals, on a global stage, the complex and multidimensional nature of contemporary framings of immigration. Greece, one of the leading refugee host countries, has sent Syrians back to Turkey in light of the EU pact between the two countries. The German Chancellor initially advocated humanitarianism in the nation's hospitality toward refugees, while simultaneously denigrating multiculturalism (Noack, 2015). The United States as well agreed to receive Syrian refugees, only to disperse them to specific government-selected locations throughout the country as part of the refugee resettlement plan (Stoltzfoos, 2016).

These contemporary responses reveal deep-rooted historical, cultural, political, and economic dimensions of immigration. They highlight the significance of one's standpoint in giving meaning to the term "immigration" in our discourse. Current perspectives on immigration are polarized between humanitarian hospitality that welcomes difference vs. economic and cultural protectionism that raise fear and distrust. It is important that immigration is understood, both as a lived experience and as a policy in nations/states on either end of this polemic. We must also explore how the voices of immigrants themselves, largely subdued in these discussions despite personal and national histories of successful immigration, might contribute to a reconceptualization of immigration.

Immigration occurs when the human response to the need for safety and well-being results in the movement of people across a national border (National Census Bureau, 2012). This framing acknowledges the systemic causes of immigration that give rise to what scholars term the "push" factors that drive immigration. "As long as there is inequality in the world, there will be migration. As long as there is starvation, there will be migration. As long as there is better chance for survival elsewhere, there will be migration" (Quintana, 2011, p. 1). Immigration is sometimes the consequence of policies in which the host community has been a participant, most evident in immigration from former colonies to the colonial host nation. Many blame United States policies and entanglements in Central American nations for the resulting migration of thousands, most notably those fleeing genocide in Guatemala. As is evident in the unfolding crisis in Syria, immigration is rarely an easy course of action for immigrants; it is fraught with difficulty and upheaval on psychological, cultural, political, economical and physical dimensions.

DIVERGENT DISCOURSES ON IMMIGRATION

Supporters of immigration recognize both the humanitarian/moral obligations of hospitality and the cultural, social, economic, and political enrichment that diversity brings. President Bill Clinton in 1998 observed that "America [sic] has constantly drawn strength and spirit from wave after wave of immigrants ... They have proved to be the most restless, the most adventurous, the most innovative, the most industrious of people" (Hernandez, 2012, p. 11). Such a framing of immigration highlights themes of resilience, courage, cross-cultural adaptation, hope, and a deep commitment to their host nation that characterize the lived experiences of first generation immigrants.

International policy discourse on immigration too often has been accompanied with an undertow of racism, classism and religious bigotry, including most recently, Islamophobia. In the past, nations such as the United States and Australia have advanced immigration policies based on race. The United States of America has restricted specific groups through the Chinese Exclusion Act of 1882, the Geary Act of 1892, the Asiatic Barred Zone Immigration Act of 1917 and a national origin quota system established in 1924. These and Australia's "White Australia" policy (1901–1973) exemplify the explicit role of racism in immigration policy. The United States government welcomed Cuban immigration following Fidel Castro's rise to power in the late 1950s with political asylum but not to Haitians deemed to be escaping poverty on boats and rafts in the 1980s. What subsequently developed into the "wet foot, dry foot" policy allowed Cubans who reached land to remain in the United States, whereas Haitians were not accorded that option (Perez, 2003). This United States immigration policy that favored lighter-skinned Cubans over their darker-skinned Haitian counterparts represents persistent leitmotifs in the nation's responses to immigration. Contemporary discourse on the immigration of Muslims underscores the importance of understanding the racial, class, and religious framing of immigration as a keyword.

In the United States, the discourse around immigration has also revolved around issues of legal vs. illegal immigration. Viewing immigration historically from a Native American perspective frames the colonists as the nation's first illegal immigrants. It is also significant that notions of legality emerge largely in the context of crossing the post-1848 southern border of the United States, rather than the northern border, or illegal status following initial legality, as pertaining to those who overstay a visa. According to the Pew Research Center, while individuals from Mexico account for 49% of unauthorized immigrants, they represent 9% of those who overstay their visas. In contrast, people from Canada—due to lax border control, few markers that designate where Canada ends and the United States begins (Nixon, 2016), and the United States' need for and desire to keep highly skilled workers (Cervantes & Guellec, 2002)—accounted for the highest number (19%) of those who overstayed a visa, with only 1% of initially unauthorized immigrants. Europe accounts for the highest number as a region (Passel & Cohn, 2016). Lawrence Downes (2007) also faults the media for exploiting the rhetoric of legality and its attendant stereotypes noting that the discourse of legality is:

> A code word for racial and ethnic hatred, it is detestable … It spreads, like a stain that cannot wash out. It leaves its target diminished as a human, a lifetime member of a presumptive criminal class … [as bigots] debate [and] rant about "illegals"—call them congenital criminals, lepers, thieves, unclean … TV ratings will go way up. (p. 411)

It is typically assumed that immigrants enter a host nation of their own volition. This was not the case for African slaves who were brought to this nation against their will, nor does it represent the experiences of many groups that were/are involuntarily transported around the world through forms of human trafficking. Emerging humanitarian crises around the world reveal that the perceived voluntariness of immigration might be better understood less as a dichotomous ascription (voluntary vs. involuntary) and more as a complex and nuanced process that captures the pain of being forced to leave one's home, the fear of the new, the courage to face the unknown, and the resilience to start life over. Thus successful immigration also becomes a matter of the receptivity of the host nation, rather than a function of solely individual effort of the immigrant. Unsuccessful immigration, as an example, could resemble the many Mexicans in the United States who voluntarily return to Mexico due to a lack of jobs and state laws that "attempt to make their lives so unbearable that they have no choice but to leave" (Alarcon, 2012, p. 1).

Critics of immigration, ironically, often descendants of the immigrants themselves, assert that immigrants will become a government's burden, take over the country, bring disease, increase crime, and destroy the economy. In the United States, classism and religious bigotry aimed against Irish and Italian Catholics, or Jewish immigrants from Germany and Poland were evident in the vitriolic descriptions of these groups as "vermin" (Koppelman, 2014, p. 74). Yet, immigrants, both voluntary and involuntary, have served to boost the nation's economy. Slavery, indentured servitude, harsh labor building railroads, in factories, plantations or in dangerous or undesired lines of work have been the dominant realities of immigration among immigrant communities in the United States (Northrup, 1995). Ironically, the economic benefit of these labor conditions accrue largely to entities that value the presence of immigrants as a social underclass. It is thus not surprising that national quota systems or temporary migrant visas emerge as national policies.

POLICY RESPONSES TO IMMIGRATION

In nations where policies support immigration from former colonies, there is pressure to assimilate, especially through proficiency in the national language verified through literacy tests. Conflating immigration with required assimilation is particularly ironic in the context of the history of the United States, where early

European immigrants themselves deemed the Native Americans "domestic foreigners" in their own land and spurned the language and culture of their hosts. Skeptics of multiculturalism view immigrants' native language, culture, and funds of knowledge as deficits that are stumbling blocks to social integration despite the evidence that multilingual, multicultural backgrounds are central to global economic success.

Not all immigrants represent a nation's poor, tired, huddled masses as embodied in the iconic welcome of the Statue of Liberty; immigrants also include highly educated professionals who spark scientific advancement and, according to Martin (2012), are responsible for three-fourths of the nation's best research university patents. Despite this diversity, immigration debates are typically framed in monolithic portrayals of immigrants, from the perspective of the host, rather than the immigrant him/herself. Issues such as whom to let in or keep out and why, whom to deport, the recent criminalization of immigrants (to the benefit of private prison companies), and even language policy are largely determined by perspectives outside of immigrant communities rather than from within.

The macro-level politics of immigration play a significant role in the educational response to immigrants. Given that one's worldview shapes one's positive or negative responses to immigration, it follows that education about and for immigrants is also likely ideologically contested. While in the USA *Plyler v. Doe* (1982) and *Lau v. Nichols* (1974) advocate for the rights of all immigrant students to be educated in public schools in a language that they understand, such legal guarantees have not always translated into equitable education. Public schools represent a transformatory agency for immigrants, who often rely on their education to be socially mobile in the United States.

National policies and public discourse and their underlying value systems typically shape educational policy and practice. Educators need to consider how these value systems impact the manner in which they educate immigrant students as well as how they teach about immigration. Where public sentiment frames immigration as an imposition, educational policies and practices that focus on assimilation dominate. Where immigration is viewed more hospitably, even as cultural enrichment, policies and practices that support cultural accommodation emerge. Thus what leaders and the media say about immigration matters in how students will learn this term. In contexts where more students are descendant of immigrants, such framing becomes crucial.

National discourse and local government practices also impact the climate and culture prevalent in schools. The Southern Poverty Law Center in association with Teaching Tolerance reported the adverse effects of the racist remarks on immigration espoused by then United States Presidential candidate Donald Trump. Children and educators reported a rise in school bullying, students' fear of attending school, and racial and ethnic conflict in the classroom. Immigration rhetoric heard at home or read on social media has caused students anxiety and stress.

> [Mexican] students worry about being deported ... [or] trapped behind a wall ... Muslim children are being called *terrorist* or *ISIS* or *bomber* ... black students ... [think they] will get sent back to Africa ... Latino students ... carry their birth certificates and Social Security cards to school because they are afraid they will be deported. (Costello, 2016, p. 5)

Communities that have support structures to facilitate the integration of immigrants will be more successful in demonstrating the positive potential of ethnic pluralism and multiculturalism. Such support services include the presence of adult education opportunities, social services, and cross-culturally competent workers in hospitable local schools and agencies.

The impact of such national sentiment is particularly evident in the example of language education. In the United States, the backlash against immigration has also resulted in the dismantling of bilingual education programs proven to be effective methods of facilitating both a bicultural identity among students and successful linguistic integration into the mainstream. Instead, most state policies support the Teaching of English as a Second Language and "English Only" mentalities that fail to tap into students' linguistic competencies in their mother tongue in order to learn a second language. Efforts such as *Proposition 227* enacted in California in 1998 banning the use of a second language in public schools epitomize the extant hostility toward immigrants. Even in Europe where, unlike in the United States, most nations espouse multilingualism as central to educational accomplishment, a key concern with immigrants has been the stipulation to learn the national language. Many nations have a literacy test integrated into applications for citizenship or immigration.

In the United States, the recent policy debate on immigration has included the plight of children. The 2014 influx of Honduran children escaping violence in their country galvanized the divergent forces around immigration. Many people viewed the young Hondurans as immigrants and felt hostility toward these children; others saw them as refugees and were not only sympathetic to their plight, but were also astonished at the children's courage and determination to reach the United States (Gomez, 2014). Emerging from this concern for the children, President Obama advocated for an immigration plan which "would have shielded undocumented parents of citizens or legal residents and childhood arrivals from deportation and allowed them to work" (Andrews, 2016, p. 1). Unfortunately, this plan was blocked by the United States Supreme Court. This is yet another setback for those calling themselves the DREAMers, a movement named after the proposed Development, Relief, and Education for Alien Minors (DREAM) Act that was meant to support the children of undocumented immigrants. Educators now must reckon with the messages that this sends to children. Why should they stay in school and be good citizens?

REPRESENTATION OF IMMIGRATION IN THE SCHOOL CURRICULUM

What shapes the perspective of immigration at a formative level is its representation in the curriculum. Positive representations of immigration can serve as an antidote to the toxic representations of the media and political demagogues. Despite the popular claims of the United States "being a nation of immigrants," there is very little evidence of the positive depiction of immigration. There is also very little discussion of the negative impact of the first waves of immigration on the indigenous populations of the Americas. As publishers and authors have the power to elect how they will present the immigrant, it is evident that "whomever controls the textbook, controls the curriculum" (Cruz, 2002, p. 327).

As literary trends often reflect societal trends and academic perspectives, such as those of researchers and educators, they may have directly or indirectly altered the context used to present immigration in social studies textbooks and curriculum, and perhaps most significantly, students' understanding. A recent review of social studies methods course textbooks for pre-service teachers and United States history high school textbooks found that while searching in the indexes, the word "immigration" was often used in association with the word "multiculturalism." Although an integral part of embracing diversity, references to multiculturalism in textbook analyses linked to culture and a student's native country rather than the immigration experience itself. As frequently seen in the indexes, the word "immigration" was used in conjunction with "debate," "citizenship," and "the process of naturalization," thus tying immigration to legality and the status of being a citizen, as well as regularly suggesting it as a topic for classroom debate. Perhaps most surprising was finding the word "immigration" unattached to the word "immigrant." Although the essence of the immigration experience is the immigrant, the word immigrant was often omitted from the indexes, as well as within the body of the text; instead, the texts substituted words "migrant," "illegal alien," or "terrorist" to reference immigrants, thereby subtly shaping attitudes toward these newcomers. What is missing in United States social studies textbooks is the concept of the immigrant, or as fittingly described, "the human face of immigration" (Costello, 2011, p. 20). Rather than focusing on "the border," or "the line between us" (Bigelow, 2006, p. 1), or *how* to teach immigrants (e.g., bilingualism, accommodations, and assimilation), pre-service students should first learn about the immigrant as an individual and examine perspective, family, and culture, and the conflicts that the immigrants may have experienced (Wallerstein, 1982). This absence of the human experience not only is a disservice to the immigrants who helped shape the United States and other global societies, but also perpetuates a subtle form of xenophobia, dehumanizes the immigrant, and reveals a missed opportunity for developing empathy with/for immigrants, in order to humanize the topic itself as well as those learning about it.

In sum, immigration as a key word must be understood in terms of its historical, cultural, economic, ideological, and social context. These contexts are often evident in the language used to demarcate political, racial, and economic borders in the keywords we discuss. For instance, terms such as *refugee*, one who seeks asylum in the host country due to a fear of persecution in their home country (United Nations High Commissioner for Refugees, 2016), contrasts with *expatriate*, one who chooses to take on an international transfer (Cerdin & Selmer, 2014)—a move that could also be viewed as either short-term or as taking an extended vacation (Lazarove, McNulty, & Reiche, 2013)—and *undocumented citizen*, a politically correct term used to describe one who holds no legal immigration documents and is therefore not a citizen (Krause, 2015). Yet they all refer to a common experience of immigration, even as we recognize that the political underpinning accompanying labels significantly alter the quality of immigration as a lived experience.

Considering the view of immigration from the perspective of immigrants might well shift discourse and labeling. In the United States, this process may well be underway. An anticipated demographic shift caused significantly by immigration will yield a nation where those of White racial identities will no longer be a majority in the United States among children by 2020 and adults by 2045 (Ware, 2015). Might this shift bring about a more humanitarian stance? Might it break down the walls of nationalism and usher in a view of a more interconnected and interdependent world? How might educators, particularly in social studies, support the development of future citizens capable of successfully leading in such a context?

DISCUSSION QUESTIONS

1. To what extent does *who* the immigrants are and *where* they are from frame discussions about immigration?
2. Is there a distinction between a refugee and an immigrant, or does the public perceive them as the same? Are refugees and immigrants treated differently?
3. How might divergent standpoints on immigration frame its discussion in schools?

4. From whose perspective do we frame our conceptions of the term "immigration"? How do these perceptions shape educational decision-making?
5. Can discussions of immigration be divorced from discussions of race?
6. How might immigration debates differ if led by immigrants themselves?
7. How do the threats of international terror reframe our discussions of immigration?

REFERENCES

Alarcon, A. (2012). Do-it-yourself deportation. *The New York Times*. Retrieved from http://www.nytimes.com/2012/02/02/opinion/do-it-yourself-deportation.html

Anderson, K. (2011). Coming to America: Focus on immigration, *School Library Journal, 57*(1), 44–45.

Andrews, T. (2016, June 27). Supreme Court's tie blocks Obama's immigration plan. *The Detroit Sports Site*, 2016. Retrieved from http://thedetroitsportssite.com/2016/06/27/supreme-courts-tie-blocks-obamas-immigration-plan/

Bigelow, B. (2006). *The line between us: Teaching about the border and Mexican immigration*. Milwaukee, WI: Rethinking Schools, Ltd.

CBS News. (2015). 30 of Donald Trump's wildest quotes: On building a wall. *CBSNEWS*. Retrieved from http://www.cbsnews.com/pictures/wild-donald-trump-quotes/14/

Cerdin, J. L., & Selmer, J. (2014). Who is a self-initiated expatriate? Towards conceptual clarity of a common notion. *The International Journal of Human Resource Management, 25*(9), 1281–1301.

Cervantes, M., & Guellec, D. (2002). The brain drain: Old myths, new realities. *Organisation for Economic Cooperation and Development Observer*, 230, 40.

Costello, M. (2011). The human face of immigration. *Teaching Tolerance, 39*, 20–27.

Costello, M. (2016). *The Trump effect: The impact of the presidential campaign on our nation's schools*. Montgomery, AL: Southern Poverty Law Center.

Cruz, B. (2002). Don Juan and rebels under palm trees: Depictions of Latin Americans in US history textbooks. *Critique of Anthropology, 22*(3), 323–342.

Downes, L. (2007, October 28). What part of 'illegal' don't you understand? *New York Times*, 2007.

Gomez, M. (2014, August 6). What we can learn from child refugees. *The Progressive*, 2014. Retrieved from http://www.progressive.org/news/2014/08/187806/what-we-can-learn-child-refugees

Hernandez, L. (2012). *Saving the American dream: Main Street's last stand*. Bloomington, IN: AuthorHouse.

Jones, S. (2016, June 30). Canadian lawmakers chant 'four more years' after Obama's speech to parliament. *CNSNews*, 2016. Retrieved from http://cnsnews.com/news/article/susan-jones/canadian-lawmakers-chant-four-more-years-after-obamas-speech-parliament

Koppelman, K. L. (2014). *Understanding human differences: Multicultural education for a diverse America* (4th ed.). Boston, MA: Allyn and Bacon.

Krause, J. (2015, December 12). Undocumented citizens? The absurd new word for illegal aliens. *The Daily Sheeple*, 2015. Retrieved from http://www.thedailysheeple.com/undocumented-citizen-the-absurd-new-word-for-illegal-aliens_122015

Lazarove, M., McNulty, Y., & Reiche, B. S. (2013). *We are not on vacation! Bridging the scholar-practitioner gap in expatriate family research*. Orlando, FL: U.S. Academy of Management Meeting Symposium.

Martin, A. (2012, June 25). Immigrants are crucial to innovation, study says. *The New York Times*, 2012. Retrieved from http://www.nytimes.com/2012/06/26/business/immigrants- played- role-in-majority-of-us-technical-patents-study-finds.html?_r=0

National Census Bureau. (2012). *International migration*. Retrieved from http://www.census.gov/population/intmigration/about/.

Nixon, R. (2016, October 16). As U.S. watched Mexico, traffickers slip in from Canada. *The New York Times*, 2016. Retrieved from http://www.nytimes.com/2016/10/17/us/northern-border-illicit-crossing.html?partner=rss&emc=rss&_r=0

Noack, R. (2015, December 14). Multiculturalism is a sham, says Angela Merkel. *Washington Post*, 2015. Retrieved from https://www.washingtonpost.com/news/worldviews/wp/2015/12/14/angela- merkel-multiculturalism-is-a-sham/

Northrup, D. (1995). *Indentured labor in the age of imperialism, 1834–1922*. New York, NY: Cambridge University Press.

Passel, J., & Cohn, D. (2016, February 3). Homeland Security produces first estimate of foreign visitors to US who overstay deadline to leave. *Pew Research Center*, 2016. Retrieved from: http://www.pewresearch.org/fact-tank/2016/02/03/homeland-security- produces-first-estimate-of-foreign-visitors-to-u-s-who-overstay-deadline-to-leave/

Perez, A. J. (2003) Wet foot, dry foot, no foot: The recurring controversy between Cubans, Haitians, and the United States immigration policy. *Nova Law Review, 28*(2), 436–465.

Quintana, E. (2011, December 31). What we owe immigrants. *Huffington Post*, 2011. Retrieved from. http://www.huffingtonpost.com/elena-quintana/undocumented- immigrants_b_1062645.html

Scott, E., & Chason, R. (2016, June 30). Obama denounces 'demagogues' in immigration debate. *CNN*, 2016. Retrieved from http://www.cnn.com/2016/06/29/politics/barack-oba demagogues-immigration

Stoltzfoos. R. (2016, April 7). First Syrian refugees hit US soil as Obama resettlement surge begins. *The Daily Caller News Foundation*, 2016. Retrieved from http://dailycaller.com/2016/04/07/first-syrian-refugees-hit-us-soil-as-obama-resettlement-surge-begins/

United Nations High Commissioner for Refugees. (2016). Refugees. *UNHCR*. Retrieved from http://www.unhcr.org/refugees.html

Wallerstein, N. (1982). *Language and culture in conflict: Problem-posing in the ESL classroom*. Reading, MA: Addison-Wesley Publishing Company.

Ware, D. (2015, March 5). Census: White children to become minority by 2020. *UPI Top News*, 2015. Retrieved from http://www.upi.com/Top_News/US/2015/03/05/Census-White-children-to-become-minority-by-2020/9751425612082/

CHAPTER THIRTY-THREE

Crossing/Erasing Borders

A Response to the Global Connections Section

CINTHIA SALINAS, UNIVERSITY OF TEXAS
MELISSA ROJAS WILLIAMS, UNIVERSITY OF TEXAS

In selecting the work of Raymond Williams and Walter Parker to emphasize "keywords" and their central and yet at times ambiguous nature, our colleagues have focused the social studies fields' attention on words that matter. Though democracy the teaching of democracy is a messy and ongoing journey, we concur and that examining keywords is fundamental to our understandings and future actions as citizens. In this short response to the work on *global* by Kennith Carano and Robert Bailey and the work on *immigration* by Dilys Schoorman and Rina Bousalis, we contend that keywords in the social studies are contextual and temporal and thus a daunting task undertaken by our colleagues. Regardless *global* and *immigration* are exceptionally relevant and compelling terms in ways that are essential to our field and our understandings.

The terms *global* and *immigration* exemplify both the importance of our terms and categorizations, phrasing and claims as well as examined and unexamined assumptions. For example, Carano and Bailey in examining the word *global* rightly assert, "Every conceptualization reflects a specific historical context, a given theoretical perspective, certain normative commitments, and particular political interests" (p. 316). The four themes that emerge in their analysis include spatial, standardized, multiple perceptions, and interconnectedness. The themes provide a valuable framework that can be used by social studies educators to deepen the employment of the term *global*. For instance, using the popular yet relatively inexplicit expression "think global, act local," the authors highlight an example of how *global* has been elevated to celebrity like status without deep consideration of its meaning.

Through the four themes we maintain that Carano and Bailey have provided us with an opportunity to consider how the "global and local" mantra can consider the "subconscious biases...of a culture of entitlement" (p. 316) as well as historical and geographic relationships between spaces. Space is in the eye of the dominant and marginalized beholder and thus "think global, act local" can produce notable thought and action. The "think global, act local" can be viewed also through the notion of standardization, which is synonymous to Americanization. One might also consider how standardization takes on an economistic if not capitalistic tone. To "think global, act local" might take on a more critical definition if teachers and students consider the contrast between differing or multiple perspectives as well as who is advantaged/disadvantaged and empowered/disempowered by a phrase that appears altruistic at face value. Finally, what might be gained in "thinking globally and acting locally" is an examination of the interconnectedness between histories, geographies, economies and so forth as tensions that undergird global as a means for the United States to gain or lose influence and dominance. The dissection of "think global, act local" through the four themes does not provide teachers and their students a singular definition or linear relationship or resolve the paradox. However, we conclude that Carano and Bailey have prompted the field to consider how the term global deserves a more thoughtful use in the social studies classroom.

For Schoorman and Bousalis *immigration* remains a word marked by "historical, cultural, political and economic dimensions." Their endeavor to examine a keyword is framed by long standing "undertow of racism, classism and religious bigotry" found with the enactment of "the Chinese Exclusion Act of 1882, the Geary Act of 1892, the Asiatic Barred Zone Immigration Act of 1917..." (p. 327). The demeaning of Italian, Catholic, Irish, Polish, and Jewish immigrants is a relatively known narrative long replaced by the demeaning of other immigrant groups. A critical analysis of contemporary immigration is ladled with "burgeoning humanitarian crisis," "economic and cultural protectionism," "push factors," and "fleeing genocide." In succinct and profound ways Schoorman and Bousalis capture the uninterrupted American practice of excluding and including immigrant groups.

As bilingual social studies educators we were particularly drawn to how bilingual education and the Development, Relief and Education for Alien Minors (DREAM) Act was central to the analysis of the keyword *immigrant*. Through a disingenuous adherence to constitutionally bindings findings of *Plyer v. Doe* (1982) and *Lau v. Nichols* (1974), Schoorman and Bousalis capture an intricate historical, social, or economic snapshot that reveals the contradictions of our nation and our failure to acknowledge the interconnectedness of humanity. The constant denial of language rights/bilingual education programs and access as well as negation of the civic identities of immigrant children who have been in the United States their entire lives are but a sampling of the xenophobia that plagues our nation. Schoorman and Bousalis unequivocally ask that social studies teacher and students focus on "issues such as whom to let in or keep out and why, whom to deport, the recent criminalization (to the benefit of private prison companies) and even language policy are largely determined by perspectives outside of immigrant communities rather than from within them" (p. 329). With great commitment, the authors implore that we all expose the inhumane and undemocratic nature of immigration discourses and policies.

The field of socials studies education is indeed in the midst of much work—considering how *global* and *immigration* merge into reconceptualizations of citizenship education. Paramount is the framing of discourses by Knight Abowtiz and Harnish (2006) that focused our attention upon more critical discourse—those that disrupt dominant and disenfranchising notions of citizenship. The keywords of *global* and *immigration* beg for such attention and are closely related to other terms and notions such as cultural citizenship (e.g., Ong, 1999; Rosaldo, 1997), participatory communal citizenship (e.g., Knight & Watson, 2014), civic identities of diverse youth (e.g., Rubin, 2007), multicultural citizenship (e.g., Dilworth, 2004), civic multicultural competence (e.g., Miller-Lane, Howard, & Halagao, 2007) and the intersectionality of citizenship with gender and race (Bondy, 2014; Vickery, 2015). Each of these bodies of work and more expose the tensions between "self making and being-made" that are inherent to the terms *global* and *immigration* (Foucault, 1989). We believe there can be vital conversations regarding identity, agency and membership within the process of claiming citizenship and being denied citizenship. Consequently, in an era in which the ubiquitous notions of *global* and *immigration* are both auspicious and undesirable perhaps social studies teachers can shape the conversation beyond nations, states, and borders and instead toward a politics of belonging.

REFERENCES

Bondy, J. (2014). "Why do I have to pledge the U.S. flag? It's not my country!": Latina youths rearticulating citizenship and national belonging. *Multicultural Perspectives, 16*(4), 193–202.

Dilworth, P. P. (2004). Competing conceptions of citizenship education: Thomas Jesse Jones and Carter G. Woodson. *International Journal of Social Education, 18*(2), 1–10.

Foucault, M. (1989). The subject and power. In H. L. Dreyfus & P. Rainbow (Eds.), *Michael Foucault: Beyond structuralism and hermeneutics* (pp. 209–228). Chicago, IL: University of Chicago Press.

Knight Abowtiz, K., & Harnish, J. (2006). Contemporary discourses of citizenship. *Review of Educational Research, 76*(4), 653–690.

Knight, M., & Watson, V. (2014). Towards participatory communal citizenship: Rendering visible the civic teaching, and actions of African American youth and young adults. *American Educational Research Journal, 51*(3), 539–566.

Miller-Lane, J., Howard, T., & Halagao, P. E. (2007). Civic multicultural competence: Searching for common ground in democratic education. *Theory and Research in Social Education, 35*(4), 551–573.

Ong, A. (1999). Cultural citizenship as subject making: Immigrants negotiate racial and cultural boundaries in the United States. In R. Torres, L. Miron, & J. Inda (Eds.), *Race, identity and citizenship: A reader* (pp. 262–293). Malden, MA: Blackwell Publishing Ltd.

Rosaldo, R. (1997). Cultural citizenship, inequality, and multiculturalism. In W. Flores & R. Benmayor (Eds.), *Latino cultural citizenship: Claiming identity, space, and rights* (pp. 1–23). Boston, MA: Beacon Press.

Rubin, B. (2007). "There's still not justice": Youth civic identity development amid distinct school and community contexts. *Teachers College Record, 109*(2), 449–481.

Vickery, A. E. (2015). It was never meant for us: Towards a black feminist construct of citizenship in social studies. *The Journal of Social Studies Research, 39*(3), 163–172.

Section X:
Civic Ideals and Practices

CHAPTER THIRTY-FOUR

Discourse

RORY P. TANNEBAUM, MERRIMACK COLLEGE

> For those of you who have been following democracy for the past 240 years, you know we have officially hit a new low in political discourse. We have sunk below "swift boat", below "secret Muslim", below "John McCain's illegitimate baby", below the Ed Sullivan theater, past the subway lines, past Hillary Clinton's secret email servers, past the founding fathers spinning in their graves, past the dinosaurs.... and we are at the center of the Earth.
>
> —STEPHEN COLBERT, MARCH 7TH, 2016, THE LATE SHOW MONOLOGUE

In a recent segment on *The Late Show*, Stephen Colbert described several candidates in the 2016 American presidential race as lacking the ability to participate in constructive conversations on issues relevant to both the presidency and the American people. Throughout the segment, Colbert took a nonpartisan approach as he showed clips and analyzed comments made by candidates throughout the year-long campaigning season. The examples shown—though clearly selected for their comedic value—depicted several candidates for the highest office in the United States in a variety of contexts calling one another names, making wild and unfounded accusations, and failing to take any real positions on major issues. Colbert finished the segment by looking at the camera and—while genuinely smiling—saying "I can't believe these are actually jokes I can make during a presidential election!"

Colbert's isolated description of the current state of political rhetoric—while certainly situated within the context of a satirical television program—serves as an interesting take on how discourse in politics currently works (or, perhaps more honestly, does *not* work). What has seemingly become valued in the political sphere during the 2016 election cycle is not collectivity and the sharing of ideas through productive conversation. Rather, politicians and pundits on both sides of the political spectrum seek to slander the opposition and increase support within their party through broad and safe position statements often lacking substantial detail or room for collaboration. Compromise, for that matter, has been sacrificed in order for a more black-and-white political conversation in which one side is "right" and the other side is "wrong."

Such a transgression is important to note, as political discourse has historically been a part of America's *progression*. Through collectivity and compromise, America—and, more broadly, the world—has shifted, adapted, and evolved over the past two and a half centuries. In this sense, the lively discussions that once defined government and society as a whole (the Lincoln-Douglas Debates, W.E.B Du Bois and Booker T. Washington, Malcolm X and Martin Luther King Jr.) all seem to be in the distant past, as the goal is to now to make a one-liner that will "trend" on social media and not offend any potential voter base. This climate of extreme partisanship is one that is neither healthy for nurturing growth nor dealing with issues of the 21st century.

The rhetoric currently occurring in the political realm is disheartening regardless of one's political affiliation and, sadly, shows no potential for improving in the near future. However, it has, in a sense, encouraged Americans to reconsider how citizens engage in public and private discourse and the expectations placed upon elected officials for compromise, open-mindedness, and collectivity through conversation. This chapter will situate these ideas within the 21st-century social studies classroom by exploring discourse to the extent in which it fits under the aims of both the social studies and, broadly speaking, various components of democratic and citizenship education. A more specific aim is to "unpack" *discourse* as a pedagogical approach in its most effective form and relate this kind of teaching to a properly functioning public (and political) sphere.

Discourse is often used in the classroom in the form of debate that can be likened to the current types of conversation occurring in the political sphere. In this sense, classroom discourse often takes the form of competition rather than collectivity, which, ultimately, does a disservice to students in that it teaches against compromise, open-mindedness, and collaboration. The classroom needs to reinvigorate discursive practices as a means for promoting "collective action" and compromise as a way to progress society and foster in a new generation of citizens (and politicians) capable of rational, progressive dialogue (Habermas, 1989; Meuwissen, 2013).

It should be noted, at this point, that students occasionally need competition to become fully engaged in content. And the purpose of this essay is to neither condemn the use of debate nor suggest competition within the classroom does not assist students in becoming citizens (especially when given the value of democratic dissent and the importance of challenging traditions for a positive change). However, the purpose of this specific chapter is to explore how collaboration in the classroom in the form of discourse is often more effective than emphasizing competition among students and aligns more properly with broad notions of democratic and citizenship education.

THE SOCIAL STUDIES AND EFFECTIVE DISCOURSE

Colbert's humorous assessment of the current state of political discourse in America is as relatable as it is interesting. On the one hand, his characterization of how politicians interact with one another seemingly reflects that of many citizens who are frustrated with the partisanship and lack of compromise coming from both major parties in the United States. Americans, for that matter, appear frustrated with a seemingly broken political system in which the discourse seems to be perpetuating the problem, not fixing it. Despite the lack of compromise or consensus stemming from such discussions, this frustration has continuously grown and has united Americans on at least one issue: that the current political sphere is often incapable of using collaboration to solve problems.

Such a view of the political sphere in America provides an interesting platform for revisiting the skills we want our students to gain prior to entering into the public sphere as participating citizens. Now more than ever, it seems, America's public schools—and, more specifically, the field of social studies education—must reexamine the skills and abilities we want our future leaders and politicians to have upon entering into the political realm (Meuwissen, 2013). Those in the field of the social studies must review and revise the expectations we have for our students regarding developing the skills to participate in rational discourse.

Despite this recent emphasis on teaching collective discourse, it should be noted that the idea of the social studies promoting various forms of dialogue in the classroom is not new, as the field has consistently maintained the need for students who are capable of engaging in collaboration and discussion among one another (Chandler & Ehrlich, 2016). Among a variety of other reasons, Parker notes that "the social studies is at the center of a good school curriculum because it is where students learn to see and interpret the world—its people, places, cultures, systems, and problems; its dreams and calamities—now and long ago" (p. 3). Because the social studies is driven largely on the notion of lifting up historically marginalized groups, promoting equity and equality, developing citizenship skills, and the construction of new knowledge, discourse is often viewed as a way to incorporate the views of various groups within a safe, diverse setting while simultaneously helping individuals grow through the construction of new knowledge

(Hess, 2009; Tannebaum, 2015). This mission has been seen in the development of the ten NCSS strands that underline the field, the recently released C3 Framework, and throughout the existing bodies of literature as put forth by both leading and emerging scholars (and, certainly, within the Common Core standards (2010) that consistently emphasize the need for students to participate in "discussion among diverse partners"). Moreover, the social studies has certainly done its part in emphasizing the need for students to learn how to collaborate with one another through various forms of verbal communication. To that end, the field of social studies education has done a solid job of acknowledging the importance of simply having students collaborate with one another within student-centered settings. An array of leading scholars within the social studies consistently write about the need for discourse as a means for achieving the lofty objectives of developing citizens capable of entering into and bettering a pluralist, democratic society (Flynn, 2009; Hess, 2009; Parker, 2010).

SO WHAT'S THE PROBLEM?

Despite such great work occurring within academia and the actual K–12 classroom, collective learning in schools often reflects the discourse Colbert humorously assessed in his segment. Rather than being used as a means for promoting progressive group-talk, discourse is often confused (or used interchangeably) with "debate"—in which individuals seek to convince someone else of their own perspectives through the exchanging of knowledge via convincing arguments (Preskill, 1997). Students are expected to prove a point or convince others that they are right and that a peer is either incorrect or incapable of participating in a conversation (Yankelovich, 2001). Such forms of classroom discourse often do a disservice to students in that they neither promote growth nor compromise to their fullest potential. Students are taught, essentially, that the most successful arguments reflect those that so often occur within the political realm: convincing others of an opinion and having neither an evolving nor bipartisan perspective. Students, therefore, learn that a conversation can be considered effective when they have a certain threshold of combativeness to argue a given point.

Though debate of this form certainly has a healthy place in a progressive democracy, teaching students that conversation should exclusively and explicitly be competitive in nature may only serve to reinforce practices resembling the politicians Colbert spotlighted as being self-serving and incapable of compromise or growth. In other words, the public sphere which exists as an arena for collaborative group-talk will be inherited by future generations of citizens who see neither the value in exchanging ideas nor working with one another to solve large, complex societal and global issues.

GROWTH THROUGH COLLECTIVE DISCOURSE

Reflecting on the idea of the public sphere being at its most efficient when participants understand how to collaborate, the prevailing notion of political theorists and educational scholars alike is that a large body of people working together is far more effective than isolated individuals with contrasting views and a refusal for compromise or collaborating (Habermas, 1989; Palmer, 1993; Rorty, 1989). Brookfield and Preskill (1999), for instance, claim that within a functioning public sphere where individuals share ideas and have evolving beliefs "a collective wisdom emerges that would have been impossible for any of the participants to achieve on their own" (p. 3). Similarly, Palmer (1993) notes, "all of us thinking together are smarter than any one of us thinking alone…" (p. 94).

In plain terms, when citizens collaborate and an inclusive environment is created, society is more likely to improve itself than when decisions are made by few individuals with limited beliefs and experiences. Regardless of the writer, there exists a clear consensus that productive discourse involves inclusivity and collaboration as a way of constructing solutions from various backgrounds, experiences, and beliefs.

On a similar—yet smaller—scale, these ideas for collective growth and progressive discourse apply to the K–12 classroom. More specifically, when a group of K–12 students works together through collaborative discourse to solve an issue or construct knowledge, the likelihood of having a powerful educational experience grows dramatically (Banks, 1993; Dewey, 1915). When students, for that matter, are exclusively exposed to the idea of debate as the prominent form of collaboration, they are, perhaps inadvertently, learning that the practices by the aforementioned politicians are *good* for society and that refusing to compromise, listen to another viewpoint, or evolve perspectives based on conversations with peers and colleagues is a strong and effective practice. Such classroom discourse promotes a "we versus them" mentality among students in regards to differing opinions, thus contrasting the views of Rorty (1989) who sees a functioning public sphere as dismantling the idea of "they" to form a more collective "we" among citizens.

Such notions of collaboration for the progression of society largely reflect the writings of Dewey who consistently viewed collectivity as a way to promote various forms of growth (Preskill, 1997). Rather than promoting a combative environment, much of Dewey's writings in the field of education centered around collaborating as a form of growth (Dewey, 1900). And though he never explicitly wrote about it, it is almost fair to assume that Dewey would say that exclusively using discourse in the form of debate could directly contrast popular views and ideals of collection action and wisdom within the public sphere. Because not only does discourse promote a collective experience in the classroom, it also works to assist with a form of social and academic growth within students that is critical to an effective educational experience.

Debate, in its most traditional sense, does not promote the type of growth Dewey and likeminded scholars have written about over the past century. Typically, debate promotes a sense of individuality in which students maintain their understandings and primarily seek to convince others that they—and they *alone*—are correct (Preskill, 1997; Yankelovich, 2001). And while students and citizens alike can both learn from a traditional debate in the form of democratic dissent (Ivie, 2008), the primary purpose for engaging in such a process often reflects different goals than those who participate in a more collaborative form of conversation. Such a practice is, in many ways, in direct contrast with the writings of Dewey; who consistently maintained the need for "growth" in students through collaboration and reflection.

Further, Dewey's continuous discussions emphasizing "growth" often explored a true democracy's ability to include perspectives from "a wide variety of backgrounds, interest groups, and sub-communities" and evolve based on the inclusion of this diversity (Dewey, 1927; Preskill 1997, p. 322). Such notions of collaboration and inquiry grounded in diversity demonstrate Dewey's (1900) strong conviction toward continuous "growth" of individuals stemming from multiple educative experiences occurring within and outside of schools. Such ideals reflect the notion that the intention of a well-constructed classroom is for students to learn from one another by listening and conversing, not evaluating one another based on differences and a "best" view (Yankelovich, 2001). A classroom should attempt to incorporate all perspectives so that students can learn from one another and formulate their own knowledge based on large-scale exposure (Banks, 1993). More specific to the aim of the social studies, discourse that is collaborative and respectful in nature helps teach students that "different" does not necessarily mean wrong.

Discourse in the classroom can and should use the diverse beliefs and experiences of students to show that differences are not always tied to various levels of "right" or "wrong" and can be used together to construct knowledge (Yankelovich, 2001). Rather, when incorporating discourse in an effective, collaborative manner, students can work directly with peers from different backgrounds and be taught to reformulate previously held opinions both about groups and opinions different from their own and learn to respect the views and values of others. Such experiences both align with principles of a truly democratic education and reflect the way a functioning society works in terms of collectivity and growth.

Collaborative discourse is a way for students to incorporate the differing perspectives of a classroom in a safe, welcoming environment. Classrooms—as Hess (2004) notes—are often the most diverse environment a young, impressionable student will experience in their youth. As such, students in the classroom have more opportunities to be exposed to a range of ideas that will help them construct their own beliefs and perspectives and, in turn, become more autonomous, critical thinkers. Because of this, students need to participate in the kind of dialogue that will best prepare them to respect one another's differences and see value in differing opinions and abstract situations.

Even when considering isolated incidents in the social studies (whether the United States should have used atomic weapons in World War II, the disappearance of the Lost Colony in Roanoke, the use of force during the Civil Rights Movement), a discussion can be enhanced for all participants if a range of opinions is integrated and if students are encouraged to evolve their views based on new evidence stemming from in-class sources. The diversity that makes up a typical classroom can promote a form of discourse that is welcoming and inclusive of various perspectives, experiences, and beliefs—but only if students are encouraged to listen to one another, remain open-minded, and evolve their perspectives in a way that a functioning society will require them to do.

CONCLUSION

Though outside of the scope of this chapter, the ability to effectively participate in discourse within society leads into questions of access to the public sphere. While access is theoretically guaranteed to all citizens, it bears noting that participation in a public sphere is also contingent on one's ability to understand the fundamental requirements and expectations for engaging in such a context. In other words, only when an individual is capable of participating in the public sphere should they reasonably be expected to do so. In many ways, the American school system is partially expected to teach students about this threshold of effective discourse in which collective action is seen as both necessary and a positive component to a functioning democracy.

The social studies, specifically, offers students opportunities to become reform-oriented citizens who participate in society by seeking to overturn the status quo, engaging in rational dialogue, and understanding their role within a democracy. And though the American school system certainly has similar aims, the social studies is positioned to lead in the development of capable citizens. The beauty of the social studies is in its inherent ability to promote collectivity within its various disciplines. Students of the social studies (when effectively engaged in the content) can work to solve abstract, complex problems where varying experiences and beliefs can be considered a positive. And, perhaps even more broadly, where the process of problem solving most closely reflects that of an effective public citizenry working toward improving society (Meuwissen, 2013). Students of the social studies can discuss issues by sharing ideas and values and, thus, gain a stronger understanding through collaboration. The social studies seems primed to provide students with opportunities that lead to such collaboration and, in a sense, practice as citizens.

The importance of collaboration through discourse among multiple parties both inside and outside of the classroom cannot be overstated within the realm of democracy and its associated principles and the social studies plays a key role for preparing students to effective participate in discourse once they have entered into the public sphere (Flynn, 2009; Hess, 2009; Meuwissen, 2013). While engaging students through competitive forms of discourse may be easier (e.g., debate), such an approach when done exclusively does students a disservice, as it promotes the individual over the collective and the lack of compromise as strong and effective. Further, if the aim of the social studies is to help create citizens capable of participating in a pluralistic 21st-century society, the classroom should serve as a location where students learn how to collaborate with one another in a manner that teaches the importance of collectivity and collaboration.

DISCUSSION QUESTIONS

1. In what ways can social studies educators teach students about collective action by studying current political rhetoric?
2. To what extent can discourse be used in the social studies classroom as a means for teaching through constructivism?
3. What role do social studies teachers have in teaching students that collaboration is critical to a vibrant society?
4. To what extent can teachers educate students on dissent as a progressive form of discourse?

REFERENCES

Banks, J. A. (1993). Multicultural education: Historical development, dimensions, and practice. *Review of Research in Education, 19*, 3–49.

Brookfield, S. D., & Preskill, S. (1999). *Discussion as a way of teaching* (Vol. 85). San Francisco: Jossey-Bass.

Chandler, P., & Ehrlich, S. (2016). The use of discussion protocols in social studies. *The Councilor: A Journal of the Social Studies, 77*(1), 1–11.

Dewey, J. (1900/1915). *The school and society: Revised edition.* University of Chicago, IL: University of Chicago Press.

Dewey, J. (1927). *The public and its problems.* New York, NY: Capricorn.

Flynn, N. (2009). Toward democratic discourse: Scaffolding student-led discussions in the social studies. *The Teachers College Record, 111*(8), 2021–2054.

Habermas, J. (1989). *The structural transformation of the public sphere* (T. Burger, Trans.). Cambridge, MA: Massachusetts Institute of Technology Press (Original work published 1962).

Hess, D. E. (2004). Discussion in social studies: Is it worth the trouble? *Social Education, 68*(2), 151–157.

Hess, D. E. (2009). *Controversy in the classroom: The democratic power of discussion.* New York, NY: Routledge Press.

Ivie, R. L. (2008). Toward a humanizing style of democratic dissent. *Rhetoric & Public Affairs, 11*(3), 454–458.

Meuwissen, K. (2013, May 2). Generating Productive political discussion in the classroom. *Huffpost College.* Retrieved from http://www.huffingtonpost.com/kevin-meuwissen/generating-productive-pol_b_2955852.html

National Governors Association Center for Best Practices & Council of Chief State School Officers. (2010). *Common core state standards.* Washington, DC: Author.

Palmer, P. J. (1993). Good talk about good teaching: Improving teaching through conversation and community. *Change: The Magazine of Higher Learning, 25*(6), 8–13.

Parker, W. C. (Ed.). (2010). Social studies education eC21. In *Social studies today: Research and practice* (pp. 1–13). New York, NY: Routledge.

Preskill, S. (1997). Discussion schooling, and the struggle for democracy. *Theory & Research in Social Education, 25*(3), 316–345.

Rorty, R. (1989). *Contingency, irony, and solidarity.* Cambridge: Cambridge University Press.

Tannebaum, R. P. (2015). *Exploring the associations preservice social studies teachers make between discussion as a pedagogical approach and democratic education: A multi-case study* (Unpublished doctoral dissertation). Clemson University, Clemson, SC.

Yankelovich, D. (2001). *The magic of dialogue: Transforming conflict into cooperation.* New York, NY: Simon and Schuster.

CHAPTER THIRTY-FIVE

Citizenship

SARAH E. STANLICK, LEHIGH UNIVERSITY

> Since the days of Greece and Rome, when the word "citizen" was a title of honor, we have often seen more emphasis put on the rights of citizenship than on its responsibilities.
>
> —Former U.S. Attorney General Robert F. Kennedy, 1962, p. 5

As Kennedy so sharply observed, citizenship is a weighted word—full of assumptions and expectations that often exist in an ambiguous space. The concept of citizenship is full of opportunity for exploration. Does citizenship have borders? Is citizenship a right bestowed or privilege to be claimed? At its most basic, does it function as a noun or as a verb? For social studies educators, citizenship can be an entree into a wide variety of issues, rights, and responsibilities that can inform and shape our students' worldview. Issues of inclusion, language, borders, barriers, equity, and access can all be examined through the lens of citizenship. Now more than ever, the ability to dialogue across borders—geographically or socially constructed—and appreciate "otherness" is a critical component to realizing a connected and interdependent humankind.

In this chapter, I explore the modes and mechanisms, definitions, and philosophical conceptions of citizenship. I will then unpack the skills of citizenship and dialogue that has timely influence and importance to free speech and inclusion debates experienced not only in the United States, but many nations around the world. Through cultivating for our students a stronger ability to exercise citizenship in the active ways alongside inquiry skills, a sense of responsibility, and an understanding of the different conceptions of citizenship, we support their ability to meaningfully sustain the very concept we explore here.

CITIZENSHIP: WHAT IS IT?

In the mid-1950s, Gallie (1956) surfaced the idea of an "essentially contested concept" to name and describe a word or phrase that can have a wide variety of interpretations depending on the interpreter (p. 107). Examples include terms such as *scholarship*, *social justice*, and, of course, *citizenship*. Citizenship can have a multitude of meanings and interpretations based on the context, country, or consciousness that perceives it. As citizens, we balance expectations of citizenship through our own lenses and senses of commitment and character. As educators, we help our students struggle with the many tensions and perceptions of citizenship in order to cultivate their own such framework.

The first construct that one must grapple with when thinking about citizenship is this: is citizenship an abstract noun that "exists" or an active noun that prompts one to "do?" Some consider citizenship to be a noun alone—a right bestowed upon an individual by various means: birth, naturalization, military service, marriage, or bloodline. This type of citizenship is often characterized as a black-and-white concept with set parameters. Philosophically, that challenge of who is and is not a citizen is much murkier. Issues of recognition, equality, and representation can still plague individuals regardless of their national citizenship, especially in cases where political upheaval or institutionalized racism or heterosexism—for example—define policy.

The Stanford Encyclopedia of Philosophy (2017) defines a citizen as "a member of a political community who enjoys the rights and assumes the duties of membership" (n. p.). Citizenship, with that definition in mind, acts as a state of existence or privilege that an individual or collective may attain or as a verb (*doing* citizenship) that calls those who consider themselves "citizens" to action as a right and responsibility (USCIS, 2016). When we talk about the concept of citizenship, rights and duties are in constant tension, as some ascribe to the idea that that rights are inherent by virtue of status while others might find them an honor to be earned. Citizenship can be seen as an independent identity and responsibility to be cultivated. Villa (2001) uses the term *Socratic citizenship* to describe the use of an iterative, active process to cultivate a lifelong citizen identity. The following section will unpack the tensions raised by these differing understandings of citizenship and how they manifest in different contexts around the world.

CITIZENSHIP: TENSIONS

In parallel with this consideration of what citizenship as a word means, debates also continue on the models of citizenship to which we should or should not aspire. Furthermore, the evolving geopolitical landscape and the influence of technology have brought us to a time ripe for reconsidering citizenship's role and meaning in the world. Globalization has also caused both strain and support of modes of citizenship as it has made possible external influences and connections economically, politically, and socially across borders in ways previously unknown.

For instance, global citizenship education has become an integral part of higher education as students are being prepared to flourish in an increasingly connected, global world (Hicks, 2003; Merryfield, 2008). (See Carano & Bailey's chapter on the keyword *Global* in this volume for a discussion of multiple formats and iterations.) Both Oxfam (1997, 2006) and UNESCO (2014) have offered curricular guidelines on global citizenship, yet the term itself is still contested. Rather than a definition, global citizenship has been increasingly conceived of as an orientation with characteristics of practice that mark a fluid process for citizenship. Building on this concept of fluidity, the idea of citizenship as process must be explored. We find ourselves in transitional times; debating the very essence of democracy, free speech, and civic engagement. Moving the paradigm of citizenship as concrete, bound certification to fluid, active, iterative process is necessary. A flourishing society needs a citizenry that can harness their agency to bring about positive social, political, and economic good. Without that agency and active engagement, despondency, futility, and powerlessness take root, further entrenching conflict and inequality.

Finally, the question of who can be a citizen must also be addressed. Debates about the very nature of citizenship have repercussions for who can and cannot be considered a citizen, what rights we have as human beings versus state citizens, and what value we place on the individual versus the collective. Immigration to the United States, for instance, has raised divisive questions of legal and illegal immigration and human rights that fuel an emotionally charged debate. In addition, refugees and asylum-seekers—those displaced by war, political upheaval, ethnic cleansing, environmental disasters, and/or disease—find themselves in a stateless position where, if we are looking at citizenship from a national citizenship model, they are not subject to the rights and responsibilities of the current place where they reside. If we look back through our history, one can see the issue of Mexican citizens in the U.S. following the Treaty of Guadalupe Hidalgo or the internment of Japanese-Americans during World War II as prime examples of human rights abuses stemming from a hard, borders-based approach to citizenship. However, if we subscribe to a cosmopolitan view of citizenship, we embrace a sense of love of humanity and recognition of the moral obligations to the rest of the world (Nussbaum, 1994). Further, the active, borderless concept of citizenship would have instead placed emphasis on responsibilities and actions, thus minimizing the nationalistic tendency to group and oppress. (See also Menon & Suleh's chapter on the keyword *Borders* in this volume). Those individuals would be considered a part of the larger humankind and have inherent rights and responsibilities by virtue of their inherent human dignity and responsibility to the collective.

CITIZENSHIP: NATIONALITY AND NATIONALISM

Citizenship as constructed through strict consideration of geopolitical borders is considered a more recent development in our world history, as it was not until the emergence of maps and physical signage delineating borders that the concept of nationalism could even be made possible (Anderson, 2006). With the invention of maps—the ability to visualize and declare borders more confidently—the divisive nature of national citizenship and nationalism became more prevalent. One could easily see a physical separation between their neighbors, and politicians could use divisive language to "other" those who were not born within the physical boundaries. National, largely border-based citizenship is a direct extension of the modern nation-state, built on the assumption that citizenship is at its core based on one's tie to a land with geopolitical edges (Tambini, 2001). Yet, Anzaldua (2012) calls our attention to the human impact of borders, actively acknowledging the social construction of power based on such borders and the hindering of the human spirit through those borders.

Nationality is a word that is oftentimes used interchangeably with citizenship, yet it does not encompass the vast umbrella of iterations and nuances that citizenship entails. National citizenship takes many forms around the world, as each nation can define the terms and conditions of that citizenship. Canada allows citizens to hold dual citizenship, yet Chile does not. In Israel, all citizens are conscripted to military service. Nationality, however, is solely the act of belonging to a specific nation or the ethnic group that comprises a political nation.

There are generally two schools of thought that influence the framing of citizenship—civic republicanism and liberal individualism. A civic republican framework, adopted by philosophers like Rousseau and Arendt, emphasizes civic self-rule and the responsibility of the citizen to work toward the common good. Rousseau (1920) sums this up succinctly: "As soon as any man says of the affairs of the State 'What does it matter to me?' the State may be given up for lost (p. 83)." Liberal-individual frameworks are more rights-engaged, with the primary motivation for citizenship being the preservation of civil liberties and rights for the individual.

Ignatieff (1987) rejects a national citizenship that assumes a national common good. Rather, he argues such citizenship as an illusion, arguing that national citizenship and the national government is only useful to the degree to which it supports and allows the ability of a nation to be a responsible world citizen. Ignatieff's argument is one of connectedness, pointing to the geopolitical, economic, and social ties that in 1987 were starting to ebb across borders, and today seem to have blurred the borders. The liberal-individual framework coupled with the transnational view of responsible citizenship forms a basis for global citizenship, which will be explored in the next section.

CITIZENSHIP: GLOBAL AND COSMOPOLITANISM

Cosmopolitanism is a paradigm that emphasizes the world as a place of borderless, open humanity to which we all belong regardless of nationality, ethnicity, race, or other demographically defined factors. The concept can be traced back to Diogenes of Sinope in the 300s BCE, who famously responded to a question about his origin by saying that he was "a citizen of the world" (Diogenes Laertius, 1979). This conceptualization of the world as a borderless humanity was developed further by the Stoics, who talked of the duality of citizenship in one's heart and of the larger humankind. Nussbaum (1997) has developed a framework of cosmopolitanism that asks us to consider the purpose of liberal education as means to engender an identity of a "citizen of humanity" beyond the borders of our geopolitical districts. She writes, "Citizens who cultivate their humanity need, further, an ability to see themselves not simply as citizens of some local region or group but also, and above all, as human beings bound to all other human beings by ties of recognition or concern" (p. 10).

Global citizenship is at its core an orientation of one's self in the globalizing world (Noddings, 2005). The modern global citizen, as described by Riley (2006), is "reflective, informed, and involved" (p. 51). Noddings (2005) offers a basic and frequently cited definition of a global citizen as one who "can live and work effectively anywhere in the world, and a global way of life would both describe and support the functioning of global citizens" (p. 5). As an operationalized framework, global citizenship suggests a set of values/attitudes, skills, and knowledge toward a borderless sense of citizenship in the world twinned with a mandate for active engagement (Noddings, 2005; UNESCO, 2014). This is not to be confused with "international citizenship," a concept of cross-border collaboration or regional participation such as the European Union where nations cooperate in a way that cedes a bit of sovereignty in return for regional benefits such as ease of travel, economic unification and standardization, military cooperation, and more.

Global citizenship is an ethos more than a hard and fast definition to be attained or developed. With that in mind, guiding principles of global citizenship, however, are agreed upon and cited by a majority of global citizenship scholars

(Merryfield, 2008; Oxfam, 1997, 2006). Oxfam (2006, p. 3) outlines a more formalized set of principles in their curriculum for K–12 education. These principles are as follows: A global citizen:

- Is aware of the wider world and has a sense of their own role as a world citizen
- Respects and values diversity
- Has an understanding of how the world works
- Is outraged by social injustice
- Participates in the community at a range of levels, from the local to the global
- Is willing to act to make the world a more equitable and sustainable place
- Takes responsibility for their actions

Andreotti (2006) advocates for critical global citizenship, an orientation that pushes individuals not only to adopt a cosmopolitan view, but also constantly challenge the system to address issues of social justice and inequity through active, engaged citizenship.

Global Citizenship Education (GCE) can take many forms, but there are a few high-quality examples to highlight. First, at Lehigh University in Bethlehem, Pennsylvania, the Global Citizenship Program exists as a backpack program that any student, regardless of major, can take to enhance their global citizen knowledge, skills, and attitudes. It starts with an introductory course on global citizenship, incorporates study abroad, mandates service-learning and globally focused coursework, and leads to a capstone project that puts active citizenship identity into practice with a project of global-local importance. Critical reflection runs through all experiential and curricular learning. At Centennial College in Toronto, Canada, all students are expected to complete a signature learning experience (SLE) that incorporates principles of social justice, global citizenship, and equity for every student that attends Centennial. Hallmarks of the program include an intention for critical thinking, reflection, social analysis and action, and professional development for faculty and staff to refine their understanding and practice of global citizenship education.

ACTIVE CITIZENSHIP AND CIVIC ENGAGEMENT

In 1952, General Lucius Clay, Director of Materiel for the Army during World War II, in an essay on demonstrations by East Berliners demanding democracy, shared these words reflecting on what it meant to be a "good citizen:"

> Like all precious possessions, freedom must be guarded carefully. I ask myself how I can best help guard it and the answer I find is in citizenship. In my view, to be a good citizen does not require the holding of public office, the achievement of either political or financial success. But it does require that I vote from conviction, that I participate in community activities to the extent that I am able, that I be honest with myself and with others. (Clay, 2009, p. 1)

Clay's words mirror the framework of a "good citizen" put forth by Westheimer and Kahne (2004): personally responsible, participatory, and justice-oriented. Such a citizen could also find themselves included in the definition of an active citizen. Active citizenship, according to Tisch and Weber (2010), affirms citizenship as an active, connected process that is synonymous with civic engagement and social activism. Tisch and Weber are not alone in this view. Palmer (2011) writes of five habits needed to engage community in the healthy functioning of democracy, spanning realms individuals and collective. The five habits (Palmer, 2011) speak to a framework for engaged citizenry, and are comprised of the following:

1. An understanding that we are all in this together
2. An appreciation of the value of "otherness"
3. An ability to hold tension in life-giving ways
4. A sense of personal voice and agency
5. A capacity to create community

While Palmer is focused on democratic engagement, the lessons for active citizenship are clear. To be an engaged part of a community—and a community that one is ultimately invested in its success—active citizenship and dialogue are essential. Further, he affirms that the "power of one" cannot lead to the cultivation of healthy communities, and it is only in partnership that we function and thrive as a society (Palmer, 2011).

This idea of citizenship as an individual process furthermore emphasizes a personal responsibility that is often not the center of our civic education—or limited to being seen as the discrete act of voting. As an example, while more learners in P-16 are engaging in service and community-engaged learning, there remains a disconnect between their long term civic identity and the transformative experiences they seemingly undertake (Mitchell, Battistoni, Keene, & Reiff, 2013). Not surprisingly, global citizenship education faces similar challenges as service learning with regard to civic engagement; students appreciate cultural diversity and enjoy travel but remain unmoved by cosmopolitanism's larger political and structural implications (Andreotti, 2006).

OPPORTUNITIES FOR CITIZENSHIP EDUCATION

When surveying these differing understandings of citizenship, it becomes apparent that strong, rounded citizenship education is a key part of the development and enrichment of young citizens. As educators, we should be concerned about seeming political apathy and be intentional about cultivating civic and community engagement of our youth. Engagement activities students experience in P-16 often do not lead to an increase in their later political participation and civic engagement (Mitchell et al., 2013; Saltmarsh, Hartley, & Clayton, 2009). In 2014, the U.S. experienced its lowest voter turnout for a federal election with only 19.9% of 18 to 29 year olds voting (CIRCLE, 2016). Further, the concept of "slacktivism," a shallow form of internet activism that is detached from active citizenship (Lee & Hsieh, 2013), has grown in the digital age and there is some evidence showing online activism to have an effect on civic decision-making. One rationale for this disconnect between citizenship in theory and practice could be that the concept of such endeavors as *doing citizenship* is not being articulated, and in some ways, civics is affirmed by some teachers and students as a box to check or, worse, an exercise in futility. Nowacek (2010) advocates for a model of citizenship across the curriculum, akin to the popular writing across the curriculum model that would weave civics into all disciplines and connect disciplinary knowledge to active citizen models. Westheimer and Kahne (2004) criticize the conservative understanding of citizenship that normally influences civic education and instead affirms the need for civic education that cultivates "personally responsible, participatory, and justice oriented" citizens (p. 237).

Citizenship education is an avenue for educators to promote and this connected view of citizenship as rights and responsibilities. Equally important, citizenship education is a way in which to enter conversations about provocative and difficult topics that have no clear answers. Such education could emphasize a strong orientation to eagerly engage in the grey. These courses and units can engage the complexities of concepts that have no clear answers and are ripe for debate. Thus, the imperative needs to be on developing the ability to have difficult discussions, hold tension, as Palmer (2011) urges us to, and be able to articulate differences and diversity in ways that are life-giving. Through an American lens, we must add to the robust nature of our engaged democratic and world citizenship.

Service-learning and Civic Engagement

When thinking about pedagogy that can directly influence and cultivate attributes of active citizen identity, service and experiential learning are essential. The National Council for the Social Studies advocates for service-learning and civic engagement as an essential component to social studies curriculum, affirming that "service-learning greatly enhances the potential for social studies teachers to fulfill their mission of educating informed and active citizens who are committed to improving society through the democratic process" (Wade, 2007). According to Bringle and Clayton (2012), service-learning and civic engagement is:

> the integration of academic material, relevant service activities, and critical reflection in a reciprocal [co-created] partnership that engages students, faculty/staff, and community members to achieve academic, civic, and personal [growth] learning objectives as well as to advance public purposes. (p. 105)

Service-learning and civic engagement can apply to contexts in local, regional, national, and international. Global citizenship curricula, for instance, typically include service learning, experiential learning, and/or study abroad, along with traditional instructional experiences that are mediated by reflection and discourse (Appleyard & McLean, 2011; Bringle & Clayton, 2012; Tarrant, 2010). In a global citizenship course, students may engage in service learning that involves a global problem on a local level, such as refugee issues. While they learn the political and logistical issues surrounding a refugee's circumstance abroad, they could also volunteer with a local organization that resettles refugees in a nearby city (Gisolo & Stanlick, 2012). An experiential exercise for global citizenship education might be a day-trip to the United Nations to listen to a briefing on transnational issues, followed by a guided reflection session to discuss the learning experience and the individual learners' impressions.

Cultivating Democratic Dialogue and Political Engagement

In addition, the debate of safe and brave spaces and the way in which we engage interpersonally in constructive dialogue is another bit of evidence of this disconnect between civic speech and active citizenship. Engagement in dialogue via social media, including the influence of algorithms tailoring our browsing experience, and the resulting development of echo chambers which limit exposure to opposing viewpoints, is harming our ability to have controversy with civility. With that in mind, this intentional troubling of the idea of citizenship to think further how dialogue, inquiry, activism, and action can balance to create an active citizen identity is more necessary today than ever before.

Villa's (2001) emphasis on cultivating Socratic citizenship is a call to harness the right and the responsibility to stay engaged critically as an active community member and to challenge structures that are unjust and/or undemocratic. This intentional, individualized process that is critical in thought and dissident in action. Such a process is key in times of flux and reconsideration, which is arguably the times in which we find ourselves currently, as issues from immigration to religious freedom to voting rights are once again dominating the larger debate in citizenry.

Global Citizenship Education

Global citizenship education is distinct from traditional definitions of citizenship and civics, which is based on the concept of defined, unitary national citizenship (Banks, 2008). Instead, global citizenship stresses cross-cultural awareness, development of personal traits such as empathy and ambiguity tolerance, social justice orientation, personal identity development, and relationship with the larger world (Hanvey, 1976; Hicks, 2003; Oxfam, 1997, 2006). For an orientation toward global citizenship, Oxfam has identified knowledge, skills, and attitudes that are essential outcomes of the GCE process (1997, 2006). These skills can be cultivated through high-impact practices such as study abroad, research, first year readings, service-learning, and experiential learning. Table 35.1 outlines the knowledge, skills, and attitudes identified through the Oxfam framework (1997, 2006) for individual learners to develop.

Table 35.1. Knowledge, Skills and Attitudes for Global Citizenship Competency

Knowledge and understanding	Skills	Attitudes and values
Social justice and equity	Critical thinking	Sense of identity and self-esteem
Diversity	Ability to argue effectively	Empathy
Globalization and interdependence	Ability to challenge injustice and inequalities	Commitment to social justice and equity
Sustainable development	Respect for people and things	Value and respect for diversity
Peace and conflict	Co-operation and conflict resolution	Concern for the environment and commitment to sustainable development
		Belief that individuals can make a difference

Source: Author adapted from *Note* below.

Note: These items have been identified as the core elements of global citizenship education that have consistently reappeared throughout literature. Those principles form the simplest definition of a global citizen (Merryfield, 2008; Noddings, 2005; Oxfam, 1997, 2006).

Digital Citizenship

A final frontier to touch upon in this chapter is the concept of digital citizenship and the need to understand our web-based spaces as potential spaces for citizenship. Mossberger, Tolbert, and McNeal (2007) defines a digital citizen as those who use the Internet effectively and regularly, which describes number that is increasing multifold. Furthermore, forces of globalization and technological growth have altered the way in which we conceive of borders, as well as the way in which we understand space and place (Bohman, 2004). Digital interactions can blur our understanding of who is an insider and an outsider, in what tribes do we belong, and how we perceive the deservingness of those we might not have considered or advocated for in the past. For instance, students in a global citizenship course could participate in online forums that deepen their experiences and helps them to develop a habit of mind of critical reflection. Pre-service teachers could participate in the UN Online Volunteering program to connect with teachers or educational non-profits around the world and hone their skills through virtual service learning projects. The space of the Internet, in its best form, can be one of dialogue, understanding, and connecting across borders in the face of injustice.

CONCLUSION

While there are many conceptions of citizenship, the tension between rights and responsibilities is a constant. What is evident is that citizenship is an iterative process—rather than a singularly bestowed right—and one that can be cultivated and challenged through a lifetime of engaged citizenry. The great opportunity for educators in this field is the ability to challenge structures of power, question longstanding forces of inequality, and open the minds of young students not to a specific political ideology or orientation, but rather to the wide range of possibilities for learners to be engaged, curious, and critical members of society. Civic education and teaching the complexity of citizenship with this in mind models the larger field of social studies as a means for inquiry-driven, critical examination of our world and ourselves.

DISCUSSION QUESTIONS

1. As an individual, what is your personal understanding of citizenship and the ways in which you demonstrate or live out that perspective in your life and your teaching?

2. Does citizenship have borders? Is citizenship a right bestowed or privilege to be claimed?
3. How do we move—and help our students move—from a more passive understanding of citizenship to a more active, participatory model?
4. Thinking about Palmer's (2011) call for us to "hold tension" to develop a strong citizenry, how do we as educators provide spaces for difficult dialogue and the sharing of diverse experiences and ideas?
5. How do we weave some of the more theoretical discussion of citizenship into everyday works? What examples do you see in your own work that do a good job of connecting theory to practice?

REFERENCES

Anderson, B. (2006). *Imagined communities: Reflections on the origin and spread of nationalism.* London: Verso Books.

Andreotti, V. (2006). Soft versus critical global citizenship education. *Policy & Practice: A Development Education Review, 3,* 40–51.

Anzaldua, G. (2012). *Borderlands/la frontera: The new mestiza* (4th ed.). San Francisco, CA: Aunt Lute.

Appleyard, N., & McLean, L. R. (2011). Expecting the exceptional: Pre-service professional development in global citizenship education. *International Journal of Progressive Education, 7*(2), 6–32.

Banks, J. A. (2008). Diversity, group identity, and citizenship education in a global age. *Educational Researcher, 37*(3), 129–139.

Bohman, J. (2004). Expanding dialogue: The Internet, the public sphere and prospects for transnational democracy. *The Sociological Review, 52*(s1), 131–155.

Bringle, R. G., & Clayton, P. H. (2012). Civic education through service learning: What, how, and why? In L. McIlrath & A. Lyons (Eds.), *Higher education and civic engagement* (pp. 101–124). New York, NY: Palgrave Macmillan US.

CIRCLE Staff. (2016). *Young voters in the 2016 general election.* Medford, MA: Tufts University.

Clay, L. (2009, November 6). Guarding the gift of freedom. *NPR: This I Believe.* Retrieved from http://thisibelieve.org/essay/16444/

Diogenes Laertius. (1979). *Lives of eminent philosophers (Vol. I–II).* Cambridge, MA: Harvard University Press.

Gallie, W. B. (1956). Essentially contested concepts. *Proceedings of the Aristotelian Society, New Series, 56*(1955–1956), 167–198.

Gisolo, G., & Stanlick, S. E. (2012). Promoting global citizenship outside the classroom: Undergraduate-refugee service learning at Lehigh University. *Journal of Global Citizenship & Equity Education, 2*(2), 98–122.

Hanvey, R. G. (1976). An attainable global perspective. *Theory into Practice, 21*(3), 162–167.

Hartley, M., Saltmarsh, J., & Clayton, P. (2010). Is the civic engagement movement changing higher education? *British Journal of Educational Studies, 58*(4), 391–406.

Hicks, D. (2003). Thirty years of global education: A reminder of key principles and precedents. *Educational Review, 55*(3), 265–275.

Ignatieff, M. (1987). The myth of citizenship. *Queen's Law Journal, 12*, 399.
Lee, Y. H., & Hsieh, G. (2013, April). Does slacktivism hurt activism?: The effects of moral balancing and consistency in online activism. In *Proceedings of the SIGCHI conference on human factors in computing systems* (pp. 811–820). Paris: Association for Computing Machinery.
Merryfield, M. M. (2008). Scaffolding social studies for global awareness. *Social Education, 72*(7), 363–367.
Mitchell, T. D., Battistoni, R. M., Keene, A. S., & Reiff, J. (2013). Programs that build civic identity: A study of alumni. *Diversity and Democracy, 16*(3), 22–23.
Mossberger, K., Tolbert, C. J., & McNeal, R. S. (2007). *Digital citizenship: The Internet, society, and participation.* Cambridge, MA: MIT Press.
Noddings, N. (2005). *Educating citizens for global awareness.* New York, NY: Teachers College Press.
Nowacek, R. S. (2010). Understanding citizenship as vocation in a multidisciplinary senior capstone. In *Citizenship across the Discipline*, ed. M.B. Smith, R.S. Nowacek, and J.L. Bernstein, 91–109. Bloomington, IN: Indiana University Press.
Nussbaum, M. C. (1994, October 1). Patriotism and cosmopolitanism. *The Boston Review*, 155–162.
Nussbaum, M. C. (1997). *Cultivating humanity: A classical defense of reform in liberal education.* Cambridge, MA: Harvard University Press.
Oxfam. (1997). *A curriculum for global citizenship.* London: Oxfam GB.
Oxfam. (2006). *Education for global citizenship: A guide for schools.* Retrieved from http://www.oxfam.org.uk/education/gc/files/education_for_global_citizenship_a_guide_for_schools.pdf
Palmer, P. J. (2011). *Healing the heart of democracy: The courage to create a politics worthy of the human spirit.* New York, NY: John Wiley & Sons.
Riley, D. R. (2006). Teaching global citizenship: Reflections on the American Indian Housing Initiative. *New Directions for Teaching and Learning, 2006*(105), 51–61.
Rousseau, J. J. (1920). *The social contract: & discourses* (No. 660). London: JM Dent & Sons.
Stanford Encyclopedia of Philosophy. (2017). Citizenship. Retrieved from http://plato.stanford.edu/entries/citizenship/
Tambini, D. (2001). Post-national citizenship. *Ethnic and Racial Studies, 24*(2), 195–217.
Tarrant, M. A. (2010). A conceptual framework for exploring the role of studies abroad in nurturing global citizenship. *Journal of Studies in International Education, 14*(5), 433–451.
Tisch, J., & Weber, K. (2010). *Citizen you: Doing your part to change the world.* New York, NY: Crown.
United Nations Educational, Scientific and Cultural Organization (UNESCO). (2014). *Global citizenship education: Topics and learning objectives.* Retrieved from http://unesdoc.unesco.org/images/0023/002329/232993e.pdf
United States Citizenship and Immigration Services (USCIS). (2016). *Citizenship rights and responsibilities.* Retrieved from https://www.uscis.gov/citizenship/learners/citizenship-rights-and-responsibilities
Villa, D. (2001). *Socratic citizenship.* Princeton, NJ: Princeton University Press.
Wade, R. C. (Ed.). (2007). *Community action rooted in history: The CiviConnections model of service-learning* (Vol. 106). Silver Spring, MD: National Council for the Social Studies.
Westheimer, J., & Kahne, J. (2004). What kind of citizen? The politics of educating for democracy. *American Educational Research Journal, 41*(2), 237–269.

CHAPTER THIRTY-SIX

Teaching Civics Amid New Discourses of Citizenship

A Response to the Civic Ideals and Practices Section

BETH C. RUBIN, RUTGERS UNIVERSITY

In this section, Tannebaum takes on the complex construct of discourse, advocating for social studies classrooms to be spaces in which students learn that discourse is critical to a progressive collective sphere in which parties work together to construct knowledge. Pointing to the all too evident shortcomings of contemporary national discourse in public and media platforms he argues that collaborative classroom discourse is more effective for developing ideal citizens than teaching students through solely through the use of debate and argument. Stanlick delves into the multiple and varied meanings of citizenship, a central key concept in social studies and one which is increasingly contested. Citizenship, she concludes, is a tension between rights and responsibilities, and an iterative process best cultivated through critical engagement. In this response, I will expand on these constructs by exploring them together.

DISCOURSE

Tannebaum describes discourse as taking place primarily on two levels—in public conversation and in classroom talk. To go even further, I would like to assert that, to some degree, we construct our worlds through talk. Through language, physical expression and markers of "thinking, feeling, believing, valuing and acting" we identify, for ourselves and for others, where we belong and with whom we identify

(Gee, 1996, p. 131). This is Discourse with a capital D, and it is central to establishing ourselves as members of social groups and "signaling" our place in society.

These constructions and identifications do not take place in a vacuum—they are enmeshed in broader historical, economic, social, cultural and political frameworks. As Abowitz and Harnish (2006) describe, "discourses are not composed of randomly chosen words and statements; rather, each discourse is a product of historical and social circumstances that provide the discursive practices—terminology, values, rhetorical styles, habits, and truths—that construct it" (p. 655). Moreover, discourse does not just *reflect* historical and social circumstances—it is a principal means by which ideas about what is right and true are constructed and spread. A hat with the words "Make America Great Again," a comedy sketch in which the president is depicted as bumbling and mean-spirited child are both part of broader, competing national discourses. Wearing the hat, finding the sketch to be funny simultaneously signal identification with particular discourses and reproduce those discourses.

What are the implications for social studies of this understanding of discourse? As educators, we should be aware of the dominant discourses of the current moment and how they are situated amid larger and longer running political, social, and historical patterns. Part of the work of the social studies is to help young people learn how to analyze and contextualize such discourses. At the "Unite the Right" march in Charlottesville, Virginia in August 2017, protesters invoked the desire to protect a statue of Confederate general Robert E. Lee; reacting to media critique of his response to the event, President Donald Trump complained that "they are trying to take away our history and our heritage." This discourse of "heritage" can be usefully analyzed as part of a longstanding racialized discourse signaling and reiterating whiteness as fundamental to national membership. Social studies is where students might develop the historical understandings and analytical tools to connect discourse to history and power in this way.

DISCOURSES OF CITIZENSHIP

Discourse is, in some senses, a link between self and setting, between identity and history; it is a way to signal and create a sense of belonging to a larger social body. In this way, discourse can be seen as deeply connected to citizenship. There are a number of discourses of citizenship that "construct the meanings of citizenship in contemporary Western cultures, particularly the United States," most prominently the civic republican and liberal discourses, and, increasingly and promisingly, critical and transnational discourses (Abowitz & Harnish, 2006, p. 653).

The civic republican discourse is focused on the transmission of the civic values of "love and service to one's political community" through participation in "pro-government" activities such as voting, respect for national symbols and, particularly since September 11, 2001, patriotism (p. 657). The liberal discourse of citizenship focuses on individual liberty, pluralism, and building the skills of civic participation, including "the deliberative values of discussion, disagreement and consensus building" (p. 663). Both of these discourses are longstanding and pervasive in civics standards and related teaching materials.

Critical and transnational discourses of citizenship challenge these more conventional discourses. Critical discourses focus on "exclusions based on gender, culture, ethnicity, nationality, race, sexuality, or socioeconomic class," seeking to extend definitions of citizenship beyond the patriotic and liberal conceptions described above (p. 666). Critical discourses reframe citizenship, taking into account the ways that inequalities are built into mainstream conceptions of the construct and challenging educators to put critical analyses of power and justice at the forefront of their civic education practices. Transnational discourses of citizenship reckon with a reality of contemporary citizenship—that young people can feel a sense of affiliation with multiple communities and that civic identity is complex, flexible and overlapping. With this in mind, Abu El-Haj (2009) proposes that "we [should] stop thinking about citizenship primarily in relation to national identifications and begin to see it as a set of critical practices—practices that give young people the tools to understand structural inequalities and work for social change within and across the boundaries of nation-states" (p. 275).

These discourses of citizenship dramatize the need for new approaches to teaching theme ten of the NCSS curriculum standards, "Civic Ideals and Practices." In these overlapping and evolving discourses, civic ideals are hotly contested and civic practices vary from unquestioning patriotic obedience to passionate resistance against government mandates. Civic ideals and practices are as varied as our population, as contentious as our history. Social studies classrooms can prepare students to critically engage with these competing discourses by discussing and learning the difficult history of the ways in which citizenship in this country has been constructed and maintained through a system of racialized inequality. As I wrote in 2015, "These are not easy discussions that lead to neat resolutions," but, as a veteran teacher told me, "Social studies seems like the only place where they are going to learn it" (Rubin, 2015, p. 29).

REFERENCES

Abowitz, K., & Harnish, J. (2006). Contemporary discourses of citizenship. *Review of Educational Research, 76*(4), 653–690.

Abu El-Haj, T. (2009). Becoming citizens in an era of globalization and transnational migration. *Theory into Practice, 48*(4), 274–282.

Gee, J. (1996). *Sociolinguistics and literacies: Ideology in discourses* (3rd ed.). London: Falmer.

Rubin, B. C. (2015). A time for social studies: Talking with young people about Ferguson and Staten Island. *Social Education, 79*(1), 22–29.

Afterword

Keywords, Windows, and Content Selection

WALTER C. PARKER, UNIVERSITY OF WASHINGTON

The editors of this collection noticed my use of Raymond Williams' concept "keywords" in the introduction to *Social Studies Today* (Parker, 2015), and they ran with it here. I had used it to point to "social studies," itself a keyword. The term organizes a social field of practice as well as a specialist community. Like most keywords, its meaning is ambiguous; the more you look into it the more the bottom falls out of what you thought was a settled meaning.

Generally, in the United States today "social studies" connotes schooling. It is a school term, and in that context, it signals a curricular federation of four areas of study: history, geography, government, and economics. "Social studies" names a *department* in (many) middle and (nearly all) high schools—the department that houses courses with names like these—and it names a *subject* in (most) elementary schools where "social studies" is an amalgamation of these four disciplines and distinct from the other amalgamated subjects: "science," "math," "language arts," "health," "art," "physical education," and so forth. Social studies is a school field of practice where curriculum controversies reflect the cultural and academic anxieties at play in society:

> Should the social studies curriculum aim to transmit the existing social order, preparing students to succeed within its norms and values, or should it aim to transform the status quo, helping students create a better society? If the latter, what sort of "better" is it? (Parker, 2015, p. 10)

Aside from this conflict over aims, another is fought over which one of the disciplines anchors the social studies curriculum and the meaning of "social studies." Neo-conservative federationists in the 1980s led by historian Diane Ravitch (1989) invented the hyphenated terms "history-social studies" and "history-social science." They were pulling history out of the mix so that it could dominate it—an unnecessary move since history already was dominant. But it was an absurd move, too: Imagine the result were it extended to the other amalgamated school subjects, resulting in "algebra-math," "physics-science," "literature-language arts," "jazz-music," and so forth. The move reflects the status anxiety experienced by the ("softer") social sciences and humanities in relation to the ("harder") natural sciences, to be sure, but also the internecine struggles among the newer and the older social sciences. Unfortunately, history's insistence on even greater supremacy did collateral damage: history not only won the contest but the rest of the social sciences, notably geography and sociology, were more or less pushed to the margins.

Keywords are key concepts, and concepts are theoretical categories—abstractions that generalize beyond a single case or context. More precisely, keywords are not concepts but concept labels. Good teachers know the difference between a concept and its label because the pedagogical challenge, always, is teaching the meaning behind the label. (It's easier to teach a vocabulary word than the concept it names.) A keyword is a name that points to a meaning. "Religion" is a word in the English language that points to a cluster of meanings; so is "democracy." The word "culture," as Williams showed in *Culture and Society* (1958) and then in *Keywords* (1976), points in so many directions as to be super slippery and, at the same time, critically important to social understanding. "Culture" was deployed by leftist scholars (e.g., Max Weber, Pierre Bourdieu, Paul Willis) in a critique of classical Marxism, a critique that would open it to the role of ideas (e.g., "religion," "democracy," "human rights") in human affairs. Ideas, then, became more than epiphenomena; they were real, they had consequences. The scare quotes around these concept labels are meant to signal the chasm between the vocabulary word (the label) and the concept (the meaning). Again, the pedagogical challenge, always, is getting beyond the term to the concept itself. This often requires teacher and student to delve into the genealogy of the concept.

Sometimes, a keyword is a "buzzword"—a fashionable idea rendered somewhat meaningless because the label is so widely and variously used. "Social justice" is a buzzword among teacher educators and their students today. "Constructivism" is another. Buzzwords bond us to other people who use the same buzzwords; their function is more affiliative than analytic. We are not engaging in critical thinking when we use them so much as we are bonding and signaling our shared interest. As Dwayne Huebner (1999) observed, these are "tokens of cohesion" (p. 217) expressed to show inclusion in a particular community and, perhaps, our opposition to or exclusion from another. Solidarity is nurtured with the use of a buzzword, but often at the expense of critical strength.

Kathy Davis (2008) provides a terrific example. She shows us how "intersectionality," the term Kimberlé Crenshaw (1989) coined to argue that the categories race and gender needed to be joined if Black women's experiences were to be described more adequately, had become such a buzzword by 2005 that it could be hailed as the most significant contribution to the field of women's studies. It had become a keyword despite/because of "the confusion which the concept evokes among those who would most like to use it in their own research" (p. 68). Davis demonstrates that some users regard intersectionality as a full-blown theory, others regard it as merely an analytic category, and still others as a technical tool in feminist discourse analysis. Others simply wanted to signal membership in the community of people who used the term.

Like most readers of this book, I teach; and teachers teach concepts. Concepts are selected strategically for instruction in a course of study—perhaps "race" and "gender" in a high school *United States History* course or "culture" and "climate" in a 3rd-grade curriculum, *Communities Near and Far,* or "inquiry" in a college social studies methods course. Particular concepts are selected from an array of possibilities because they are judged to be key to a course of study, "key" for two reasons. They are central to the subject matter of that curriculum—central in the way a star anchors a solar system of planets and moons or in the way the entrée centers a meal (the other dishes are "sides"). Second, they are key because they are generative, alive. In Philip Phenix's (1962) phrase, these concepts "lead on and out" (p. 278). They give students powers to think outside the boxes of their upbringing and their local circumstances. They empower them to interpret and maybe even to interrupt the status quo. In this way, conceptual knowledge is liberating.

Consequently, keywords are a practical matter in teaching and learning. Has the teacher selected concepts with care? Will they open windows onto the social world and provide students with new and unsettling ways to think about it? Are they potentially mind-altering, leading "on and out"? This kind of knowledge is in an epistemic category of its own, and it is what young people are sent to school to learn. Vygotsky (1986) called it theoretic knowledge, and educational researchers call it disciplinary knowledge, meaning that it is constructed and revised in specialist communities under norms of peer-review, criticism, and fallibilism. At home young people learn a different kind of knowledge—what Vygotsky called everyday knowledge. This knowledge is less abstract and more context-dependent, more "cultural" and less "scientific." The distinction is useful, and the great task of teaching is to articulate the two, building what Geneva Gay (2013) calls "meaningfulness bridges" (p. 66) between students' everyday funds of knowledge and the key concepts of the social studies. If the curriculum is loaded with students' everyday knowledge, then it's all mirrors, so to speak—too few windows and too little liberation.

Keywords, windows, and content selection. They go together. In a series of research-and-development studies of Advanced Placement social studies courses (e.g., Parker, Valencia, & Lo, 2018), my colleagues and I have been striving to deepen learning in courses known mainly for breadth-speed-test. This work has required us and our teacher-collaborators to pay close attention above all else to content selection. Which few concepts will anchor the course and, if learned in depth, carry the rest of the course topics with them? Which key concepts will lead on and out, giving students the intellectual powers to think the not-yet-thought?

REFERENCES

Crenshaw, K. (1989). Demarginalizing the intersection of race and sex: A Black feminist critique of antidiscrimination doctrine, feminist theory, and antiracist politics. *University of Chicago Legal Forum, 14*, 538–554.

Davis, K. (2008). Intersectionality as buzzword. *Feminist Theory, 9*(1), 67–85.

Gay, G. (2013). Teaching to and through cultural diversity. *Curriculum Inquiry, 43*(1), 48–70.

Huebner, D. E. (1999). The tasks of the curricular theorist. In V. Hillis (Ed.), *The lure of the transcendent* (pp. 212–230). Mahwah, NJ: Lawrence Erlbaum.

Parker, W. C. (Ed.). (2015). *Social studies today: Research and practice* (2nd ed.). New York, NY: Routledge.

Parker, W. C., Valencia, S. W., & Lo, J. C. (2018). Teaching for deeper political learning: A design experiment. *Journal of Curriculum Studies, 50*(2) 252–277.

Phenix, P. H. (1962). The use of the disciplines as curriculum content. *The Educational Forum, 26*(3), 273–280.

Ravitch, D. (1989). The plight of history in American schools. In P. Gagnon (Ed.), *Historical literacy: The case for history in American education* (pp. 51–68). New York, NY: Macmillan.

Vygotsky, L. S. (1986). *Thought and language*. Cambridge, MA: MIT Press.

Williams, R. (1958). *Culture and society: 1780–1950*. New York, NY: Columbia University Press.

Williams, R. (1976/2014). *Keywords: A vocabulary of culture and society*. Oxford: Oxford University Press.

Contributors

Erin C. Adams
Erin C. Adams is Assistant Professor of Elementary Social Studies Education at Kennesaw State University. Drawing on poststructural theories and theorists, her work is primarily concerned with economic education, citizenship, and subjectivity.

Robert W. Bailey
Dr. Robert W. Bailey's research interests have grown out of his early career experience as a state child abuse investigator and later as a secondary school teacher and focus on social justice and education as a transformative and progressive force. Dr. Bailey currently teaches at a Title I public high school.

Whitney G. Blankenship
Whitney G. Blankenship is Associate Professor of Educational Studies & History at Rhode Island College. Her research interests include historical thinking, technology integration in social studies, and curriculum history.

Daniel T. Bordwell
Daniel T. Bordwell is a Graduate Instructor at the University of Minnesota and a high school teacher. This praxis affords him an opportunity to see research in to practice. His research interests include exploring manifestations of identity, gender, and sexuality in social studies classrooms, curricula, and pedagogies.

Rina Bousalis

Rina Bousalis is Assistant Professor of Social Studies Education at Florida Atlantic University. She has authored articles in numerous peer-reviewed journals on issues related to immigration, multiculturalism, human rights, and U.S. history.

Kristy Brugar

Dr. Kristy Brugar is Associate Professor at the University of Oklahoma where she teaches social studies education courses. Her research interests include interdisciplinary instruction (social studies/history, literacy, and visuals) and teacher development. Her work has been published in social studies and literacy journals.

Erik Jon Byker

Erik Jon Byker, Ph.D., is Associate Professor in the Department of Reading and Elementary Education at the University of North Carolina at Charlotte. Erik teaches instructional design and social studies methods courses. His research agenda is comparative and international in scope and he has conducted ethnographic field studies across the globe.

Kenneth T. Carano

Kenneth T. Carano is Associate Professor of Social Studies Education at Western Oregon University. He is a former secondary social studies teacher and Returned Peace Corps Volunteer. His scholarship interests focus on social justice frameworks, which prepare students to become critically literate citizens in an increasingly interconnected world.

Jeffrey Craig

Jeffrey Craig has a Ph.D. in Mathematics Education from Michigan State University. His work focuses on numeracy as a transdisciplinary translation of mathematics education, irrevocably tied to the social world.

Kristen E. Duncan

Kristen E. Duncan is Assistant Professor of Secondary Social Studies Education at Clemson University. Her research focuses on the ways Black teachers help their students navigate systems of white supremacy. Her scholarship can be found in numerous journals and edited books.

Tommy Ender

Tommy Ender is the Inclusive Excellence Post-Doctoral Fellow at Loyola University Maryland. His research examines how identity informs critical teaching pedagogies within social studies.

Colleen Fitzpatrick
Colleen Fitzpatrick is a Teacher Scholar Postdoctoral Fellow at Wake Forest University. Her research interests center on teaching religion and teaching in religious contexts.

Amanda Geiger
Amanda Geiger is a social studies teacher at Leon High School specializing in government and economics.

Amy J. Good
Amy J. Good, Ph.D. is Associate Professor and graduate programs director in the Reading and Elementary Department at the University of North Carolina at Charlotte. Amy teaches various methods courses at the undergrad, graduate, and doctorate level. Her research interests include social studies education, National Board Certification, and seamless technology integration.

Delandrea Hall
Delandrea Hall is a doctoral student at The University of Texas at Austin in the Curriculum and Instruction, Social Studies Department. Her K–12 experience includes eleven years as a high school social studies teacher in the Dallas area. Her research interests center around examining the ways racialized and gendered experiences inform the pedagogical decisions of teachers of color, specifically Black women in social studies, with a focus on pre-college economics education and students' understandings of economics.

Anne-Lise Halvorsen
Anne-Lise Halvorsen is Associate Professor in the Department of Teacher Education at Michigan State University. Her research and teaching interests are elementary social studies education, project-based learning, the history of education, the integration of social studies and literacy, and teacher preparation in the social studies.

Jason Harshman
Jason Harshman is Assistant Professor of Social Studies and Global Education at the University of Iowa. His research examines the intersections of geography and citizenship, along with teaching and learning for global competence in K–12 and teacher education. He coedited the book *Research in Global Citizenship Education*.

Mark Helmsing
Mark Helmsing is Assistant Professor in the Graduate School of Education at George Mason University. A member of various editorial boards for journals and book series, Mark publishes extensively on aspects of affect and emotion related to learning history and heritage in schools, museums, and popular culture. His current research examines the affective and emotional aspects of teaching and learning about war and genocide. Reach Mark on Twitter @markhelmsing.

Mary Beth Henning
Mary Beth Henning is Professor of Social Studies Education at Northern Illinois University. She recently edited the book *Innovations in Economic Education: Promising Practices for Teachers and Students, K–16*. She is president of the Illinois Council for Social Studies and helped author the 2016 Illinois Social Science Learning Standards.

Wayne Journell
Wayne Journell is an associate professor at the University of North Carolina at Greensboro. His research primarily focuses on the teaching politics and political processes in K–12 education. He is currently editor of *Theory & Research in Social Education*, the premier research journal in the field of social studies education.

Eli Kean
Eli Kean earned their Ph.D. in Curriculum, Instruction and Teacher Education from Michigan State University. Eli draws on sociology, philosophy, and history to critically analyze curriculum and pedagogical practice, with particular attention to gender discourses within classroom spaces, and seeks to transform education into a liberatory space for transgender individuals.

Stacey L. Kerr
Stacey L. Kerr is Assistant Professor of Geography & Environmental Studies at Central Michigan University. Her research uses spatial and feminist theories to think about geography and teacher education.

Daniel G. Krutka
Daniel G. Krutka is Assistant Professor of Social Studies Education at the University of North Texas. A former high school social studies teacher, Dan has published widely on citizenship education and the role social media might play in cultivating more democratic and educational experiences. He is an active podcaster (VisionsOfEd.com) who will respond to your tweets at @dankrutka.

Jodi Latremouille
Jodi Latremouille is a doctoral candidate in Educational Research at the Werklund School of Education, University of Calgary, and a sessional instructor in the Master of Education program at Thompson Rivers University. Her research interests include hermeneutics, ecological and feminist pedagogy, social and environmental justice, life writing, and poetic inquiry.

Sara A. Levy
Sara A. Levy is Associate Professor of Education at Wells College. Her research focuses on heritage narratives, emotion in the social studies classroom, and difficult histories.

Megan List
Megan List is Assistant Professor of Curriculum and Instruction, specializing in social studies, at Youngstown State University, in Youngstown Ohio. She researches LGBT issues, is the director of the YSU Women and Gender Resource Center, and enjoys knitting.

Jane C. Lo
Jane C. Lo is Assistant Professor of Social Science Education in the School of Teacher Education at Florida State University. Her research focuses on the political engagement of youth, social studies curriculum development, and civic education. She is interested in how young people learn to become productive citizens in the polity.

Lance E. Mason
Lance E. Mason is Associate Professor of Education at Indiana University Kokomo. He has published widely in social studies and philosophy of education journals about the connections between media, democracy, and education.

J.B. Mayo, Jr.
J.B. Mayo, Jr. is Associate Professor of Social Studies Education at the University of Minnesota. His research interests center on the inclusion of LGBTQ histories in standard social studies curriculum, students' identity formation in GSAs, intersections of racialized identities and sexual orientation, and the lived experiences of queer teachers.

Sajani Jinny Menon
Sajani Jinny Menon is a Ph.D. candidate at the University of Alberta and a member of the university's Centre for Research for Teacher Education and Development. For Jinny, a multiplicity of knowing, re-presenting, and sharing knowledge is integral to re-stor(y)ing humane practices and understandings. Her research interests include: curriculum studies, children's literature, issues of diversity, women's studies, children, youth and families, and narrative inquiry.

Scott Alan Metzger

Scott Alan Metzger is Associate Professor of Social Studies Education at Penn State University. He has published in *Theory & Research in Social Education* and other journals on history and media and also is editor (with Lauren Harris) of *The Wiley International Handbook of History Teaching and Learning*.

Matthew T. Missias

Dr. Matthew T. Missias is the owner of Cultivated Learning, LLC and part time faculty at the Brooks College of Interdisciplinary Studies at Grand Valley State University. His research explores how emerging and early stage teachers experience teaching and learning, and the role of imagination in understanding pedagogical possibilities. His areas of expertise include: Qualitative research methodologies, teachers and teaching, social studies and history education, and curriculum theory.

Ryan D. Oto

Ryan D. Oto is a Ph.D. student in Curriculum and Instruction at the University of Minnesota. He currently teaches social studies full-time and researches the ways discussions of identity take shape in classroom spaces, particularly how pedagogic and curricular changes affect the productive capacity of classrooms as sites of anti-oppressive action.

Walter C. Parker

Walter C. Parker is Professor of Social Studies Education and (by courtesy) Political Science at the University of Washington in Seattle. He is the editor of *Social Studies Today* (2015) and the author of *Social Studies in Elementary Education* (2017, with Terry Beck).

Kim Pennington

Kim Pennington is an assistant professor of Education at the University of Central Oklahoma. She taught high school social studies for 18 years and is the recipient of numerous K–12/higher education teaching awards. Her research and service interests include recruitment and support of urban educators in the Oklahoma City area.

Gabriel A. Reich

Gabriel A. Reich is Associate Professor of History/Social Studies Education at Virginia Commonwealth University. He has published in articles in a variety of academic journals on history assessment, and the collective memory of the U.S. Civil War.

E. Wayne Ross

E. Wayne Ross is Professor in the Department of Curriculum and Pedagogy at the University of British Columbia in Vancouver, Canada. His most recent book is *Rethinking Social Studies* (Information Age Publishing, 2017).

Beth C. Rubin
Beth C. Rubin is Professor at Rutgers GSE. She uses ethnographic methods to explore how youth civic identity takes shape within local contexts marked by historical and contemporary inequalities, and designs and studies innovations that attend to this critical, sociocultural understanding of youth civic learning. Access her publications at https://rutgers.academia.edu/BethRubin

Muna Saleh
Muna Saleh is a recent Ph.D. graduate of the University of Alberta's Department of Elementary Education. Her doctoral studies included a two-year narrative inquiry alongside Canadian Muslim girls and their mothers. Her research interests include: multiperspectival narrative inquiry, familial curriculum-making, mothering and motherhood studies, and the experiences of Muslim children, youth, and families with exceptionalities. She is currently Assistant Professor in the Faculty of Education at Concordia University of Edmonton and is the author of "Stories We Live and Grow By: (Re)Telling Our Experiences as Muslim Mothers and Daughters."

Cinthia Salinas
Dr. Cinthia Salinas is a professor at the University of Texas at Austin in Curriculum and Instruction in Social Studies Education. Her research and teaching focus in the social studies includes critical historical thinking and broader understandings of citizenship in elementary bilingual and secondary immigrant ESL classroom settings.

Dilys Schoorman
Dilys Schoorman is Professor and Chair of the Department of Curriculum, Culture and Educational Inquiry at Florida Atlantic University. Her community engagement in South Florida offers her authentic opportunities for exploring the experiences of recent immigrant populations as part of a broader commitment to educator preparation for equity and social justice.

Sarah B. Shear
Sarah B. Shear is Assistant Professor of social studies education at Penn State University-Altoona. Her primary research focuses on teaching and learning social studies within Indigenous contexts, especially teacher decision-making to include or exclude Indigenous content in social studies lessons. Sarah's other research includes examining race(ism) and settler colonialism in social studies curriculum, teacher education, and qualitative research methodologies.

Sarah E. Stanlick
Sarah E. Stanlick is the founding director of Lehigh University's Center for Community Engagement and professor of practice in Sociology and Anthropology. She previously taught at Centenary University and served as Research Associate to former U.S. Ambassador to the United Nations, Samantha Power, at the Harvard Kennedy School.

Christine R. Stanton
Christine R. Stanton is Associate Professor of Education at Montana State University. Her interests focus on social studies education for social justice, Indigenous knowledges, participatory research and filmmaking, and community-engaged methodologies. She has published in journals such as *Theory and Research in Social Education, Curriculum Inquiry,* and *Qualitative Inquiry.*

Gabriel P. Swarts
Gabriel P. Swarts is Assistant Professor of Social Studies in the School of Teacher Education at the University of Wyoming. Swarts' scholarly interests and publications include experiential learning and identity formation, information and communication technologies, citizenship education, democratic living and moral philosophy.

Rory P. Tannebaum
Rory P. Tannebaum is Assistant Professor of Education at Merrimack College in North Andover, Massachusetts. His research interests focus on the development of reform-oriented preservice social studies teachers through powerful teacher education. He can be contacted at TannebaumR@merrimack.edu.

Stephanie van Hover
Stephanie van Hover is Professor of Social Studies Education at the Curry School of Education at the University of Virginia. Her research explores teaching and learning history in standards-based settings.

Cathryn van Kessel
Cathryn van Kessel is Assistant Professor of Social Studies Education and Curriculum Studies at the University of Alberta. Her research interests include conceptualizations of evil in the context of education, teaching for social change, philosophy in/of education, youth studies, popular culture, and terror management theory.

Amanda E. Vickery
Amanda E. Vickery is Assistant Professor of Teacher Preparation at Arizona State University. She has published in numerous journals exploring how Black women social studies teachers utilize experiential and community knowledge to reconceptualize the construct of citizenship. She is a former middle school history teacher.

Annie McMahon Whitlock
Annie McMahon Whitlock is Associate Professor of Elementary Education and the Elementary Education Program Coordinator at the University of Michigan-Flint. Her research is centered on teaching social studies through civic engagement, place-based inquiry, and integrating language arts and literature. She has served as the President of the Michigan Council for the Social Studies.

Melissa Rojas Williams
Melissa Rojas Williams is a doctoral student in the Social Studies Department at the University of Texas at Austin. Her interests are in LatCrit, Bilingual Teacher social studies pedagogy, and bilingual/biliteracy studies.

Nakeshia N. Williams
Nakeshia N. Williams is Assistant Professor of Educator Preparation at North Carolina A&T State University. She teaches diversity and social studies methods courses to undergraduate and graduate teacher candidates. She has published in numerous education journals on multicultural education, equity, access, and achievement of PK–12 students.

Ashley N. Woodson
Ashley N. Woodson is a mother, other-mother, and qualitative researcher. Her scholarship examines Black adolescents' civic imaginations, and radical possibilities for civic education. She is Assistant Professor of Social Studies Education at the University of Missouri-Columbia.

COUNTERPOINTS

Studies in Criticality

General Editor
Shirley R. Steinberg

Counterpoints publishes the most compelling and imaginative books being written in education today. Grounded on the theoretical advances in criticalism, feminism, and postmodernism in the last two decades of the twentieth century, Counterpoints engages the meaning of these innovations in various forms of educational expression. Committed to the proposition that theoretical literature should be accessible to a variety of audiences, the series insists that its authors avoid esoteric and jargonistic languages that transform educational scholarship into an elite discourse for the initiated. Scholarly work matters only to the degree it affects consciousness and practice at multiple sites. Counterpoints' editorial policy is based on these principles and the ability of scholars to break new ground, to open new conversations, to go where educators have never gone before.

For additional information about this series or for the submission of manuscripts, please contact:

Shirley R. Steinberg
c/o Peter Lang Publishing, Inc.
29 Broadway, 18th floor
New York, New York 10006

To order other books in this series, please contact our Customer Service Department:

(800) 770-LANG (within the U.S.)
(212) 647-7706 (outside the U.S.)
(212) 647-7707 FAX

Or browse online by series:
www.peterlang.com